<<<<< THE POT LUCK >>>

PUB

QUIZ

BOOK

Published in 2020 by Welbeck
An Imprint of Welbeck Non-Fiction Limited,
part of Welbeck Publishing Group
Based in London and Sydney.
www.welbeckpublishing.com

Text © Welbeck Non-Fiction Limited,
part of Welbeck Publishing Group

First published by Carlton Books in 2019

A CIP catalogue record for this book is available from the British Library

ISBN 978-1-78739-263-2

Printed and bound in Great Britain

10 9 8 7 6 5 4 3

Content in this book was previously published in
The Best Pub Quiz Book Ever! Vol 3

MIX
Paper | Supporting
responsible forestry
FSC® C171272
www.fsc.org

<<<<< THE POT LUCK >>>>>

PUB QUIZ BOOK

MORE THAN 8,000 QUIZ QUESTIONS TO
BE ENJOYED AT HOME OR IN THE PUB!

WELBECK

Contents

Introduction

Quizzes are strange things. If you were to stroll up to some poor bloke on the street – let's say it's a Saturday lunch time, and he's out with the wife doing the weekly shopping, trying to get it over and done with so he can make it back home for kick-off – and start firing questions at him, one after the other, he'd probably take it pretty badly. He'd be nervous, irritated, and looking for quick ways to escape the maniac who latched on to him. If you take a moment to picture it ("Quick, mate, what would you ride in a velodrome? What colour is an aubergine?"), you'll see how ludicrous it sounds. If he doesn't lamp you one, he'll probably run off screaming in terror.

However, get the same bloke later on the same Saturday, down the pub with his mates after the match, and then you leap up and start firing the same questions at him, at the very least he's going to rise to the challenge and prove he's the equal of your questions. If you've taken the time to sort things out with the landlord in advance, and you're asking the whole pub, you'll have a crowd of people enthralled, hanging on your every word, and not just our bloke. Even if – and this is the best part – there's absolutely no prize at the end of it. We all love glory, after all, and what could be more glorious than proving you've got the keenest mind in the bar? It beats getting on to a horse and charging at a cannon hands down.

This is the latest in our popular quiz book series and it keeps getting better and better. Inside these hallowed covers, you'll find more than 8,000 questions covering a stunning range of topics, divided into laughably easy, reasonably medium, and brain-shreddingly hard. At the back, you'll also find a comprehensive set of guidelines on how to prepare for and run a successful quiz of your own down the local, and some handy answer sheet templates to photocopy and give out to contestants. There is one important thing you have to remember though, and that is never, ever, under any circumstances, give out your own pens.

More importantly than that though – seriously for a minute – when you are going to be running a quiz, prepare properly beforehand. Don't just take this book along and read out of it (because apart from anything else, some other wise guy might have bought a copy too, and be checking the answers). Note down all the questions and all the answers, and make sure you've got everything. If an answer makes you think "hang on a moment, is that right?" then double-check it to make sure that it is not only correct, but it is the only correct answer. While every possible effort has been undertaken to make absolutely sure that every answer is accurate, there is a slight possibility that an error may have crept in and the answer is wrong. Nothing is more humiliating than telling people who are right that they are wrong, in front of a lot of other people who will remember it and tease you about it mercilessly for the next three years. If you've made sure of your answers, you'll be absolutely 100% safe, not just 99.99% safe.

So, there you go. Wade in, and have fun. After all, that's what it's all about.

Easy Questions

The whole point of these questions is that they are, well, easy. As in not hard. That means that they shouldn't give you, or anyone else who speaks the same language, any problems. If you get these questions right, that's really not much to be proud of. In fact, it's close to the truth that getting these questions wrong is something to be worried about. If you find yourself doing badly on these questions, there are many possible reasons. The first thing to check is that you're looking at the correct answer block. If you've made that mistake, it'll throw your results right out. Alternatively, you may be extremely drunk. If reading this short introduction is proving tricky, that could be the cause. Try again later. Another possible cause is that you might only be three or four years old – again, try again later, only make it much later. Finally, you may have been born in the wilds and have spent your life being raised by a friendly family of otters, in which case you can be forgiven for your ignorance. They're nice creatures, but they're really not much cop when it comes to hits of the 90s.

So, when you're devising a quiz for people, you might like to soften them up with a few of these questions, ease them into the groove, fatten them for the kill, and lots of other clichés that mean you're gently preparing people for something nasty. If nothing else, it'll make sure that even the bloke in the corner who's so hammered he can't stand will get one or two points, and save face. Tomorrow, he may even be grateful enough to buy you a drink for being so considerate. It's worth a shot, so to speak...

Quiz 1 | Animal World

Answers – page 10

LEVEL 1

1 Which land mammal has the largest ears?
2 Which wild animal is the domesticated dog descended from?
3 Are mammals warm-blooded or cold-blooded?
4 Which part of the body has a crown and a root?
5 What is another name for the larynx?
6 Do tigers hunt in packs or alone?
7 Which group of animals shares its name with an archbishop?
8 What type of creature is an Aylesbury?
9 What was the first animal to be domesticated?
10 Cheviot and Suffolk are both types of what?
11 Shrews have acute sense of smell and hearing to compensate for which weak sense?
12 The opossum and the skunk are famous for what?
13 What colour is a grizzly bear?
14 The llama is native to which continent?
15 Which part of a human's body has a cornea?
16 A leveret is a young what?
17 What part of a basset hound is particularly long?
18 Which northerly US state is famous for the brown bear?
19 Does the moose live in a warm or cold climate?
20 Are crocodiles carnivorous or herbivores?
21 Which farm animals chew the cud?
22 Which primate species is the closest genetic cousin to humanity?
23 Where is a human's jugular vein?
24 Are most animals vertebrates or invertebrates?
25 How many young does a kangaroo usually produce at any one time?
26 What part of the body of a Manx cat is missing which is present on most other cats?
27 Which bear is the largest meat-eating land animal?
28 What do all mammals feed their babies on?
29 Which part of a human includes loops and whorls?
30 In which hemisphere do penguins live in the wild?

Answers | TV: Cops & Robbers *(see Quiz 2)*

1 Idris Elba. 2 EastEnders. 3 Tommy. 4 Jonathan Creek. 5 Z Cars. 6 Heartbeat.
7 Yorkshire. 8 Police surgeon. 9 Poirot. 10 Cornwall. 11 Lewis. 12 Maigret.
13 Tosh. 14 Taggart. 15 Wainthropp. 16 Frost. 17 Hill St. Blues. 18 Adam.
19 Nail. 20 Sherlock Holmes. 21 Chef. 22 Manchester. 23 PD James. 24 Kojak
(Telly Savalas). 25 Midsomer Murders. 26 Miami. 27 John Thaw. 28 New York.
29 Line of Duty. 30 Paris.

Quiz 2 — TV: Cops & Robbers

Answers – page 9

LEVEL 1

1 Who plays DCI John Luther?
2 Michael French left which soap to become a Crime Traveller?
3 In "Murphy's Law", is Murphy named Mick, Pat or Tommy?
4 Which sleuth Jonathan was created by David Renwick?
5 Which early police serial is found at the end of the alphabet?
6 Which Yorkshire police series did Nick Berry leave in 1997?
7 In which county was "Dalziel & Pascoe" originally set?
8 "Dangerfield" deals with what type of police personnel?
9 David Suchet played which Belgian Agatha Christie detective?
10 In which English county does "Wycliffe" take place?
11 Which assistant to Morse was missing from the show in 1998?
12 Michael Gambon played which French detective in the 1990s?
13 How was "The Bill's" DC Lines, played by Kevin Lloyd, better known?
14 Which Glasgow detective was played by Mark McManus?
15 Which Hetty has a sidekick called Geoffrey?
16 What is the surname of detective Jack played by David Jason?
17 Which police station's blues were led by Captain Frank Furillo?
18 What is the first name of Commander Dalgliesh, created by PD James?
19 Which Jimmy starred in "Evita" and played Geordie Spender?
20 Which Victorian sleuth from Baker Street was played by Jeremy Brett?
21 In "Pie in the Sky", which profession did Henry combine with policing?
22 In which northern city was "City Central" set?
23 How is Cordelia Gray's creator Baroness James better known?
24 Which bald TV cop was "Friends" Jennifer Aniston's godfather?
25 In which series might DC Ben Jones be called on to help solve murders?
26 Where did Sonny Crockett aka Don Johnson sort out Vice?
27 Who has played Jack Regan and Morse?
28 In which city was "Cagney & Lacey" set?
29 Which series has characters called Steve Arnott and Kate Fleming?
30 In which city did Maigret operate?

| Answers | Animal World *(see Quiz 1)* |

1 (African) elephant. 2 Wolf. 3 Warm blooded. 4 Tooth. 5 Voice box. 6 Alone. 7 Primate. 8 Duck. 9 Dog. 10 Sheep. 11 Sight. 12 Offensive smell. 13 Brown. 14 (South) America. 15 Eye. 16 Hare. 17 Its ears. 18 Alaska. 19 Warm. 20 Carnivorous. 21 Cows. 22 Chimpanzee. 23 Neck. 24 Invertebrates. 25 One. 26 Tail. 27 Polar bear. 28 Milk. 29 Fingerprints. 30 Southern.

1   Which movie actress's second marriage was to director Sam Mendes?
2   Raymond Blanc is famous for being what?
3   Which Betty became the House of Commons' first woman Speaker?
4   In 2006 where did Prince William start military training?
5   Which one time husband and wife actors were dubbed Ken and Em?
6   Which trendy homeware store did Terence Conran found in the 60s?
7   Which part of you would you ask Nicky Clarke to cut off?
8   How was Yorkshire-based murderer Peter Sutcliffe better known?
9   Which celebrity daughter was named after the song "Chelsea Morning"?
10   Which ex-Wimbledon champ did Andre Agassi marry?
11   Which 90s PM was in a university pop group called Ugly Rumours?
12   Who is taller, Kylie Minogue or Naomi Campbell?
13   Who launched Virgin Cola and Virgin PEPs ?
14   Which singer Sarah was once Mrs Andrew Lloyd Webber?
15   Which rock star became dad to Alistair at the age of 60 in 2005?
16   Which Monica was intimately associated with Bill Clinton?
17   Was Joan Collins born in the 1920s, 1930s or the 1940s?
18   Which ex-British party leader has the same first names as Bill Clinton?
19   Which model Jerry had a cameo role in "Batman"?
20   Did actress Gwyneth Paltrow call her daughter Apple, Banana or Peach?
21   Which football club do Ant and Dec support?
22   Which Scot Andrew was the Sunday Times editor from 1983 to 1994?
23   John Prescott became Deputy Leader of which political party?
24   Which Prime Minister had twins called Mark and Carol?
25   The names Saatchi and Saatchi are associated with which industry?
26   Who was the last Beatle to marry twice?
27   What title does the brother of the late Princess Diana have?
28   What type of shops did Tim Waterstone found?
29   Which designer Vivienne is famous for her outrageous clothes?
30   Whoopi Goldberg's real name is Caryn Johnson – true or false?

Answers	Pot Luck 1 *(see Quiz 4)*

1 Donkey. 2 Italy. 3 90th. 4 Kirsty Young. 5 Poppy. 6 48. 7 Lah. 8 A calf. 9 China. 10 Frank Sinatra. 11 Chequered. 12 Ed Sheeran. 13 C. 14 Bach. 15 Ellen MacArthur. 16 Orange. 17 11. 18 Blue. 19 Dublin. 20 Florence Nightingale. 21 Pumpkin. 22 Bill Haley & the Comets. 23 London. 24 Hans Christian Andersen. 25 The twins. 26 Shropshire. 27 Grapes. 28 Tennis. 29 Sound and noise. 30 New York.

1 What kind of animal is Eeyore in the children's classic?
2 Which country produces Parmesan cheese?
3 The Queen celebrated which landmark birthday in 2016?
4 Which Kirsty replaced Sue Lawley on "Desert Island Discs"?
5 Which flower is linked with Remembrance Sunday?
6 How many sides are there in a dozen quadrilaterals?
7 Which note follows the musical note "soh"?
8 What name is given to a young elephant?
9 In which country was acupuncture developed?
10 Which singer was known affectionately as "Old Blue Eyes"?
11 Which flag in motor racing signals the end of the race?
12 Whose first studio album was called "+"?
13 Which vitamin is found in oranges and lemons?
14 Which composer had the forenames Johann Sebastian?
15 In February 2005, who became the fastest female to sail solo around the world?
16 What kind of fruit is a satsuma?
17 How many players are in a hockey team?
18 What colour is the shade of cobalt?
19 The Abbey Theatre is in which Irish city?
20 Which nurse was called "The Lady with the Lamp"?
21 What was Cinderella's coach made from?
22 Who rocked around the clock in 1955?
23 Which zoo is found in Regent's Park?
24 Who wrote "The Ugly Duckling"?
25 What is the Zodiac sign Gemini also called?
26 Shrewsbury is the county town of which county?
27 Which fruit when dried produces raisins?
28 In which sport did Ivan Lendl achieve fame?
29 What is measured in decibels?
30 Where is the headquarters of the United Nations?

Answers | Rich & Famous: Names *(see Quiz 3)*

1 Kate Winslet. 2 Chef/Restaurateur. 3 Boothroyd. 4 Sandhurst. 5 Kenneth Branagh and Emma Thompson. 6 Habitat. 7 Hair. 8 Yorkshire Ripper. 9 Chelsea Clinton. 10 Steffi Graf. 11 Tony Blair. 12 Naomi Campbell. 13 Richard Branson. 14 Brightman. 15 Rod Stewart. 16 Lewinsky. 17 1930s. 18 William Jefferson Hague. 19 Hall. 20 Apple. 21 Newcastle United. 22 Neil. 23 Labour. 24 Margaret Thatcher. 25 Advertising. 26 Paul McCartney. 27 Earl Spencer. 28 Bookshops. 29 Westwood. 30 True.

1 Messrs Docherty, Atkinson and Ferguson have all managed which team?
2 Who was the first football boss to marry one of her former players?
3 Which club sacked Jose Mourinho as manager at the end of 2018?
4 Between 2010 and 2018, who won European Player of the Year three times?
5 Which was the first Rovers side to win the Premier League?
6 Graham Taylor was likened to a turnip after a defeat in which Scandinavian country?
7 In 2018, who took over from Arsène Wenger as manager of Arsenal?
8 In which Asian country did Gary Lineker play club football?
9 What colour are the stripes on Newcastle Utd's first choice shirts?
10 Which side moved from Roker Park to the Stadium of Light?
11 Was Alan Shearer sold to Newcastle for £5 million, £15 million or £25 million?
12 In which country was George Best born?
13 What is the nationality of Dennis Bergkamp?
14 Which Premier League keeper fractured his skull in a game in 2006?
15 Which English club did Mo Salah join in 2017?
16 Son Heung-min became the most expensive Asian player in history when he signed for which club?
17 Which Paul was the first black player to captain England?
18 Who was known as El Tel when he managed Barcelona?
19 Who in 1997 became Arsenal's all-time leading goalscorer?
20 How is the Football Association Challenge Cup better known?
21 Which Welshman Ian said living in Italy was like "living in a foreign country"?
22 Which club did Jürgen Klopp manage before Liverpool?
23 Which colour links shirts at Liverpool, Middlesbrough and Southampton?
24 Which Brian managed Nottingham Forest for 18 years?
25 Gareth Southgate finished his playing career at which club?
26 Which Charlton brother was the first to be knighted?
27 Which Eric was the first overseas PFA Player of the Year winner?
28 Who was dubbed Duncan Disorderly?
29 Where did England finish in the 2018 World Cup?
30 Pep Guardiola became manager of which club in 2016?

Answers | Pot Luck 2 *(see Quiz 6)*

1 Austria. 2 Fawn. 3 Plums. 4 Charles M. Schulz. 5 Ant & Dec. 6 Me. 7 Sand.
8 Beatrix Potter. 9 Hampshire. 10 La Marseillaise. 11 Lion. 12 Ebony. 13 Ireland.
14 Golf. 15 Aardvark. 16 Bull. 17 Bayeux. 18 Beef. 19 Poppy. 20 Prince Edward.
21 Eight. 22 An angle. 23 Twiggy. 24 Bury its head. 25 Or Nearest Offer. 26 A
clear soup. 27 Purplish red. 28 Apple. 29 West Ham. 30 Nottinghamshire.

Quiz 6

Pot Luck 2

Answers – page 13

LEVEL 1

1 Vienna is the capital of which European country?
2 What name is given to a young deer?
3 Which fruit when dried produces prunes?
4 Who drew the Peanuts cartoons?
5 Which duo won the NTA's Most Popular TV presenters five times at the start of this century?
6 Which musical note follows ray?
7 What do you find in a bunker on a golf course?
8 Who wrote "The Tale of Peter Rabbit"?
9 Winchester is the county town of which county?
10 What is the name of the French National Anthem?
11 Which animal was Androcles very friendly with?
12 Which black wood is used for piano keys?
13 Which island is affectionately called the Emerald Isle?
14 In which sport is the Ryder Cup competed for?
15 What type of creature is Arthur in the CBBC series of the same name?
16 Which animal is linked with the Zodiac sign Taurus?
17 Which town is home to the Bayeux Tapestry?
18 What kind of meat can be silverside and topside?
19 What is the first name of Jamie Oliver's eldest daughter?
20 What is the name of the Queen's youngest son?
21 How many notes are there in an octave?
22 What do you measure with a protractor?
23 Who is Dame Lesley Lawson better known as?
24 What is it said an ostrich does, if it thinks it is in danger?
25 After a selling price, what do the initials O.N.O. stand for?
26 Which type of soup is a consommé?
27 What colour is magenta?
28 What type of fruit is an Orange Pippin?
29 Which London-based football club are known as "The Hammers"?
30 In which county is Sherwood Forest?

Answers	**Sport: Football UK** *(see Quiz 5)*

1 Manchester Utd. 2 Karren Brady. 3 Manchester United. 4 Cristiano Ronaldo. 5 Blackburn. 6 Sweden. 7 Unai Emery. 8 Japan. 9 Black & white. 10 Sunderland. 11 £15 million. 12 Northern Ireland. 13 Dutch. 14 Petr Cech. 15 Liverpool. 16 Tottenham Hotspur. 17 Ince. 18 Terry Venables. 19 Ian Wright. 20 FA Cup. 21 Rush. 22 Borussia Dortmund. 23 Red. 24 Clough. 25 Middlesbrough. 26 Bobby. 27 Cantona. 28 Duncan Ferguson. 29 Fourth. 30 Manchester City.

14

Quiz 7

Hobbies & Leisure 1

Answers – page 16

1 The art of self-defence aikido originated in which country?
2 Which Bank Holiday comes immediately before Easter Day?
3 What is the Japanese art of paper folding called?
4 Where might you be entertained by a redcoat?
5 Which reptiles feature in a popular board game?
6 Which is bigger, Disneyland or Disneyworld?
7 What do you play baccarat with?
8 Which leisure park Towers are near Stoke on Trent?
9 In which game is the object to gain checkmate?
10 What is the minimum number of players in a cribbage game?
11 Which quiz board game involves the collection of coloured wedges?
12 Brass rubbing usually takes place in what type of building?
13 You navigate to a location with GPS and try to find a container hidden there – what is this activity called?
14 In which English city could you watch Rovers and City play football?
15 Which part of a pub shares its name with an area of a law court?
16 Which End of London is famous for its theatres?
17 Microlighting takes place in what sort of craft?
18 What name is given to the hours that a pub can open to sell alcohol?
19 What type of music is celebrated at the CMA awards?
20 What colour is the L on a normal learner driver's L plate?
21 What sort of accommodation is provided in a B & B?
22 Knitting needs needles, what does crochet need?
23 Which pier is to the north of Blackpool's central pier?
24 What type of castle do young children enjoy jumping up and down on?
25 "The dogs" involves races of which breed?
26 What colour are the segments on a roulette wheel?
27 Which Planet is a celebrity-founded restaurant chain?
28 What colour are Scrabble tiles?
29 Which gambling game's best hand is Royal flush?
30 What colour is the M on the McDonalds logo?

| **Answers** | Pot Luck 3 *(see Quiz 8)* |

1 Green. 2 Fish. 3 Friar Tuck. 4 Brideshead Revisited. 5 Leo. 6 Johnny Ball. 7 Public Limited Company. 8 Switzerland. 9 Bear. 10 Alexandra. 11 April. 12 76. 13 Pancakes. 14 On board ship. 15 A snake. 16 Iceni. 17 Yellow/orange. 18 Apple. 19 George Orwell. 20 Isle of Wight. 21 1960s. 22 Before they're hatched. 23 Holland. 24 Saturday. 25 A pup. 26 Malta. 27 Dark. 28 Eucalyptus leaves. 29 White coffee. 30 The Tower of London.

1 If you mix blue and yellow paint what colour is made?
2 What is usually eaten with Tartare Sauce?
3 Who was Robin Hood's priest?
4 Jeremy Irons and Anthony Andrews starred in which 1981 TV drama?
5 Which sign of the Zodiac is normally shown as a lion?
6 Who is Zoe Ball's famous father?
7 What do the initials plc stand for after a company name?
8 Berne is the capital of which European country?
9 What type of creature was Baloo in "The Jungle Book"?
10 Which London palace is also called "Ally Pally"?
11 St George's Day is in which month?
12 How many trombones led the big parade according to the song?
13 What are crêpes Suzettes a type of?
14 Where does a purser usually work?
15 What is a black mamba?
16 Boudicca was queen of which ancient tribe?
17 What colour is ochre?
18 What kind of fruit is a russet?
19 Who wrote the novel "Animal Farm"?
20 On which island is Osborne House, home of Queen Victoria?
21 In which decade did Yuri Gagarin become the first man in space?
22 When must you not count your chickens, according to the proverb?
23 Which country makes Gouda cheese?
24 What day of the week is the Jewish Sabbath?
25 What name is given to a young seal?
26 Which island was awarded the George Cross in 1942?
27 Is presenter Carol Vorderman's hair light or dark?
28 What does a koala have for its main source of food?
29 What is café au lait?
30 Where are the Crown Jewels kept?

Quiz 9 | Pop Divas | Answers – page 18

1 Which Spice Girl advertised Milky Bars as a child?
2 Who sang "I Will Always Love You" from the movie "The Bodyguard"?
3 Who kissed Britney Spears and Christina Aguilera on stage at an MTV awards show?
4 Who put her famous Union Jack dress up for auction?
5 Who had a No.1 single with "Toxic"?
6 Which female R&B artist wrote "A Rose Is Still A Rose" for Aretha Franklin?
7 Janet and La Toyah are from which famous family?
8 What is the first name of the Welsh singer from Catatonia?
9 What was Madonna's surname at birth?
10 Which 60s singer's first hit was written by the Rolling Stones?
11 Heather Small found fame with which band?
12 What is the surname of sisters Kylie and Dannii?
13 In which year was Amy Winehouse born?
14 Who rose to fame as lead singer of the Supremes?
15 Who had hits with "Respect" and "Chain of Fools"?
16 Whose debut album was called "19"?
17 Who sang the themes to three Bond films, including "Goldfinger"?
18 How many members does Little Mix have?
19 How did the Bangles Walk?
20 Of which group was Beyoncé originally a member?
21 Which 60s singer hosted "Surprise Surprise"?
22 Which Capstan sang with the B52s and guested with REM?
23 Who was the lead singer for Blondie?
24 Which musical instrument is Vanessa Mae famous for?
25 Where was Rihanna born?
26 Alanis Morissette and Celine Dion are from which country?
27 Who sang about "Baboushka" and "Wuthering Heights"?
28 In which decade did Bananarama have their first hit?
29 Miss Nurding dropped her surname and became known as whom?
30 Her first name means "love" in Albanian – who is she?

Answers | **Pot Luck 4** (see Quiz 10)

1 July. 2 Bull/cow. 3 Cider. 4 Michael Palin. 5 A savoury snack. 6 1969. 7 Venice. 8 Mount Ararat. 9 Forbidden fruit. 10 A will. 11 France. 12 Norwich City. 13 Vincent van Gogh. 14 Aries. 15 Calligraphy. 16 Harley Street. 17 Pinocchio. 18 Tanks. 19 Friday. 20 A bird. 21 Taskmaster. 22 Cherry. 23 17. 24 September. 25 Devon. 26 Baptism. 27 Eric Morecambe. 28 Arsenal. 29 Hippopotamus. 30 Colin Firth.

Quiz 10 Pot Luck 4

Answers – page 17

1 St Swithin's Day is in which summer month?
2 Who or what is an Aberdeen Angus?
3 What drink did writer Laurie Lee share with Rosie?
4 Which ex-Python Palin published his diaries in autumn 2006?
5 What are pretzels?
6 Did man first land on the moon in 1966, 1969 or 1972?
7 In which Italian city is St Mark's cathedral?
8 On which Mount is the resting place of Noah's Ark?
9 Which fruit tastes sweetest according to the proverb?
10 What does a testator make, in law?
11 Which country produces Camembert cheese?
12 Which football team is known as "The Canaries"?
13 Which Dutch painter cut off his ear?
14 Which Zodiac sign is normally associated with the ram?
15 What is the study of handwriting called?
16 Which London street is associated with the medical profession?
17 Which wooden puppet was written about by Carlo Collodi?
18 Shermans, Grants and Cromwells are all types of what?
19 Which day of the week is the Muslim Holy Day?
20 What is a quail?
21 Greg Davies and Alex Horne present which show?
22 Which fruit is used to make kirsch?
23 How old should you be to apply for a car driving licence in the UK?
24 In what month is Michaelmas Day?
25 Which county has Exeter as its county town?
26 For which religious ceremony is a font normally used?
27 Who was born John Eric Bartholomew?
28 Which football club's nickname is the Gunners?
29 Which animal has a name which means "river horse"?
30 Which Colin starred in the movie "Hope Springs"?

Answers	Pop Divas *(see Quiz 9)*

1 Emma (Baby Spice). 2 Whitney Houston. 3 Madonna. 4 Geri Halliwell. 5 Britney
Spears. 6 Lauryn Hill. 7 Jackson. 8 Cerys. 9 Ciccone. 10 Marianne Faithfull. 11 M
People. 12 Minogue. 13 1983. 14 Diana Ross. 15 Aretha Franklin. 16 Adele.
17 Shirley Bassey. 18 Four. 19 Like an Egyptian. 20 Destiny's Child. 21 Cilla Black.
22 Kate. 23 Debbie Harry. 24 Violin. 25 Barbados. 26 Canada. 27 Kate Bush.
28 1980s. 29 Louise. 30 Dua Lipa.

1 Which early Spielberg blockbuster was about a shark?
2 What was Daniel Craig's first movie as James Bond?
3 In which 1990s musical film did Madonna change costume 85 times?
4 What was the name of the movie based on TV's "The X Files"?
5 Which Julianne played opposite Anthony Hopkins in "Hannibal"?
6 Martin Scorsese made a film about the Gangs Of which city?
7 "The Fellowship of the Ring" was based on which book?
8 Which creatures dominated "Jurassic Park"?
9 What was "Crocodile Dundee's" homeland?
10 "Hook" was based on which children's book?
11 Which lizard-like monster's name is a mix of the Japanese words for
   gorilla and whale?
12 Who left Kramer in the 1970s movie with Hoffman and Streep?
13 "From Here to Eternity" is set before the Japanese attack on where?
14 "Raging Bull" was about which sport?
15 Which film was an abbreviation of Extra Terrestrial?
16 "The Empire Strikes Back" was a sequel to what?
17 "Raiders of the Lost Ark" was about which Mr Jones?
18 Robin Hood was Prince of what in the 1991 blockbuster?
19 Was "Snow White and the Seven Dwarfs" released before or after World
   War II?
20 Where was Gary Oldman Lost in the 1998 hit movie?
21 Which Caped Crusader was the subject of one of the top 1980s films?
22 Which watery film succeeded "Waterworld" as the most costly to make?
23 Gene Kelly was An American ... where in the Vincente Minnelli movie?
24 Which star of "Grease" and "Saturday Night Fever" is a qualified pilot?
25 Was "The Sting" a hit in the 1950s, 70s or 90s?
26 Which Disney animal movie was a 1994 blockbuster set in Africa?
27 "Amadeus" told the story of which composer?
28 "Home Alone" shot which child star to fame?
29 Was "Schindler's List" in colour or black and white?
30 Which Kevin played Mariner in "Waterworld"?

Answers	Pot Luck 5 *(see Quiz 12)*

1 Switzerland. 2 Charles. 3 Golden Hind. 4 The Gondoliers. 5 Thrillers. 6 Fleet
Street. 7 Suffolk. 8 V-shaped. 9 St Patrick. 10 Pisces. 11 National Trust. 12 Emily
Blunt. 13 4. 14 Darren Gough. 15 Reindeer. 16 Golf. 17 Olivia. 18 Rome.
19 Alpha. 20 A dog. 21 France. 22 Lawn. 23 Herbs. 24 Green. 25 Small Island.
26 A newspaper. 27 Eel. 28 Seaweed. 29 The Sound of Music. 30 Dorchester.

1 Which country produces Gruyère cheese?
2 Who was invested as Prince of Wales in 1969?
3 Francis Drake's ship Pelican was renamed what?
4 Which opera by Gilbert and Sullivan is set in Venice?
5 Did John le Carré write thrillers or romantic fiction?
6 Which London Street was home to several British newspapers?
7 Which county has Ipswich as its county town?
8 What shape are the teeth on pinking shears?
9 Which Saint is commemorated on the 17th of March?
10 Which Zodiac sign is normally associated with two fishes?
11 What organization which protects historic buildings was founded in 1895?
12 Who plays Mary Poppins in "Mary Poppins Returns"?
13 In snooker, how many points is the brown ball worth?
14 Who was the first cricketer to win TV's "Strictly Come Dancing"?
15 What kind of animals were Cupid, Donner and Blitzen?
16 In which sport would you use a caddie?
17 What was the top girls' name in 2017?
18 According to the proverb, which Italian city was not built in a day?
19 What is the first letter of the Greek alphabet?
20 What is a Shih-Tzu?
21 Which country does the wine claret come from?
22 In tennis, what does the initial L in LTA stand for?
23 What kind of plants are sage, lovage and basil?
24 Which London park is the name of a colour?
25 Andrea Levy wrote the award-winning novel titled "Small" what?
26 If you bought "Le Figaro" in France what would you be buying?
27 An elver is a young what?
28 What is kelp?
29 Which film featured the Von Trapp Family?
30 What is the county town of Dorset?

Answers	The Movies: Blockbusters *(see Quiz 11)*

1 Jaws. 2 Casino Royale. 3 Evita. 4 The X Files. 5 Julianne Moore. 6 New York.
7 The Lord of the Rings. 8 Dinosaurs. 9 Australia. 10 Peter Pan. 11 Godzilla.
12 Kramer. 13 Pearl Harbor. 14 Boxing. 15 E.T. 16 Star Wars. 17 Indiana Jones.
18 Thieves. 19 Before. 20 Space. 21 Batman. 22 Titanic. 23 Paris. 24 John
Travolta. 25 70s. 26 The Lion King. 27 Mozart. 28 Macaulay Culkin. 29 Black &
white. 30 Costner.

1 Chrome, Explorer, Firefox and Safari are types of what?
2 What company did Bill Gates found?
3 What are the first names of the Super Mario Brothers?
4 On a computer keyboard, the copy command is Ctrl plus which letter?
5 What is the name of the software which products files that end in .ppt?
6 What is Amazon's virtual assistant called?
7 In which country is the consumer electronics company Sony headquartered?
8 Would you find a motherboard inside a computer or on its keyboard?
9 What did Tim Berners-Lee invent in 1990?
10 Which social media network has a blue bird as its symbol?
11 In what country is the telecommunications company Nokia based?
12 Nano, Shuffle and Touch are types of what?
13 What does WWW stand for?
14 On a computer keyboard, the paste command is Ctrl plus which letter?
15 The Google technology which provides panoramas of city streets is called what?
16 What is Apple's virtual assistant called?
17 What service does Microsoft Outlook offer?
18 Which name is a combination of 'instant camera' and 'telegram'?
19 What do Americans call their mobile phone?
20 If you are paid to promote products to your social media followers, what are you known as?
21 Of which social network was Mark Zuckerberg a founder?
22 What is a Snapchat multimedia message called?
23 He founded Apple and died in 2011 – who was he?
24 How long are Instagram stories available for viewing?
25 In 2018 what did the BBC change the name of its audio app to?
26 .jpg and .png are usually what sort of files?
27 What is Amazon's electronic book reader called?
28 How many characters were originally permitted in a tweet?
29 Who invented the first computer and called it the Difference Engine?
30 On social networks, what do you use to label or find content on a specific subject?

Answers | Pot Luck 6 *(see Quiz 14)*

1 Volcanoes 2 Insects. 3 The Boy Scout Movement. 4 Shrove Tuesday. 5 Pink.
6 Sagittarius. 7 Gorillaz. 8 Badger. 9 Newcastle United. 10 Romeo and Juliet.
11 England. 12 Egypt. 13 Little Acorns. 14 Nazareth. 15 A tutu. 16 The Simpsons.
17 Clouds. 18 In water. 19 Wood. 20 John Cleese. 21 Ontario. 22 Adolf Hitler.
23 Chelsea. 24 Blood. 25 Venice. 26 Silence. 27 Warwickshire. 28 A toad.
29 Gladys Knight. 30 Blonde.

1 What is the theme of the French amusement park Vulcania?
2 What does a Venus fly-trap trap?
3 Which movement was founded by Lord Baden-Powell?
4 What day precedes Ash Wednesday?
5 In snooker, is the pink ball or the brown ball of higher value?
6 Which sign of the Zodiac is pictured by an archer?
7 "Dare" was the first No.1 single for which band?
8 Which animal is often given the name Brock?
9 Which football club's nickname is the Magpies?
10 Which Shakespeare play features the Capulets and Montagues?
11 Which country was called Albion by Greeks and Romans?
12 In which country is the battle site of El Alamein?
13 Great oak trees grow from what, according to the proverb?
14 Which town did Jesus grow up in?
15 What is the name of the dress worn by a ballerina?
16 Which long-running TV series features Marge and Homer?
17 Stratus, Cirrus and Cumulus are all types of what?
18 Where do mosquitoes lay their eggs?
19 What are clogs traditionally made from?
20 Which actor played Basil Fawlty in "Fawlty Towers"?
21 Toronto is the capital of which Canadian province?
22 Who wrote "Mein Kampf"?
23 Which football team plays at Stamford Bridge?
24 What do your arteries carry from your heart?
25 In which northern Italian city is the Doge's Palace?
26 If speech is silver, what is golden according to the proverb?
27 Which county cricket team plays at Edgbaston?
28 What is a natterjack?
29 Which Gladys sang the theme song to the 007 movie "Licence to Kill"?
30 Was Renee Zellwegger a blonde or brunette in "Bridget Jones's Diary"?

Answers	**Technology** *(see Quiz 13)*

1 Web browser. 2 Microsoft. 3 Mario and Luigi. 4 C. 5 PowerPoint. 6 Alexa.
7 Japan. 8 Inside. 9 World Wide Web. 10 Twitter. 11 Finland. 12 iPod. 13 World
Wide Web. 14 V. 15 Street View. 16 Siri. 17 Email. 18 Instagram. 19 Cell phone
or cell. 20 Influencer. 21 Facebook. 22 A snap. 23 Steve Jobs. 24 24 hours. 25
Sounds. 26 Image files. 27 Kindle. 28 140. 29 Charles Babbage. 30 Hashtag.

1 Which detective did Dr Watson assist?
2 The cover of Peter Kay's "The Sound of Laughter" is a spoof of which film poster?
3 Mrs Beeton was most famous for writing on what subject?
4 Are Penguin books hardbacks or paperbacks?
5 Was St Trinian's a school for boys or girls?
6 What type of animal is Winnie the Pooh?
7 What relation was Charlotte to Emily and Anne Brontë?
8 Who is Agatha Christie's most famous female detective?
9 What is the name of the book of scripts from "The Catherine Tate Show"?
10 In which building does the murder take place at the start of "The Da Vinci Code"?
11 Who's "Winter Collection" of recipes sold 1.5 million copies in just eight weeks?
12 What sort of Factory is associated with Roald Dahl's Charlie?
13 In which book are there four accounts of Jesus's life called gospels?
14 Which African president's autobiography was called "Long Walk to Freedom"?
15 Who wrote "Cook with Jamie"?
16 What was "Schindler's Ark" renamed when it was made into a film?
17 Where was Douglas Adams' Hitchhiker's Guide to?
18 What type of tales did the Grimm brothers write?
19 What is the nationality of novelist Maeve Binchy?
20 Which novelist Dame Catherine died in 1998?
21 Who wrote "And It's Goodnight from Him..." about himself and his late comedy partner?
22 Who was Ian Fleming's most famous secret agent creation?
23 Whom did Laurie Lee write of in the title "Cider with..."?
24 Which football coach's World Cup Story 1998 caused an outrage over breaches of confidentiality?
25 Which Stephen is famous for horror writing such as "The Shining"?
26 What was Dick Francis's profession before he turned to writing?
27 What was Bram Stoker's most famous monstrous creation?
28 In which century did Charles Dickens live?
29 Which comedian Ben wrote "Gridlock" and "Popcorn"?
30 Which Frederick's first success was "The Day of the Jackal"?

| **Answers** | **Pot Luck 7** *(see Quiz 16)* |

1 November. 2 The tail. 3 Elvis Presley. 4 An alkali. 5 A small wood. 6 Hamlet.
7 Angels. 8 Conservatives. 9 Afrikaans. 10 Kenya. 11 Willow. 12 Seven. 13 An eyrie. 14 Threadneedle Street. 15 Doncaster. 16 The Osbournes. 17 £1. 18 Ballet.
19 Violet. 20 Adder. 21 Nepal. 22 Agoraphobia. 23 Mercury. 24 Pasta.
25 Spencer. 26 The Hours. 27 Norwich. 28 A news agency. 29 Mars. 30 Somerset House.

Quiz 16 Pot Luck 7

Answers – page 23

1 In which month is Thanksgiving celebrated in America?
2 Where is the rattle in a rattlesnake?
3 Whose "Are You Lonesome Tonight" was back in the UK charts in 2005?
4 What is the opposite of an acid?
5 What is a spinney?
6 Who said, "To be or not to be, that is the question"?
7 In the Bible, what were seraphim and cherubim?
8 Which political party had Benjamin Disraeli as a leader?
9 Which South African language derives from the Dutch settlers?
10 Which country has Nairobi as its capital?
11 Cricket bats are traditionally made from which wood?
12 How many colours are in the spectrum?
13 What name is given to the home of an eagle?
14 On which Street is the Bank of England?
15 The St Leger is run at which Yorkshire racecourse?
16 Which real rock family includes Ozzy, Sharon and Kelly?
17 Which coin was first introduced in the UK in 1983?
18 For what type of dancing did Anna Pavlova achieve fame?
19 What colour is an amethyst?
20 What is the only poisonous snake in Britain?
21 Which country is native homeland to the Gurkha troops?
22 Which phobia is the fear of open spaces?
23 Which chemical is also known as quicksilver?
24 Penne, rigatoni and tagliatelle are all types of what?
25 What did the initial "S" stand for in Winston S. Churchill?
26 Did Nicole Kidman win an Oscar for "The Days", "The Hours" or "The Weeks"?
27 Which Norfolk city stands on the River Wensum?
28 What is Reuters?
29 Who was god of war in Roman mythology?
30 In 2018–19, which London venue held a "Peanuts" exhibition?

Answers | Books (see Quiz 15)

1 Sherlock Holmes. 2 The Sound of Music. 3 Cooking. 4 Paperbacks. 5 Girls. 6 Bear. 7 Sister. 8 Miss Marple. 9 Am I Bovvered. 10 Louvre. 11 Delia Smith. 12 Chocolate. 13 Bible. 14 Nelson Mandela. 15 Jamie Oliver. 16 Schindler's List. 17 The Galaxy. 18 Fairy tales. 19 Irish. 20 Cookson. 21 Ronnie Corbett. 22 James Bond. 23 Rosie. 24 Glenn Hoddle. 25 King. 26 Jockey. 27 Dracula. 28 19th. 29 Elton. 30 Forsyth.

1 Mark Spitz won seven Olympic golds at record speeds doing what?
2 In 2018, in Berlin, Eliud Kipchoge broke what record in two hours, one minute and 39 seconds?
3 How many seasons did Alan Shearer play for Newcastle – 3, 6 or 10?
4 Lynn Davies broke the British record in which jump event?
5 David Campese was leading try scorer for which country?
6 Which Sally was a world record hurdler and 1992 Olympic champion?
7 Who was made England's youngest ever football coach in 1996?
8 Did Roger Bannister run the first four-minute mile in Oxford or Cambridge?
9 Was Martina Hingis 13, 15 or 17 when she first won Wimbledon doubles?
10 Who was the first Rugby Union player to win 100 England caps?
11 Which Nigel was the first to win both F1 and Indy Car world championships?
12 Which record breaker Sebastian went on to become a Tory MP?
13 Which Tony made the first televised hole in one in Britain?
14 How many Olympic gold medals did Usain Bolt win?
15 Which Steve was six times World Snooker Champion in the 1980s?
16 For which former Iron Curtain country did Marita Koch break records?
17 Jerry Rice set a career touchdown record in which sport?
18 How many events were in Daley Thompson's speciality event?
19 Which Pete equalled Borg's five Wimbledon singles wins in 1998?
20 Which Gareth became Wales's youngest ever Rugby captain in 1968?
21 Alain Prost was the first to win the F1 world title for which country?
22 Bob Beamon held which Olympic jump record for over 20 years?
23 Who was Britain's only Men's 100m world record holder between 1983 and 1993?
24 Which David did Graham Gooch overtake to become England's highest-scoring Test player?
25 World record breaker Kip Keino is from which continent?
26 Did Nadia Comaneci first score a perfect Olympic 10 at 14, 18 or 21?
27 Which golfer Jack was first to achieve 15 career professional majors?
28 Colin Jackson was a world record holder in which event?
29 Who was the first player to score 100 goals in the Premier League?
30 Duncan Goodhew held British records in which sport?

Answers | Pot Luck 8 *(see Quiz 18)*

1 Leicester City. 2 Gin. 3 Taj Mahal. 4 Dingoes. 5 Actor/Actress. 6 Violins. 7 Greece. 8 June. 9 Bridges. 10 May. 11 Alan Bleasdale. 12 A stipend. 13 Red. 14 Kite mark. 15 New York. 16 Albatross. 17 Coronation Street. 18 Sherry. 19 The worm. 20 Paul McCartney. 21 Bread. 22 45. 23 In the mouth. 24 Andrew Lloyd Webber. 25 St Paul's Cathedral. 26 Vertical. 27 Victoria Coren Mitchell. 28 Sugar, almonds. 29 99 years old. 30 Magpie.

Quiz 18 Pot Luck 8

Answers – page 25

LEVEL 1

1 Which football club's nickname is the Foxes?
2 Which alcoholic drink contains juniper as a flavour?
3 By what name is the mausoleum at Agra, India normally known?
4 Which dogs are a serious pest in Australia?
5 What would your profession be if you were a member of Equity?
6 Which instruments did Antonio Stradivari produce?
7 Which country is famous for moussaka?
8 In which month is Father's Day in the UK?
9 Pontoon and suspension are both types of which construction?
10 What did the "M" stand for in Louisa M. Alcott's name?
11 Who wrote the TV drama "Boys from the Blackstuff"?
12 What is a salary paid to a clergyman called?
13 What colour is cochineal?
14 The British Standards Institute uses what mark as a sign of approval?
15 Which American city is served by Kennedy Airport?
16 Which bird has the largest wing span?
17 Which soap is set in the city which hosted the 2002 Commonwealth Games?
18 What kind of drink is Amontillado?
19 What does an early bird catch, according to the proverb?
20 Which Beatle's daughter is a dress designer?
21 Bloomers and baps are both types of what?
22 How many years are there in four and a half decades?
23 Where are your incisors?
24 Who, together with Tim Rice, wrote "Evita"?
25 Where is Lord Nelson buried?
26 On a staircase are the risers flat or vertical?
27 Who presents "Only Connect"?
28 What are the two ingredients of marzipan?
29 How old was evangelist Billy Graham when he died in 2018?
30 Which black and white bird is usually accused of stealing?

Answers	Sport: Record Breakers *(see Quiz 17)*

1 Swimming. 2 Marathon. 3 10 years. 4 Long jump. 5 Australia. 6 Gunnell.
7 Glenn Hoddle. 8 Oxford. 9 15. 10 Jason Leonard. 11 Mansell. 12 Coe.
13 Jacklin. 14 Nine. 15 Davis. 16 East Germany. 17 American football. 18 Ten.
19 Sampras. 20 Edwards. 21 France. 22 Long jump. 23 Linford Christie. 24 Gower.
25 Africa. 26 14. 27 Jack Nicklaus. 28 Hurdles. 29 Alan Shearer. 30 Swimming.

1 Is 0207 the dialling code for central Manchester or central London?
2 The name of which mobile network provider is a number?
3 If you dial 1471 whose number are you given?
4 Which four or five letters can preface access to an Internet website?
5 What is the normal size of a floppy disk?
6 NDR is a broadcasting company from which country?
7 What are held in the hands to communicate through semaphore?
8 The fingertips represent which five letters in sign language?
9 112 is an alternative to which number?
10 A modem connects a computer to what?
11 Qantas Airways originated in which country?
12 Which cross-Channel link has its French terminus at Coquelles?
13 Tresco airport links which Isles to the UK?
14 What does a letter c enclosed in a circle stand for?
15 Which country has the most Internet users in the world?
16 What does D stand for in IDD?
17 Which character divides the person from the place in an email address?
18 Which type of clock works from shadows?
19 Numbers beginning with 0800 usually cost how much to the caller?
20 On a standard keyboard which letter is to the right of Q?
21 Combinations of which two signs are used in Morse code?
22 On a standard keyboard which letter is to the right of Z?
23 In texting what does TMI stand for?
24 Which number do you ring to contact a BT operator?
25 Where is Cathay Pacific Airways based?
26 What is the American version of the British postcode?
27 With BT calls, what is the daytime period, Monday to Friday?
28 What does "I" stand for in IT?
29 What is the internet code for the United Kingdom?
30 Ryanair is a budget airline from which country?

1 Choux, puff and short are all types of what?
2 Who was the more unpleasant – Dr Jekyll or Mr Hyde?
3 Generally what is Hatton Gardon in London famous for?
4 What colour is carmine?
5 What are tweeters and woofers?
6 Which ceremony is associated with orange blossom?
7 Which pink bird sleeps on one leg?
8 Which mountain overlooks Cape Town, South Africa?
9 Which British film company used a symbol of a man striking a gong?
10 In "Peanuts", what is Snoopy's bird friend called?
11 What is the Spanish word for a young or single lady?
12 Where was the news agency Tass based?
13 At which club did Mick McCarthy take over from Glenn Hoddle?
14 Who was the first Jewish Prime Minister in Britain?
15 Comedian Barry Humphries plays which female character?
16 Which colony ceased to be British in June 1997?
17 Where would you be if you were in a transept?
18 What is the list of the subjects to be discussed at a meeting called?
19 Which Prince served in the Falklands War?
20 In the old saying, how many makes a crowd if two are company?
21 Conference and Cornice are types of which fruit?
22 Which animal needs "Taming" in the title of the Shakespeare play?
23 Aboard which ship in 1620 did the Pilgrim Fathers sail to America?
24 Which Helen was a star of the movie "Gosford Park"?
25 What colour is angelica?
26 What connects singer Kate Bush with novelist Emily Brontë?
27 What is the capital of Barbados?
28 What is a wife of a sultan called?
29 What word describes something being next to last?
30 Which British studios were famed for their horror movies of the 1950s, 60s and 70s?

Answers	Science: Communication *(see Quiz 19)*

1 London. 2 Three. 3 The last person to have called you. 4 http or https. 5 3.5ins.
6 Germany. 7 Flags. 8 Vowels. 9 999. 10 Telephone. 11 Australia. 12 Channel
Tunnel. 13 Scilly Isles. 14 Copyright. 15 China. 16 Dialling. 17 @. 18 Sundial.
19 Nothing. 20 W. 21 Dots & dashes. 22 X. 23 Too Much Information. 24 100.
25 Hong Kong. 26 Zip. 27 7 am to 7 pm. 28 Information. 29 .uk. 30 Ireland.

1 Which country did ABBA come from?
2 Which 70s pop movie with John Travolta was re-released in 1998?
3 Which band did Diana Ross leave at the start of the decade?
4 T Rex was led by which singer?
5 What colour was Debbie Harry's hair which named her band?
6 "Maggie May" provided whom with his first No.1?
7 Kiki Dee's biggest 70s hit was with whom?
8 Where did Supertramp have Breakfast in 1979?
9 Who was lead singer with the Boomtown Rats?
10 Who cleaned Wimbledon Common and cleaned up in the charts in '74?
11 What went with Peaches in the 70s charts?
12 Who had a posthumous hit with "Way Down"?
13 Song for whom was Elton John's first instrumental hit?
14 Which World Cup football squad did Rod Stewart have a hit with?
15 Which Rollers had two No.1s in 1975?
16 Who had a single hit from the album "Bat Out of Hell"?
17 Izhar Cohen and Alphabeta won Eurovision for which country?
18 Which brothers included Wayne, Donny and Little Jimmy?
19 Whose first hit was "Wuthering Heights"?
20 Which 70s B side for Queen became a football anthem?
21 Which ABBA hit became the name of an Alan Partridge spoof?
22 Which Gary's first hit was as Tubeway Army?
23 Which hostel did the Village People visit in the 70s?
24 How many performers made up The Carpenters?
25 Which football side had a hit with "I'm Forever Blowing Bubbles"?
26 "Tubular Bells" is credited with establishing which record label?
27 Which band were "Part of the Union"?
28 Which Bryan founded Roxy Music?
29 Who celebrated his "Ding-A-Ling" in song?
30 Who had the last 70s Xmas No.1 with "Another Brick in the Wall"?

1 What is the profession of Geraldine Grainger of Dibley?
2 How do Men Martin Clunes and Neil Morrissey behave in the sitcom?
3 In which country is "Kath & Kim" set?
4 Alphabetically which of the characters in "Friends" comes first?
5 "Whatever Happened to the Likely Lads?" was the sequel to what?
6 Which sitcom classic was about self-sufficiency in Surbiton?
7 How did Hyacinth pronounce "Bucket" in "Keeping Up Appearances"?
8 Which show about Grace Brothers' store had a rerun in 1998?
9 What was the sequel to "Yes Minister"?
10 Which sitcom about the Trotters was originally to be called Readies?
11 Which series featured the character David Brent?
12 Which Penelope alias Audrey was "To the Manor Born"?
13 How many children feature in the sitcom about Bill and Ben Porter?
14 Which Ronnie played Arkwright in "Open All Hours"?
15 Ian McShane starred in which sitcom about a shady antiques dealer?
16 In which historical sitcom did Baldrick first appear?
17 Which show was originally to have been called "Your Bottom"?
18 Which Felicity was the star of "Solo"?
19 In which sitcom did Joanna Lumley play champagne-swilling Patsy?
20 What are the names of the Birds in "Birds of a Feather"?
21 In "Dad's Army", who called Sgt Wilson Uncle Arthur?
22 Frasier was a spin-off from which series based in a Boston bar?
23 Which Craig co-wrote and starred in "The Royle Family"?
24 Which wartime sitcom featured Rene and Edith Artois?
25 Who played Jean, husband of Lionel, in "As Time Goes By"?
26 "Goodnight Sweetheart" is set in the 1940s and which other decade?
27 Which series was based on Butlin's and Pontin's?
28 What was Anton Rodgers' legal job in "May to December"?
29 Which Family is a sitcom with ex-Mrs Merton Caroline Aherne?
30 What is Mrs Victor Meldrew's first name?

Answers | Pop: 70s *(see Quiz 21)*

1 Sweden. 2 Grease. 3 The Supremes. 4 Marc Bolan. 5 Blonde. 6 Rod Stewart.
7 Elton John. 8 America. 9 Bob Geldof. 10 The Wombles. 11 Herb. 12 Elvis Presley.
13 Guy. 14 Scottish. 15 Bay City Rollers. 16 Meat Loaf. 17 Israel. 18 Osmond.
19 Kate Bush. 20 We are the Champions. 21 Knowing Me Knowing You. 22 Numan.
23 YMCA. 24 Two. 25 West Ham. 26 Virgin. 27 Strawbs. 28 Ferry. 29 Chuck
Berry. 30 Pink Floyd.

1 Red Admirals, Fritillaries and Tortoiseshells are all what?
2 Which pie is Melton Mowbray renowned for?
3 Which has more rainfall, the Sahara or Antarctica?
4 Which sport would you see at Chepstow?
5 Which brothers made the first manned powered aero flight in 1903?
6 Who is the main male character in the novel "Lorna Doone"?
7 What was sold by an apothecary?
8 Who presents BBC2's "Later" music show?
9 Which animals live in an earth or lair?
10 Along with white, what colours appear on the Italian flag?
11 Which snake is it said Cleopatra used to poison herself?
12 How many ships came sailing by according to the carol?
13 Who presented the very first series of "Big Brother"?
14 What is chipboard made from?
15 Catherine Zeta Jones and Michael Douglas sued about photos from which event?
16 What is a poinsettia?
17 In the novel what kind of animal was Tarka?
18 Bruges is the capital of which part of Belgium?
19 Which characters sang "The Bare Necessities" in "The Jungle Book"?
20 Which football club's nickname is the Baggies?
21 How many wings does a bee have?
22 In which decade did Britain convert to decimal currency?
23 Sardinia is part of which country?
24 What are collected by a philatelist?
25 What colour is the background of the Scottish flag?
26 What flavour is crème de menthe?
27 What type of bird are Ring, Turtle and Collared?
28 Who is Sooty and Sweep's female friend?
29 Which is the highest female singing voice?
30 Which sea is called La Manche by the French?

Answers | **Pot Luck 11** *(see Quiz 24)*

1 12. 2 Stop bleeding. 3 The King and I. 4 Canada. 5 Sir Cliff Richard. 6 Tower of London. 7 Blue/violet. 8 Suffolk. 9 General Strike. 10 Cricket. 11 Russian. 12 Australia. 13 24. 14 Sturgeon. 15 Heart. 16 White. 17 Madness. 18 Spirit level. 19 Anna Sewell. 20 Maundy money. 21 Kayaks. 22 Oranges. 23 All for one and one for all. 24 Tracey Thorn. 25 Windsor. 26 A Sharp. 27 Oliver. 28 Cambridge. 29 Red/white. 30 Zoe Ball.

1 How many episodes of "Fawlty Towers" were made?
2 What is a tourniquet used for in First Aid?
3 Which musical is based on a book called "Anna and the King of Siam"?
4 The chipmunk is native to America and which other country?
5 Who was pop's first Knight?
6 Where in London is the ceremony of the keys held each night?
7 What colour is indigo?
8 Which East Anglian county is often called "Constable Country"?
9 In 1926 which General crisis happened in England?
10 Which sport links Ted Dexter, Peter May and Ray Illingworth?
11 What was the nationality of composer Rimsky-Korsakov?
12 Budgerigars are native to which country?
13 How many carats in pure gold?
14 Caviar comes traditionally from which fish?
15 What does a cardiologist study?
16 What colour are Aylesbury ducks?
17 Which band played on BBC1's 2018 into 2019 New Year coverage?
18 What is used to check something is level by a builder?
19 Who wrote the novel "Black Beauty"?
20 What does the Queen give out on the day before Good Friday?
21 What are the sealskin boats used by Eskimos called?
22 What did Nell Gwyn sell when Charles II first saw her?
23 What was the motto of the Three Musketeers?
24 Who wrote the memoir "Bedsit Disco Queen"?
25 Which castle is in the royal county of Berkshire?
26 If a musical note is lowered by a flat, what raises it?
27 What was the top boys' name in 2017?
28 In which city is the River Cam?
29 Apart from blue, what other two colours appear on the Dutch flag?
30 Who took over the Radio 2 breakfast show from Chris Evans in 2019?

Answers | Pot Luck 10 *(see Quiz 23)*

1 Butterflies. 2 Pork Pie. 3 The Sahara. 4 Horse racing. 5 Wright Brothers. 6 John Ridd. 7 Medicines/Drugs. 8 Jools Holland. 9 Fox. 10 Red/green. 11 Asp. 12 Three. 13 Davina McCall. 14 Small pieces of wood. 15 Their wedding. 16 Flower/Shrub. 17 Otter. 18 Flanders. 19 Baloo and Mowgli. 20 West Bromwich Albion. 21 Four. 22 1970s. 23 Italy. 24 Stamps. 25 Blue. 26 Peppermint. 27 Dove. 28 Soo. 29 Soprano. 30 The English Channel.

1 Is Holy Island off the east or west coast of England?
2 What is a native of Aberdeen called?
3 Is London's Docklands, north, south, east or west of the city?
4 The Angel of the North was erected next to which major road?
5 Which English gorge takes its name from a nearby village famous for its cheese?
6 Which county has the abbreviation Beds?
7 St Anne's lies to the south of which British seaside resort?
8 Which Royal residence stands by the river Dee?
9 In which country is the UK's highest mountain?
10 What sort of an institution in London is Bart's?
11 On a London Tube map the Central Line is what colour?
12 In which Scottish city did you find the Gorbals?
13 Which motorway links London to Winchester?
14 Which Isle off the south coast of England is a county in its own right?
15 What is Britain's most southerly country?
16 Norwich is the administrative centre of which county?
17 In which city did the National Trust buy the childhood home of Paul McCartney?
18 Which motorway runs almost parallel to the A4?
19 In October 2018, in which UK county did a new fracking site open?
20 What is Britain's largest international airport?
21 In which county is Land's End?
22 What colour are most London buses?
23 Which motorway goes from Lancashire to Yorkshire east to west?
24 What is the background colour of road signs to tourist sites?
25 In which part of the UK is "Land of My Fathers" a traditional song?
26 Winchester is the adminstrative seat of which county?
27 Aston University is near which Midlands city?
28 Most of the Lake District is in which county?
29 What red flower does Lancs have?
30 In which city is the Barbican Centre?

Answers | Pot Luck 12 *(see Quiz 26)*

1 Harry Potter. 2 Mozart. 3 A peach. 4 Sark. 5 Brown. 6 He who laughs last.
7 1953. 8 Carpets. 9 Diagonally. 10 Spain. 11 Wahaca. 12 Black/Yellow. 13 A vixen. 14 Cakes. 15 Edmund. 16 Afghanistan. 17 Colour. 18 Isle of Wight.
19 A fish. 20 39. 21 Blackberry. 22 Zambezi. 23 Herring. 24 Marie Antoinette.
25 Everton. 26 Victor Hugo. 27 Puffin. 28 Red, yellow & blue. 29 Four. 30 Italy.

1 Daniel Radcliffe played which famous boy on screen?
2 Who composed the opera "The Marriage of Figaro"?
3 What type of fruit is a nectarine?
4 Which of the four Channel Islands is the smallest?
5 What colour is sepia?
6 Who, according to the proverb, laughs longest?
7 In which year was Everest conquered?
8 Which house furnishing is associated with the town of Kidderminster?
9 How does a bishop move in chess?
10 The drink sangria comes from which European country?
11 Thomasina Miers founded which restaurant chain?
12 What two colours other than red appear on the Belgian flag?
13 What is a female fox called?
14 What is sold in a patisserie?
15 Who is Peter's brother in "The Lion, the Witch and the Wardrobe"?
16 .af is the internet code for which country?
17 What can a chameleon lizard change?
18 The rocks called The Needles are close to which island?
19 What is a barracuda?
20 How many steps were there in the title of the novel by John Buchan?
21 A loganberry is a cross between a raspberry and what?
22 Which river are the Victoria Falls on?
23 Sardines and pilchards are part of which fish family?
24 Which French Queen was executed in the French Revolution?
25 Which football club's nickname is the Toffees?
26 Who wrote "The Hunchback of Notre Dame"?
27 Which seabird is associated with Lundy Island?
28 What are the three primary colours in art?
29 How many wings does a moth have?
30 From which country does the football team Juventus come from?

Answers	**Geography: The UK** *(see Quiz 25)*

1 East. 2 Aberdonian. 3 East. 4 A1. 5 Cheddar. 6 Bedfordshire. 7 Blackpool. 8 Balmoral. 9 Scotland. 10 Hospital. 11 Red. 12 Glasgow. 13 M3. 14 Isle of Wight. 15 England. 16 Norfolk. 17 Liverpool. 18 M4. 19 Lancashire. 20 Heathrow. 21 Cornwall. 22 Red. 23 M62. 24 Brown. 25 Wales. 26 Hampshire. 27 Birmingham. 28 Cumbria. 29 Rose. 30 London.

1 Whom was tennis star Martina Hingis named after?
2 Which lauded football star was born Edson Arantes do Nascimento?
3 Which French footballer David advertised L'Oreal hair products?
4 Golfer Ernie Els is from which African country?
5 Which British tennis player was born on Greg Rusedski's first birthday?
6 Jonah Lomu plays for which international side?
7 Athlete Kelly Holmes was formerly a member of which armed service?
8 Which Paula had a hat-trick of London Marathon wins this millennium?
9 Which snooker champ Ray was nicknamed Dracula?
10 Whom did Andy Murray beat to win his first Olympic gold medal?
11 Who won BBC Sports Personality of the Year in 2018?
12 Which Monica was stabbed in the back by a fanatical Graf supporter?
13 What sport did Michael Jordan play?
14 Which racing driver was first to clock up more than 75 F1 wins?
15 In which sport was Lizzy Yarnold a double Olympic gold medal winner?
16 Which three-time Grand National winner died in 1995?
17 Which Greg rejected a maple leaf for a Union Jack in the 1990s?
18 Who founded the book known as the cricketer's Bible?
19 Rachael Heyhoe-Flint is a famous name in which sport?
20 What was Greg Rutherford's athletics event?
21 Which Princess won the 1971 European Three Day Event?
22 What nationality is footballer Zlatan Ibrahimović?
23 Which temperamental tennis player was dubbed Superbrat?
24 Which Jenny was the first woman to train a Grand National winner?
25 Where was multiple Tour de France winner Chris Froome born?
26 Which boxer's catchphrase was "Know what I mean 'Arry"?
27 Which disappearing horse won the Derby in 1981?
28 Who founded the Stewart motor racing team?
29 What was cricket umpire Harold Bird's nickname?
30 Who became the first black manager of a Premier League club when he took over at Chelsea in 1996?

| **Answers** | Pot Luck 13 *(see Quiz 28)* |

1 Four. 2 Loire. 3 Weatherfield. 4 Cornwall. 5 South-south-east. 6 Thomas Hardy.
7 Slavery. 8 King. 9 Red/White. 10 USA. 11 Seven. 12 Kew. 13 Hadrian's Wall.
14 Purple. 15 Mont Blanc. 16 Venice. 17 June. 18 Malta. 19 Grey. 20 Apple.
21 Queen's Counsel. 22 The Black Death/Bubonic Plague. 23 Types of rhubarb. 24 A
spring tide. 25 Argentina. 26 Daisy. 27 West Ham. 28 Pigeon racing. 29 Melon.
30 Switzerland.

1 How many wings does a butterfly have?
2 Which river is the longest in France?
3 In which fictional town does "Coronation Street" take place?
4 In which county is Bodmin Moor?
5 Which compass point is opposite north-north-west?
6 Which Thomas wrote "The Mayor of Casterbridge"?
7 Which trade was abolished in 1807 in the British Empire?
8 Which chess piece should be protected at all costs?
9 What two colours are on the Austrian flag?
10 In which country was there a North v. South civil war from 1861–65?
11 How many players are in a netball team?
12 Where in Britain are the Royal Botanic Gardens?
13 Which ancient wall crosses England from Wallsend to Solway?
14 What colour is an aubergine?
15 Which mountain is the highest in the Alps?
16 The artist Canaletto was associated with which Italian city?
17 In which month is the Trooping of the Colour?
18 Which island is also called the George Cross Island?
19 Which colour is linked to Sir Ian McKellen's character Gandalf?
20 Cox, Braeburn and Gala are all kinds of which fruit?
21 In legal terms, what do the initials QC stand for?
22 Which disaster struck England in the 1340s?
23 What links Champagne and Timperley Early?
24 What is the opposite of a neap tide?
25 Which country lies immediately east of Chile?
26 Who was asked to ride "a bicycle made for two" in the song?
27 Jermain Defoe joined Tottenham Hotspur from which other London club?
28 The National Homing Union is involved with which leisure pursuit?
29 What kind of fruit can be cantaloupe?
30 Which country as well as France is Lake Geneva in?

Answers	Sport: Who's Who? *(see Quiz 27)*

1 Martina Navratilova. 2 Pele. 3 Ginola. 4 South Africa. 5 Tim Henman. 6 New Zealand. 7 Army. 8 Paula Radcliffe. 9 Reardon. 10 Roger Federer. 11 Geraint Thomas. 12 Seles. 13 Basketball. 14 Michael Schumacher. 15 Skeleton. 16 Red Rum. 17 Rusedski. 18 Wisden. 19 Cricket. 20 Long jump. 21 Anne. 22 Swedish. 23 John McEnroe. 24 Pitman. 25 Nairobi, Kenya. 26 Frank Bruno. 27 Shergar. 28 Jackie Stewart. 29 Dickie Bird. 30 Ruud Gullit.

1 Who went straight to No.1 in 1981 with "Stand and Deliver"?
2 What colour Door gave Shakin' Stevens an 80s hit?
3 Which ex-Beatle had a hit with Stevie Wonder in 1982?
4 Whose album "Thriller" provided several hit singles?
5 Who was KC's backing Band?
6 Which Scot had chart success after Esther Rantzen's "The Big Time"?
7 Which BBC Radio station banned "Relax"?
8 Ravel's "Bolero" charted because of which skaters' Olympic success?
9 Which actor Robert was named in a Bananarama song title ?
10 Which Superstar Rat sang "Love Me Tender"?
11 Which Alison's nickname was Alf?
12 Which Elaine and Barbara topped the charts in 1985?
13 Which Mrs Andrew Lloyd Webber had a hit with "Pie Jesu"?
14 David Bowie and Mick Jagger had a hit after which Concert?
15 Elton John charted with "Nikita" at the same time as Sting had which coincidental hit?
16 Who had hits as part of Visage and Ultravox?
17 Who told you that you were "In the Army Now"?
18 Who fronted Culture Club?
19 Graham McPherson of Madness was known as what?
20 Which Kim reached No. 2 in 1981, 24 years after dad Marty?
21 Which Spanish singer had the UK's first chart topper in Spanish?
22 David Sylvian was part of which Asian-sounding band?
23 Who was the first ventriloquist in the charts with Orville?
24 Who teamed up with Annie Lennox in The Eurythmics?
25 Who was the then oldest man in the charts with "New York New York"?
26 Who joined Cliff Richard for his 80s "Living Doll"?
27 Which TV puppets sang "The Chicken Song"?
28 Which red-haired Royal liked "Lady in Red"?
29 Which future England coach joined Waddle on "Diamond Lights"?
30 Who had a Xmas No.1 in 1988 after 30 years in the charts?

Answers | Pot Luck 14 (see Quiz 30)

1 Eton. 2 Raymond Briggs. 3 13. 4 Soft fruit. 5 Peter Kay. 6 A soliloquy. 7 Isle of Man. 8 Kim Sears. 9 Oranges. 10 French. 11 Horse Guards Parade. 12 Drugs. 13 Your Old Kit Bag. 14 Hats. 15 Honey. 16 Five. 17 Distillery. 18 His tools. 19 The Jordan. 20 Needles. 21 Blackbird. 22 Richard I. 23 Whales. 24 American Football. 25 Capricorn. 26 Pears. 27 November. 28 Lisa. 29 Robert. 30 Harp.

Quiz 30 | Pot Luck 14

1 Which school did Prince Harry attend when he was 13?
2 Which cartoonist was the creator of "The Snowman"?
3 How many are there in a baker's dozen?
4 What would you find in a punnet?
5 Who featured on Tony Christie's 2005 smash hit "Amarillo"?
6 What is a Shakespearan speech or scene with only one actor called?
7 Douglas is the capital town of which Isle?
8 What was the maiden name of Andy Murray's wife?
9 The Spanish city of Seville is famous for which fruit?
10 What is the nationality of pianist Richard Clayderman?
11 Where does the Trooping of the Colour take place in London?
12 Pharmacology is the study of what?
13 Where, according to the song, should you pack up your troubles?
14 What is usually kept in a band-box?
15 What is the main ingredient in the drink mead?
16 In music, how many lines are there in a stave?
17 What name is given to the building where whisky is made?
18 According to the proverb, a bad workman always blames what?
19 Jesus Christ was baptised in which river?
20 What are inserted into the body during acupuncture?
21 According to rhyme which bird pecked off the maid's nose?
22 Which King was known as the "Lionheart"?
23 Beluga, Sperm and Blue are all types of what?
24 Which sport is played on a grid iron?
25 Which Zodiac sign is known as the sign of the goat?
26 What is perry made from?
27 In which month is the State Opening of Parliament in England?
28 Who is Bart Simpson's older sister?
29 What is Judge Rinder's first name?
30 Which musical instrument is a national emblem of Ireland?

Answers | Pop: The 80s *(see Quiz 29)*

1 Adam and the Ants. 2 Green. 3 Paul McCartney. 4 Michael Jackson. 5 Sunshine Band. 6 Sheena Easton. 7 Radio One. 8 Torvill & Dean. 9 Robert de Niro. 10 Roland. 11 Moyet. 12 Paige, Dickson. 13 Sarah Brightman. 14 Live Aid. 15 Russians. 16 Midge Ure. 17 Status Quo. 18 Boy George. 19 Suggs. 20 Kim Wilde. 21 Julio Iglesias. 22 Japan. 23 Keith Harris. 24 Dave Stewart. 25 Frank Sinatra. 26 The Young Ones. 27 Spitting Image. 28 Duchess of York. 29 Hoddle. 30 Cliff Richard.

1 Which batter mix is an accompaniment to roast beef?
2 Where was restaurateur Yotam Ottolenghi born?
3 What colour wine is Beaujolais Nouveau?
4 What colour is the flesh of an avocado?
5 What is the traditional colour for the outside of a stick of rock?
6 Would you eat or drink a Sally Lunn?
7 What type of egg is covered in sausage meat?
8 Scrumpy is a rough form of what?
9 Which mashed vegetable tops a shepherd's pie?
10 Which food has given its name to a road network near Birmingham?
11 Is a Spotted Dick a first course or a pudding?
12 Which fruit is associated with tennis at Wimbledon?
13 Champagne originated in which country?
14 Is a Melton Mowbray pie sweet or savoury?
15 What is a pistachio?
16 What sort of fruit is in a teacake?
17 Since 2017, who has co-presented "The Great British Bake Off" with Sandi Toksvig?
18 Which is more substantial, afternoon tea or high tea?
19 If you ate al fresco would you be indoors or out of doors?
20 What is the usual shape of a Camembert cheese?
21 Which soft pulpy peas are eaten with fish and chips?
22 What type of food may be served clotted?
23 What would you make in a cafetière?
24 What type of drink is Bristol Cream?
25 Is chowder a soup or a pudding?
26 A "pinta" is usually a pint of what?
27 Should red wine normally be drunk chilled or at room temperature?
28 Is there milk in a cappuccino coffee?
29 Are you more likely to eat a croissant at breakfast or supper?
30 What country does kimchi come from?

| **Answers** | **Pot Luck 15** *(see Quiz 32)* |

1 Edward. 2 Jamie Oliver. 3 Everton. 4 Films. 5 Ferrari. 6 Hillary Clinton. 7 Eyes. 8 A fool. 9 101 Dalmatians. 10 Baghdad. 11 B. 12 Four years. 13 Portugal. 14 Parkinson. 15 Wood. 16 Fish. 17 Beta. 18 Ear, nose and throat. 19 Assisi. 20 Stitches. 21 Cancer. 22 Tammy Wynette. 23 Brown. 24 New Zealand. 25 St Bernard. 26 California. 27 21. 28 Michael and John. 29 Norway. 30 Liz Pichon.

Quiz 32 | Pot Luck 15

Answers – page 39

LEVEL 1

1 Which English King was also called "The Confessor"?
2 Who has children called Poppy, Daisy, Petal, Buddy and River?
3 Which football team play their home games at Goodison Park?
4 PG, 15 and 18 are all classifications for what?
5 Which manufacturer was the first to achieve more than 100 F1 Grand Prix wins?
6 How is US lawyer Hillary Roddam better known?
7 In Cockney rhyming slang, what are your mince pies?
8 According to the proverb, who is soon parted from his money?
9 From which Disney film does Cruella De Vil come from?
10 What is the capital of Iraq?
11 Which letter describes a soft lead pencil?
12 How long is an American president's term of office?
13 The Azores are a part of which European country?
14 Which Michael began his TV chat shows back in 1971?
15 What are the bars on a xylophone made from?
16 What is a mud skipper?
17 What is the second letter of the Greek alphabet?
18 In medicine, what do the initials ENT stand for?
19 With which Italian town is Saint Francis linked?
20 Blanket, back and buttonhole are all types of what?
21 Which Zodiac sign is known as the sign of the crab?
22 Whose life story was called "Stand By Your Man"?
23 Which wire is live in modern three-core electric cable?
24 From which country other than Australia did Anzac troops come from?
25 Who is the patron saint of mountaineers?
26 In which state of the US is the resort of Palm Springs?
27 How many consonants are in the English alphabet?
28 In "Peter Pan" what are the names of Wendy's brothers?
29 The port of Bergen is in which European country?
30 Who wrote the Tom Gates children's books?

Answers	**Food & Drink 1** *(see Quiz 31)*

1 Yorkshire pudding. 2 Jerusalem. 3 Red. 4 Green. 5 Pink. 6 Eat. 7 Scotch egg. 8 Cider. 9 Potato. 10 Spaghetti (junction). 11 Pudding. 12 Strawberries. 13 France. 14 Savoury. 15 Nut. 16 Currants and/or other dried fruit. 17 Noel Fielding. 18 High tea. 19 Out of doors. 20 Round. 21 Mushy peas. 22 Cream. 23 Coffee. 24 Sherry. 25 Soup. 26 Milk. 27 Room temperature. 28 Yes. 29 Breakfast. 30 Korea.

1 Levi Strauss founded the first company to manufacture what?
2 J. Robert Oppenheimer is associated with the invention of which explosive device?
3 Who invented the ballpoint pen?
4 What did Alexander Fleming discover?
5 What nationality was Samuel Morse, inventor of Morse code?
6 The inventor of cornflakes was called what?
7 Richard Gatling invented the first working what?
8 What form of travel did the Montgolfier brothers pioneer?
9 Benjamin Franklin had a common vision problem – what did he invent?
10 Igor Sikorsky invented which flying vehicle?
11 What did Wilhelm Röntgen discover?
12 Who invented the electric light bulb?
13 What object did Mikhail Kalashnikov invent and give his name to?
14 Guglielmo Marconi is associated with the invention of what technology?
15 What nationality was Johannes Gutenberg, inventor of movable type for printing?
16 Who is credited with inventing the telephone?
17 In what field was Karl Benz a pioneer?
18 What form of travel did the Wright brothers pioneer?
19 What nationality was Blaise Pascal, inventor of the barometer?
20 Isaac Singer invented which domestic machine?
21 George Eastman's invention was the basis for the moving picture industry – what was it?
22 In which decade did it television become widely available?
23 What form of power did Nikola Tesla work on and help develop?
24 Did Thomas Edison register around 1,100 or 11,000 patents?
25 Rudolf Diesel invented what?
26 What type of clothing is named after Charles Macintosh?
27 When was the first mobile phone call made – 1973 or 1993?
28 What nationality was Alessandro Volta, inventor of the electric battery?
29 It made life much easier for the parents' of small babies – what did Marion Donovan invent?
30 Was the ice cream cone invented in Italy, Iceland or America?

Answers	**Pot Luck 16** *(see Quiz 34)*

1 Confessions. 2 Egg whites. 3 Betjeman. 4 Liquid or gas. 5 Edinburgh. 6 11.
7 Gabriel. 8 Mods. 9 Drei. 10 Winnie The Pooh. 11 Canute. 12 Victor. 13 Alan
Coren. 14 Snapdragon. 15 Sheffield. 16 Quickly. 17 Fountain pen. 18 Italy.
19 Estimated Time of Arrival. 20 Wine. 21 Rocky Horror Show. 22 Loch Ness Monster.
23 Ken Loach. 24 The All Blacks. 25 The sparrow. 26 Brazil. 27 James Herriot. 28
Poland. 29 Play. 30 2012.

1 What was made "On a Dance Floor" according to Madonna's album title?
2 What is sugar added to, to make meringues?
3 Which poet laureate Sir John died in 1984?
4 What can pass through something if it is porous?
5 In which Scottish city are the Rebus novels set?
6 How many Oscars did "Titanic" win – 6, 11 or 14?
7 In the Bible, which angel foretold the birth of Jesus?
8 What youth group took to wearing parkas?
9 What is the German word for the number three?
10 Which children's favourite bear said he had "very little brain"?
11 Which English king reputedly commanded the sea to retreat?
12 What is the letter "V" if A is Alpha and B is Bravo?
13 Who was the presenter of "Only Connect"'s famous father?
14 What is a popular name for the flower the antirrhinum?
15 Which Yorkshire city were Pulp from?
16 In music what does presto mean?
17 What object was invented by Lewis Waterman in 1884?
18 Tuscany is in which European country?
19 In the world of flying, what do the initials ETA stand for?
20 What is retsina?
21 Dr Frank-N-Furter is a character in which musical?
22 Which monster first hit the headlines in 1933?
23 Who directed "Cathy Come Home"?
24 What are the New Zealand rugby union team called?
25 According to the rhyme, who killed Cock Robin?
26 The Samba originated in which South American country?
27 Who wrote "It Shouldn't Happen to a Vet"?
28 The port of Gdansk is in which country?
29 Would you eat, play or sit on a sitar?
30 When did Andy Murray win his first Olympic gold medal?

1 Which ex-James Bond has "Scotland Forever" tattooed on his arm?

2 Which Jools starred in "Spiceworld: The Movie"?

3 Which Irish-born 007 starred in "Tomorrow Never Dies"?

4 Which Grease actor danced with Princess Diana at the White House?

5 Which sleuth did Albert Finney play in Agatha Christie's "Murder on the Orient Express"?

6 Which top-selling rapper made his movie debut in "8 Mile"?

7 Who was the star of "Moonwalker" after being in The Jackson Five?

8 Which bespectacled US actor/director directed the musical "Everyone Says I Love You"?

9 What type of hat was Charlie Chaplin most famous for?

10 Who is Emma Forbes' actor/director dad?

11 Who was named after her home town of Winona?

12 Which knighted pop singer wrote the music for "The Lion King"?

13 Hayley Mills is the daughter of which knighted actor?

14 Who separated from husband Bruce Willis in 1998?

15 Which newspaper magnate bought 20th Century-Fox in 1985?

16 Who was Sid played by Gary Oldman in "Sid and Nancy"?

17 What name usually associated with a schoolbag did Woody Allen give his son?

18 Which Welsh actor Sir Anthony bought part of Mount Snowdon in 1998?

19 Which pop star Tina starred in "Mad Max Beyond Thunderdome"?

20 Which Ms Foster swapped her real first name from Alicia?

21 In rhyming slang what financial term is Gregory Peck?

22 Which child star was Shirley MacLaine named after?

23 Who appeared first at Madame Tussaud's, Harrison Ford or Hugh Grant?

24 Who starred as Steed in the film version of "The Avengers"?

25 Which boxer played himself in "The Greatest"?

26 What was the surname of Chico, Harpo, Groucho and Zeppo?

27 Who sang "It's Not Unusual" in "Mars Attacks!"?

28 Which actress appeared on the cover of "The Sound of Music" movie DVD?

29 Judi Dench played which character known by a letter in the Bond movies?

30 "There's Something About Mary" and "Gangs of New York" starred which actress?

1 In December 2005, which pop legend was remembered 25 years after his murder?

2 Who wrote the novel "You Only Live Twice"?

3 Which English county has a border with only one other county?

4 What collective name is given to the structure of bones in the body?

5 The drink port takes its name from which town?

6 What colour is normally associated with ecological groups?

7 What is the hardest substance known to man?

8 Which people are associated with the Jolly Roger flag?

9 What is the French word for the number two?

10 Alphabetically, which is the second of the 12 calendar months?

11 With which sport do we associate a half nelson?

12 In a Steven Spielberg movie if A stood for Artificial what did I stand for?

13 What was the result of the final Ashes Test match of the 2005 series?

14 Which country did the paso doble dance originate in?

15 What type of food can be pilau?

16 In which American city is a 500-mile motor race run annually?

17 Which cartoon cat never manages to catch Tweetie Pie?

18 What is Britain's busiest ferry passenger port?

19 What kind of animal is a hind?

20 What can pass through something if it is translucent?

21 Which Tony first became MP for Sedgefield in 1983?

22 How many sides do seven hexagons have?

23 Was "Crackerjack" shown on BBC or ITV?

24 Who played James Bond in "Die Another Day"?

25 Which country does the drink sake come from?

26 For which sport is Pat Eddery famous?

27 What colour is saffron?

28 In children's books and on TV, what kind of animal is Babar?

29 David Attenborough's "The Blue Planet" was about life in what type of location?

30 What term is used in golf to indicate the stroke rating for each hole?

Answers | The Movies: Who's Who? *(see Quiz 35)*

1 Sean Connery. 2 Holland. 3 Pierce Brosnan. 4 John Travolta. 5 Poirot. 6 Eminem. 7 Michael Jackson. 8 Woody Allen. 9 Bowler. 10 Bryan Forbes. 11 Winona Ryder. 12 Sir Elton John. 13 Sir John Mills. 14 Demi Moore. 15 Rupert Murdoch. 16 Vicious. 17 Satchel. 18 Hopkins. 19 Turner. 20 Jodie Foster. 21 Cheque. 22 Shirley Temple. 23 Harrison Ford. 24 Ralph Fiennes. 25 Muhammad Ali. 26 Marx. 27 Tom Jones. 28 Julie Andrews 29 M. 30 Cameron Diaz.

1 What is a bookmaker's licensed premises called?
2 What shape is the target in archery?
3 Where on a dartboard is the bull?
4 Which cubes are necessary for a game of craps?
5 Which direction do you go if you are abseiling?
6 What sort of Park is at Whipsnade?
7 Which locomotive identification hobby shares its name with a controversial 1990s movie?
8 In which game do you aim to call "House!"?
9 Yoga was developed from which nation's religion?
10 Is scuba practised above or below the water's surface?
11 From which part of a vehicle might you sell goods to raise cash?
12 What name is given to a small piece of land rented for growing food?
13 In the UK most Bank Holidays fall on which day of the week?
14 Which commodities would you buy at a PYO centre?
15 What does E stand for in NEC?
16 What colour is the baize on a snooker table?
17 Which word precedes sport to describe killing animals for recreation?
18 What type of weapon is used in fencing?
19 What is the name of a coach trip where few know the destination?
20 If you practised on a pommel horse where would you probably be?
21 The Chamber of Horrors is in which London waxworks museum?
22 Which weekly draw is run by Camelot?
23 Are bonsai trees smaller or larger than average?
24 Which club moved to The Riverside in the 1990s?
25 What sort of establishment is a greasy spoon?
26 Who is a tied house usually tied to?
27 What is the type of billiards played in pubs called?
28 The Summer Bank Holiday takes place in which month in the UK?
29 Which name for an expert in a particular hobby is the same as a padded jacket?
30 What does Y stand for in DIY?

Answers	**Pot Luck 18** *(see Quiz 38)*

1 70s. 2 Tommy Walsh. 3 Cuba. 4 Springfield. 5 Seven. 6 Toboggan. 7 Goliath. 8 On water – it's a boat. 9 Countdown. 10 Elephant. 11 Tower Bridge. 12 Their gills. 13 Meat. 14 Six. 15 Possession. 16 Green & Yellow. 17 Nephews. 18 Ein. 19 Liverpool. 20 Catherine wheel. 21 Victoria. 22 Adrenaline. 23 Mineral water. 24 Baldrick. 25 Bergman. 26 650. 27 Rome. 28 Yellow. 29 Moses. 30 Six.

1 Did Britain join the EEC in the 60s, 70s or 80s?
2 Which "Ground Force" presenter was the tallest of the original three?
3 The Rumba originated in which country?
4 Where do the cartoon Simpsons live?
5 How many edges are there around a 50-pence coin?
6 What type of vehicle is seen on the Cresta Run?
7 Which Biblical giant was killed by David?
8 Where would you find a useful junk?
9 Dictionary expert Susie Dent featured regularly on which programme?
10 Which animal does ivory predominantly come from?
11 Which London bridge opens upwards to let tall ships through?
12 Fish breathe through what?
13 What was sold at London's Smithfield market?
14 How many noughts are there in the written number one million?
15 According to the saying, what is "nine points of the law"?
16 What colour is earth in modern three-core electric cables?
17 What relation are Huey, Dewey and Louie to Donald Duck?
18 What is the German word for the number one?
19 In which city was the Channel 4 soap "Brookside" set?
20 Which firework is named after a saint?
21 Which Queen became Empress of India in 1876?
22 What hormone is injected by an epi-pen?
23 Vichy is famous for which drink?
24 Which "Blackadder" character had a fascination for turnips?
25 Which Ingrid was the mother of Isabella Rossellini?
26 How many centimetres are there in six and a half metres?
27 The Vatican City is within which other capital city?
28 What colour is the shade of jonquil?
29 In the Bible, who was found in the bulrushes?
30 How many points does a snowflake have?

Answers	Hobbies & Leisure 2 *(see Quiz 37)*

1 Betting shop. 2 Circular. 3 Centre. 4 Dice. 5 Downwards. 6 Animal Park.
7 Trainspotting. 8 Bingo. 9 Indian. 10 Below. 11 Car boot. 12 Allotment. 13 Monday.
14 Fruit and vegetables (Pick Your Own). 15 Exhibition. 16 Green. 17 Blood. 18 Sword.
19 Mystery tour. 20 Gym. 21 Madame Tussaud's. 22 The National Lottery. 23 Smaller.
24 Middlesbrough. 25 Cafe. 26 Brewery. 27 Bar billiards. 28 August. 29 Anorak.
30 Yourself.

Quiz 39 TV: Famous Faces

1 Who travelled from "Pole to Pole" and "Around the World in 80 Days"?

2 Which former "Newsnight" presenter was nicknamed Paxo?

3 Clive James hails from which Commonwealth country?

4 Who was born John Cheese and changed his name by one letter?

5 Would you expect Brendan Cole to cook, dance or sing on TV?

6 Which David and Jonathan hosted the 1998 Election coverage?

7 Which "Gardener's World" presenter wrote a novel "Mr MacGregor"?

8 Which Kate won an OBE for her reporting in Beijing and the Gulf?

9 Which famous part of her did Rachel of "Friends" advertise?

10 Who was Mel and Sue's co-presenter on the BBC version of "The Great British Bake Off"?

11 Which Sir David's catchphrase is "Hello, good evening and welcome"?

12 Who worked with amateur chefs on "Hell's Kitchen"?

13 Which Paula gave interviews on her bed in "The Big Breakfast"?

14 Which Irishman took over from Terry Wogan as presenter of "The Eurovision Song Contest"?

15 Which practical joker Jeremy first hosted "You've Been Framed"?

16 What did Tomasz Schafernaker train as?

17 Is Paul Ross the brother, son or no relation of Jonathan Ross?

18 In 2006, which "Top Gear" presenter suffered a near fatal high-speed crash?

19 Which stock cube did Lynda Bellingham advertise?

20 How were TV cooks Clarissa and Jennifer better known?

21 Which professional dancer won "Strictly Come Dancing" 2018?

22 Who was the footballing team captain on "They Think It's All Over"?

23 Who is actor Rafe Spall's famous TV dad?

24 Ian McCaskill retired from presenting what in 1998?

25 Which American comedian takes other comedians to get coffee in a car?

26 Which former Beatle did Morecambe and Wise refer to as Bongo?

27 What are the first names of Reeves and Mortimer?

28 Which Judith did Anthea Turner replace on "Wish You Were Here"?

29 Which "Match of the Day" presenter took on a Radio 2 show in 1998?

30 Who played Angie Watts in the early episodes of "EastEnders"?

Answers | Pot Luck 19 *(see Quiz 40)*

1 Athletics. 2 Champion. 3 Dr John Reid. 4 Joseph. 5 Grievous Bodily Harm.
6 Like a lamb. 7 Ron. 8 Five. 9 Caribbean. 10 India. 11 Growing of crops.
12 Mae West. 13 On the shoulder. 14 King Charles. 15 Green. 16 Animal.
17 Boutique. 18 "Rocky Horror Show". 19 Grand National. 20 Mg. 21 2000.
22 December. 23 Phoenix. 24 Leather. 25 Five. 26 John Lennon. 27 Democrats & Republicans. 28 Fame Academy. 29 Dix. 30 Harry Corbett.

1 For which sport is Paula Radcliffe famous?
2 In the TV song, who was the "Wonder Horse"?
3 Which doctor became Home Secretary in Tony Blair's government?
4 Which of Jacob's sons had a coat of many colours, in the Bible?
5 In crime what do the initials G.B.H. stand for?
6 According to the saying, how will March go out if it comes in like a lion?
7 Did Rupert Grint play Harry or Ron in the Harry Potter films?
8 After how many years must an election be held in Britain?
9 Jamaica is in which sea?
10 Which country does the musical instrument the sitar come from?
11 Which kind of farming is arable farming?
12 Which famous film star gave her name to a life jacket?
13 Where would you wear an epaulette?
14 Which kind of spaniel was named after a king?
15 What colour sits between yellow and blue in the rainbow?
16 Is a jellyfish a mineral, vegetable or animal?
17 In the 60s what was Biba?
18 Which musical is a humorous tribute to science fiction B movies?
19 In 1993, which horse race was made void after a false start?
20 Which two letters form the symbol for the element magnesium?
21 How many centimetres are there in twenty metres?
22 Which month of the year in Britain includes the shortest day?
23 What is the capital of the US state of Arizona?
24 What is prepared in a tannery?
25 How many lines are there in a limerick?
26 Which member of the Beatles sang "Imagine"?
27 Which are the two main political parties in America?
28 What sort of "Academy" did Cat Deeley co-host?
29 What is the French word for the number ten?
30 Did Harry Corbett, Harry H. Corbett or Ronnie Corbett work with Sooty?

1 What's the name of the policeman in "Balamory"?
2 Which Stephen narrates "Pocoyo"?
3 What was the follow-up to "How!"?
4 Tom Baker was the longest-serving Doctor in which sci-fi series?
5 Which children's favourite has the number plate PAT 1?
6 What is Lola's brother called in the animation based on the Lauren Child books?
7 Which Engine's friends were Terence the Tractor and Bertie the Bus?
8 Does Tom or Jerry have the furrier coat?
9 What cuddly creatures are Uncle Bulgaria and Orinoco?
10 What was Worzel Gummidge?
11 Are Smurfs blue or orange?
12 Which Street teaches about letters and numbers?
13 What sort of creature is Pingu?
14 Which family is headed by Homer?
15 What colour is Teletubby Laa-Laa?
16 Which Bear was found in a London railway station?
17 What is Popeye's occupation?
18 What is the name of the superhero character in "Gigglebiz"?
19 What is the most number of presenters "Blue Peter" has at once?
20 Matthew Corbett said goodbye to which puppet companion in 1998?
21 What sort of animal was Huckleberry?
22 Who is the narrator of "In the Night Garden"?
23 Who is Dastardly's canine sidekick?
24 "On Your Marks" and "Art Attack" are about what subject?
25 Spot is chiefly what colour?
26 Is "Crush" a game show or a drama?
27 What sort of animal is Garfield?
28 What is Casper?
29 What does Rupert Bear wear on his feet in the 2006 series?
30 Are "Thunderbirds" birds, child actors or puppets?

Answers | Pot Luck 20 *(see Quiz 42)*

1 The mice. 2 Sports trophy (golf). 3 American Indians. 4 Questions. 5 Spanish. 6 Wallace and Gromit. 7 David Schwimmer. 8 Six. 9 Advent. 10 A kimono. 11 Mount Sinai. 12 Johnny Depp. 13 Althorp Park. 14 Quotient. 15 Hiroshima. 16 Three. 17 Plane crash. 18 Germany. 19 Boxing. 20 Neuf. 21 Tiger. 22 Tuxedo. 23 Battle of Hastings. 24 Rabbit. 25 Terry Waite. 26 Yellow. 27 Victory in Europe. 28 168. 29 The eye. 30 Anne Frank.

1 According to the proverb, what plays when the cat's away?
2 Did Harry Vardon give his name to a disease, a sports trophy or a fruit?
3 Which people wore moccasins originally?
4 What does Q mean in FAQ?
5 What is the main spoken language in Mexico?
6 "Shaun the Sheep" was a spin-off from which animation?
7 Which "Friends" star was the voice of the neurotic giraffe in "Madagascar"?
8 How many noughts are there in the written number fifty-two million?
9 Which season comes just before Christmas in the Christian calendar?
10 Which long dress is traditionally worn by Japanese women?
11 In the Bible, on which mountain was Moses told the commandments?
12 Who was Captain Jack Sparrow in the movie "Pirates of the Caribbean"?
13 At which Park is Princess Diana buried?
14 What does the Q stand for in IQ?
15 Where was the first atomic bomb dropped on 6 August 1945?
16 How many times has Andy Murray won BBC Sports Personality of the Year?
17 In 1993, what disastrous event boosted Emmerdale viewing figures?
18 Hanover, Westphalia and Bavaria are all parts of which country?
19 For which sport is Chris Eubank famous?
20 What is the French word for the number nine?
21 Which animal in the poem by Blake was described as "burning bright"?
22 What do Americans call a dinner jacket?
23 In which battle was King Harold killed?
24 What type of animal can be Dutch, Angora and Chinchilla?
25 Who was a Beirut hostage with John McCarthy and Brian Keenan?
26 What colour was the "itsy bitsy teeny weeny bikini" in the pop song?
27 What do the initials VE stand for in VE Day?
28 How many hours are there in a week?
29 Which part of the body can suffer from an astigmatism?
30 Which Jewish girl kept a diary while hidden in Amsterdam in 1942?

Answers | **Children's TV** *(see Quiz 41)*

1 PC Plum. 2 Stephen Fry. 3 How 2. 4 Doctor Who. 5 Postman Pat. 6 Charlie. 7 Thomas the Tank Engine. 8 Tom. 9 Wombles. 10 Scarecrow. 11 Blue. 12 Sesame Street. 13 Penguin. 14 The Simpsons. 15 Yellow. 16 Paddington. 17 Sailor. 18 Captain Adorable. 19 Four. 20 Sooty. 21 Hound. 22 Derek Jacobi. 23 Muttley. 24 Art & crafts. 25 Yellow. 26 Game show. 27 Cat. 28 Ghost. 29 Trainers. 30 Puppets.

Quiz 43 | The Movies: Greats | Answers – page 52

1 Which great screen dancer is on the cover of "Sgt Pepper"?
2 Which wartime classic starred Ingrid Bergman and Humphrey Bogart?
3 Who was Jamie Lee Curtis's actor father?
4 Cary Grant was born in which west country port?
5 Was Rita Hayworth a blonde or a redhead?
6 Was it Bob Hope or Bing Crosby who was born in south London?
7 Which monster was arguably Boris Karloff's most famous role?
8 How was dancer Eugene Curran Kelly better known?
9 Who was the original "Candle in the Wind" dedicated to?
10 Which Anthony starred as the lead character in "Psycho"?
11 Which Sir Alec starred in, and had a share of the profits of, "Star Wars"?
12 Who was taller, Rock Hudson or Mickey Rooney?
13 Which James starred in "Harvey" and "The Philadelphia Story"?
14 Which Italian-born actor is best known for silent movies such as "The Sheikh"?
15 Which Citizen was the subject of Orson Welles' first film?
16 Lauren Bacall was the wife of which Humphrey?
17 Tough guy Frank J. Cooper adopted which first name?
18 Which Joan starred in "Whatever Happened to Baby Jane"?
19 How was Ruth Elizabeth Davis better known?
20 Which Charlie was a founder of the film studio United Artists?
21 Bing Crosby had just finished a round of which game when he died?
22 William Claude Dunkenfield used his first two initials to become who?
23 Jane and Peter are the children of which screen great Henry?
24 Which Katharine enjoyed a long on and off screen relationship with Spencer Tracy?
25 Which Doris enjoyed popularity in films with Rock Hudson?
26 He was born John Uhler Lemmon III but how is he known in films?
27 Who is Michael Douglas's famous actor father?
28 In which German capital was Marlene Dietrich born?
29 Did Clark Gable die during his last film in the 40s, 50s or 60s?
30 Greta Garbo was born in which Scandinavian capital?

| **Answers** | **Pot Luck 21** *(see Quiz 44)* |

1 1970s. 2 An ill wind. 3 Harvey Keitel. 4 Beef cattle. 5 Windsor. 6 Runnymede.
7 Washington. 8 Around your waist. 9 Neun. 10 Egypt. 11 J. 12 Jack.
13 Origami. 14 Circus. 15 Dutch. 16 Krypton. 17 Trousers. 18 The teeth.
19 Spain. 20 900. 21 Jennifer Aniston. 22 The Archers. 23 Cavalier. 24 Easter.
25 Pink. 26 France. 27 Arachnophobia. 28 The skin. 29 Horses. 30 90th.

1 Charting again in 2004, in which decade was ABBA's "Waterloo" first a hit?
2 What kind of wind blows no good according to the proverb?
3 Which Harvey starred in Quentin Tarantino's "Reservoir Dogs"?
4 What type of animal can be Charolais, Galloway and Simmental?
5 Which is the largest castle in Britain?
6 Where did King John sign the Magna Carta?
7 In which capital is the Capitol Building?
8 Where would you wear a cummerbund?
9 What is the German word for the number nine?
10 Which country had eleven kings called Rameses?
11 What appears most as the initial letter in calendar month names?
12 According to the rhyme, who fixed his head with vinegar and brown paper?
13 What name is given to the Japanese craft of paper folding?
14 Billy Smart and Chipperfields provided what type of entertainment?
15 What was the nationality of diarist Anne Frank?
16 What was the name of Superman's home planet?
17 Who or what are Oxford Bags?
18 What part of your body is covered by orthodontics?
19 Paella is a traditional dish from which country?
20 How many seconds are in a quarter of an hour?
21 Which "Friends" star has advertised L'Oreal?
22 Bridge Farm and Brookfield Farm feature in which long-running soap?
23 What type of person was Laughing in the famous portrait?
24 Which festival follows Lent in the Christian calendar?
25 What colour is the Financial Times?
26 Brittany and Picardy are parts of which country?
27 Which phobia describes the fear of spiders?
28 In medicine, what does a dermatologist specialise in?
29 Suffolk Punch, Shires and Clydesdales are all types of what?
30 David Attenborough celebrated which landmark birthday in 2016?

Answers	The Movies: Greats *(see Quiz 43)*

1 Fred Astaire. 2 Casablanca. 3 Tony Curtis. 4 Bristol. 5 Redhead. 6 Bob Hope.
7 Frankenstein's monster. 8 Gene Kelly. 9 Marilyn Monroe. 10 Perkins. 11 Guinness.
12 Rock Hudson. 13 Stewart. 14 Rudolph Valentino. 15 Citizen Kane. 16 Bogart.
17 Gary. 18 Crawford. 19 Bette Davis. 20 Chaplin. 21 Golf. 22 W.C. Fields.
23 Fonda. 24 Hepburn. 25 Day. 26 Jack Lemmon. 27 Kirk Douglas. 28 Berlin.
29 60s. 30 Stockholm.

1 In which country would you find Jerez?
2 How would you travel if you left for France from a hoverport?
3 In which Sea is the island of Majorca?
4 In which country is Cologne?
5 Does London or Rome have the higher population?
6 The province of Flanders is in which country?
7 Which landlocked country is divided into cantons?
8 In which city would you find the Parthenon?
9 Bohemia is part of which Republic, formerly part of Czechoslovakia?
10 Is Schiphol an airport or a river in the Netherlands?
11 Which island is in the Bay of Naples?
12 Where is the Black Forest?
13 What type of country is Monaco?
14 Andorra lies between France and which other country?
15 In which Sea does Cyprus lie?
16 Belarus and Ukraine were formerly part of which huge republic?
17 What is the English name for the city known to Italians as Venezia?
18 Is Sweden a kingdom or a republic?
19 Vienna lies on which river?
20 Is Ibiza part of the Canaries or the Balearics?
21 In which Circle does about a third of Finland lie?
22 The Hague is the seat of government of which country?
23 Crete and Corfu belong to which country?
24 Which Scandinavian country is opposite Norway and Sweden?
25 Is Europe the second largest or the second smallest continent?
26 Which country marks the most westerly point of mainland Europe?
27 The Iberian Peninsula consists of Portugal and which other country?
28 Which French city is mainland Europe's largest?
29 What are the Balkans, the Apennines and the Pyrenees?
30 Which island is known to the French as Corse?

Quiz 46 | Pot Luck 22

1 Which Pamela featured in the "Borat" movie?
2 In Bruce Springsteen songs what goes before In The USA and To Run?
3 Which famous cricket commentator died of a heart attack in January 1994?
4 Which Lou wrote and sang "A Perfect Day"?
5 Was Liz Hurley born in the 50s, 60s, or 70s?
6 What colour sits between blue and violet in the rainbow?
7 Which Tory MP earned the name Goldilocks?
8 Which Harry created the character of Frank Doberman?
9 Which insects include drones, queens and workers?
10 Has a violin four, six or eight strings?
11 Which actor Peter played crumple-coated cop Columbo?
12 What is the capital of the US state of Utah?
13 Where did Peter Mayle spend a year of his life?
14 In which county was the Plymouth Brethren founded?
15 Athena, Nike and Zeus were all what?
16 The movie "Starter for Ten" is about a student's ambition to be on which TV show?
17 In football what is the real first name of the keeper unkindly nicknamed "Calamity" James?
18 Which Derby is run at the Curragh?
19 Who had a best friend with the politically incorrect name of Big Ears?
20 A lateen sail is what shape?
21 Revie, Robson and Taylor have all managed which team?
22 Which valuable things were made by Thomas Sheraton?
23 On TV, Sabrina is the name of the Teenage... what?
24 Which musical instrument does Larry Adler play?
25 Tony Banks was Minister for what in Tony Blair's first Cabinet?
26 What type of crazy cops were created by Mack Sennett?
27 What do XL stand for in Roman numerals?
28 What's the foodie stage name of sizeable singer Marvin Lee Aday?
29 Brady, Macari and Stein have managed which Scottish football club?
30 What kind of animal is a fox terrier?

Answers | Geography: Euro Tour (see Quiz 45)

1 Spain. 2 Hovercraft. 3 Mediterranean. 4 Germany. 5 London. 6 Belgium.
7 Switzerland. 8 Athens. 9 Czech Republic. 10 Airport. 11 Capri. 12 Germany.
13 Principality. 14 Spain. 15 Mediterranean. 16 USSR. 17 Venice. 18 Kingdom.
19 Danube. 20 Balearics. 21 Arctic Circle. 22 Netherlands. 23 Greece.
24 Denmark. 25 Second smallest. 26 Portugal. 27 Spain. 28 Paris. 29 Mountain ranges. 30 Corsica.

1 Where is water stored in a cactus plant?
2 Are most conifers evergreen or deciduous?
3 Ceps and chanterelles are types of what?
4 Flax is grown to produce which fabric?
5 Which drug is obtained from the coca plant?
6 Bamboo is the tallest type of what?
7 Which Mexican drink comes from the agave plant?
8 Is it true or false that laurel has poisonous leaves?
9 The petiole is on which part of a plant?
10 What colour is cuckoo spit?
11 What colour are the flowers on a gorse bush?
12 Which perennial herb can be grown to create lawns?
13 What goes before lavender and holly to make another plant's name?
14 What can be obtained from the cassava plant which would have gone in a typical school dinner pudding?
15 Harebells are usually what colour?
16 Does a polyanthus have a single or several blooms?
17 Which ingredient in tonic water comes from the bark of the cinchona?
18 Which plants would a viticulturist grow?
19 Wild cornflowers are usually what colour?
20 Which paintbrush cleaner is found in the resin of a conifer?
21 Which pear has the most protein?
22 In the garden what would you use secateurs for?
23 Do peanuts grow on trees or low plants?
24 What colour is chlorophyll?
25 In which Gardens is the Princess of Wales Conservatory?
26 Cacti are native to which continent?
27 What would you find in an arboretum?
28 Which fast grower is nicknamed the mile-a-minute vine?
29 Which yellow flower is nicknamed the Lent lily?
30 Which trees carry their seeds in cones?

Answers | Pot Luck 23 *(see Quiz 48)*

1 A will. 2 Four. 3 Giles Coren. 4 Both died in plane crashes. 5 Zwanzig. 6 Bryan Adams. 7 A cactus. 8 Struay. 9 Street-Porter. 10 Australia. 11 World War II. 12 Black. 13 Landscape gardening. 14 A size of paper. 15 Edward Woodward. 16 A herb. 17 River Niagara. 18 Snow White. 19 Horse racing. 20 Beef. 21 Purple. 22 Three. 23 Alaska. 24 Burgundy. 25 Simple Simon. 26 Luke and Matt Goss. 27 A kind of plum. 28 Celebrity Big Brother. 29 Lizzie. 30 Flattery.

1 If you die intestate you have not made what?
2 What's the least number of Mondays that can occur in July?
3 Who is the presenter of "Only Connect"'s famous brother?
4 What links the singers Buddy Holly and Otis Redding?
5 What is the German word for the number twenty?
6 Who had a No.1 UK hit with "Everything I Do, I Do It for You"?
7 What is a prickly pear?
8 In the CBeebies series, what island does Katie Morag live on?
9 Media person Janet Bull changed her last name to what in her search for "yoof"?
10 Bob Hawke was prime minister of which country?
11 The movie "Enigma" was set during which world conflict?
12 What colour is sable in heraldry?
13 For what was Capability Brown famous?
14 What is foolscap?
15 On TV who played the Equaliser?
16 What kind of plant is marjoram?
17 On which River are the Niagara Falls?
18 Which Disney movie includes the song "Heigh-Ho"?
19 For which sport is Willie Carson famous?
20 Sirloin, rump and topside are all joints of which meat?
21 What colour is Tinky Winky in the Teletubbies?
22 How many leaves are on a shamrock?
23 Which American state is the largest in area?
24 What is usually the colour of an EU passport?
25 According to the nursery rhyme, who met a pieman going to the fair?
26 Which two brothers made up the group Bros?
27 What is a bullace?
28 On which show did Chantelle Houghton first find fame?
29 A Model T Ford was nicknamed Tin what?
30 According to the proverb, imitation is the sincerest form of what?

Answers | **Plant World** *(see Quiz 47)*

1 Stem. 2 Evergreen. 3 Fungi. 4 Linen. 5 Cocaine. 6 Grass. 7 Tequila. 8 True.
9 Leaf stalk. 10 White. 11 Yellow. 12 Camomile. 13 Sea. 14 Tapioca. 15 Blue.
16 Several. 17 Quinine. 18 Vines. 19 Blue. 20 Turpentine. 21 Avocado.
22 Cutting, pruning. 23 Low plants. 24 Green. 25 Kew. 26 America. 27 Trees.
28 Russian Vine. 29 Daffodil. 30 Conifers.

1 What type of sport is eventing?
2 In which county was Lewis Hamilton born?
3 Phidippides was the first runner of which 26-mile race?
4 Which Stephen was the then youngest ever winner of a professional snooker title in 1987?
5 Did Evander Holyfield box at heavyweight or welterweight?
6 Which country did Virginia Leng represent at the Olympic Games?
7 FC Porto play football in which country?
8 At the USPGA Championships, what game is played?
9 Did Shane Warne first play English county cricket for Essex or Hampshire?
10 At which sport might you see the American Williams sisters play?
11 Does the Le Mans 24-hour race take place in summer or winter?
12 In swimming, is freestyle usually performed on the back or front?
13 Which country won the first 25 America's Cup trophies in yachting?
14 In which sport is there a Foil discipline?
15 How was boxer Rocco Francis Marchegiano better known?
16 Caber tossing is native to which country?
17 In what year did Arsenal's Emirates Stadium open?
18 For which national rugby side did Gavin Hastings play?
19 Magic Johnson found fame at which US sport?
20 Which horse race is sometimes called just The National?
21 What was tennis's Billie Jean Moffitt's married name?
22 Which Jackie's record of Grand Prix wins did Alain Prost pass in 1987?
23 Which heavyweight Mike knocked out 15 of his first 25 pro opponents in the first round?
24 In what year did Alex Ferguson retire as Manchester United manager?
25 In which sport is a ball hit through a hoop with a mallet?
26 What is Scottish long-distance runner Liz Lynch's married name?
27 What does the first F in FIFA stand for?
28 F1 driver Jacques Villeneuve is from which country?
29 Which winter sport can be alpine or Nordic?
30 Is the Oaks a race for colts or fillies?

Answers	**Pot Luck 24** *(see Quiz 50)*

1 Two. 2 Mean. 3 Lettuce. 4 2016. 5 An even number. 6 Green. 7 Little Britain. 8 The mirror. 9 Half a pound of tuppenny rice. 10 Eight. 11 A bullfrog. 12 Penny Black. 13 Judas. 14 Half a crown. 15 The Banger Sisters. 16 One. 17 The Alps. 18 Gold. 19 Pepper. 20 Westminster Abbey. 21 A knot. 22 Coffee. 23 Victory. 24 Bread. 25 Green. 26 The harp. 27 Blue. 28 White Star Line. 29 A filament. 30 Queen Victoria.

1 How many people perform a pas de deux in a ballet?
2 If T is time what is M in G.M.T.?
3 Cos and Iceberg are varieties of which salad plant?
4 In what year did Theresa May become leader of the Conservative Party?
5 What type of number will you always get if you add two odd numbers together?
6 In movies is Shrek blue, green or purple?
7 Which TV series featured the Thai bride Ting Tong?
8 Who told the Queen that Snow White was the "fairest of them all"?
9 What is mixed with half a pound of treacle in "Pop Goes the Weasel"?
10 How many furlongs are there in a mile?
11 In the song, what was good friend Jeremiah?
12 What was the common name for the first postage stamp?
13 Which biblical character had the second name Iscariot?
14 What was the name for two shillings and sixpence?
15 In which film are Goldie Hawn and Susan Sarandon a pair of 50 something ex-groupies?
16 How many hooks do you use for crochet?
17 The Matterhorn is in which European mountain range?
18 What did Fort Knox originally store?
19 Steak au poivre is steak covered in what?
20 Where did the Queen's Coronation take place?
21 If you asked a Scout to make a sheep-shank, what would he make?
22 What drink is the main export from Brazil?
23 What was the name of Admiral Nelson's ship?
24 Chapatti is a kind of Indian what?
25 What colour is the door of the pub the Rovers Return?
26 Which stringed instrument has the most strings in an orchestra?
27 What colour is connected with the River Danube?
28 Which shipping line did Titanic belong to?
29 What is the name of the glowing curly wire in a light bulb?
30 At the start of the 20th century who was Queen of England?

Answers | **Sporting Chance 1** *(see Quiz 49)*

1 Equestrian. 2 Hertfordshire. 3 Marathon. 4 Hendry. 5 Heavyweight. 6 Great Britain. 7 Portugal. 8 Golf. 9 Hampshire. 10 Tennis. 11 Summer. 12 Front. 13 USA. 14 Fencing. 15 Rocky Marciano. 16 Scotland. 17 2006. 18 Scotland. 19 Basketball. 20 Grand National. 21 King. 22 Stewart. 23 Tyson. 24 2013. 25 Croquet. 26 McColgan. 27 Federation. 28 Canada. 29 Skiing. 30 Fillies.

1 Which "Grease" classic begins "I got chills, they're multiplyin'"?
2 Which Madonna hit contains the words, "Ring, ring ring"?
3 What is the first line of "Nessun Dorma"?
4 What did Tina Turner sing after "Do I love you, my oh my"?
5 What follows the Beatles' "will you still need me, will you still feed me"?
6 Which song begins, "I feel it in my fingers, I feel it in my toes"?
7 In "Candle in the Wind 1997" how are England's hills described?
8 How many times is "submarine" sung in the chorus of "Yellow Submarine"?
9 Which hit began "Oh my love, my darlin', I hunger for your touch"?
10 Which song's second line is "and so I face the final curtain"?
11 Which song begins "First I was afraid I was petrified"?
12 In which song did Tammy Wynette complain "Sometimes it's hard to be a woman"?
13 Which Slade Xmas hit has the line "Everybody's having fun"?
14 In the "Titanic" song what follows, "Near, far, wherever you are, I believe..."?
15 What follows Bryan Adams' "Everything I do"?
16 Which Dire Straits hit begins "Here comes Johnny"?
17 What follows "Two little boys had two little....."?
18 Which charity hit has the line "Feed the world"?
19 What follows The Spice Girls' "swing it, shake it, move it, make it"?
20 Which ABBA hit states "I was defeated you won the war"?
21 What do neighbours become in the original "Neighbours" theme song?
22 What follows "I believe for every drop of rain that falls"?
23 Which football anthem speaks of "Jules Rimet still gleaming"?
24 Which song's second chorus line is "I just called to say I care"?
25 Which Evita song begins, "It won't be easy, you'll think it strange"?
26 What did Boy George sing after singing karma five times?
27 Which "Lion King" song began "From the day we arrive on the planet"?
28 Which Simon & Garfunkel hit begins "When you're weary, feeling small"?
29 Which traditional song has the line, "The pipes, the pipes are calling"?
30 What are the last three words of Queen's "We are the Champions"?

Answers | Pot Luck 25 *(see Quiz 52)*

1 The Peril. 2 Shaun the Sheep. 3 Mint. 4 Soldier Sailor. 5 Calais. 6 Horse racing.
7 August. 8 Berkshire. 9 Trombone. 10 Tuesday. 11 VAT. 12 Bulb. 13 Three.
14 Cricket. 15 Andrew Lloyd Webber. 16 Quentin Crisp. 17 Minestrone. 18
Champagne. 19 Little girls. 20 Patience. 21 Melbourne. 22 Silver. 23 Ganges. 24
Tannic/Tannin. 25 Boots. 26 A house. 27 Please. 28 Red. 29 Nose. 30 Sherry.

Quiz 52 | Pot Luck 25

Answers – page 59

1 If Dennis is the Menace what is Beryl?
2 "Timmy Time" was a spin-off from which children's TV show?
3 Which sweet flavoured herb is often used to accompany roast lamb?
4 According to the rhyme, which two characters followed Tinker Tailor?
5 Which French port is closest to Britain?
6 To see which sport could you go to Towcester?
7 Lammas Day is in which month?
8 In which county is the Royal Military Academy at Sandhurst?
9 Which brass instrument has a sliding, adjustable tube?
10 Which day's child is "full of grace" according to the traditional rhyme?
11 Which present-day tax replaced Purchase Tax in 1973?
12 Is a snowdrop grown from a bulb or seed?
13 How many national parks are there in Wales?
14 For which sport is David Gower famous?
15 Who composed the music for "Cats"?
16 Who called their autobiography "The Naked Civil Servant"?
17 Which soup is made from a variety of vegetables and pasta?
18 What sort of drink is Moet & Chandon?
19 Maurice Chevalier "thanked heaven" for what?
20 Which has smaller cards, an ordinary pack or a patience pack?
21 Which Australian city stands near the mouth of the Yarra river?
22 What colour is argent in heraldry?
23 The city of Calcutta stands on which river?
24 Tea contains which acid?
25 Which high street chemist's shop opened its first store in 1877?
26 What are you probably buying if you are gazumped?
27 What does the Italian "per favore" mean?
28 What colour, together with yellow, is the Spanish flag?
29 The symbol for Comic Relief is a red what?
30 What kind of drink can be Bristol Cream?

Answers | Pop: Karaoke *(see Quiz 51)*

1 You're the One that I Want. 2 Wannabe. 3 Nessun dorma, nessun dorma. 4 River deep mountain high. 5 When I'm sixty-four. 6 Love is All Around. 7 Greenest. 8 Six. 9 Unchained Melody. 10 My Way. 11 I Will Survive. 12 Stand by Your Man. 13 Merry Christmas Everybody. 14 That the heart does go on. 15 I do it for you. 16 Walk of Life. 17 Toys. 18 Do They Know It's Christmas? 19 Who do you think you are?. 20 Waterloo. 21 Good friends. 22 A flower grows. 23 Three Lions. 24 I Just Called to Say I Love You. 25 Don't Cry for Me Argentina. 26 Chameleon. 27 Circle of Life. 28 Bridge Over Troubled Water. 29 Danny Boy. 30 Of the world.

Quiz 53 TV Times 1

LEVEL 1

1 Which is the female half of Mulder and Scully?
2 Who first presented "Deal or No Deal" on Channel 4?
3 What is the subject of the Channel 4 show "Hooked"?
4 "Torchwood" is an anagram of which series of which it is a spin-off?
5 Who took over from David Dimbleby as "Question Time" presenter in 2019?
6 Who narrates CBeebies series "Little Charley Bear"?
7 What would Peter Cockcroft talk about on TV?
8 Who took over "Gardener's World" from the late Geoff Hamilton?
9 In "Game of Thrones", what is Hodor's real name – Wycliffe or Wylis?
10 Maureen Rees found TV fame at what type of School?
11 In "Coronation Street", who murdered Maxine Peacock in 2003?
12 Which letters does TV's Kavanagh have after his name?
13 From 2003 to 2015, David Mitchell and Robert Webb starred in which Channel 4 sitcom?
14 Who played Lou Beale in the early episodes of "EastEnders"?
15 Which TV presenter is Johnny Ball's daughter?
16 Which Mary founded the Clean Up TV campaign in 1964?
17 Which female pop quintet launched Channel 5?
18 Does Oz Clarke specialise in food or drink?
19 Who played the older Queen Elizabeth II in "The Crown"?
20 Where were the shorts "Mid Morning Matters with Alan Partridge" first shown?
21 Other than John Cleese's character, what was the other Basil in "Fawlty Towers"?
22 What links Terry Wogan, Les Dawson and Lily Savage?
23 Which part of the country is served by Anglia Television?
24 "Ground Force" offered a viewer a makeover in which part of the home?
25 Whom does the true crime documentary series "Making a Murderer" focus on?
26 "It's good to talk" was the ad slogan of which phone company?
27 In "Coronation Street", what was the name of Hilda Ogden's husband?
28 Which broadcasting corporation is known as Auntie?
29 How many studio judges are there on "The X Factor"?
30 Who is the human half of Wallace and Gromit?

Answers | Pot Luck 26 *(see Quiz 54)*

1 Tom Cruise. 2 The farmer's wife. 3 Gooseberry. 4 Diamonds. 5 Broken. 6 All Saints. 7 1984. 8 Apples. 9 Rutland. 10 1985. 11 Boston. 12 Hops. 13 Pears. 14 Saviour's Day. 15 Jennifer Lopez. 16 White. 17 He was married. 18 The Doge. 19 Eight. 20 Dance steps. 21 A plant. 22 Richard. 23 Red. 24 Birmingham. 25 Three. 26 Bank of England. 27 Goodwood. 28 Champagne. 29 A bulb. 30 New York.

Quiz 54 Pot Luck 26

Answers – page 61

1 Who is older – Leonardo DiCaprio or Tom Cruise?
2 According to the nursery rhyme, who cut off the three mice tails?
3 Is a person on their own with a couple called a raspberry or a gooseberry?
4 What is mined at Kimberley in South Africa?
5 What does a German mean if he says something is "kaput"?
6 Who had a No.1 UK hit in September 1998 with "Bootie Call"?
7 Which George Orwell novel has a year as its title?
8 Cider is made from which fruit?
9 What was the smallest county in England until 1974?
10 In what year was "EastEnders" first broadcast?
11 What is the capital of the US state of Massachusetts?
12 What is dried in Kentish oast houses?
13 Which fruit can be served Belle Hélène?
14 Which Day gave Cliff Richard a No.1 for Christmas 1990?
15 In "Out of Sight" which Jennifer starred along with George Clooney?
16 What colour along with red and blue is the Luxembourg flag?
17 What happened to Solomon Grundy on Wednesday, according to the rhyme?
18 Historically speaking, who was the chief magistrate of Venice?
19 On the Union Jack, how many blue triangles are there?
20 What does a choreographer plan?
21 What is a yucca?
22 In pop music, who is Jagger's long-time writing partner?
23 What colour is Po in the "Teletubbies"?
24 "Crossroads" was set near which major city?
25 How many people are in a boat in a rowing coxed pair race?
26 What is sometimes called the "Old Lady of Threadneedle Street"?
27 Which race meeting is known as "Glorious"?
28 What was invented by Dom Peter Perignon, a French monk?
29 Is a tulip grown from seed or a bulb?
30 Which American city has the Yankees and Mets baseball teams?

1 Scully. 2 Noel Edmonds. 3 Fishing. 4 Doctor Who. 5 Fiona Bruce. 6 James Corden. 7 Weather. 8 Alan Titchmarsh. 9 Wylis. 10 Driving School. 11 Richard Hillman. 12 QC. 13 Peep Show. 14 Anna Wing. 15 Zoe Ball. 16 Whitehouse. 17 The Spice Girls. 18 Drink. 19 Olivia Colman. 20 YouTube. 21 Rat. 22 Blankety Blank. 23 East Anglia. 24 Garden. 25 Steven Avery. 26 BT. 27 Stan. 28 BBC. 29 Three. 30 Wallace.

62

1 What is the surname of German F1 drivers Ralf and Michael?
2 Which jump event did Carl Lewis specialise in as well as sprinting?
3 When did Andy Murray win his second Olympic gold medal?
4 Is professional badminton an indoor or outdoor game or both?
5 What was the professional name of boxer Joe Louis Barrow?
6 Which much-capped England Rugby star Matt took part in a TV dancing contest?
7 Which team won the Ryder Cup in 2018 – Europe or USA?
8 Which sport is David Brailsford involved in – swimming or cycling?
9 Which horned animal name does Leeds' Rugby Super League team have?
10 In which sport might you hit another living thing with a crop?
11 Peter O'Sullevan commentated on which sport?
12 Which rugby side shares its name with stinging insects?
13 Which red flower is the emblem of the England rugby union team?
14 In which country is the golfing venue Valderrama?
15 Which motoring Grand Prix is held at the Hungaroring?
16 What's the highest score in darts from three different doubles?
17 In which country is the oldest football league in the world?
18 Which area of New York has a Globetrotters basketball team?
19 Which Bin was introduced for Rugby League players in 1983?
20 How many disciplines are there in a biathlon?
21 In which Sheffield theatre were the World Snooker Championships first held in 1977?
22 In which country was judo coincidentally added to the Olympic programme?
23 In badminton what were goose feathers used for?
24 What is the usual surface of the lane in ten-pin bowling?
25 Which German Men's Wimbledon champion was born on Billie Jean King's 23rd birthday?
26 Which Lennox of the UK became undisputed world heavyweight champ?
27 On what surface is curling played?
28 Which animal is on top of Rugby's Calcutta Cup?
29 In which sport would you wear a judogi?
30 What type of sporting event was The Rumble in the Jungle?

1 In what year was Jeremy Corbyn elected leader of the Labour Party?
2 What is a tam-o'-shanter?
3 Which organ is particularly affected by hepatitis?
4 Who played the title role in the film "Educating Rita"?
5 On which river estuary does Swansea stand?
6 The letters F.R.A.M. mean a Fellow of which Royal Academy?
7 For which sport was Duncan Goodhew famous?
8 The raven is traditionally associated with which Tower?
9 Who played Inspector Clouseau in the original "Pink Panther" films?
10 Was Condoleezza Rice born in the 1950s, 1960s or 1970s?
11 What is a cockchafer?
12 Which animal isle is in the River Thames?
13 Where did a famous battle take place in 1066?
14 Which elephants are the larger - African or Indian?
15 Which English musician and comedian married Tuesday Weld?
16 Who was the female lead in the movie "Enigma"?
17 What kind of mammal is a chamois?
18 In which city is Pushkin Square?
19 Does coq au vin contain red or white wine?
20 Which TV series is set in Sun Hill police station?
21 During the Gulf War, who was the leader of Iraq?
22 Who played Pauline Fowler in the early episodes of "EastEnders"?
23 Which car maker has the same name as a London bridge?
24 Which animal should you take by the horns, according to the proverb?
25 How many pins are in the back row of a ten-pin bowling triangle?
26 Which city is further north – Bristol or Sheffield?
27 Which of Chippendale, Ming and Wedgwood is not a type of pottery?
28 How much gold is there in a one-pound coin?
29 What are a pig's feet called?
30 Of which country's coast is the world's largest coral reef?

Answers | **Sporting Chance 2** *(see Quiz 55)*

1 Schumacher. 2 Long jump. 3 2016. 4 Indoor. 5 Joe Louis. 6 Matt Dawson.
7 Europe. 8 Cycling. 9 Rhinos. 10 Equestrianism. 11 Horse racing. 12 Wasps.
13 Rose. 14 Spain. 15 Hungarian. 16 114. 17 England. 18 Harlem. 19 Sin bin.
20 Two. 21 Crucible. 22 Japan. 23 Shuttlecock. 24 Wood. 25 Boris Becker.
26 Lennox Lewis. 27 Ice. 28 Elephant. 29 Judo. 30 Boxing match.

Quiz 57   Movies: The Brits

Answers – page 66

1 What was the Spice Girls' first film?
2 Who with The Shadows starred in "The Young Ones"?
3 Which movie told of redundant steel workers becoming strippers?
4 "The Bridge on the River Kwai" prisoners are imprisoned by whom?
5 Nick Hornby's "Fever Pitch" is about which game?
6 Which Kenneth directed and starred in "Hamlet"?
7 "The Blue Lamp" preceded which TV series about PC George Dixon?
8 A BAFTA is a British Award for film and what?
9 What nationality was The ... Patient in the 1996 Oscar winner?
10 Who directed the 2013 movie "Philomena"?
11 Mrs Blake Edwards won an Oscar for "Mary Poppins"; who was she?
12 What is the nationality of Sir Anthony Hopkins?
13 In which part of the UK was "Trainspotting" set?
14 Which one-time British Transport Minister twice won an Oscar?
15 Which Sir Richard directed "Chaplin"?
16 Which 1994 British hit shot Hugh Grant to superstardom?
17 Which Emma wrote the screenplay for "Sense & Sensibility"?
18 Jenny Agutter found fame in which movie about an Edwardian family?
19 Is Helena Bonham Carter a British Prime Minister's or a US President's granddaughter?
20 Elizabeth Taylor was twice married to this Welsh actor; who was he?
21 Who was born Maurice Micklewhite?
22 Which Julie was Oscar nominated in 1998?
23 Which Ewan plays the young Obi Wan Kenobi in Episode I of "Star Wars"?
24 In which film did Tom Conti play Pauline Collins' Greek lover?
25 In 2008, who directed "Slumdog Millionaire"?
26 Linus Roache's father has played which "Coronation Street" character since the soap began?
27 Who or what was the film "Wilde" with Stephen Fry about?
28 Which famous graffiti artist directed "Exit Through The Gift Shop"?
29 In which part of the UK was Robert Carlyle born?
30 Hot Chocolate's "You Sexy Thing" was the theme for which 1997 film?

Answers   Pot Luck 28 *(see Quiz 58)*

1 France. 2 Windsor Castle. 3 Yogi Bear. 4 Lime. 5 Badminton. 6 Oysters.
7 Watford. 8 Five. 9 Johnny Cash. 10 Coronation. 11 Flock together. 12 Poet.
13 True. 14 Javelin. 15 Cornwall. 16 A catamaran. 17 Eeyore. 18 L. S. 19 An
apple. 20 Europe, Asia. 21 Elizabeth I. 22 Yachting. 23 Yugoslavia. 24 Goat.
25 Leeds. 26 Peppermint. 27 The humming bird. 28 Cricket. 29 Ballerina.
30 Bottom.

1 The Dauphin was heir to which European throne?
2 Which castle was partly damaged by fire in 1992?
3 Which bear had a friend called Boo Boo?
4 What is another name for a linden tree?
5 Which sport is named after a place which is famous for horse trials?
6 The precious stone, a pearl, can be found in what?
7 Elton John was famously chairman of which football club?
8 How many senior titles (excluding over-35 events) are contested each Wimbledon?
9 The movie "Walk the Line" was about which singer?
10 At which ceremony is a Monarch given their crown?
11 According to the saying, what do birds of a feather do?
12 Was Ted Hughes a dancer, painter or poet?
13 Alex Ferguson managed the Scottish national football team – true or false?
14 For which sport is Tessa Sanderson famous?
15 Prince Charles is Duke of which English county?
16 What is a yacht with two hulls called?
17 Which character from "Winnie The Pooh" lost his tail?
18 What two initials did northern artist Lowry have?
19 What did William Tell shoot from his son's head with a crossbow?
20 Which continents are separated by the Urals?
21 Who was England's Queen when Shakespeare was alive?
22 Cowes on the Isle of Wight is famous for which sport?
23 Which country was formerly ruled by President Tito?
24 Which animal's milk is used to make cheese called Chevre?
25 Which city is further North – Lincoln or Leeds?
26 What flavour is Kendal's most famous cake?
27 Which is the only bird that can fly backwards?
28 What is John Major's favourite sport?
29 What was Natalie Portman's character's profession in the 2010 movie "Black Swan"?
30 Which part of your body is a character in Shakespeare's "A Midsummer Night's Dream"?

Answers | **Movies: The Brits** *(see Quiz 57)*

1 Stephen Frears. 2 Cliff Richard. 3 The Full Monty. 4 Japanese. 5 Football. 6 Branagh. 7 Dixon of Dock Green. 8 Television. 9 English. 10 Stephen Fears. 11 Julie Andrews. 12 Welsh. 13 Scotland. 14 Glenda Jackson. 15 Attenborough. 16 Four Weddings and a Funeral. 17 Thompson. 18 The Railway Children. 19 British Prime Minister's. 20 Richard Burton. 21 Michael Caine. 22 Christie. 23 McGregor. 24 Shirley Valentine. 25 Danny Boyle. 26 Ken Barlow. 27 Oscar Wilde. 28 Banksy. 29 Scotland. 30 The Full Monty.

1 What sort of security device is a Chubb?
2 An Entryphone would normally be found at the entrance to what?
3 What in the bedroom would have a TOG rating?
4 What colour is Copydex adhesive?
5 What is the abbreviation for volt?
6 Is pine a soft or hard wood?
7 Which machine tool is used for turning wood?
8 Do weft fibres run across the width or the length of a fabric?
9 What goes between a nut and the surface to protect it?
10 Soldering joins two pieces of what?
11 Cushions, curtains etc. are referred to as what sort of furnishings?
12 Should silk be washed in hot or cool water?
13 Which tool can be band, hand or hack?
14 E numbers refer to additives to what?
15 Is an emery cloth rough or smooth?
16 Which device turns off an appliance when a temperature is reached?
17 A rasp is a type of what?
18 Is Araldite a strong or light glue?
19 In which sort of bank would you deposit waste glass?
20 Canning, bottling and freezing are types of what?
21 What would a bradawl produce in wood?
22 Batik is a type of dyeing on what?
23 What would you normally make in a percolator?
24 Where is the door on a chest freezer?
25 A bedsit usually consists of how many rooms?
26 What type of electrical devices are "white goods"?
27 Is a kilogram less or more than two pounds in weight?
28 What colour does silver turn when it is tarnished?
29 Which wood is darker, mahogany or ash?
30 What does the ply of a yarn refer to?

1 Who was the last President of the USA elected in the 1980s?
2 Which city is further North – Cardiff or Sheffield?
3 Which plant helps to take away the sting of a stinging nettle?
4 The River Forth flows into which Sea?
5 Who was Jeremy Corbyn's predecessor as leader of the Labour Party?
6 Which country was ruled by Chairman Mao?
7 What name is given to the imaginary lines drawn from north to south on a map?
8 Which sweets were "made to make your mouth water"?
9 Who starred in the movie "Florence Foster Jenkins" with Meryl Streep?
10 Thomas Sheraton was a designer and manufacturer of what?
11 Which came first, zips, velcro or buttons?
12 Which horse named after a drink won the Grand National three times?
13 What was the name of Donald Duck's girlfriend?
14 What is the name of Bill Gates's wife?
15 What is the fat of a whale called?
16 Which is the warmest sea in the world, The Red, Med or Dead?
17 Who wrote the pop anthem "Knockin' on Heaven's Door"?
18 Who or what flock together according to the saying?
19 What is the flavour of a Devil's Food Cake?
20 Which cowboy had a horse called Trigger?
21 For which event is Daley Thompson famous?
22 Which King put his seal on the Magna Carta?
23 Which is nearest to Ireland, England, Scotland or Wales?
24 Who is Kieran Culkin's brother, famed as a movie child star?
25 Which actress played Jessica Fletcher in "Murder She Wrote"?
26 What colour balls were used at Wimbledon before yellow balls?
27 Where would you expect to hear the prologue in a play?
28 Which of the following will not dissolve in water: salt, sugar or sand?
29 How many teats does a cow have normally?
30 Was the Flying Fortress a plane or a train?

Answers | Home & D-I-Y (see Quiz 59)

1 Lock. 2 Block of flats. 3 Duvet. 4 White. 5 V. 6 Soft. 7 Lathe. 8 Width.
9 Washer. 10 Metal. 11 Soft furnishings. 12 Cool. 13 Saw. 14 Food. 15 Rough.
16 Thermostat. 17 File. 18 Strong. 19 Bottle bank. 20 Preserving. 21 Hole.
22 Fabric. 23 Coffee. 24 Top. 25 One. 26 Large kitchen appliances, such as freezers
and washing machines. 27 More. 28 Black. 29 Mahogany. 30 Its thickness.

1 Which football anthem was co written by Skinner and Baddiel?
2 What is the surname of Oasis brothers Noel and Liam?
3 Whom was "Candle in the Wind 1997" dedicated to?
4 Which Zoo sang "Spaceman" in 1996?
5 In which drama series did chart toppers Robson & Jerome find fame?
6 Isaac, Taylor and Zac make up which boy band?
7 Who said "Eh Oh" on the their first smash hit?
8 Whose album of "Urban Hymns" hit the top spot?
9 Which 90s band were named after an area of London?
10 "Knockin' on Heaven's Door" was released after which 1996 tragedy?
11 Which single was released by Robson & Jerome and two years later by The Three Tenors?
12 Who was "Older" in the 90s after a long-running battle with Sony?
13 Who were "Back for Good" in 1995 before disbanding?
14 Whose death propelled "Bohemian Rhapsody" back to the charts?
15 Which Peter had a No.1 with "Flava"?
16 Who had a No.1 with Nilsson's "Without You"?
17 Who backed Katrina on her 1997 Eurovision winner?
18 Which Damon fronted Blur?
19 Who starred in and sang on the soundtrack of "The Bodyguard"?
20 In September '98 Celine Dion released an album in which language?
21 Which toy provided Aqua with a No.1?
22 Which country singer John died flying his plane in 1997?
23 Who had a daughter Lourdes Maria in 1996?
24 Which band's name is a US emergency number?
25 Dana International won Eurovision '98 for which Middle East country?
26 Oasis were formed in which UK city?
27 Who had a huge hit with "Drop Dead Gorgeous"?
28 Which Darren appeared in the 90s version of "Summer Holiday"?
29 In which county were Blur formed?
30 "My Heart Will Go On" came from which smash hit film?

Answers | Pot Luck 30 *(see Quiz 62)*

1 Tasmania. 2 Balsawood. 3 Tennis. 4 The candlestick maker. 5 Up. 6 Roald Dahl.
7 Hindu. 8 St David. 9 USA. 10 1940s. 11 Davy Crockett. 12 Polo. 13 Shoes.
14 South Pacific. 15 George Bush. 16 Sean Hughes. 17 Australia. 18 Jessica. 19 St
Ives. 20 Alan Davies. 21 Four. 22 Jacobites. 23 Touché. 24 Rainbow. 25 Avon.
26 David Cameron. 27 Black and yellow. 28 Javelin. 29 One. 30 Chester.

1 Which Australian state is named after its discoverer Abel Tasman?
2 Which very soft wood is popular with model makers?
3 Which sport was played by Gabriela Sabatini?
4 According to the nursery rhyme, who joined the butcher and baker?
5 Do bananas grow pointing up or down?
6 Who wrote "Charlie and the Chocolate Factory"?
7 The River Ganges is sacred to the people of which religion?
8 Which Saint is the patron saint of Wales?
9 Which country was the 1994 football World Cup Final played in?
10 Was Terry Venables born in the 1940s, 1950s or the 1960s?
11 Which American hero wore a hat with a racoon tail hanging from the back?
12 Which sport is played on the largest pitch: cricket, football or polo?
13 What are or were winkle pickers?
14 Which part of an ocean shares its name with a musical?
15 Who was American president immediately before Bill Clinton?
16 Which Sean was was the star of "Sean's Show" on TV?
17 Does Nicole Kidman come from Australia or Austria?
18 What is the middle name of Sarah Parker, famed for "Sex and the City"?
19 Where was the person going, who met a man with seven wives?
20 Which Alan portrayed the character Jonathan Creek?
21 In the neck of a violin how many tuning pegs are there?
22 What were supporters of James II and his Stuart descendants called?
23 What is shouted by people when they make contact in fencing?
24 Which children's TV programme featured Bungle and Zippy?
25 Which English county shares its name with a beauty products range?
26 Who was Theresa May's predecessor as leader of the Conservative Party?
27 What colour is Rupert the Bear's scarf?
28 For which sport was Fatima Whitbread famous?
29 How many players take part in a game of patience at any one time?
30 Which city is further North – Bristol or Chester?

1 Which former leader went on trial in his own country in October 2005?
2 In which country were the Borgias a powerful family?
3 Benazir Bhutto was Prime Minister of which Muslim state?
4 Which Al was crime boss of Chicago during Prohibition?
5 Which South African shared the Nobel Peace Prize with FW de Klerk in 1993?
6 What was President John F. Kennedy's wife called?
7 In what area of London was the Victorian serial killer Jack the Ripper active?
8 In which country was Terry Waite imprisoned?
9 Roman Emperor Hadrian gave his name to what in Britain?
10 Which animals did Hannibal use to frighten the Romans?
11 Hirohito was Emperor of which country during WWII?
12 Which Russian word for Caesar was used by Russian monarchs?
13 What was T.E. Lawrence's sobriquet?
14 Which Russian revolutionary took his name from the River Lena?
15 In which century did Columbus discover America?
16 Which 11thC Scottish king was the subject of a Shakespeare play?
17 In which country of the UK was David Livingstone born?
18 Which British admiral Horatio was born in Norfolk?
19 Where is Botany Bay?
20 Which country put the first woman in space?
21 Which journalist John was imprisoned in Beirut with Brian Keenan?
22 What was Argentinean vice president Eva Duarte's married name?
23 Ho Chi Minh founded the Communist Party in which country?
24 Angela Merkel became leader in which country?
25 Which outspoken TV chef received an OBE in the 2006 New Year's Honours?
26 In which country was Joan of Arc born?
27 Where was the tomb of Tutankhamun discovered in 1922?
28 Which famous Indian monument was built by Shah Jahan?
29 Zulu leader Buthelezi became a government minister where?
30 Which nurse is famous for her work during the Crimean War?

Answers	Pot Luck 31 *(see Quiz 64)*

1 Arsenal. 2 Marzipan. 3 Cookery. 4 Two. 5 22. 6 Putty. 7 Roger Bannister.
8 Ballet. 9 Glasgow. 10 Eleven. 11 Right. 12 A skateboard. 13 Carrot.
14 Gymnasts. 15 Billy Butlin. 16 The sea. 17 A fiddle. 18 English Heritage.
19 Canada. 20 19th. 21 Collar bone. 22 Victoria. 23 The service. 24 Forget.
25 Grass. 26 Kill You. 27 Val Kilmer. 28 1990s. 29 The knight. 30 Red and black.

Quiz 64 | Pot Luck 31

Answers – page 71

1 Which English team made their first Champions League final appearance in 2006?
2 What name is given to the almond coating often on a Christmas cake?
3 What type of TV programmes are presented by Nadiya Hussain?
4 How many Bank Holidays are there in May?
5 How many yards are there between the wickets in cricket?
6 What sticky paste usually holds glass in a window?
7 Who was the first person to run a mile in under four minutes?
8 What is performed by the Russian Bolshoi company?
9 Which Scottish city has the biggest population?
10 How many players can a team have on the field in American football?
11 On a UK coin does Elizabeth II face left or right?
12 What has a kicktail and four wheels?
13 Which vegetable, high in vitamin A, is said to be good for the eyes?
14 What kind of athletes perform a flic-flac?
15 Who set up England's biggest chain of holiday camps?
16 Neptune was the god of what?
17 According to the saying, which instrument can you be as fit as?
18 Which body manages Stonehenge?
19 Which is biggest – the USA, Germany or Canada?
20 Was basketball developed in the 17th, 18th or 19th century?
21 What is the common name for the clavicle?
22 Africa's biggest lake is named after which British queen?
23 What is the name given to the first hit in a game of tennis?
24 What do elephants never do according to the saying?
25 Bamboo is a very large variety of what?
26 What will too much love do, according to Brian May?
27 In the movies, which Val replaced Michael Keaton as Batman?
28 In which decade was "Hollyoaks" first broadcast?
29 Which chess piece is shaped like a horse's head?
30 What two colours are Dennis the Menace's sweater?

Answers	People & Places *(see Quiz 63)*

1 Saddam Hussein. 2 Italy. 3 Pakistan. 4 Capone. 5 Nelson Mandela. 6 Jackie.
7 Whitechapel. 8 Lebanon. 9 Hadrian's Wall. 10 Elephants. 11 Japan. 12 Tsar.
13 Lawrence of Arabia. 14 Lenin. 15 15th century. 16 Macbeth. 17 Scotland. 18 Nelson. 19 Australia. 20 USSR. 21 McCarthy. 22 Peron. 23 Vietnam. 24 Germany. 25 Gordon Ramsay. 26 France. 27 Egypt. 28 Taj Mahal. 29 South Africa. 30 Florence Nightingale

1 On which type of show is Ainsley Harriott most likely to appear?
2 Which Carol was the first presenter of "Changing Rooms"?
3 Which series looks at the love lives of Carrie, Charlotte and Samantha?
4 Which programme is often referred to simply as Corrie?
5 Which Zoe succeeded Gaby Roslin on "The Big Breakfast"?
6 Which impersonator Rory starred in "Who Else"?
7 Who played Yosser Hughes in TV drama "Boys from the Blackstuff"?
8 Do the Royle Family live in London, Manchester or Newcastle?
9 In which country was "Ballykissangel" set?
10 Which actor played Thomas Magnum in "Magnum PI"?
11 Who was the BT housewife in the ads as played by Maureen Lipman?
12 In which show did David Jason call Nicholas Lyndhurst a plonker?
13 Which Rik was involved in a quad bike accident in 1998?
14 Which "Have I Got News for You?" star's real name is Paul Martin?
15 Which Helen appeared nude on the cover of Radio Times to celebrate her 50th birthday?
16 Who was the taller in the Peter Cook and Dudley Moore partnership?
17 Which comic Griff has been involved in restoring buildings?
18 Who is Paul O'Grady's blonde, cigarette-smoking alter ego?
19 What was the occupation of Bramwell in the TV series?
20 Was "Dragon's Den" about business plans or wildlife?
21 Who is Reeves' TV comedy partner?
22 In which show would you see the neighbour-from-hell Dorien Green?
23 How many children were there in the "Brady Bunch" family?
24 What is the first name of "Prime Suspect" writer La Plante?
25 Which morning show did Chris Evans and Gaby Roslin present?
26 Which TV astronomer was born Patrick Caldwell-Moore?
27 The game show "Boys and Girls" was introduced by which Vernon?
28 Who presented "The Full Wax"?
29 Which Victorian drama series has a hospital called The Thrift?
30 In the CBeebies series, who is the voice of Rastamouse?

Quiz 66 | Pot Luck 32

Answers – page 73

1 Alex Ferguson failed to win the Premier League in his last season as a manager – true or false?
2 What are the metal loops that you place your feet in when horse riding?
3 Which bank is a dangerous sand bar in the North Sea?
4 Which magician was married to Debbie McGee?
5 Whose official plane is Air Force One?
6 What does the letter P stand for in ESP?
7 Which group of countries did the Vikings come from?
8 How many Popes have been English – one, two or three?
9 What colour was Kojak's hair?
10 What kind of programmes are Hanna and Barbara famous for?
11 What is a man-made lake in which water is stored called?
12 What type of creature is a Black Widow?
13 Which overture has a date in its title and includes cannons and bells?
14 On what date did the St. Valentine's Day Massacre take place?
15 Which Tony won the first "I'm a Celebrity Get Me Out of Here"?
16 Melbourne is the capital of which Australian State?
17 How many walls surround a squash court?
18 In the Bible, who parted the sea?
19 Fiji is in which ocean?
20 Which part of your body has a coating of enamel?
21 In "Austin Powers International Man of Mystery" who was the leading actress?
22 Who milked the cow with the crumpled horn, in the rhyme?
23 Which parts of the Venus de Milo's body are missing?
24 In which city beginning with H was the 2005 World Athletics Championship held?
25 Would a vermicide be used to kill worms or mice?
26 How many presidents' faces are carved into Mount Rushmore?
27 Which green stone was buried by the Chinese with their dead?
28 How many New Testament Gospels are there?
29 What word describes a picture made from sticking scraps on to a background?
30 Which English coin was nicknamed the tanner?

Answers	TV Times 2 *(see Quiz 65)*

1 Cookery. 2 Smillie. 3 Sex and the City. 4 Coronation Street. 5 Ball. 6 Bremner.
7 Bernard Hill. 8 Manchester. 9 Ireland. 10 Tom Selleck. 11 Beattie. 12 Only Fools
and Horses. 13 Mayall. 14 Paul Merton. 15 Mirren. 16 Peter Cook. 17 Griff Rhys
Jones. 18 Lily Savage. 19 Doctor. 20 Business plans. 21 Mortimer. 22 Birds of a
Feather. 23 Six. 24 Lynda. 25 The Big Breakfast. 26 Patrick Moore. 27 Vernon Kay. 28
Ruby Wax. 29 Bramwell. 30 Reggie Yates.

1 What force makes the Earth orbit the Sun?

2 What colour is the Great Spot on Jupiter?

3 Is Jupiter larger or smaller than Earth?

4 Which gas is present in the Earth's atmosphere which is not present on any other planet?

5 A solar eclipse occurs when the Moon gets between Earth and what?

6 Which is the seventh planet from the Sun?

7 What is the layer around the Earth called?

8 What is the name given to matter so dense that even light cannot escape its pull?

9 Which planet's name comes nearest the end of the alphabet?

10 Herschel planned to name Uranus after the King; which one?

11 What would you find on a celestial map?

12 Is the science of celestial bodies, astrology or astronomy?

13 Which colour in the rainbow has the shortest name?

14 Which TV programme called space The Final Frontier?

15 Were the first US Shuttle flights in the 1950s, 60s, or 80s?

16 Which show with Reeves & Mortimer shared its name with another term for meteors?

17 What is a group of stars which make a recognisable pattern called?

18 What does "S" stand for in NASA?

19 In which decade was the US's first satellite launched?

20 What is the English name for the lunar sea Mare Tranquillitas?

21 Castor and Pollux are two stars in which constellation?

22 John Young ate which item of fast food in space in 1968?

23 Was Apollo a US or USSR space programme?

24 Prior to being an astronaut was John Glenn in the Air Force or the Marines?

25 How long does it take the Earth to orbit the Sun?

26 Mishka, the 1980 Olympic mascot, was the first of which toy in space?

27 How is Ursa Major better known?

28 How many times did Gagarin orbit the Earth on his first space flight?

29 What travels at 186,272 miles per second?

30 Edward White was the first American to walk where?

Quiz 68 | Pot Luck 33

Answers – page 75

1 In "Last of the Summer Wine", which part was played by Kathy Staff?
2 What colour is Dipsy in the "Teletubbies"?
3 An aftershock can sometimes follow what natural disaster?
4 For which sport was Sue Barker famous?
5 Which day's child is "fair of face" according to the traditional rhyme?
6 Which tradesman from Seville is featured in the title of an opera?
7 Which Scottish comic actor Robbie featured in the first Harry Potter movie?
8 In legend, who or what was Excalibur?
9 Which London club did football's Ian Wright join from Arsenal?
10 Which university is the oldest in England?
11 St Stephen's Day is generally known by what other name?
12 Did Sacha Baron Cohen's character Borat sport a moustache or a full beard?
13 What is a peregrine?
14 Who was Tony Blair's first Northern Ireland Minister?
15 What are the two main colours of the Argentinean flag?
16 What type of word is produced when you put two other words together?
17 Which actor links "Play Misty for Me" and "Pale Rider"?
18 What type of fruit is a morello?
19 With which board game are Karpov and Kasparov associated?
20 Sizewell in Suffolk is associated with which form of power?
21 Which gas is the full name for marsh gas?
22 "I, Partridge" was a spoof autobiography of which character?
23 In the Bible, who was Adam and Eve's firstborn son?
24 Keith Duffy joined "Coronation Street" from which Irish boy band?
25 Which character in "Coronation Street" was played by Violet Carson?
26 The song "Tomorrow" comes from which musical?
27 In which Italian city is the Rialto Bridge?
28 How many noughts are in the written number one hundred million?
29 What is the most lasting symbol of the French Exhibition of 1889?
30 Royal Sovereign is a type of which soft fruit?

| **Answers** | **Science & Nature: Space** *(see Quiz 67)* |

1 Gravity. 2 Red. 3 Larger. 4 Oxygen. 5 The Sun. 6 Uranus. 7 Atmosphere.
8 Black Hole. 9 Venus. 10 George. 11 Stars. 12 Astronomy. 13 Red. 14 Star
Trek. 15 80s. 16 Shooting Stars. 17 Constellation. 18 Space. 19 1950s. 20 Sea of
Tranquillity. 21 Gemini. 22 Burger. 23 USA. 24 Marines. 25 A year. 26 Teddy bear.
27 Great Bear. 28 Once. 29 Light. 30 Space.

1 Which Oscar winner became a Labour MP?

2 Which actress received an Oscar for "Erin Brokovich"?

3 Which actress Ms Berry won an Oscar for "Monster's Ball"?

4 In 2018, who won Best Actress for her role in "Three Billboards Outside Ebbing, Missouri"?

5 "Braveheart" was set in which country?

6 Who won Best Actor for "The Silence of the Lambs"?

7 Who directed "Schindler's List"?

8 Which British actor Jeremy was a winner with "Reversal of Fortune"?

9 Was it Tom Hanks or Tom Cruise who won in 1993 and again in '94?

10 Sonny's ex-wife won Best Actress in "Moonstruck"; who was she?

11 Which Susan won for "Dead Man Walking"?

12 Which foot is named in the title of the movie with Daniel Day-Lewis?

13 Was Clint Eastwood Best Actor or Best Director for "Unforgiven"?

14 How often are the Oscars presented?

15 Which keyboard instrument gave its name to a film with Holly Hunter?

16 Kathy Bates won with "Misery" based on which Stephen's novel?

17 Which Kate was Oscar-nominated for "Titanic"?

18 Did Madonna receive one, two or no nominations for "Evita"?

19 What was Best Picture when Tom Hanks won Best Actor for "Forrest Gump"?

20 Which Al was Best Actor for "Scent of a Woman"?

21 Which Shirley won an Oscar at the age of five?

22 For which film did James Cameron win a 1997 Oscar?

23 Which British movie about the 1924 Olympics was a 1980s winner?

24 Which Oscar winner based in India holds the record for most extras?

25 Which son of Kirk Douglas won for "Wall Street"?

26 "Platoon" was about which Asian war?

27 Which Ralph was an "English Patient" winner?

28 "Talk to the Animals" came from which movie about a Doctor?

29 For her role in "The Hours" actress Nicole Kidman wore a false what?

30 Which film was announced as the 2017 Best Picture winner – but wasn't the winner?

Answers	**Pot Luck 34** *(see Quiz 70)*

1 Gaz. 2 Rosary. 3 Winston Churchill. 4 University. 5 Herod. 6 Jonathan Ross. 7 Five of a kind. 8 Cat. 9 M. 10 Salmon. 11 Arquette. 12 Finland. 13 Badminton. 14 Walking distance. 15 12. 16 Nigella Lawson. 17 100. 18 The Office. 19 Huit. 20 Notting Hill. 21 Blue. 22 Squirrel. 23 Five. 24 Germany. 25 Golf. 26 Deadly nightshade. 27 The Matrix. 28 Mars. 29 Supper. 30 Blue.

Quiz 70 | Pot Luck 34

Answers – page 77

LEVEL 1

1 Actor Robert Carlyle led "The Full Monty" as which character?
2 What does a Catholic call the string of beads used when praying?
3 In 2018 Gary Oldman won an Oscar for his portrayal of which British politician?
4 In what type of educational establishment was "Educating Rita" set?
5 In the Bible, which King tried to get the baby Jesus put to death?
6 Which top-earning presenter replaced Barry Norman on BBC's Film programme?
7 What is the highest ranking hand in Poker Dice?
8 In cartoons, what type of animal is Sylvester?
9 Which letter represents 007's boss?
10 Which fish leap up river to get to their spawning grounds?
11 What name did Courteney Cox add to her name after marrying actor David?
12 In which country did saunas originate?
13 A shuttlecock is used in which game?
14 What is measured by a pedometer?
15 How many creatures give their names to Chinese years?
16 Who wrote the best-selling "How to be a Domestic Goddess"?
17 How many decades are there in a millennium?
18 Which comedy was set in the offices of the Wernham Hogg paper merchants?
19 What is the French word for the number eight?
20 In which part of London is there an annual famous carnival?
21 If put in an alkaline solution, what colour does litmus paper become?
22 Which animal lives in a drey?
23 If December 1 is a Tuesday, how many Wednesdays are in the month?
24 Did Beethoven come from Austria, Germany or Holland?
25 For which sport is Sam Torrance famous?
26 Belladonna is also known by which deadly name?
27 "The Matrix Reloaded" was the first sequel to which movie?
28 The month March is named after which Roman god?
29 Leonardo da Vinci's religious painting featured The Last... what?
30 What colour is connected to neutral in modern three-core electric cable?

Answers | The Movies: The Oscars *(see Quiz 69)*

1 Glenda Jackson. 2 Julia Roberts. 3 Halle Berry. 4 Frances McDormand. 5 Scotland. 6 Anthony Hopkins. 7 Steven Spielberg. 8 Irons. 9 Hanks. 10 Cher. 11 Sarandon. 12 Left Foot. 13 Director. 14 Once a year. 15 The Piano. 16 King. 17 Winslet. 18 None. 19 Forrest Gump. 20 Pacino. 21 Temple. 22 Titanic. 23 Chariots of Fire. 24 Gandhi. 25 Michael. 26 Vietnam. 27 Fiennes. 28 Dolittle. 29 Nose. 30 La La Land.

122

Quiz 71 | Hobbies & Leisure 3 | Answers – page 80 | LEVEL 1

1 Which part of the body names a millennium feature on the London skyline?
2 Which sport would you watch at Aintree?
3 Are there more chairs at the start or end of a game of musical chairs?
4 What links a novice's ski slope and a garden centre?
5 What name is given to the promotional scheme to save points for cheaper plane travel?
6 Stem, chain and French knot are what?
7 What colour would a Sloane Ranger's wellies be?
8 The initials RSVP come from a request in which language ?
9 What colour are most road signs on UK motorways?
10 In which UK county might you holiday on the Broads?
11 What is the name of the most famous theatre in London's Drury Lane?
12 In which city is the exhibition centre Olympia?
13 What would you hire at Moss Bros?
14 Butlin's was the first type of what?
15 What is the flower-shaped ribbon awarded at gymkhanas called?
16 What is a less formal name for a turf accountant?
17 Which magazine's title is the French word for "she"?
18 On which summer bank holiday is the Notting Hill Carnival held?
19 Which public track can be used for horses but not traffic?
20 On which date in May was May Day traditionally?
21 Does a busker entertain indoors or out of doors?
22 In which month would you celebrate Hogmanay?
23 In golf, what is usually meant by the nineteenth hole?
24 What is a horse chestnut called when it's used in a children's game?
25 Which card game has two forms called auction and contract?
26 What craft involves rolling and shaping strips of paper to create decorative designs?
27 Are seats in the circle of a theatre on the ground or first floor?
28 Where would a shopper be if they went to M&S?
29 If you wore jodhpurs you'd probably be about to do what?
30 On which ground in north-west England do you watch Test cricket?

1 Who described 1992 as an "annus horribilis"?
2 In which country would you see the Great and Little Orme?
3 According to Rudyard Kipling the female of what is deadlier than the male?
4 Which country hosted football's 1966 World Cup?
5 Which "Jailhouse" song gave Elvis another No.1 in 2005?
6 What falls out if you have alopecia?
7 In "Peanuts", what was Lucy's little brother called?
8 Who live at Home Hill?
9 How does James Bond like his Martini served?
10 Which Richard was the first knighted New Zealand cricketer?
11 Europe's first motorway was built in which country?
12 What rude noise is the English equivalent of a Bronx Cheer?
13 What was Schindler's first name in the film "Schindler's List"?
14 In which South American country was Ayrton Senna born?
15 If January 1 was on a Thursday what day would February 1 be?
16 What colour was The Pimpernel created by Baroness Orczy?
17 Shanklin and Sandown are on which Isle?
18 Which Boys had a No.1 in the 1980s with "Always On My Mind"?
19 Who was the male half of the Torvill and Dean partnership?
20 What kind of animal was Korky from the Dandy comic?
21 Does Ewan McGregor come from Ireland or Scotland?
22 IDEAL is an anagram of the first name of which famous cook?
23 In what year did Bradley Wiggins win BBC Sports Personality of the Year?
24 Which singer Michael had a No.1 with "Earth Song"?
25 Sodium chloride is better known as which condiment?
26 Was Brother Cadfael a fictional medieval or Victorian detective?
27 Which Prime Minister's son did Emma Noble become engaged to?
28 Which doll has a boyfriend called Ken?
29 Which Gordon replaced Martin O'Neill as Celtic manager?
30 If Lions are playing Wallabies what sport are you watching?

Answers	Hobbies & Leisure 3 *(see Quiz 71)*

1 (London) Eye. 2 Horse racing. 3 Beginning. 4 Nursery. 5 Air miles. 6 Embroidery stitches. 7 Green. 8 French. 9 Blue. 10 Norfolk. 11 Theatre Royal. 12 London. 13 Formal dress. 14 Holiday camp. 15 Rosette. 16 Bookie. 17 Elle. 18 August Bank Holiday. 19 Bridleway. 20 First. 21 Out of doors. 22 December. 23 The clubhouse bar. 24 Conker. 25 Bridge. 26 Quilling. 27 First floor. 28 Marks & Spencer. 29 Horse riding. 30 Old Trafford.

1 Who replaced Len Goodman as head judge on "Strictly Come Dancing" in 2017?
2 Who was the host of the variety show "Lenny Goes to Town"?
3 Which medical drama takes place in Holby's A & E department?
4 Which former Friend became a "Top Gear" presenter?
5 What is the name of Catherine Tate's schoolgirl character?
6 What is presented to the 'victim' at the end of "This is Your Life"?
7 What is Lorraine Kelly's morning TV show called?
8 Steve Irwin was famous for hunting which creatures?
9 "The Jerry Springer Show" comes from which country?
10 "Newsround" is aimed at which group of viewers?
11 In which series set in Ireland did barmaid Assumpta meet a sad end?
12 Which near silent walking disaster was created by Rowan Atkinson?
13 Whose chat show features the red chair?
14 Which Geoff gardened at Barnsdale?
15 Which series was dubbed "Barewatch" and "Boobwatch"?
16 Which charity campaign has Pudsey Bear as its mascot?
17 Which Michael's 70s chat show was revived in 1998?
18 In which Practice have doctors Kerruish, Glover and Attwood worked?
19 Which was broadcast later, "Newsnight" or "News at Ten"?
20 Who substituted for Ant on 2018's "I'm a Celebrity… Get Me Out of Here"?
21 Which reality show did Danny Dyer's daughter Dani win in 2018?
22 What follows Police, Camera…, in the show about awful drivers?
23 Who played Den Watts in the early episodes of "EastEnders"?
24 Which drama series where Robson and Jerome found fame is about army life?
25 On which day of the week does the so-called God slot take place?
26 On TV, what is "The Royal"?
27 Which Cilla Black series made dreams come true?
28 In which city is "Peaky Blinders" set?
29 Which "Torchwood" star was a "How Do You Solve a Problem Like Maria?" judge?
30 Which Files feature Mulder and Scully?

Quiz 74 | Pot Luck 36

Answers – page 81

1 Which comic did Dan Dare first appear in?
2 Golfer Ian Woosnam comes from which country?
3 Mumbai, Chennai and Kolkata are major cities in which country?
4 Which inventor Michael appeared on a £20 note?
5 Gouache is a type of what?
6 The notorious Klaus Barbie was the Butcher of where in France?
7 Which county do the Arctic Monkeys come from?
8 What shape is something if it is campanulate?
9 Was "Cutting It" set in a butcher's, a hair salon or a hospital?
10 Which Robin was the spoof film "Men in Tights" about?
11 Which word can go in front of BISCUIT, CLOSET and COLOUR?
12 As which character was "Coronation Street" actor Bruce Jones the neighbour from hell?
13 Which ticking instrument keeps perfect time for a musician?
14 Was the Automobile Association founded before or after World War I?
15 Which nation came back to international rugby in 1993?
16 Which is bigger, A3 or A4 paper?
17 Which band featured Noddy Holder and Dave Hill?
18 The mesosphere and the stratosphere are layers of what?
19 With which country are Walloons associated?
20 What links a chocolate bar, a planet and a god of war?
21 "Aliens" and "Alien Evolution" were sequels to which movie?
22 In which part of the body are the smallest bones?
23 In Greek legend, who had a bad hair day with snakes on her head?
24 What is the common name for seasonal allergic rhinitis?
25 What was the first name of Wacky Racer Mr Dastardly?
26 Was Chris Tarrant born in the 1940s or the 1960s?
27 Operation Overlord was the codename for the 1944 Allied invasion of where?
28 Who took a "Careless Whisper" to No.1 in the 1980s?
29 What is the name of the line of latitude that runs around the centre of the earth?
30 Which Scottish loch is reputed to be home to a monster?

Answers | TV Times 3 (see Quiz 73)

1 Shirley Ballas. 2 Lenny Henry. 3 Casualty. 4 Matt LeBlanc. 5 Lauren. 6 Book.
7 Lorraine. 8 Crocodiles. 9 USA. 10 Children. 11 Ballykissangel. 12 Mr Bean.
13 Graham Norton. 14 Hamilton. 15 Baywatch. 16 Children in Need. 17 Parkinson.
18 Peak Practice. 19 Newsnight. 20 Holly Willoughby. 21 Love Island. 22 Action.
23 Leslie Grantham. 24 Soldier Soldier. 25 Sunday. 26 Hospital. 27 Surprise Surprise.
28 Birmingham. 29 John Barrowman. 30 The X Files.

82

Quiz 75 Performing Arts

Answers – page 84

1 Who sang a "Barcelona" duet with Freddy Mercury?
2 Which composer wrote the "Four Seasons"?
3 Which branch of performing is Michael Flatley famous for?
4 In which country was the Halle Orchestra founded?
5 Which dancer Wayne toured in 1998 to mark his 50th birthday?
6 Who composed the incidental music for Ibsen's play "Peer Gynt"?
7 Which writers of comic opera are referred to as G&S?
8 Which playwright was known as the Bard of Avon?
9 Billy Smart was associated with what type of entertainment?
10 In which country is an eisteddfod held?
11 Which Circle is a professional association of conjurors?
12 Which charity gala with many different performers is held in November and attended by the Royal Family?
13 Which Lord Andrew wrote the musical "Whistle Down the Wind"?
14 In Rodgers and Hammerstein who wrote the music?
15 In which country was the Bolshoi Ballet founded?
16 Which famous Paul wrote the oratorio "Ecce Cor Meum"?
17 The stage musical "Wicked" is a retelling of which film and book?
18 At what time of year would you go and watch a nativity play?
19 Which Monty Python-based musical opened in the UK in the autumn of 2006?
20 The Last Night of the Proms takes place in which month?
21 A person playing a pantomime dame is usually which sex?
22 What type of singing made Maria Callas famous?
23 What was the surname of US musical composers George and Ira?
24 What is the final concert at the Promenade Concerts called?
25 "Matilda the Musical" is based on a book by which children's author?
26 Which Sir Noel wrote and starred in his plays and musicals?
27 What is the first name of Scarborough-based playwright Ayckbourn?
28 Opera singer Lesley Garrett is from which county?
29 Do you stand or sit for the Hallelujah Chorus from "The Messiah"?
30 In panto how do you respond to "Oh yes it is!"?

Answers | Pot Luck 37 *(see Quiz 76)*

1 50 Cent. 2 Arsenal. 3 Bill Wyman. 4 H.G. 5 Felicity. 6 Pub. 7 Pottery. 8 Long-haired. 9 James Bond. 10 Goldie Hawn. 11 Wok. 12 The Archers. 13 Beef. 14 Horse. 15 Spoons. 16 Hello. 17 Nigel. 18 King Edward. 19 Crawford. 20 Arkansas. 21 Canada. 22 Etna. 23 Smoking. 24 Deer. 25 Outside. 26 Two (South Australia & New South Wales). 27 Moonlight Serenade. 28 New Testament. 29 Jeroboam. 30 Bronx.

1 Which rapper works with G-Unit?
2 England football star Ashley Cole began his career at which London club?
3 Who is older, Bill Wyman or the Prince of Wales?
4 What are the two initials of early 20th Century sci-fi writer Wells?
5 Which Kendall starred in the sitcom "Solo"?
6 Craig Cash's "Early Doors" was set in what type of establishment?
7 What did Clarice Cliff make?
8 Is an Afghan hound short-haired or long-haired?
9 Which secret agent was created by Ian Fleming?
10 Kate Hudson is the daughter of which actress Goldie?
11 What is a round-bottomed Chinese cooking pan called?
12 In which radio series is there a pub called The Bull?
13 What sort of meat is usually in a hamburger?
14 What type of animal is a palomino?
15 What is Uri Geller famous for bending?
16 Would you say Bonjour to a French person when you say hello
   or goodbye?
17 Violinist Kennedy chose to drop which first name professionally?
18 Which monarch gave his name to a type of potato?
19 Which Michael created the Phantom in Lloyd Webber's musical?
20 Is Bill Clinton's home state Arkansas or Arizona?
21 In which country is Hudson Bay?
22 Which Sicilian mountain is Europe's highest volcano?
23 ASH is a pressure group against what?
24 Which animal might be fallow or red?
25 Would you find a gazebo inside or outside your home?
26 How many Australian states have South in their names?
27 Was Glenn Miller's theme tune "Moonlight Sonata" or
   "Moonlight Serenade"?
28 Is the book of Jude in the Old or New Testament?
29 Which is larger, a magnum of champagne or a Jeroboam?
30 Which tough area of New York gives its name to a gin, vermouth and
   orange cocktail?

Answers | Performing Arts *(see Quiz 75)*

1 Montserrat Caballé. 2 Vivaldi. 3 Dance. 4 UK. 5 Sleep. 6 Edvard Grieg. 7 Gilbert & Sullivan. 8 William Shakespeare. 9 Circus. 10 Wales. 11 Magic Circle. 12 Royal Variety Show. 13 Lloyd Webber. 14 Rodgers. 15 Russia. 16 Paul McCartney. 17 The Wizard of Oz. 18 Christmas. 19 Spamalot. 20 September. 21 Male. 22 Opera. 23 Gershwin. 24 Last Night of the Proms. 25 Roald Dahl. 26 Coward. 27 Alan. 28 Yorkshire. 29 Stand. 30 "Oh no it isn't!".

1 How often is the World Cup held?
2 Did Jimmy Greaves ever play in a World Cup Final?
3 Who won the last World Cup of the 20th century?
4 What colour shirts were England wearing when they won in 1966?
5 Who became known sarcastically as The Hand of God?
6 Who was sent off in France 98 and fled to Posh Spice in New York?
7 Which side from Great Britain did not make France 98?
8 Which 1966 World Cup veteran resigned as Republic of Ireland manager in 1995?
9 Which British side did Brazil play in the first match of France 98?
10 Which European country hosted the 2006 tournament?
11 Which country did Louis Saha play for in the 2006 World Cup?
12 Who were beaten finalists in the last World Cup of the 20th century?
13 In France 98 which Caribbean side were called the Reggae Boys?
14 Who was the manager of the England football team during the 2018 World Cup?
15 Which former Man Utd keeper played in the 2006 Final?
16 Which German boss Jurgen resigned after the 2006 tournament?
17 In France 98 whom did Suker play for?
18 Who was the only Englishman to lift the World Cup before 2000?
19 Which central American country was the first to host the World Cup twice, in 1986?
20 Which ex-World Cup manager's autobiography is "An Englishman Abroad"?
21 What colour are Brazil's shirts?
22 Who were the only non-Europeans to win the World Cup in the 90s?
23 Who was England's youngest player in France 98?
24 What colour-coded hair was seen on the Nigerian team in France 98?
25 Which Gary was top scorer in the 1986 World Cup?
26 In which month did France 98 finish?
27 Which Scandinavian side was third in the 1994 US tournament?
28 Which South American side knocked England out of France 98?
29 In which city did France 98 begin and end?
30 Where did the 2018 World Cup take place?

Answers	Pot Luck 38 *(see Quiz 78)*

1 Lancashire. 2 L.B. 3 Kent. 4 Rum. 5 Locum. 6 Argentina. 7 Dog.
8 Northamptonshire. 9 DH Lawrence. 10 Apple. 11 Germany. 12 Italy. 13 Alan Titchmarsh. 14 Gunnell. 15 Ernie Wise. 16 China. 17 Westlife. 18 Potter. 19 Holly. 20 Colin Farrell. 21 Cuckoo. 22 Tenor. 23 Bit. 24 Addams. 25 Chris de Burgh. 26 Tennis. 27 Alice (in Wonderland). 28 Sleeve. 29 Celine Dion. 30 Perambulator.

Quiz 78 | Pot Luck 38

Answers – page 85

1 Michael Atherton played for which county cricket club?
2 Which were the initials of US President Johnson?
3 In which county is Ashford International station?
4 Does a pina colada contain rum or gin?
5 Which word for a duty doctor is a Latin name for place holder?
6 Which country's Rugby Union side are the Pumas?
7 Is a Dandie Dinmont, a dog, a cat or a horse?
8 In which county is the stately home of Althorp?
9 Which controversial author used the initials for his first names David Herbert?
10 What sort of fruit flavour does Calvados have?
11 In which country were BMWs first made?
12 St Francis of Assisi is patron saint of which country?
13 Which Alan presented the TV programme "How to be a Gardener"?
14 Which Sally was British women's team captain in the 1996 Olympics?
15 Which late comedian was the one with "short, fat hairy legs"?
16 Which country was once called Cathay?
17 Which boy band had a No.1 with their version of Billy Joel's "Uptown Girl"?
18 Which Dennis created "The Singing Detective"?
19 Which Buddy did Alvin Stardust sing about?
20 Which Irishman Colin starred in the movie "Phone Booth"?
21 Which bird lays its eggs in the nests of other birds?
22 Was the singer Mario Lanza a bass, baritone or tenor?
23 What name is given to the part of the bridle in a horse's mouth?
24 Wednesday and Pugsley are part of which family?
25 Christopher Davidson found fame as a singer as which Chris?
26 Maria Bueno was famous for which sport?
27 In fiction, which girl swam in a pool of her own tears?
28 A raglan forms which part of a garment?
29 Who had a huge 1995 hit with "Think Twice"?
30 Pram is an abbreviation of which word?

Answers | **Sport: Football World Cup Fever** *(see Quiz 77)*

1 Every four years. 2 No. 3 France. 4 Red. 5 Diego Maradonna. 6 David Beckham.
7 Wales. 8 Jack Charlton. 9 Scotland. 10 Germany. 11 France. 12 Brazil.
13 Jamaica. 14 Gareth Southgate. 15 Fabien Barthez. 16 Jurgen Klinsman.
17 Croatia. 18 Bobby Moore. 19 Mexico. 20 Bobby Robson. 21 Yellow. 22 Brazil.
23 Michael Owen. 24 Green. 25 Lineker. 26 July. 27 Sweden. 28 Argentina.
29 Paris. 30 Russia.

1 Which Yasser founded the PLO?
2 Which Kennedy announced he was running for President in 1960?
3 Nikita Krushchev was head of state of which Union?
4 In which Italian city were the 1960 summer Olympics held?
5 Whose Lover was the subject of a court case in book form?
6 The USSR sent its first man where in April 1960?
7 Which Russian dancer Rudolf defected to the West?
8 Across which former European capital was a Wall built?
9 Which drug taken by pregnant mothers caused abnormalities in babies?
10 Which Harold became Labour leader in 1963?
11 Of where did Neil Armstrong say, "The surface is like fine powder"?
12 What were mailbags containing over £1 million stolen from?
13 Caroline was the name of Britain's first offshore pirate what?
14 Which British WWII leader died in 1965?
15 What sort of champion was Arkle?
16 Which communist country had its famous Red Guards?
17 Which knighted football star retired aged 50?
18 Who launched the Queen Elizabeth II – QE2 – on Clydebank?
19 Which model Jean was called The Shrimp?
20 Which homeless charity was set up after TV's "Cathy Come Home"?
21 What product was banned from TV advertising on health grounds?
22 Which Rolling Stone singer was best man at David Bailey's wedding?
23 Which notorious East End gangland twins were jailed for murder?
24 Which rock star married Patricia Beaulieu?
25 Which capital was said to swing in the 60s?
26 Which Martin famously gave his "I have a dream" speech?
27 If Mods rode scooters, who rode motorbikes?
28 LBJ was President of which country?
29 How were Ian Brady and Myra Hindley known?
30 Which actress Marilyn was found dead in her bungalow near Hollywood?

Answers	Pot Luck 39 *(see Quiz 80)*

1 Thaw. 2 Florin. 3 Actress. 4 Chris Evans. 5 1980. 6 Bluto. 7 Yes. 8 Liverpool.
9 Portuguese. 10 André Previn. 11 Mile. 12 Harman. 13 Ten. 14 26. 15 The Kinks.
16 Greek gods. 17 Buffy the Vampire Slayer. 18 Borzoi. 19 Nissan. 20 Birmingham.
21 Fox. 22 Cyrillic. 23 British Prime Ministers. 24 Champion. 25 Mick Hucknall.
26 Penicillin. 27 Catherine Zeta Jones. 28 Golf. 29 Duck. 30 McCartney.

Quiz 80 | Pot Luck 39

Answers – page 87

LEVEL 1

1 Which John married actress Sheila Hancock?
2 Which pre-decimal coin had the value of two shillings?
3 What does Emma Stone's character aspire to be in "La La Land"?
4 Which TV presenter's shows have had Toothbrush and Breakfast in their titles?
5 Were the Olympic Games last held in Russia in 1960, 1980 or 1988?
6 Who is Popeye's rival?
7 Was Sir Walter Scott Scottish?
8 Which English football side was managed by the late Bob Paisley?
9 What is the main language in Brazil?
10 Whom did Morecambe and Wise call Andrew Preview?
11 Which is greater in distance, a mile or a kilometre?
12 Which MP Harriet was axed in Tony Blair's first Cabinet reshuffle?
13 How many national parks are there in England?
14 How many red cards are there in a standard pack of cards?
15 Ray Davies was writer and singer with which band?
16 Adonis, Apollo and Poseidon were all what?
17 Tara and Willow featured in which occult-based series?
18 Which dog is larger – a borzoi or a corgi?
19 The Micra was made by which car company?
20 "Crossroads" was set near which major city?
21 A vixen is the female of which animal?
22 Which alphabet is used by Muscovites?
23 What links the names Chamberlain, Heath and Wilson?
24 Which jockey Bob fought back from cancer to win the Grand National?
25 Who is Simply Red's lead singer?
26 Which was the first antibiotic to be discovered?
27 Which Welsh actress won an Oscar for her role in "Chicago"?
28 For which sport is Sunningdale famous?
29 A Muscovy is what type of bird?
30 Which musical Paul got involved with frogs and Rupert Bear?

Answers	**Past Times: The 60s** *(see Quiz 79)*

1 Arafat. 2 John. 3 Soviet. 4 Rome. 5 Lady Chatterley's. 6 Space. 7 Nureyev.
8 Berlin. 9 Thalidomide. 10 Wilson. 11 The Moon. 12 Train. 13 Radio station.
14 Churchill. 15 Horse. 16 China. 17 Sir Stanley Matthews. 18 Queen Elizabeth II.
19 Jean Shrimpton. 20 Shelter. 21 Cigarettes. 22 Mick Jagger. 23 Kray twins.
24 Elvis Presley. 25 London. 26 Luther King. 27 Rockers. 28 USA. 29 Moors
murderers. 30 Monroe.

1 Which actor was nicknamed "Bogey"?
2 Which actor Marlon was paid $18 million for nine minutes in "Superman" in 1978?
3 Which western star John first acted as Duke Morrison?
4 Which Samuel starred as a gangster in "Pulp Fiction"?
5 Which Bruce starred in "The Jackal"?
6 Which Kiwi won an Oscar for his role in "Gladiator"?
7 Tough guy Robert de Niro sang about New York in which film?
8 Which lager did "Crocodile Dundee" star Paul Hogan advertise?
9 Which Vietnam veteran Oliver directed "Platoon"?
10 Which star of "The Godfather" bought an island called Tetiaroa?
11 Which Martin was assigned to assassinate Brando in "Apocalypse Now"?
12 What did George C. Scott refuse to do about his Oscar for "Patton"?
13 Gene Hackman played cop Popeye Doyle in which classic thriller?
14 Ray Liotta played a member of which criminal organisation in "Goodfellas"?
15 Which Bruce was the psychiatrist in "The Sixth Sense"?
16 Was Charles Bronson one of ten or fifteen children?
17 Is Bruce Willis a cop or a soldier in the "Die Hard" movies?
18 Which hell raiser Oliver released a single "Lonely for a Girl" in 1965?
19 Lee Marvin headed a Dirty cast of how many in the 1967 movie?
20 Which singer who died in 1998 was the tough guy captain in "Von Ryan's Express"?
21 How many gunfighters were hired in The Magnificent film of 1960?
22 On what vehicle did Steve McQueen try to flee in "The Great Escape"?
23 Which Sylvester starred in "Judge Dredd"?
24 What is the first name of "Reservoir Dogs" director Tarantino?
25 Which tough guy Arnold has appeared on a postage stamp of Mali?
26 Which Mel starred in the "Lethal Weapon" series of films?
27 Which bare-headed actor was in "The Magnificent Seven" and "The King and I"?
28 Which Clint got the part in "Dirty Harry" when Sinatra pulled out?
29 Which James Bond has an actor son called Jason?
30 Was "The Untouchables" with Kevin Costner set in the 20s, 40s or 60s?

Answers Pot Luck 40 *(see Quiz 82)*

1 Tennis. 2 Heart. 3 Chris Tarrant. 4 West Yorkshire (Guiseley). 5 Frog. 6 Dingle. 7 Rot away. 8 Five. 9 Ten. 10 Aberdeen. 11 Becoming. 12 Belgium. 13 Black Bess. 14 Purdy. 15 Eric Clapton. 16 Marylebone. 17 Bahamas. 18 The Taming of the Shrew. 19 Margaret Thatcher. 20 Uluru. 21 John Hurt. 22 Cornwall. 23 English. 24 British Prime Minister. 25 Himalayas. 26 Vingt. 27 Aircraft. 28 Wizzard. 29 Blue. 30 France.

Quiz 82 Pot Luck 40

LEVEL 1

Answers – page 89

1 For which sport is Billie-Jean King famous?
2 According to the proverb, absence makes which organ grow fonder?
3 Who hosted ITV's "Who Wants to be a Millionaire"?
4 In what county was Harry Ramsden's first chip shop?
5 Which species of creature includes the most poisonous animal in the world?
6 Which soap family included Lisa, Marlon and Shadrach?
7 If something is biodegradable, what will it do?
8 How many noughts are in the written number two hundred thousand?
9 Every how many years is a National Census taken in Britain?
10 Where are you if you visit the Granite City?
11 What was Michelle Obama's bestselling 2018 memoir called?
12 In which country is the town of Spa?
13 What was the name of Dick Turpin's horse?
14 In the "New Avengers", which character was played by Joanna Lumley?
15 Which guitarist is nicknamed "Slowhand"?
16 In cricket, what does the initial M stand for in MCC?
17 Nassau is the capital of which group of islands?
18 In which Shakespeare play does Kate marry Petruchio?
19 Who was Tory leader immediately before John Major?
20 What is Ayers Rock also known as?
21 Who played Quentin Crisp in the 1975 TV film "The Naked Civil Servant"?
22 Which English county boasts the longest coastline?
23 What nationality was Bridget in "Bridget Jones's Diary"?
24 Eden, Heath and MacDonald have all held which important position?
25 In which mountain range is Mount Everest?
26 What is the French word for the number twenty?
27 What are DC-10s and 747s?
28 "See My Baby Jive" was a 70s No.1 for which magic-sounding group?
29 What colour is azure in heraldry?
30 Which country is immediately south of Belgium?

Answers | The Movies: Tough Guys *(see Quiz 81)*

1 Humphrey Bogart. 2 Brando. 3 John Wayne. 4 Jackson. 5 Willis. 6 Russell Crowe.
7 New York, New York. 8 Fosters. 9 Stone. 10 Marlon Brando. 11 Sheen.
12 Accept it. 13 French Connection. 14 Mafia. 15 Bruce Willis. 16 Fifteen. 17 Cop.
18 Reed. 19 Dozen. 20 Frank Sinatra. 21 Seven. 22 Motorcycle. 23 Stallone.
24 Quentin. 25 Schwarzenegger. 26 Gibson. 27 Yul Brynner. 28 Eastwood.
29 Sean Connery. 30 20s.

1 In which country did black activist Steve Biko die in 1977?
2 Which US President was brought down by the Watergate scandal?
3 What did a policeman use to hide a streaker's embarrassment in a famous incident at Twickenham in 1974?
4 Which London-born comic Charlie was knighted?
5 Which tree population was decimated by a Dutch disease?
6 Did Skytrain provide cut price tickets by air 'or rail?
7 Who succeeded John Paul I as Pope?
8 The New English version of which Book was published in 1970?
9 Which Czech tennis star Martina defected to the West?
10 In which country did Pol Pot conduct a reign of terror?
11 Which Sebastian was a record-breaking middle-distance runner?
12 Which father of twins was the husband of the British PM?
13 Which princess was sportswoman of the year in 1971?
14 The Queen celebrated how many years on the throne in her Jubilee?
15 Which Lord disappeared after his nanny was murdered?
16 Who beat four male candidates to become Tory leader in 1975?
17 Which war ended with the fall of Saigon in 1975?
18 Which country's athletes were murdered at the 1972 Olympics?
19 John Curry won Olympic gold on what surface?
20 In which county did a Ripper carry out horrific murders?
21 Which Lord and Royal uncle was murdered off Ireland?
22 Which Mother won a Nobel Peace Prize?
23 Charles de Gaulle died after being president of which country?
24 Were Sunderland in the first or second division when they won the FA Cup in 1973?
25 Where was the monarchy restored after the death of Franco?
26 In 1971 the first British soldier was killed in which British province?
27 Evonne Goolagong from which country won Wimbledon in 1971?
28 Which Chris was Jimmy Connors' fiancée when he first won Wimbledon?
29 Which James succeeded Harold Wilson as Prime Minister?
30 David Steel became leader of which political party in 1976?

Answers	Pot Luck 41 *(see Quiz 84)*

1 Orange. 2 Jennifer Saunders. 3 Madonna. 4 London & Birmingham. 5 Unchained Melody. 6 Goldcrest. 7 18. 8 Martin. 9 Liffey. 10 1940s. 11 Pam St Clement. 12 Red Indian tribes. 13 Take That. 14 White. 15 Four. 16 Mind. 17 Alfred Hitchcock. 18 Five. 19 Charles Dickens. 20 Hutch. 21 China. 22 Northumberland. 23 MW. 24 Green. 25 A king. 26 Yorkshire. 27 Food. 28 Angostura Bitters. 29 Jennifer Aniston. 30 Queensland.

1 In international football, what is the main colour of Holland's shirts?
2 Who is older – Ruby Wax or Jennifer Saunders?
3 "Into the Groove" gave a first UK No.1 for which singer?
4 Which two cities were linked by the M1 when it first opened?
5 Which song was a British No.1 for Jimmy Young, the Righteous Brothers, Robson & Jerome and Gareth Gates?
6 What is Britain's smallest songbird?
7 How many sides are there in a pair of nonagons?
8 Which George was the main producer of The Beatles' hits?
9 What river flows through the city of Dublin in Ireland?
10 Was Joanna Lumley born in the 1940s, 50s or 60s?
11 Who played Pat Butcher in "EastEnders"?
12 Mohawk, Seminole and Sioux are all names of what?
13 Which star group was Jason Orange a member of?
14 Is Riesling a red or white wine?
15 How many Teletubbies are there?
16 Russell Crowe starred in the movie "A Beautiful" what?
17 Who links the films "Rebecca", "Psycho" and "Vertigo"?
18 What's the most number of Sundays that could occur in December?
19 Which author created the reclusive character Miss Havisham?
20 On TV, did David Soul play Starsky or Hutch?
21 Do more people live in China or India?
22 What is England's most north easterly county?
23 Is Radio 5 Live broadcast on MW or FM?
24 What colour is verdigris which appears on copper or brass?
25 Who is killed if regicide is committed?
26 Ridings used to divide which county?
27 Is Robert Carrier linked with food, theatre or sport?
28 Pink gin is gin flavoured with what?
29 Who played the character Rachel in "Friends"?
30 Brisbane is the capital of which Australian state?

1 Blackbirds are members of the thrush family – true or false?

2 What kind of bird features in Helen Macdonald's memoir "H is for Hawk"?

3 Which island in the Bristol Channel derives its name from the Norse for puffin island?

4 Which common garden bird has a bright blue cap and pale yellow breast?

5 Which bird famously lays its eggs in other birds' nests?

6 Which type of bird is known for its excellent eyesight and hearing?

7 Would you spot a kingfisher in a wood or beside a river?

8 What bird featured in the music hall song "My Old Man"?

9 A pintail is a type of duck – true or false?

10 What colour is the cap of a coal tit?

11 What kind of bird catches the worm?

12 Which birds can be found at the Tower of London?

13 Its Latin name is pica pica and it is said to like shiny objects – what is it?

14 Which composer wrote the musical work "The Lark Ascending"?

15 Is the UK's most common bird of prey a buzzcock or a buzzard?

16 What is the largest living bird in the world?

17 Which wonderful bird's beak can hold more than his belly can?

18 What physical features do chaffinches and bullfinches have in common?

19 Where do British swallows spend the winter?

20 Who wrote the book "Jonathan Livingston Seagull"?

21 Which bird topped the RSPB's 2018 Big Garden Birdwatch survey?

22 In the song, which bird sang in Berkeley Square?

23 When were laws making it illegal to kill birds of prey passed in the UK – 1934, 1954 or 1974?

24 Albatrosses are native to the UK – true or false?

25 Alfred Hitchcock based his horror film "The Birds" on a short story by which author?

26 Which comedian's 2018 live tour was called Larks in Transit?

27 Who played the female lead in the 2010 movie "Black Swan"?

28 What kind of bird was Kes in the Ken Loach film of the same name?

29 WWhen male and female birds look distinctly different it's called dimorphic – true or false?

30 What kind of bird was the animated character Woody?

Answers   **Past Times: The 80s** *(see Quiz 86)*

1 Margaret Thatcher. 2 London. 3 Eggs. 4 Johnson. 5 North Sea. 6 King's Cross.
7 Neil Kinnock. 8 Duchess of Windsor. 9 Zeebrugge. 10 Philippines. 11 South Africa.
12 Prince Andrew. 13 Runner. 14 Wembley. 15 Morecambe. 16 Parkinson.
17 Bradford. 18 Liberal Democrats. 19 The Smiths. 20 Greenham. 21 Harrods.
22 Bjorn Borg. 23 Car accident. 24 Dallas. 25 Falklands. 26 Tyson.
27 Champion. 28 Reagan. 29 New York. 30 Kindergarten.

1 Which serving British PM survived an assassination attempt?

2 In which city did the SAS storm the Iranian embassy?

3 Edwina Currie resigned over what type of farm food?

4 Which Ben was disqualified from the Seoul Olympics for drug taking?

5 In which Sea did the oil rig Piper Alpha catch fire?

6 Which north London Tube station was gutted by fire in 1987?

7 Who was Labour leader when Thatcher had her third election victory?

8 Which late Duchess's jewels were auctioned for over £30 million?

9 The Herald of Free Enterprise sank off which Belgian port?

10 President Marcos was ousted in a rebellion in which island country?

11 Desmond Tutu became an archbishop in which country?

12 Who was the second of the Queen's sons to marry in the 80s?

13 Was Zola Budd a swimmer, a runner or a gymnast?

14 At which UK stadium was the Live Aid concert held?

15 Which Eric, half of a classic comedy duo, died in 1984?

16 Which Tory minister Cecil resigned in a scandal in 1983?

17 In which Yorkshire city's football ground was there a fatal fire in '85?

18 What is the full name of the Lib Dems, formed in 1989?

19 Which Manchester band was fronted by Steven Morrissey?

20 At which Common was there a camp against cruise missiles?

21 Outside which London store did a bomb explode in December 1983?

22 Which Swedish tennis star retired aged 26?

23 In what type of accident was Princess Grace of Monaco killed?

24 Which soap asked the audience "Who shot JR?"?

25 Which war in the South Atlantic was Britain involved in?

26 Which Mike became the youngest heavyweight boxing champion?

27 Which Bob rode Aldaniti to a Grand National win in 1981?

28 Which US president was the victim of an assassination attempt?

29 In which city was Beatle John Lennon murdered?

30 Where was Lady Diana Spencer working when photographed in a seemingly see-through skirt?

---

1 Whose album "True Blue" was No.1 in 28 countries?
2 What was The Spice Girls' first No.1?
3 Whose charity hit included "Something About the Way You Look Tonight"?
4 Which of Madonna's two hits from "Evita" got higher in the charts?
5 What was the name of Dua Lipa's 2018 hit with Calvin Harris?
6 In which decade did the UK singles charts begin?
7 Who as well as The Troggs charted with "Love is All Around"?
8 Which wartime song charted with Robson & Jerome's "Unchained Melody"?
9 Which father and daughter had a No.1 with "Somethin' Stupid"?
10 "I Bet You Look Good on the Dancefloor" was a 2005 No.1 for which band?
11 Which football team charted with "Come On You Reds"?
12 Whose "Release Me" spent a record number of weeks in the charts?
13 Was Celine Dion's "Power of Love" the same as Jennifer Rush's or Frankie Goes to Hollywood's?
14 Who was the first all-female band to have three consecutive No.1s?
15 The soundtrack from which film musical topped the album charts in 2018?
16 Who hit the top spot with "Cotton Eye Joe"?
17 Which musical did Boyzone's No.1 "No Matter What" come from?
18 Whose first solo number one hit was 2003's "Crazy in Love"?
19 Billboard is a list of best-selling records where?
20 "Stickwitu" was the second No.1 for which girl group?
21 Which family were at No.1 with "Do the Bartman"?
22 Which Scandinavian country do chart toppers Aqua come from?
23 Who accompanied Vic Reeves on his No.1 hit "Dizzy"?
24 Whose '96 No.1s were "Firestarter" and "Breathe"?
25 Which Boys' first No.1 was "West End Girls"?
26 Which artist had the most entries in the UK's Official Singles chart in 2018?
27 A 2018 hit for Lady Gaga and Bradley Cooper, which movie was "Shallow" from?
28 Which Bee Gees number one shared its name with a US state?
29 "Love Me for a Reason" charted for The Osmonds and which band?
30 Who wrote the series "Crocodile Shoes" and its chart songs?

Answers | Geography: World tour *(see Quiz 91)*

1 Nile. 2 Pope. 3 West. 4 Afghanistan. 5 Bombay. 6 Abominable. 7 Australia.
8 Southern. 9 India. 10 Peru. 11 Caribbean. 12 Zimbabwe. 13 Suez. 14 Coast.
15 Pacific. 16 South Africa. 17 Abraham Lincoln. 18 Arizona. 19 Australia.
20 Sahara. 21 Monarchy. 22 Africa. 23 Danube. 24 Atlantic. 25 Iran. 26 Arctic
Circle. 27 Southern. 28 Hungary. 29 China. 30 Canada.

1 Sir Paul McCartney was awarded the freedom of which city?
2 Which legendary band released "The Wall"?
3 Which soul star Ray has the nickname The Genius?
4 Which Shirley was dubbed the Tigress from Tiger Bay?
5 Supermodel Rachel Hunter married which superstar Rod?
6 Which ex-Police singer founded the Rainforest Foundation in 1988?
7 Who does not use her surname Ciccone?
8 Which brother completed the Gibb trio with Maurice and Robin?
9 "Hung Up" gave a 12th No.1 single for which superstar?
10 Which rock superstar was Lisa Marie Presley's second husband?
11 Which female sang on Westlife's "When You Tell Me that You Love Me"?
12 In 2005 which Robbie Wiliams song was voted best in 25 years of BRIT awards?
13 Which drummer's solo album "No Jacket Required" was a best-seller?
14 Which Rolling Stone did not normally play an instrument on stage?
15 Which group was heard on the soundtrack of "Saturday Night Fever"?
16 Whose hits range from "The Laughing Gnome" to "Space Oddity"?
17 Who sang "You Don't Bring Me Flowers" with Barbra Streisand?
18 Which Queen of Soul sang the best version of "Nessun Dorma" according to Pavarotti?
19 Which band would you find The Edge and Bono in?
20 Who lived in a mansion called Graceland?
21 Which boys liked "California Girls"?
22 Whose "Streets of Philadelphia" was his highest hit at the time in 1994?
23 Which Stevie dropped the tag Little and had hits well into adulthood?
24 Which Tina recorded Bond theme "Goldeneye"?
25 Which superstar founded the Rocket record label?
26 All Lionel Richie's early hits were on which record label?
27 Which Scottish football fan has the first names Roderick David?
28 Which Roy charted with "Crying" with kd lang four years after his death?
29 Which Barbra did actor James Brolin marry in 1998?
30 Which Barry's song "Copacabana" became a musical?

Answers | Pop: Charts (see Quiz 87)

1 Madonna. 2 Wannabe. 3 Elton John. 4 Don't Cry for Me Argentina. 5 One Kiss.
6 1950s. 7 Wet Wet Wet. 8 The White Cliffs of Dover. 9 Frank & Nancy Sinatra.
10 Arctic Monkeys. 11 Manchester United. 12 Engelbert Humperdinck. 13 Jennifer
Rush's. 14 Spice Girls. 15 The Greatest Showman. 16 Rednex. 17 Whistle Down the
Wind. 18 Beyoncé. 19 USA. 20 The Pussycat Dolls. 21 The Simpsons. 22 Denmark.
23 The Wonder Stuff. 24 Prodigy. 25 Pet Shop. 26 Drake. 27 A Star is Born. 28
Massachusetts. 29 Boyzone. 30 Jimmy Nail.

1 What organisation did the sitcom "W1A" satirise?
2 Which ex-newspaper editor Piers became a star presenter on American TV?
3 The Sporting Life devotes itself to which sport?
4 Which radio and TV listings magazine is published by the BBC?
5 Which independent radio station specialises in classical music?
6 Is "The Archers" on Radio 1 or Radio 4?
7 In 2011, which judge was appointed to chair a public inquiry into the press?
8 In what year did the "News of the World" close?
9 In 2018 who retired as editor of the "Daily Mail"?
10 In which north of England city is Granada TV based?
11 What sort of column tells of stories and rumours about celebrities?
12 "Gavin and Stacey" was originally broadcast on which channel?
13 Is GQ for men or women?
14 Which Rebekah was the first female to edit "The Sun" newspaper?
15 On which shelf would someone buy an "adult" magazine?
16 What does FT stand for in the name of the financial daily newspaper?
17 What is the Daily Mail's Sunday paper called?
18 Who or what owns the "Guardian" newspaper?
19 Which corporation is known as Auntie?
20 Which magazine about celebs is based on the Spanish mag Hola!?
21 Which Rupert founded Sky Television?
22 Which page in a newspaper is famous for its nude photos?
23 Arianna Huffington was one of the founders of what?
24 Which satirical magazine shares its name with the nickname for a detective?
25 Rupert Bear is linked with which newspaper?
26 Border TV serves the borders of which two countries?
27 What professional person would read The Lancet?
28 How often does the magazine Take A Break appear?
29 Which comic Ricky was a pioneer in podcasting?
30 Which Sir David co-founded LWT and TV-am?

Answers | Celebs: The Royals *(see Quiz 90)*

1 Stark. 2 Brother-in-law. 3 Some of her dresses. 4 Anne. 5 Helen Mirren. 6 Princess Michael of Kent. 7 Margaret. 8 Panorama. 9 Eton. 10 Bulimia. 11 Sarah, Duchess of York. 12 The Tig. 13 Andrew. 14 The Queen. 15 Britannia. 16 Miss. 17 Balmoral. 18 Laura. 19 Christmas. 20 Candle in the Wind. 21 Grace Kelly. 22 USA. 23 Westminster. 24 Monaco. 25 Photographer. 26 Paris. 27 Windsor. 28 Queen Victoria. 29 Navy. 30 Anne.

Quiz 90 | Celebs: The Royals | Answers – page 97

1 Which famous actress Koo was romantically linked to Prince Andrew?
2 What relation was Prince Philip to Princess Margaret?
3 What did the Princess of Wales sell at auction in 1997?
4 What is the Princess Royal's real first name?
5 Who played the Queen in a 2006 film about the death of Princess Diana?
6 What is the title of the wife of Prince Michael of Kent?
7 Which Princess was prevented from marrying divorced Peter Townsend in the 1950s?
8 On which programme did Princess Diana say her marriage had been "a bit crowded"?
9 Prince Harry followed Prince William to which school in 1998?
10 Which dietary illness did Princess Diana allegedly suffer from?
11 Who is the mother of Princesses Beatrice and Eugenie?
12 What was Meghan Markle's blog called?
13 Who is older, Prince Andrew or Prince Edward?
14 Which Royal is always referred to as Her Majesty?
15 Which Royal yacht was decommissioned in 1997?
16 Is Princess Anne's daughter a Princess, or a Miss?
17 Where is the Queen's holiday home north of the border?
18 What is the first name of Princes William and Harry's step sister?
19 At which time of year does the Queen always make a TV broadcast?
20 What did Elton John sing at Princess Diana's funeral?
21 Which wife of Prince Rainier of Monaco was an Oscar winner?
22 Was Charles and Camilla's first overseas tour together to Russia or USA?
23 In which Abbey did Prince Andrew and Sarah Ferguson marry?
24 Prince Albert succeeded to which throne in 2005?
25 Which profession is shared by Lords Snowdon and Lichfield?
26 In which city was Princess Diana tragically killed?
27 Which castle was reopened in 1998 after being damaged by fire?
28 Who was the last British monarch of the 19th century?
29 Before his marriage was Prince Philip in the army or the navy?
30 Which Princess was married to Captain Mark Phillips?

Answers | The Media (see Quiz 89)

1 BBC. 2 Piers Morgan. 3 Horse racing. 4 Radio Times. 5 Classic FM. 6 Radio 4.
7 Leveson. 8 2011. 9 Paul Dacre. 10 Manchester. 11 Gossip column. 12 BBC3.
13 Men. 14 Rebekah Wade. 15 Top shelf. 16 Financial Times. 17 Mail on Sunday.
18 The Scott Trust. 19 BBC. 20 Hello! 21 Murdoch. 22 Three. 23 Huffpost.
24 Private Eye. 25 Daily Express. 26 England & Scotland. 27 Doctor. 28 Weekly.
29 Ricky Gervais. 30 Frost.

1 Which long river has White and Blue tributaries?
2 Which religious leader is head of state of the Vatican?
3 Is Perth on the west or east coast of Australia?
4 Which country was the centre of operations for the Taliban?
5 Does Bombay or Tokyo have the higher population?
6 What sort of Snowman is another name for the Himalayan yeti?
7 What is the world's smallest, flattest and driest continent?
8 Is Argentina in the northern or southern half of South America?
9 Pakistan and Bangladesh both border which country?
10 Which country's name is an anagram of PURE?
11 The West Indies lie in which sea?
12 Zambia is a neighbour of which country which also begins with Z?
13 Which Egyptian canal links the Red Sea and the Mediterranean?
14 Is Ghana on the African coast or wholly inland?
15 Which ocean is the world's deepest?
16 In which country is the homeland of KwaZulu?
17 Who is commemorated at Washington's Lincoln Memorial?
18 Which US state has the zipcode (postcode) AZ?
19 New South Wales is in which country?
20 Which African desert is the world's largest?
21 Is Swaziland a monarchy or a republic?
22 Mount Kilimanjaro is the highest point of which continent?
23 Which river runs through Belgrade, Budapest and Vienna?
24 Which ocean lies to the east of South America?
25 Which Islamic Republic used to be called Persia?
26 Two thirds of Greenland lies in which Circle?
27 Is Namibia in northern or southern Africa?
28 In which country in Europe could you spend a forint?
29 Which People's Republic has the world's largest population?
30 Alberta is a province of which country?

Medium Questions

For the majority of pub quiz situations, these questions are going to be your primary line of attack. They're tricky enough to make people think about the answer, but they're not so mind-straining that your audience is going to walk off feeling humiliated. And that's important. The majority of folks in the pub are going to know roughly half of the answers to these questions, and where people fall down totally will be in subjects that they know nothing about. If you're setting a quiz for lone contestants, make good use of these questions.

If you're working with teams, you may find that this section is a little on the simple side still. Pick any four people from the bar, and you'll find that between them, they have at least some knowledge of most areas. That means that scores for teams on this sort of material should be around the 75% mark, which leaves plenty of room for doing well or doing badly, but still lets everyone feel good about themselves.

So, either way, use these questions wisely. Rely on their power to help you out of a sticky situation (although that might just be beer on the pub carpet), and you won't go far wrong. They will provide the backbone of your quiz.

1 Stamp duty is normally paid on the sale of what?
2 In which country is Aceh province, scene of the 2004 tsunami?
3 What does a BACS system transfer?
4 Who wears a chasuble?
5 Who or what is your doppelganger?
6 Emphysema affects which part of the body?
7 Which term for school or university is from the Latin meaning "bounteous mother"?
8 Which salts are hydrated magnesium sulphate?
9 What was the last No.1 single made by Steps?
10 What did Plaid Cymru add to its name in 1998?
11 Which punctuation mark would an American call a period?
12 How many national parks are there in the UK?
13 Where were the Elgin Marbles from originally?
14 Which song starts, "Friday night and the lights are low"?
15 According to legend, what will happen to Gibraltar's ape population if the British leave?
16 Is BST before or behind GMT?
17 Which river flows through the city of Edinburgh in Scotland?
18 How many valves does a bugle have?
19 What name is given to the compulsive eating disorder?
20 What is a Blenheim Orange?
21 Which childhood disease is also called varicella?
22 What do citronella candles smell of?
23 Which part of the anatomy shares its name with a punctuation mark?
24 Which tax did council tax immediately replace?
25 Which English archbishop signs his name Ebor?
26 Which saint was born in Lourdes?
27 Which proposal for a single currency shares its name with a bird?
28 Where is the auditory canal?
29 Where is a fresco painted?
30 How long must a person have been dead to qualify for a blue plaque?

Answers	Sport: Cricket *(see Quiz 2)*

1 Viv Richards. 2 Surrey. 3 Tony Lewis. 4 Trevor McDonald. 5 Terrence. 6 Kapil Dev.
7 Somerset. 8 Denis Compton. 9 Shakoor Rana. 10 Dennis Lillee. 11 Dickie Bird.
12 Wilfred Rhodes. 13 Graham Alan Gooch. 14 Langer & Hayden. 15 Headingley.
16 Mutthiah Muralitharan. 17 William Gilbert. 18 David Gower. 19 1740s.
20 Lancashire. 21 Sunglasses. 22 Sunil Gavaskar. 23 Hansie Cronje. 24 Don
Bradman. 25 Four. 26 Imran Khan. 27 Antigua. 28 The Times. 29 Sri Lanka.
30 Left.

1 Which West Indian batsman represented Antigua in the 1979 World Cup?
2 Which county did Jack Hobbs play for?
3 Which former test cricketer became President of the MCC in 1998?
4 Which newsreader has written biographies of Viv Richards and Clive Lloyd?
5 What is Ian Botham's middle name?
6 Which Indian was the second bowler to reach 400 Test wickets?
7 Which English county did Viv Richards play for?
8 Which cricketer was the first British sportsman to appear in a major advertising campaign?
9 Which umpire did Gatting publicly argue with in Faisalabad?
10 Which Australian was the first man to take 300 wickets in Test cricket?
11 Which famous umpire played for Yorkshire and Leicestershire?
12 Which all-rounder took 100 wickets and scored 1,000 runs in 16 seasons between 1903 and 1926?
13 Which cricketer's initials are GAG?
14 In Aussie opening partnerships, who are Justin and Matthew?
15 At which ground did England beat South Africa to clinch the 1998 series?
16 David Lloyd was reprimanded for criticising which Sri Lankan bowler in 1998?
17 What were WG Grace's first two names?
18 Whose record did Graham Gooch pass when he became England's leading run scorer?
19 Which decade do the first widely accepted laws of cricket date from?
20 Who won the 1998 NatWest Trophy?
21 In 1996 Darren Gough became the first England bowler to bowl wearing what?
22 Which Indian cricketer scored 10,122 runs in 125 matches between 1971 and 1987?
23 Who captained the South Africans on their 1998 England tour?
24 Which cricketer's bat was auctioned for £23,000 in 1997?
25 How many balls were there in an over up until 1889?
26 Who captained Pakistan in the 1992 World Cup victory?
27 On which island did Brian Lara make his record-breaking 375?
28 In which newspaper was it announced that English cricket had died, leading to competition for the Ashes?
29 In which country is Khettarama Stadium?
30 Which hand does David Gower write with?

1 Which "EastEnders" funeral took place at Christmas 2005?
2 Why does a glow worm glow?
3 Which comedy actor swam the Channel for Sports Relief in 2006?
4 What river flows through the city of Toledo in Spain?
5 Cambodian leader Saloth Sar was better known by what name?
6 How many holes are most major golf tournaments played over?
7 In the song, what colour rose is linked with Texas?
8 Tokai wine comes from which country?
9 In which month did Samuel Pepys begin his famous diary?
10 Whom was Lord Lucan said to have murdered?
11 Mont Blanc stands in France as well as which other country?
12 William Wilkins designed which London gallery?
13 Which city has an American football team called the Cowboys?
14 Which is the world's oldest surviving republic?
15 Which Latin words did HM the Queen use to describe the year 1992?
16 Which cave is the most famous on the Scottish Isle of Staffa?
17 Cars with the international vehicle registration SF come from where?
18 Number 22 in bingo is represented by a pair of little what?
19 What is the core of an ear of maize called?
20 What was the title of the Eurovision winner for Bucks Fizz?
21 How many did Arsenal score to win the first FA Cup Final decided on penalties?
22 Which country's stamps show the word "Hellas"?
23 Who were the subject of the Cat and Mouse Act of 1913?
24 How many points are scored for a motor racing Grand Prix win?
25 What is the largest structure ever made by living creatures?
26 Papworth Hospital is in which county?
27 Who said, "Float like a butterfly, sting like a bee"?
28 Which magazine was first published in the 1840s and last in the 1990s?
29 Which road is crossed by the horses during the Grand National?
30 Which religious ceremony comes from the Greek word for "to dip"?

Answers	The Movies: All Action *(see Quiz 4)*

1 Goldeneye. 2 Platoon. 3 Jeremy Irons. 4 Ridley Scott. 5 Charles Bronson. 6 Jim Carrey. 7 Best Director. 8 Wesley Snipes. 9 Live and Let Die. 10 Faye Dunaway. 11 Donald Pleasence. 12 Chadwick Boseman. 13 Rihanna. 14 Marseilles. 15 Apollo 13. 16 Bruce Willis. 17 Popeye Doyle. 18 James Caan. 19 Irish. 20 Brad Pitt. 21 Lost in Space. 22 Phil Collins. 23 Cabbie. 24 Paul & Linda McCartney. 25 JFK. 26 Sean Bean. 27 Gal Gadot. 28 Arnold Schwarzenegger. 29 Six. 30 Leonardo DiCaprio.

Quiz 4 — The Movies: All Action

Answers – page 103

1 Which Bond film shares its name with Ian Fleming's Jamaican home?
2 What was the third of Oliver Stone's films about Vietnam?
3 Which English Oscar winner was the villain in "Die Hard III"?
4 Which Brit directed "Black Hawk Down" and "Hannibal"?
5 Who played Bernardo in "The Magnificent Seven" and Danny Velinski in "The Great Escape"?
6 Who was The Riddler in "Batman Forever"?
7 Which Oscar did Kevin Costner win for "Dances with Wolves"?
8 Who played the defrosted super-villain in "Demolition Man"?
9 What was Roger Moore's first Bond film in 1973?
10 Who had her first major starring role in "Bonnie & Clyde"?
11 Who plays the President in "Escape from New York"?
12 Who plays T'Challa/the Black Panther in the 2018 movie "Black Panther"?
13 In 2018's "Ocean's 8" heist movie, who played the character Nine Ball?
14 Where was "French Connection II" set?
15 Astronaut Jim Lovell was portrayed by Tom Hanks in which film?
16 Who heads the crew which saves the world in "Armageddon"?
17 Whom did Gene Hackman play in "The French Connection"?
18 Who played Sonny Corleone in "The Godfather" and its sequel?
19 What nationality cop did Sean Connery play in "The Untouchables"?
20 Who co-starred with Morgan Freeman in "Seven"?
21 Which 1998 film of a 60s cult TV series starred Gary Oldman and William Hurt?
22 Who played the train robber of the title role in "Buster"?
23 What was Mel Gibson's job in the 1997 thriller "Conspiracy Theory"?
24 Which husband and wife were Oscar nominated for the song from "Live and Let Die"?
25 Which Oliver Stone movie with Kevin Costner was about events prior to Kennedy's assassination?
26 Which Yorkshireman played the IRA terrorist in "Patriot Games"?
27 Who plays the title role in the 2017 version of "Wonder Woman"?
28 Who was the construction worker who had flashbacks in "Total Recall"?
29 As of the end of 2018, how many Tom Cruise "Mission Impossible" films had been released?
30 Who played two roles in the 90s version of "The Man in the Iron Mask"?

Answers | Pot Luck 2 (see Quiz 3)

1 Nana Moon. 2 To attract mates. 3 David Walliams. 4 Tagus. 5 Pol Pot. 6 72.
7 Yellow. 8 Hungary. 9 January. 10 Sandra Rivett. 11 Italy. 12 The National Gallery.
13 Dallas. 14 San Marino. 15 Annus horribilis. 16 Fingal's Cave. 17 Finland.
18 Two little ducks. 19 A corncob. 20 Making Your Mind Up. 21 5 (in 2005).
22 Greece. 23 Suffragettes. 24 25 points. 25 The Great Barrier Reef.
26 Cambridgeshire. 27 Muhammad Ali. 28 Punch. 29 Melling Road. 30 Baptism.

1 Who wrote the book which TV show "Pretty Little Liars" is based on?
2 Who was voted Beard of the Year 2006?
3 Spy writer David J. Cornwell writes under which name?
4 What is the unit of measurement for the brightness of stars?
5 Which "-ology" is the study of birds' eggs?
6 Which Dire Straits album included "Money for Nothing"?
7 Who were Janet, Pam, Barbara, Jack, Peter, George and Colin?
8 In which country would you be to visit Agadir?
9 What name is given to a bell tower not attached to a church?
10 Van Pelt is the surname of which "Peanuts" character?
11 What is the best hand in a game of poker?
12 The Virgin record label was launched by which instrumental album?
13 Was Madonna's "Confessions on a Dance Floor" a No.1 album in 5, 15 or 25 countries?
14 In the official conker rules, how many strikes per turn are allowed?
15 Which country celebrated its bicentenary in 1988?
16 What word commonly describes a spasm of the diaphragm?
17 Daniel Carroll found theatrical fame under which name?
18 Whose first performed work was the radio play "The Ruffian on the Stair"?
19 Who lit the funeral pyre of Mrs Indira Gandhi?
20 Which recently discovered element has the symbol Mc?
21 Which comedian plays the role of Brian Potter in "Phoenix Nights"?
22 John Sentamu was Bishop of where, before becoming Archbishop of York?
23 Switzerland's Mont Cervin is better known by what name?
24 Who wrote the novel "Where Eagles Dare"?
25 Which England cricket captain had the middle name Dylan?
26 What do the initials CND stand for?
27 What is the collective name for a group of frogs?
28 Who was the first act to have seven consecutive US No.1 singles?
29 Eton school is in which county?
30 Which country was first to host Summer and Winter Olympics in the same year?

Answers | Food & Drink 1 *(see Quiz 6)*

1 Fish. 2 Kirschwasser. 3 Gin. 4 Sugar. 5 November. 6 Curry powder. 7 Greece.
8 Halal. 9 20. 10 Kiwi fruit. 11 Gelatine. 12 Spice. 13 Mrs Beeton. 14 Nut.
15 Coca-Cola. 16 Turmeric. 17 Clarified butter. 18 Carrot. 19 Bloody Mary.
20 Wheat gluten. 21 Michael Mosley. 22 Aluminium. 23 Bergamot. 24 Antonio
Carluccio. 25 Black. 26 Tana. 27 Poisonous raw. 28 Mushroom. 29 Cherry.
30 Milk.

1 What type of food is gravadlax?
2 Which type of brandy is made from cherries?
3 Which spirit is Pimm's No.1 based on?
4 Aspartame is an alternative to what when added to food?
5 In which month does Beaujolais Nouveau arrive?
6 Which powder includes turmeric, fenugreek, chillies and cumin?
7 Which country produces more than 70% of the world's olive oil?
8 What name is given to food prepared according to Muslim law?
9 How many standard wine bottles make up a Nebuchadnezzar?
10 Which fruit is also called the Chinese gooseberry?
11 Agar agar is a vegetarian alternative to what?
12 What is sumac – a grain or a spice?
13 How is cook Isabella Mary Mayson better known?
14 What sort of food is a macadamia?
15 Atlanta is the headquarters of which drinks company?
16 Which bright yellow-orange powder is made from the root of a member of the ginger family?
17 What is ghee?
18 Caraway is related to which family of vegetables?
19 Which queen's nickname is the name of a cocktail?
20 What is the main ingredient of the vegan meat alternative, seitan?
21 Which TV presenter is credited with popularising the 5:2 diet?
22 What are most beer and soft drinks cans made from?
23 Which flavour is traditionally used in Earl Grey tea?
24 Which London-based Italian chef, known as "the godfather of Italian gastronomy" died in 2017?
25 What colour are fully ripened olives?
26 What is TV chef Gordon Ramsay's wife called?
27 Why do cashew nuts have to be roasted to be eaten?
28 What is a morel?
29 What is a morello?
30 Which drink did Bob Geldof advertise?

Answers | Pot Luck 3 *(see Quiz 5)*

1 Sara Shepard. 2 Monty Panesar. 3 John le Carré. 4 Magnitude. 5 Oology. 6 Brothers in Arms. 7 The Secret Seven. 8 Morocco. 9 A campanile. 10 Lucy. 11 Royal flush. 12 Tubular Bells. 13 25. 14 Three. 15 Australia. 16 Hiccough. 17 Danny La Rue. 18 Joe Orton. 19 Rajiv Gandhi. 20 Moscovium. 21 Peter Kay. 22 Birmingham. 23 The Matterhorn. 24 Alistair MacLean. 25 Bob Willis. 26 Campaign for Nuclear Disarmament. 27 An army (or colony). 28 Whitney Houston. 29 Berkshire. 30 France.

1 The illness pertussis is more commonly called what?
2 Who wrote the novel "Angels and Demons", featuring the Large Hadron Collider?
3 Which rock is the largest monolith in the world?
4 Which Spanish team were the first winners of the European Cup?
5 What type of animal can be Texel and Romney Marsh?
6 Where would you hurt if you were kicked on the tarsus?
7 The Bee Gees were born on which island?
8 What action does a dromophobic fear?
9 In which country is the world's second highest mountain, K2?
10 What nationality is Salman Rushdie?
11 ROYGBIV is an acronym for remembering what?
12 Which tanker went down on the Seven Stones reef off Land's End?
13 Which large forest is the nearest to London's Liverpool Street Station?
14 Which hit by Judy Collins entered the UK charts on eight occasions?
15 What is Ryan Gosling's character's profession in "La La Land"?
16 In which decade did Constantinople become Istanbul?
17 How many bridesmaids attended Princess Diana?
18 Which poet gave his name to a Cape to the south of Brisbane?
19 Which Russian town produced deformed sheep after a 90s disaster?
20 What is Paul McCartney's first name?
21 Which drug took its name from the Greek god of dreams?
22 Which is the largest borough in the city of New York?
23 Which doll's name gave Aqua a No.1 hit?
24 What is the name of Paul Daniels' former assistant and wife?
25 What is examined using an otoscope?
26 What is measured on the Mercalli Scale?
27 Along with Doric and Ionic, what is the third Greek order of architecture?
28 What is lowered by a Beta Blocker?
29 How many pieces does each backgammon player use?
30 A Blue Orpington is a type of what?

Answers   **Animal World** *(see Quiz 8)*

1 Suffocation. 2 Sett. 3 Velvet. 4 Black. 5 Dachshund. 6 It cannot bark.
7 Afrikaans. 8 Mauritius. 9 Antelope. 10 Snow leopard. 11 Fight. 12 Squirrel.
13 One. 14 Cattle. 15 Hearing. 16 32. 17 Fawn. 18 Hooves. 19 Blood of birds
and mammals. 20 Sheep. 21 Pink. 22 White. 23 Japan. 24 Caribou. 25 Lemurs.
26 White / cream. 27 V shape. 28 Elk. 29 Sand. 30 Border collie.

1 How do the anaconda's victims die?
2 What is the badger's system of burrows called?
3 What is the skin on a deer's antlers called?
4 What colour face does a Suffolk sheep have?
5 Which small breed of dog has a German name meaning badger dog?
6 What is unusual about the sound of the dingo?
7 Aardvark means "earth pig" in which African language?
8 On which island was the dodo formerly found?
9 What is an impala?
10 What type of leopard is another name for the ounce?
11 Pit bull terriers were bred to do what?
12 To which family does the prairie dog belong?
13 Does the Indian rhinoceros have one or two horns?
14 Bovine Spongiform Encephalitis is a fatal disease of which animals?
15 Tinnitus affects which of the senses?
16 How many teeth do human adults have?
17 What is the most common colour of a Great Dane?
18 What does an ungulate animal have?
19 What do vampire bats feed on?
20 Lanolin is a by product of which domestic animal?
21 If a mammal has albinism what colour are its eyes?
22 What colour are dalmatians when they are born?
23 The tosa is a dog native to which country?
24 What is the reindeer of North America called?
25 Which group of primates are found only on Madagascar?
26 What colour is the coat of a samoyed?
27 What shaped mark does an adder have on its head?
28 What is another name for the wapiti?
29 What do alligators lay their eggs in?
30 Which dog do shepherds now most commonly use for herding sheep?

| **Answers** | Pot Luck 4 *(see Quiz 7)* |

1 Whooping cough. 2 Dan Brown. 3 Ayers Rock. 4 Real Madrid. 5 Sheep.
6 Ankle. 7 Isle of Man. 8 Crossing the road. 9 Pakistan. 10 British. 11 Colours
of the rainbow. 12 Torrey Canyon. 13 Epping Forest. 14 Amazing Grace. 15 Jazz
pianist. 16 1930s. 17 Five. 18 Byron. 19 Chernobyl. 20 James. 21 Morphine.
22 Queens. 23 Barbie. 24 Debbie McGee. 25 Ear. 26 Earthquakes. 27 Corinthian.
28 Blood pressure. 29 15. 30 Chicken.

Quiz 9   Pot Luck 5

Answers – page 110   **LEVEL 2**

1 In which US state is Death Valley?
2 Which Sea does the River Jordan flow into?
3 What river flows through Vienna, Bratislava, Budapest and Belgrade?
4 The West Yorkshire rhubarb triangle lies between Morley, Rothwell and where?
5 Which BBC magazine was launched in 1929?
6 What did Captain Cook call the Islands of Tonga?
7 Which celebrity was murdered in 1980 outside New York's Dakota Building?
8 Who played Lennie Godber in the TV series "Porridge"?
9 Which naval base is situated in Hampshire?
10 The pins used in skeletal surgery are made of what metal?
11 What is Marc Bolan's son's Christian name?
12 Which war is the first for which there are photographic records?
13 Writer Mary Westmacott is better known by what name?
14 Who or what was a ducat?
15 Which day is the last quarter day in a calendar year in England?
16 Which actor links "The Charmer" with "Dangerfield"?
17 In the Bible, who was Jacob's youngest son?
18 What was suffragette Mrs Pankhurst's Christian name?
19 In which sport is the Plunkett Shield competed for?
20 Which animal has breeds called Roscommon, Kerry Hill, Ryedale?
21 Which two countries was the Cod War of the 1970s between?
22 What colour are Rupert Bear's trousers?
23 Caboc, Dunlop and Morven are cheeses from which country?
24 Which animal can be red, arctic, bat-eared and fennec?
25 Newman Noggs appears in which Charles Dickens novel?
26 What name is given to the base of your spine?
27 Whom did Andy Murray beat to win his second Olympic gold medal?
28 Which actress links the films "Ghostbusters" and "Alien"?
29 Perth is the capital of which state?
30 Which word describes both a blunt sword and a very thin sheet of metal?

Answers   Geography: The UK *(see Quiz 10)*

1 Brighton. 2 Newport 3 South Kensington. 4 Stoke Mandeville. 5 Suffolk. 6 1.1 million. 7 Newgate. 8 Canary Wharf (Isle of Dogs). 9 Salopian. 10 Army exercises. 11 Essex & Suffolk. 12 Bristol. 13 M6. 14 Glastonbury. 15 Big Ben. 16 Blackpool. 17 Windscale. 18 Mersey. 19 Clyde. 20 Nottingham. 21 Wiltshire. 22 Edinburgh. 23 Petticoat Lane. 24 Papworth. 25 Hyde Park. 26 Aberdeen. 27 Bath. 28 Straits of Dover. 29 Castle. 30 Bristol.

Quiz 10 | Geography: The UK | Answers – page 109

1 Which seaside resort has Lanes and a nudist beach?
2 After Cardiff and Swansea, what is the third largest city in Wales?
3 In which part of London is the Natural History Museum?
4 Where is the National Spinal Injuries Unit?
5 In which county is Sizewell nuclear power station?
6 What is the approximate population of Birmingham as of late 2018?
7 The Old Bailey is on the site of which former prison?
8 Where in London would a Canary sit on Dogs?
9 What is a native of Shropshire called?
10 What is Salisbury Plain primarily used for?
11 In which two counties is Constable Country?
12 Where is the Clifton Suspension Bridge?
13 Spaghetti Junction is on which road?
14 Which Somerset town is said to be the burial place of King Arthur?
15 Which bell was named after Benjamin Hall?
16 Which pleasure beach was the UK's top tourist attraction in 2005?
17 What was the former name of Sellafield?
18 The city of Liverpool is on which river?
19 Holy Loch is an inlet of which river?
20 Which city has an annual Goose Fair?
21 In which English county is Europe's largest stone circle?
22 Which castle is at the west end of the Royal Mile?
23 How is the Sunday market in London's Middlesex Street better known?
24 Which Cambridgeshire hospital is famous for its transplant surgery?
25 Speaker's Corner is on the corner of what?
26 Where is the administrative headquarters of the Grampian region?
27 Which city has a famous Royal Crescent?
28 The Goodwin Sands are at the entrance to which straits?
29 What type of historic structures can be found at Framlingham, Orford and Windsor?
30 Where is Temple Meads railway station?

Answers | Pot Luck 5 *(see Quiz 9)*

1 California. 2 Dead Sea. 3 Danube. 4 Wakefield. 5 The Listener. 6 The Friendly Islands. 7 John Lennon. 8 Richard Beckinsale. 9 Gosport. 10 Titanium. 11 Roland Bolan. 12 Crimean. 13 Agatha Christie. 14 A coin. 15 Christmas Day. 16 Nigel Havers. 17 Benjamin. 18 Emmeline. 19 Cricket. 20 Sheep. 21 Iceland and Britain. 22 Yellow check. 23 Scotland. 24 Fox. 25 Nicholas Nickleby. 26 Coccyx. 27 Juan Martin del Potro. 28 Sigourney Weaver. 29 Western Australia. 30 Foil.

1 In what year was David Attenborough born?
2 What is his middle name?
3 What relation was actor and film director Richard Attenborough?
4 At which university did he study?
5 What subject did he gain a degree in at university?
6 In which branch of the military did he do his national service?
7 What was the first natural history programme that he was involved in?
8 Where was the BBC's Natural History Unit established in 1957?
9 In 1965, he was appointed controller of which TV channel?
10 When colour was introduced on his channel in 1967, which sport did he start televising?
11 Which 1969 series about Western culture, presented by Alan Clarke, did he commission?
12 From whom did he commission the 1973 series "The Ascent of Man"?
13 When was "Life on Earth" first broadcast?
14 In what country were the mountain gorillas he was filmed interacting with in "Life on Earth"?
15 Does he eat meat?
16 Which 1987 episode did BBC viewers vote best wildlife documentary of all time?
17 Which 1993 series investigated the natural history of Antarctica?
18 Which 2005 series looked at the evolution and habits of invertebrates?
19 What colour featured in titles of the 2001 and 2017 series exploring oceans?
20 What was the DVD boxset of all his "Life" series called?
21 With 14.1 million viewers, which series was the UK's most watched in 2017?
22 Emperor penguins, lions, wolves and tigers – what other animals featured in 2018's "Dynasties"?
23 In what year did he receive a knighthood?
24 What is the title of his autobiography?
25 What is Radio 4's "Tweet of the Day", which he presented, based around?
26 How many species have been named after him?
27 This research vessel was ultimately named the "Sir David Attenborough", but what did the public vote for it to be called?
28 What has he said is the strangest delicacy he's tasted on his travels?
29 Which animal does he wish he could bring back to life?
30 What has he said he never goes travelling without?

| **Answers** | Pot Luck 6 *(see Quiz 12)* |

1 Docklands. 2 Rainfall. 3 David Bowie. 4 Everglades. 5 A waterhole. 6 21.
7 Asia Minor. 8 Will Carling. 9 Loose rocks. 10 Jude Law. 11 Dysentery. 12 Trilby.
13 Corinth Canal. 14 London. 15 Elizabeth Bennet. 16 Football match. 17 Bhopal.
18 Hudson Bay. 19 155. 20 Stevie Wonder. 21 Cadbury's. 22 Agnes Baden-Powell.
23 1990. 24 Stereophonics. 25 Dodecanese. 26 Clay. 27 Vogue. 28 September
15th. 29 1972. 30 The Queen was pregnant.

Quiz 12 | Pot Luck 6

Answers – page 111

1 Canary Wharf is in which London development?
2 What does a pluviometer measure?
3 Which superstar was a former member of the group the King Bees?
4 Which Florida national park has a highway called Alligator Alley?
5 What do Australians mean when they talk about a billabong?
6 How old was Billy the Kid when he died?
7 What was the former name of Turkey?
8 Julia Smith became the wife of which famous sportsman?
9 What on a mountainside is scree?
10 Who was Kate Winslet's co star in "All the King's Men"?
11 What killed Sir Francis Drake?
12 What type of hat took its name from a novel by George DuMaurier?
13 The Aegean Sea is linked to the Ionian Sea by which canal?
14 Florence Nightingale was given the Freedom of which city in 1908?
15 Who is the heroine in Jane Austen's "Pride and Prejudice"?
16 What game started the 1969 war between El Salvador and Honduras?
17 In the 80s two thousand people were killed by a gas leak in which Indian town?
18 Which Bay is the largest in the world?
19 What is the highest break in snooker with the advantage of a free black ball?
20 Which blind music star ran for Mayor of Detroit in 1989?
21 Bournville was established for the workers of which company?
22 Who was responsible for setting up the Girl Guides movement?
23 In what year was Nelson Mandela released from prison?
24 Which band's album title reasoned "You Gotta Go There To Come Back"?
25 Rhodes is the largest of which group of islands?
26 What is a sumo wrestling ring made from?
27 The film "Dick Tracy" was promoted by which Madonna single?
28 The Battle of Britain is remembered on which date?
29 Which year did John Lennon perform his final live concert?
30 The 1959 Royal Variety Performance was cancelled for what reason?

Answers | **Sir David Attenborough** *(see Quiz 11)*

1 1926. 2 Frederick. 3 Brother. 4 Cambridge. 5 Natural sciences. 6 Navy. 7 Animal Patterns (producer). 8 Bristol. 9 BBC2. 10 Snooker. 11 Civilisation. 12 Jacob Bronowski. 13 1979. 14 Rwanda. 15 No. 16 Meerkats United. 17 Life in the Freezer. 18 Life in the Underground. 19 Blue (Blue Planet). 20 Life on Land. 21 Blue Planet II. 22 Chimpanzees. 23 1985. 24 Life on Air. 25 Birdsong. 26 15. 27 Boaty McBoatface. 28 Toasted caterpillars. 29 The dodo. 30 Front door key.

1 Which Ponchielli piece features in "Fantasia"?
2 Which US-born Australian was the voice of John Smith in "Pocahontas"?
3 In which year was the Best Animated Feature Oscar first awarded?
4 Who voiced Elsa and sang "Let It Go" in "Frozen"?
5 What colour are Mickey Mouse's gloves?
6 Perdita and Pongo are what type of animals?
7 How many Oscars, in total, was Disney given for "Snow White and the Seven Dwarfs"?
8 Where is the 2015 animated film "Inside Out" set?
9 Who is the best-known rabbit in "Bambi"?
10 Featuring Elton John songs, what was the highest-grossing animation movie of the 1990s?
11 Which of the Gabor sisters was a voice in "The Aristocats"?
12 Who created Tom and Jerry at MGM in the 40s?
13 What did Dumbo do immediately before his ears grew so big?
14 Which film of a fairy tale features the song "Bibbidy Bobbidy Boo"?
15 Which part did Kathleen Turner voice in "Who Framed Roger Rabbit?"?
16 Which Disney film was the first with a synchronised soundtrack?
17 "Colours of the Wind" was a hit song from which movie?
18 Which film with an animated sequence featured Angela Lansbury using her magic powers against the Nazis?
19 Who sings "He's a tramp" in "Lady and the Tramp"?
20 When you crack and shake a Minion, what happens?
21 Who voiced Gnomeo in "Gnomeo and Juliet"?
22 Which 1990 film was about pizza-loving, sewer dwelling reptiles?
23 Which was the first film to feature, appropriately enough, computer-animated sequences?
24 What type of orphaned creature featured in "The Land Before Time"?
25 Which was the first animated film in the 90s which Tim Rice won an Oscar for?
26 Which dancer commissioned Hanna and Barbera to do an animation sequence in "Anchors Aweigh" in 1945?
27 Which Tchaikovsky ballet piece features in "Fantasia"?
28 In which film does Shere Khan appear?
29 Which characters made their debut in "Puss Gets the Boot" in 1940?
30 Who was the voice of Stuart in "Stuart Little 2"?

Answers | **Pot Luck 7** (see Quiz 14)

1 Cuba. 2 California. 3 Blueberry. 4 Vodka and orange juice. 5 Canada. 6 Skin.
7 Spain. 8 1940s. 9 Willow. 10 Cricket. 11 Australia. 12 Julian Clary. 13 Scotland and England. 14 Sesame seeds. 15 A. 16 Asbestos. 17 King Lear. 18 Government Issue. 19 Violet. 20 Acetylene. 21 Redcurrants. 22 A river bed. 23 USA.
24 Carbon. 25 Sue Townsend. 26 The bark. 27 Mega. 28 Gumbo. 29 Mark Knopfler. 30 Both married their cousins.

Quiz 14 | Pot Luck 7

Answers – page 113

LEVEL 2

1 Cars with the international vehicle registration C come from where?
2 The Paul Getty Museum is in which American state?
3 What is the American equivalent of an English bilberry?
4 What is added to Galliano to make a Harvey Wallbanger?
5 Which country is nearest to where the Titanic was found?
6 An average man has twenty square feet of what about his person?
7 In which country were the last summer Olympics of the 20th century in Europe?
8 In which decade was Cassius Clay – later Muhammad Ali – born?
9 From which tree family is the basket-making osier a member?
10 Which sport other than rugby is played for the Currie Cup?
11 In which country is the Great Sandy Desert?
12 Who had "Sticky Moments on Tour"?
13 The Cheviot hills run along the boundary between which countries?
14 Which seeds are in the sweet, Halva?
15 What note does an orchestra tune to?
16 What dangerous substance is sometimes known as woolly rock?
17 Which Shakespeare play was banned during George III's time of madness?
18 Before being used as a name for US soldiers, what did "GI" stand for?
19 What is the flowery name of the daughter of Jennifer Garner and Ben Affleck?
20 Which gas is produced by adding water to calcium carbide?
21 Which berries are used in a Cumberland sauce?
22 What is a wadi?
23 In which country is the Potomac River?
24 Which element has the highest melting point?
25 Which Adrian Mole creator wrote "Queen Camilla"?
26 Which part of a tree gives Angostura Bitters its taste?
27 What is the metric word for a million?
28 What is the southern American stew of rice and okra called?
29 Which famous pop guitarist performed with the Notting Hillbillies?
30 What links scientists Charles Darwin and Albert Einstein?

Answers | **Movies: Animation** *(see Quiz 13)*

1 Dance of the Hours. 2 Mel Gibson. 3 2002. 4 Idina Menzel 5 White.
6 Dalmatians. 7 Eight. 8 Inside the mind of an 11-year-old girl. 9 Thumper. 10 The Lion King. 11 Eva. 12 Hanna & Barbera. 13 He sneezed. 14 Cinderella. 15 Jessica Rabbit. 16 Steamboat Willie. 17 Pocahontas. 18 Bedknobs & Broomsticks. 19 Peggy Lee. 20 It glows in the dark. 21 James McAvoy. 22 Teenage Mutant Ninja Turtles. 23 Tron. 24 Dinosaur. 25 Aladdin. 26 Gene Kelly. 27 Nutcracker Suite. 28 Jungle Book. 29 Tom & Jerry. 30 Michael J. Fox.

Quiz 15 — Books 1

Answers – page 116

LEVEL 2

1 Where according to the Bible is the site of the final battle between nations which will end the world?
2 In which Dickens novel did Uriah Heep appear?
3 "Old Possum's Book of Practical Cats" is composed of what?
4 What was the title of Yuval Noah Harari's 2014 bestseller?
5 In which book did John Braine introduce Joe Lampton?
6 What type of book is the OED?
7 What is the subject of Desmond Morris's "The Naked Ape"?
8 What type of books did Patricia Highsmith write?
9 Which detective first appeared in "A Study in Scarlet" in 1887?
10 The sequel to "Peter Pan" was called "Peter Pan in" what?
11 Which Gothic horror story has the alternative title "The Modern Prometheus"?
12 For what types of book is Samuel Pepys famous for?
13 Who wrote "The Female Eunuch" in 1970?
14 In which county were Jane Austen and Charles Dickens born?
15 Who wrote the memoir "Naked at the Albert Hall"?
16 In "Charlie and the Chocolate Factory", what is Charlie's surname?
17 Which ex-jockey wrote a book of short stories called "Field of Thirteen"?
18 Whose horror stories include "Carrie" and "The Shining"?
19 Which "Sex & the City" star wrote the teen advice book "Being a Girl"?
20 Who wrote "Das Kapital"?
21 Which publisher reissues out-of-print works by women writers, with grey covers?
22 Which writer and politician bought poet Rupert Brooke's house?
23 Which fictional barrister was created by John Mortimer?
24 Whose first novel, "A Woman of Substance" became a best-seller?
25 The "Dummies" advice books are coloured black and what other main colour?
26 "The Day of the Jackal" is about an assassination plot on whom?
27 For which Salman Rushdie book did the Ayatollah impose a fatwa?
28 Who is the central character in William Boyd's "Any Human Heart"?
29 To five years, how old was Mary Wesley when her first bestseller was published?
30 Award-winning novelist Ben Okri hails from which country?

Answers | Pot Luck 8 *(see Quiz 16)*

1 Cross Fell, Cumbria. 2 Agatha Christie. 3 27. 4 Henry Cooper. 5 Wolf Alice.
6 Hyde Park. 7 1966. 8 Phone cards. 9 Steve Davis. 10 Graeme Hick. 11 Sullivan.
12 Tottenham Hotspur. 13 20th. 14 Nevada. 15 Five. 16 Pavlova. 17 Volga.
18 Asparagus. 19 Clint Eastwood. 20 Mack Sennett. 21 Michael Henchard. 22 The
alphabet. 23 Ronald Reagan. 24 Montreux. 25 Rhodes. 26 2008 US Open. 27 Mr
Men. 28 Lily. 29 Tea. 30 1960s.

115

Quiz 16 | Pot Luck 8

1 What is the highest point of the Pennines?

2 2006 marked the 30th anniversary of the death of which crime writer?

3 How many years was Nelson Mandela held in prison?

4 Which British boxer was the first to win three Lonsdale belts outright?

5 Who won the 2018 Mercury Music Prize for "Visions of a Life"?

6 In which London park is Rotten Row?

7 When was the homelessness drama "Cathy Come Home" first broadcast?

8 What will a green phone kiosk only take for payment?

9 Which snooker star was nicknamed "Interesting" by "Spitting Image"?

10 In 1988 who scored 405 not out at Taunton?

11 Who died first, Gilbert or Sullivan?

12 Which was the first London football club to win a European title?

13 In which century did Joan of Arc become a saint?

14 Which American state is called the "Gambling State"?

15 Did John Glenn's first spaceflight last five, ten or 24 hours?

16 Which dessert is named after a famous ballerina?

17 Which river flows from northern Moscow to the Caspian Sea?

18 A Bruxelloise sauce is flavoured with which vegetable?

19 Who was the leading actor in "Play Misty for Me" with Jessica Walker?

20 Who created the Keystone Kops?

21 Who was the Mayor of Casterbridge in the Thomas Hardy novel?

22 What does an alphabetarian study?

23 Who became US President in the year John Lennon died in New York?

24 In which Swiss resort are the Golden Rose TV accolades awarded?

25 Which island is the largest of the Dodecanese group?

26 What was Andy Murray's first Grand Slam final?

27 What characters were created by Roger Hargreaves?

28 To which flower family does garlic belong?

29 Which drink can be green, black and oolong?

30 In which decade was the first American Superbowl?

---

1 What colour is the flesh of a cantaloupe melon?
2 Simnel cake was traditionally eaten on which Sunday?
3 What is the fishy ingredient in Scotch woodcock?
4 What is a champignon?
5 Which spirit is Russia famous for producing?
6 What alcoholic drink is made in Hakushu, Yoichi and Yamazaki?
7 What is added to pasta to make it green?
8 Which drink is grown in the Douro basin and exported from Oporto?
9 Which cooking pot boils food at a higher temperature than boiling point?
10 What is another name for dietary fibre?
11 Which sauce/salad shares its name with Latin big-band music?
12 Where did satsumas originate?
13 What are cornichons?
14 Puerto Rico and Jamaica are the main producers of which spirit?
15 What colour is cayenne pepper?
16 What type of pastry is used to make a steak and kidney pudding?
17 Which drink is served in a schooner?
18 What is a Laxton's Superb?
19 Which seafood, usually fried in breadcrumbs, is the Italian name for shrimps?
20 Tofu and TVP come from which bean?
21 Tartrazine colours food which colour?
22 What is added to whisky to make a whisky mac?
23 Where would you buy a pint of Shires?
24 What colour is Double Gloucester cheese?
25 Which Mexican drink is distilled from the agave plant?
26 Which black, gourmet fungus is a native of France's Perigord region?
27 Which expensive vinegar is aged in wooden barrels?
28 Which grain is whisky made from?
29 What is red wine made with that white wine is not?
30 Vermouth is wine flavoured with what?

1 Which was Kylie's first UK No.1 of the new millennium?

2 Kylie voiced Florence in which 2006 movie?

3 Which tour was postponed when Kylie was diagnosed with cancer?

4 Which city does Kylie come from?

5 Which word completes her hits, "I Believe In ..." and "Giving ... Up"?

6 In 2001 which release returned her to No.1 in the album charts?

7 Kylie moved to which UK label that launched The Beatles?

8 What was Kylie's first single to contain the word "Love"?

9 What is Kylie's star sign?

10 Who had the original hit with "The Loco-Motion"?

11 Which ABBA classic did Kylie cover when closing the Sydney Olympics?

12 Which fungus-linked word names her early Australian recording label?

13 Which Kylie hit has the same title as a 2005 hit by Erasure?

14 Which charted first, "Chocolate" or "In Your Eyes"?

15 Which major British festival did Kylie pull out of in 2005?

16 Which No.1 was promoted with a video showing Kylie in gold hot pants?

17 She played what colour of fairy in the movie "Moulin Rouge"?

18 What was Kylie's first Top Ten single with a colour in the title?

19 What was her 2018 album called?

20 She had a 1988 hit single with a cover of "The Loco-Motion" – who sang it originally?

21 What word completes her children's book, "The Showgirl..."?

22 What was Kylie's first million-seller single in the UK?

23 What kind of "Language" featured in the title of Kylie's 2003 hit album?

24 Love Kylie was the name of a range of what?

25 Kylie's first hit duet was with which artist?

26 Both "Chocolate" and "Slow" featured on which album?

27 In which decade of the twentieth century was Kylie born?

28 Kylie started off with how many consecutive Top Ten hits – 3, 9 or 13?

29 In which TV series did she play a cameo as Epponnee Rae?

30 What was the one-word title of Kylie's first album?

Answers	**Food & Drink 2** *(see Quiz 17)*

1 Orange. 2 Mothering Sunday. 3 Anchovies. 4 Mushroom. 5 Vodka. 6 Japanese Whisky. 7 Spinach. 8 Port. 9 Pressure cooker. 10 Roughage. 11 Salsa. 12 Japan. 13 Gherkins (pickled cucumbers). 14 Rum. 15 Red. 16 Suet pastry. 17 Sherry. 18 Apple. 19 Scampi. 20 Soya. 21 Yellow. 22 Ginger wine. 23 Ambridge. 24 Orange-red. 25 Tequila. 26 Truffle. 27 Balsamic. 28 Malted barley. 29 Skins of the grape. 30 Bitter herbs.

1 Who supposedly brought about the downfall of Barings Bank?
2 Which country was the first to legalise abortion?
3 Which Eurovision-winning group formed the Polar Music Company?
4 Luis Saha joined Man Utd from which club?
5 Mount Elbert is the highest peak in which American mountain range?
6 Adam and Eve were the main characters in which work by John Milton?
7 What was Jeremy Irons' character called in 1981's TV drama "Brideshead Revisited"?
8 Whose murder conviction was overturned after 45 years in 1998?
9 Which famous riding school is in Austria?
10 What colour traditionally is an Indian wedding sari?
11 Which county first won the Benson and Hedges Cricket Cup twice?
12 Which Copenhagen statue is a memorial to Hans Christian Andersen?
13 Which Derbyshire town is famous for the church with a crooked spire?
14 The Parthenon in Athens was built as a temple to whom?
15 In what year was the last "Peanuts" cartoon published (for the first time)?
16 Which glands produce white blood cells?
17 What sort of creature is a guillemot?
18 What was the first film Bogart and Bacall starred in together?
19 Which role did Billie Piper play in "Dr Who"?
20 Which girl's name gave the Damned their only top ten hit?
21 Which chess piece can only move diagonally?
22 What is a taikonaut?
23 William "Fatty" Foulkes played which sport?
24 Which oil company was founded by John D. Rockefeller?
25 At which Southwark inn did Chaucer's Canterbury Pilgrims meet?
26 Joseph Marie Jacquard is most remembered for which invention?
27 Before Winston Churchill went bald, what colour was his hair?
28 The word micro is what fraction in the metric system?
29 Which county included WG Grace as a team member?
30 Which musical instrument was first developed by Bartolomeo Cristofori?

Answers | **Past Law & Order** *(see Quiz 20)*

1 Haiti. 2 Bluebeard. 3 20th (1941). 4 Ruth Ellis. 5 Dr Crippen. 6 Philip Lawrence.
7 Official Secrets Act. 8 Lester Piggott. 9 Slavery. 10 Director of Public Prosecutions.
11 Cape Town. 12 St Valentine's Day. 13 Nick Leeson. 14 Michael Howard.
15 Iceland. 16 Back to Basics. 17 Treason. 18 Colditz. 19 Ethiopia didn't have electricity. 20 Cromwell Street. 21 Richard I. 22 Jack Straw. 23 Louise Woodward.
24 Road rage attack. 25 Robert Maxwell. 26 Peter Sutcliffe. 27 The Butcher of Lyon.
28 The Ritz. 29 Monster. 30 The Clintons.

1 Which country had the private security force the Tontons Macoutes?
2 What was the nickname of mass murderer Gilles de Rais who killed six of his seven wives?
3 In which century was the last execution at the Tower of London?
4 Which woman was hanged in 1955 for murdering David Blakely?
5 Cora was the wife of which doctor who murdered her?
6 In the 1990s which London head teacher was killed outside his school?
7 Which Act bans the disclosure of confidential items from government sources by its employees?
8 Which world-famous jockey was jailed in 1987 for tax evasion?
9 What did abolitionism seek to abolish?
10 What is the DPP, a post created in 1985?
11 Robben Island was a prison near which city?
12 Which Day saw seven of Bugs Moran's gang murdered by members of Al Capone's, disguised as policemen?
13 Whose crime was recounted in the film "Rogue Trader"?
14 Which one-time Home Secretary led his party in the 2005 general election?
15 The Althing is the parliament of which country?
16 Which phrase used by John Major in 1993 was used as a slogan to return to traditional British values?
17 In 1965 capital punishment was abolished except for which crime?
18 How was the prison camp Oflag IVC near Leipzig better known?
19 In what way was Ethiopian Emperor Menelik III thwarted in bringing the electric chair to his country?
20 What was the Gloucester street where Rose & Frederick West lived?
21 Robin Hood is said to have lived in Sherwood Forest during the reign of which king?
22 Which Home Secretary took his son to the police after allegations of drug selling?
23 Which British nanny's US trial was televised after a baby died in her care?
24 Why was the death of Stephen Cameron in 1996 a tragic first?
25 Who fell from the Lady Ghislaine leaving debts behind him?
26 What is the real name of the criminal dubbed The Yorkshire Ripper?
27 What was the nickname of Nazi war criminal Klaus Barbie?
28 Jonathan Aitken's court case centred on a stay in which Paris hotel?
29 Which 2004 movie starred Charlize Theron playing a real-life serial killer?
30 In the US whose involvement in the Whitewater affair had lengthy repercussions?

Answers	Pot Luck 9 *(see Quiz 19)*

1 Nick Leeson. 2 Iceland. 3 ABBA. 4 Fulham. 5 The Rockies. 6 Paradise Lost.
7 Charles Ryder. 8 Derek Bentley. 9 The Spanish Riding School. 10 Scarlet.
11 Leicestershire. 12 The Little Mermaid. 13 Chesterfield. 14 Athena. 15 2000.
16 Lymph glands. 17 Bird. 18 To Have and Have Not. 19 Rose Tyler. 20 Eloise. 21 The Bishop. 22 Chinese astronaut. 23 Football. 24 Standard Oil. 25 The Tabard Inn.
26 The Jacquard loom. 27 Red. 28 A millionth. 29 Gloucestershire. 30 The piano.

1 What nationality was the spy Mata Hari?
2 The Dickens work Edwin Drood is different for what reason?
3 Which Australian soap star had the biggest-selling UK single in 1988?
4 What were the Boston Tea Party protesters against?
5 What is a Wessex Saddleback?
6 Who succeeded Gerhard Schroeder as German Chancellor?
7 Lyncanthropy involves men changing into what?
8 Which city's American football team is known as the Vikings?
9 Queen Wilhelmina who died in 1962 was Queen of which country?
10 The pop band America were formed in which country?
11 In curling how many shots at the target is each player allowed?
12 What was Janet Street-Porter's beastly last name before marriage?
13 Which Band Aid No.1 hit was written by Midge Ure and Bob Geldof?
14 Which late singer became the third biggest-selling singles act of 2005?
15 Which American symbol was famously painted by Jasper Johns?
16 In fencing how many hits must a male fencer score for a win?
17 In gin rummy how many cards are dealt per player?
18 What nationality was the inventor of the Geiger counter?
19 Before it moved to Wales on which London hill was the Royal Mint?
20 In which century was the first circumnavigation of the earth?
21 Which is further south, Cardiff or Oxford?
22 Which river rises in the Black Forest?
23 Which road vehicle takes its name from the Hindu God Jagganath?
24 In which South American country is the condor sacred?
25 The first modern Olympics were held in which city?
26 Whom did Michael Sheen play in "Fantabulosa"?
27 What have you on your mouth if you suffer from herpes labialis?
28 Prince Edward resigned from which part of the military in 1987?
29 Mike Burden is the sidekick to which TV detective?
30 It ended in 2006, but in which city was the first ever "Top of the Pops" recorded?

Answers | Communications *(see Quiz 22)*

1 Stansted. 2 Leeds. 3 Philips. 4 Decibel. 5 Seattle. 6 Telephone handset. 7 Trans Siberian. 8 Paris. 9 999 service. 10 Nothing. 11 Service. 12 Acoustics. 13 123. 14 You've Got M@il. 15 Video Cassette Recorder. 16 LL Zamenhof. 17 FBI's. 18 Derbyshire. 19 A12. 20 ADA. 21 Dundee. 22 Grand Canal. 23 Alaska. 24 A. 25 M62. 26 Some insects. 27 8. 28 Moscow. 29 Madam Mayor. 30 Channel Tunnel.

Quiz 22 | Communications

Answers – page 121

1 What is Britain's third largest airport?
2 Which northern city has the dialling code 0113?
3 Which company launched the CD-i in 1992?
4 dB is the symbol for what?
5 Where in America was the on-line bookstore Amazon first based?
6 An acoustic coupler allows computer data to be transmitted through what?
7 Which railway links European Russia with the Pacific?
8 Which city linked up with London by phone in 1891?
9 Which vital communications link began in July 1937?
10 How much is the maximum charge for postage in Andorra?
11 What does S stand for in ISP?
12 What is the science of sound and its transmission called?
13 What number do you dial for the speaking clock?
14 Which Tom Hanks movie had sometimes an email address symbol in its title?
15 What is a VCR?
16 He used the pseudonym Dr Esperanto, but what was the real name of the creator of this 'universal' language?
17 On whose website did Leslie Ibsen Rogge appear, leading to his arrest?
18 In which county is East Midlands airport?
19 Which A road links London with East Anglia?
20 Which computer language was named after Ada Augusta Byron?
21 Which is the nearest city to the Tay road bridge?
22 Which waterway does Venice's Rialto bridge span?
23 Which state is the northern terminus of the Pan American highway?
24 In France all motorways begin with which letter?
25 Which motorway links Hull and Leeds?
26 Which living creatures can you send through the post?
27 How many bits are there in a byte?
28 In which city is the TASS news agency based?
29 How would you verbally address a Mayor who is a woman?
30 Which tunnel goes from Cheriton to Sangatte?

Answers | Pot Luck 10 *(see Quiz 21)*

1 Dutch. 2 It is not finished. 3 Kylie Minogue. 4 Tea taxes. 5 Pig. 6 Angela Merkel. 7 Wolves. 8 Minnesota. 9 Holland. 10 England. 11 2. 12 Bull. 13 Do They Know It's Christmas. 14 Elvis Presley. 15 The stars & stripes. 16 Five. 17 10. 18 German. 19 Tower Hill. 20 16th. 21 Cardiff. 22 Danube. 23 Juggernaut. 24 Peru. 25 Athens. 26 Kenneth Williams. 27 Cold Sores. 28 The Marines. 29 Reg Wexford. 30 Manchester.

Quiz 23 — Pot Luck 11

LEVEL 2

1 Who had a No.1 UK hit with "The Reflex"?
2 In English what is the only anagram of the word ENGLISH?
3 Which rules are American football played to?
4 In which South African city was the 1995 Rugby Union World Cup Final?
5 Which musical was based on the play "Pygmalion"?
6 If you suffer from bulimia, what do you have a compulsive urge to do?
7 In Greek mythology, who was the son of Thetis and Peleus?
8 Which triangular-shaped Indian pastry contains meat or vegetables?
9 Which part of Spain is named after its many castles?
10 The range of the pH scale is zero to what?
11 Which everyday objects can be decorated with the King's Pattern?
12 Stage performer Boy Bruce the Mighty Atom became known as who?
13 Which Russian word means "speaking aloud"?
14 What recently discovered element has the symbol Ts?
15 What is the name of the world's largest Gulf?
16 At which UK oil depot was there a massive fire in December 2005?
17 Ouzo is what flavour?
18 What does a trishaw driver do with his legs?
19 Which hospital did TV Doctor Kildare work at?
20 Which is the slowest swimming stroke?
21 What nickname do Tottenham Hotspur and Preston North End share?
22 What does E stand for in "E-numbers"?
23 In Peter Pan which part of Peter was kept in a drawer?
24 What word links an ice cream holder and a brass instrument?
25 Who performed "Sgt Pepper" to open Live 8 with Paul McCartney?
26 In which Dickensian drama did Gillian Anderson play Lady Dedlock?
27 What is the epicarp of an orange?
28 Who was George W. Bush's first Secretary of State?
29 Which three Time Travel films were directed by Robert Zemeckis?
30 Which European country has the only active volcanoes in Europe?

Answers | Pop Music: The 70s *(see Quiz 24)*

1 Love Me for a Reason. 2 Pigeon. 3 1975. 4 Eddie Holman. 5 Dawn. 6 Ray Stevens. 7 Heart. 8 Squeeze. 9 January. 10 The Kinks. 11 10538. 12 Matthews Southern Comfort. 13 Leo Sayer. 14 Your Song. 15 The Floral Dance. 16 Minnie Riperton. 17 Sweet Sensation. 18 Paul Simon. 19 Nathan Jones. 20 B A Robertson. 21 Rainbow. 22 New York. 23 Transformer. 24 Summer Nights. 25 The Commodores. 26 Rivers of Babylon. 27 Midnight. 28 In the Summertime. 29 Donna Summer. 30 Eye Level.

1 Which 70s hit by the Osmonds gave Boyzone a hit in '94?
2 Which Lieutenant's only UK No.1 hit was "Mouldy Old Dough"?
3 In what year was Bruce Springsteen's "Born to Run" album released?
4 "(Hey There) Lonely Girl" was the only UK hit for which vocalist?
5 Tony Orlando sang in which group that had a girl's name?
6 The craze for streaking gave a No.1 to which Ray?
7 Which part of the body was mentioned in the title of a Blondie hit?
8 Who were "Up The Junction" in 1979?
9 Which month links Pilot and part of a song title for Barbara Dickson?
10 Whose hits from 1970 include "Victoria" and "Apeman"?
11 What was the number of ELO's Overture in their first hit?
12 The No.1 UK hit "Woodstock" was a one-hit wonder for which group?
13 Who had a No.1 single in 2006, but first charted with "The Show Must Go On"?
14 Which Elton John 70s hit with a two-word title returned to the Top Ten in 2002?
15 What links Terry Wogan and the Brighouse and Rastrick Brass Band?
16 "Loving You" was a high-pitched No. 2 UK hit for which female singer?
17 Which group had a No.1 UK hit with "Sad Sweet Dreamer"?
18 Who wanted to be taken to the Mardi Gras?
19 Which 1971 Supremes hit was later a hit for Bananarama?
20 Who had hits with "Bang Bang" and "Knocked It Off" in 1979?
21 The 1979 No. 6 hit "Since You've Been Gone" was a hit for whom?
22 Which US city was named twice in a Gerard Kenny hit from 1978?
23 "Walk on the Wild Side" appeared on which 1972 Lou Reed album?
24 In which song do the chorus beg, "Tell me more, tell me more!"?
25 Which group had hits in the 70s with "Easy", "Still" and "Sail On"?
26 What was on the other side of Boney M's "Brown Girl in the Ring"?
27 What time was Gladys Knight's train leaving for Georgia?
28 Which Mungo Jerry hit was used in an anti drink-drive campaign?
29 Which disco-style singer had the word Love in the title of four of her first five Top Ten hits?
30 Which No.1 from 1972 was the theme for the Van der Valk series?

1 If a bridge player has a Yarborough, what is the top scoring card?
2 Which desert covers a large area in North Africa?
3 In the Grand National, how many times did Red Rum run?
4 Which was the first railway terminus in London?
5 Which term is used when a mortgage is more than the value of a house?
6 Whose hits include "Slave to Love" and "This is Tomorrow"?
7 What is a Clouded Yellow?
8 How was Agatha Miller better known?
9 El Paso is in which American state?
10 Which road leads from Westminster to Blackfriars along the north bank of the Thames?
11 The first player to score 100 Premier League goals played for which club?
12 In which board game is FIDE the governing body?
13 A BBC estimate said half the population had watched which live event in 2005?
14 In which year did TV soap "EastEnders" first appear?
15 What is the Mirror of Diana, located in Northern Italy?
16 Beta Vulgaris is the Latin name for which crop?
17 Which film featured the Joe Cocker hit "Up Where We Belong"?
18 Who wrote the opera from which "Here Comes the Bride" is taken?
19 Lime Street Station is in which English city?
20 Cars with the international vehicle registration IS come from where?
21 Which magazine, established in 1922, claims to be the most widely read in the world?
22 What happened to Ken Barlow's second wife in "Coronation Street"?
23 What type of fruit is a Laxton Superb?
24 Who plays grandma Kumar at No. 42?
25 A sericulturist breeds which creatures?
26 Did early TV have 405 or 625 lines?
27 What term describes the fineness of yarns?
28 Where do mice live who are proverbially poor?
29 Joseph Grimaldi achieved everlasting fame as what?
30 Who made history in 1982 by going to an Anglican service in Canterbury Cathedral?

Answers	**World Football** *(see Quiz 26)*

1 Japan. 2 Lazio. 3 Ruud Gullit. 4 Gary Lineker. 5 Australia. 6 Croatia. 7 Barcelona. 8 Prague. 9 Graham Poll. 10 Mario Zagallo. 11 Benfica. 12 Germany. 13 Davor Suker. 14 Argentina. 15 DC United. 16 Uruguay. 17 North Korea (holds 150,000). 18 Edson Arantes do Nascimento. 19 Italy. 20 Aron Gunnarsson. 21 Emmanuel Petit. 22 Ivory Coast. 23 Zinedine Zidane. 24 Dennis Bergkamp. 25 Matthias Sammer. 26 St Denis. 27 Dunga. 28 Stanley Matthews. 29 Marco Materazzi. 30 Alexi Lalas.

1 In which country is the club Grampus Eight?
2 Which Italian team did Gazza play for?
3 Who was Dutch captain when they won the European Championship in 1988?
4 Who was leading scorer in the 1986 World Cup finals?
5 Which international side did Venables manage after England?
6 Who won the third-place final in the 1998 World Cup?
7 Which side did Cruyff move to from Ajax in 1973?
8 Dukla and Sparta are from which European city?
9 In 2006, which British ref. showed three yellow cards to the same player?
10 Which Brazilian football coach was sacked after France '98?
11 Which Portuguese side did Graeme Souness manage?
12 Which country ran a full-page "thank you" ad in The Times after Euro 96?
13 Who won the Golden Boot in the 1998 World Cup?
14 Cesar Menotti managed which victorious World Cup side?
15 At the end of his career, which MLS side did Wayne Rooney leave Everton for?
16 Penarol is a club side in which country?
17 In which country is the football stadium with the largest capacity?
18 What is Pele's full name?
19 Who, with England and Holland, was eliminated from France 98 on penalties?
20 Which Cardiff City player captained the Iceland team to the 2016 European Championships qualifiers?
21 Who scored the last goal in France 98?
22 Which team beat Ghana on penalties to lift the 2015 African Nations Cup?
23 Who received the Golden Ball as outstanding player of the 2006 World Cup?
24 Which star won most Premier League Player of the Month awards in 1997/98?
25 Which German won European Player of the Year in 1996?
26 In which stadium was the opening match of France 98?
27 Who captained Brazil in the 1998 World Cup Finals?
28 Who was the first European Footballer of the Year?
29 Who scored Italy's open play goal in the 2006 World Cup Final?
30 Which US star of the 1994 World Cup became the first American player to take part in Italy's Serie A?

Answers | Pot Luck 12 *(see Quiz 25)*

1 Nine. 2 Sahara. 3 Five. 4 Euston Station. 5 Negative equity. 6 Bryan Ferry's. 7 A Butterfly. 8 Agatha Christie. 9 Texas. 10 The Embankment. 11 Blackburn (Alan Shearer). 12 Chess. 13 Live 8 concert. 14 1985. 15 A lake. 16 Sugar beet. 17 An Officer and a Gentleman. 18 Wagner. 19 Liverpool. 20 Iceland. 21 Reader's Digest. 22 She committed suicide. 23 An apple. 24 Meera Syal. 25 Silkworms. 26 405. 27 Denier. 28 Church. 29 A clown. 30 The Pope.

1 In what year was Lewis Hamilton BBC Sports Personality of the Year?
2 From which novel by EM Forster does the phrase 'Only connect' come?
3 Which group had a No.1 UK hit in 1992 with Ebenezer Goode?
4 In which sport were Jack Broughton and James Figg champions?
5 Which Aldous Huxley novel is set in the seventh century AF?
6 Which instrument was Jose Feliciano famous for playing?
7 Which Queen was played in films by Jean Simmons and Bette Davis?
8 On the TV show "Only Connect", what would be missing from this list – lion, eye of Horus, horned viper, two reeds and water?
9 Which musical instruments represent Peter in "Peter and the Wolf"?
10 Who presented "Restoration Village" on TV?
11 A glaive was what kind of weapon?
12 In which century was the first Indianapolis 500 first held?
13 In which country do soldiers wear skirts called fustanella?
14 What can be done if an object is scissile?
15 Which film studios were founded by Harry, Sam, Albert and Jack?
16 Which word can describe a listening device, an illness and an insect?
17 Which famous actress starred in "Courage of Lassie" and "Lassie Come Home"?
18 Who was older when he died, Benny Hill or Richard Burton?
19 What ill-fated personal transport was invented by Sir Clive Sinclair?
20 What type of fruit is a jargonelle?
21 Which part of the head is studied by a phrenologist?
22 Whose ancestral home is Woburn Abbey?
23 Who wrote the poem "Four Quartets"?
24 Which children's game is played on the fingers with looped string?
25 Jane Harris and Nel Mangel appeared in which soap?
26 Brassica Rapa is the Latin name for which vegetable?
27 Who wrote the music and lyrics to the "Rocky Horror Show"?
28 Which two letters are in the internet code for Malta?
29 Excess bile pigment in the bloodstream causes which illness?
30 Whom was Dennis Bergkamp named after?

Answers   Blockbusters *(see Quiz 28)*

1 Five. 2 Brad Pitt. 3 The Robe. 4 Francis Ford Coppola. 5 Normandy. 6 M*A*S*H.
7 Hearst. 8 Crocodile Dundee. 9 James Caviezel. 10 Midnight Cowboy. 11 Dan
Aykroyd. 12 The English Patient. 13 Vito Corleone. 14 Pierce Brosnan. 15 Derek.
16 Gone with the Wind. 17 Wall Street. 18 Braveheart. 19 Dune. 20 John Huston.
21 Terminator II. 22 Gore Verbinski. 23 All About Eve. 24 1930s. 25 Goldblum.
26 Jim Carrey. 27 Carrie Fisher. 28 Celine Dion. 29 The Last Samurai. 30 Cop.

Quiz 28 | Blockbusters

Answers – page 127

1 How many crew members were there in the Nostromo in "Alien"?
2 Who had dental work done to chip his teeth before playing Tyler Durden in "Fight Club"?
3 Which 1953 film was the first made in Cinemascope?
4 Who directed "The Godfather" and all its sequels?
5 "Saving Private Ryan" dealt with events in which part of France?
6 Which anti-war comedy did Robert Altman direct?
7 Which newspaper magnate was said to be the model for Orson Welles' Citizen Kane?
8 Which 80s film was the most profitable in Australian history?
9 Who played Christ in Mel Gibson's "The Passion of the Christ"?
10 What was John Schlesinger's first US film, made in 1969 with Dustin Hoffman and Jon Voight?
11 Who starred in, and co-wrote "Ghostbusters"?
12 Which film starred Juliette Binoche and Kristin Scott Thomas?
13 What was the name of Marlon Brando's character in "The Godfather"?
14 Which James Bond actor starred in "Dante's Peak"?
15 In the 2001 film "Zoolander", what was Zoolander's first name?
16 In which classic did Olivia de Havilland play Melanie Wilkes?
17 In which film did Michael Douglas say "Greed is good"?
18 What was Mel Gibson's first film as actor, director and producer?
19 Which David Lynch space epic was based on the work of Frank Herbert?
20 Who was directing "The African Queen" when his daughter Anjelica was born?
21 Which sequel had the subtitle "Judgment Day"?
22 Who directed the first three "Pirates of the Caribbean" movies?
23 What was the last film before Titanic to win 14 Oscar nominations?
24 In which decade was "Gone with the Wind" made?
25 Which Jeff was the mathematician in "Jurassic Park"?
26 Who became a human cartoon in "The Mask"?
27 Who played Princess Leia in the "Star Wars Trilogy"?
28 Who sang the theme song for "Titanic"?
29 In which movie did Tom Hanks play Captain Nathan Algren?
30 What was Michael Douglas' profession in "Basic Instinct"?

Answers Pot Luck 13 *(see Quiz 27)*

1 2014. 2 Howard's End. 3 The Shamen. 4 Boxing. 5 Brave New World. 6 Guitar.
7 Elizabeth I. 8 Twisted flax (question symbols). 9 Violins. 10 Griff Rhys Jones.
11 A sword. 12 20th. 13 Greece. 14 It can be cut. 15 Warner Brothers. 16 A bug.
17 Elizabeth Taylor. 18 Richard Burton. 19 Sinclair C5. 20 A pear. 21 The skull.
22 Dukes of Bedford. 23 TS Eliot. 24 Cat's Cradle. 25 Neighbours. 26 Turnip.
27 Richard O'Brien. 28 mt. 29 Jaundice. 30 Denis Law.

Quiz 29

TV: Cops & Robbers 2

Answers – page 130

LEVEL 2

1 Which TV cop actress was christened Ilynea Lydia Mironoff?
2 What is the name of the actress who played Sarah Lund in "The Killing"?
3 Which show features DCI Michael Jardine?
4 What was Paul Nicholls' first major series after leaving "EastEnders"?
5 Who was Don Johnson's character in "Miami Vice"?
6 What was the name of law enforcer Michael Knight's computer buddy?
7 Which character did Keeley Hawes play in "Line of Duty"?
8 Which series featured the Wentworth Detention Centre?
9 Who played the TV version of the "Avengers" role portrayed by Uma Thurman on the big screen?
10 Which member of the Ruth Rendell Mysteries cast also scripted some of the shows?
11 In which series did the character Charlie Barlow first find fame?
12 Which "Blue Peter" presenter played Dangerfield's son in the police surgeon series?
13 In which 90s series did Neil Pearson star as Det. Sup. Tony Clark?
14 What rank does John Luther hold?
15 What was Fitz's full name in "Cracker"?
16 Peter Falk played which offbeat TV cop?
17 Which real crime series was based on the German "File XY Unsolved"?
18 In which series did Rowan Atkinson appear as a police officer?
19 Who was the British half of "Dempsey and Makepeace"?
20 Which long-running show increased the length of episodes in 1998 to one hour in a bid to improve ratings?
21 What was Carey Mulligan's character called in David Hare's 2018 police drama "Collateral"?
22 "The Body in the Library" was the first in an 80s series about which sleuth?
23 Which series began with an Armchair Theatre production "Regan"?
24 Loretta Swit was replaced by Sharon Gless in which US series?
25 Who played barrister Kavanagh in the TV series?
26 Which detective was based at Denton police station?
27 How long did the "Morse" episodes usually last?
28 Who played Saga Noren in "The Bridge"?
29 In which series did Charlie Hungerford appear?
30 Which series was based on the Constable novels by Nicholas Rea?

Answers | **Pot Luck 14** *(see Quiz 30)*

1 Hamlet. 2 Central Park Zoo, New York. 3 Take That. 4 Surrey. 5 Elizabeth I.
6 Tim Minchin. 7 Tutti Frutti. 8 A boat. 9 Rockall. 10 Portillo. 11 Fox. 12 Rudyard Kipling. 13 Van Gogh. 14 Trams. 15 George I. 16 Safe. 17 Chaka Khan.
18 Peter Davison. 19 Sonic. 20 Michel Platini. 21 Scurvy. 22 Time. 23 Glucose.
24 Sheridan. 25 Texas. 26 Best Supporting Actress. 27 July, August. 28 Fairy tales.
29 Terry Pratchett. 30 Much.

Quiz 30 | Pot Luck 14

Answers – page 129

1 In which Shakespeare play does a ghost walk on the battlements?
2 In "Madagascar" where do the animals escape from?
3 Which group had No.1 hits with "Babe" and "Pray" in 1993?
4 Charterhouse Public School is found in which county?
5 Miranda Richardson played whom in the second "Blackadder" series?
6 Who wrote the music and lyrics for "Matilda the Musical"?
7 Which 1987 TV series featured the ageing rock band The Majestics?
8 What is a gallivat?
9 Which British island is 230 miles west of the Hebrides in the Atlantic?
10 Which Michael lost his Enfield seat in the 1997 general election?
11 A skulk is the collective name for a group of which animal?
12 Who wrote "How the Leopard Got His Spots"?
13 Who painted the picture called "Irises"?
14 On which forms of transport would you find knifeboards?
15 Handel's "Water Music" was composed for which English King?
16 Michael C. Hall starred in which 2018 TV adaptation of a Harlan Coben novel?
17 Who had UK hits with "Ain't Nobody" and "I'm Every Woman"?
18 Georgia Moffett is the daughter of which ex-"Dr Who"?
19 Which boom is produced by breaking the sound barrier?
20 From 1983–85 which Frenchman was European Footballer of the Year?
21 What disease are you suffering if you are scorbutic?
22 Dr Stephen Hawking wrote the bestselling brief history of what?
23 What is the other name for grape-sugar?
24 Who wrote the play "The School for Scandal"?
25 Which band made the hit albums "White on Blonde" and "The Hush"?
26 The film "The Piano" received Oscars for Best Actress and Best what?
27 In a single calendar year which two consecutive months total most days?
28 What did Charles Perrault collect?
29 Who was the author of the best-selling "Discworld" sci-fi novels?
30 Which member of Robin Hood's gang was the son of a miller?

1 What are the three Baltic states?
2 In which country does the Douro reach the Atlantic?
3 What is the capital of Catalonia?
4 What is Northern Ireland's chief non-edible agricultural product?
5 What do the Germans call Bavaria?
6 Which European capital stands on the river Liffey?
7 What is the Eiffel Tower made from?
8 How is the Danish region of Jylland known in English?
9 In which forest does the Danube rise?
10 Which was the first country to legalise voluntary euthanasia?
11 What covers most of Finland?
12 In which country is the world's highest dam?
13 What is the capital of the Ukraine?
14 What is a remarkable feature of the caves at Lascaux in SW France?
15 What is Europe's highest capital city?
16 Where is France's Tomb of the Unknown Soldier?
17 Which area of the Rhone delta is famous for its nature reserve?
18 In which country would you find Kerkyra?
19 What are the two official European languages of Luxembourg?
20 The Magyars are the largest ethnic group of which country?
21 Where is Castilian an official language?
22 Abruzzi is a mountainous region of which country?
23 Which is the largest of the Balearic Islands?
24 On which island was the Mafia founded?
25 What is the UK's chief Atlantic port?
26 Tallinn is the capital of which Baltic state?
27 What is the main religion of Albania?
28 In which country would you meet Walloons?
29 In which country was the Millau Viaduct built?
30 Which country has Larisa and Volos amongst its chief towns?

1 Which animal can be described as ursine?
2 Who was older when he died, Graham Hill or James Hunt?
3 Which prize for fiction was instigated in 1969?
4 Which Jackie Wilson hit was No.1 nearly thirty years after it was made?
5 A tarpon is a type of what?
6 In 2016 which Radio 4 magazine programme celebrated its 70th birthday?
7 If something is vernal, what is it connected with?
8 Where do Southend United football club play their home games?
9 How did both James I's mother and son die?
10 The sidewinder belongs to which group of snakes?
11 Who played Super Hans in "Peep Show"?
12 Which was the first commercial jet aircraft in the world?
13 Jazz musician John Coltrane played which instrument?
14 In March 2005, who became the first person to fly a plane solo, non-stop around the globe without refuelling?
15 Which part was played by Audrey Hepburn in the film "My Fair Lady"?
16 Wapentakes, hundreds and hides were all areas of what?
17 What is the collective name for a litter of piglets?
18 Who gave Pip his wealth in "Great Expectations"?
19 Who wrote the novel "Jurassic Park"?
20 How many squares have pieces on them at the start of a chess game?
21 In which London park are The Holme, The Broad Walk and Winfield House?
22 What does the differential on a car allow the driving wheels to do?
23 The abbreviation GDP stands for what?
24 The Gulf of Sidra is located off the coast of which continent?
25 Which day of the week is named after the Norse goddess Freya?
26 Winnipeg is the capital of which Canadian province?
27 What type of creature is a flying fox?
28 Cristiano Ronaldo joined Man Utd from which club?
29 In which decade was the Guinness Book of Records first published?
30 In a calendar year what is the first quarter day in England?

Answers	Euro Tour *(see Quiz 31)*

1 Estonia, Latvia and Lithuania. 2 Portugal. 3 Barcelona. 4 Flax. 5 Bayern.
6 Dublin. 7 Iron. 8 Jutland. 9 Black Forest. 10 Netherlands. 11 Trees.
12 Switzerland. 13 Kiev. 14 Cave paintings. 15 Madrid. 16 Under L'Arc de Triomphe. 17 Camargue. 18 Greece. 19 French & German. 20 Hungary. 21 Spain.
22 Italy. 23 Majorca. 24 Sicily. 25 Liverpool. 26 Estonia. 27 Muslim. 28 Belgium.
29 France. 30 Greece.

1 Which US President's father was a former Ambassador in the UK?

2 Edith Cresson was which country's PM from 1991–92?

3 The Downing Street Declaration in 1993 involved the Prime Ministers of which two countries?

4 Which family died at Ekaterinburg in 1918?

5 Which school provided the UK with 19 Prime Ministers before 2000?

6 In which war did British soldiers first wear balaclava helmets?

7 Which mountaineer was the first person since Scott to reach the South Pole overland, in 1958?

8 The "Bomb Plot" of 1944 failed to assassinate whom?

9 What was the minimum age for joining the UK Home Guard in WWII?

10 Which former US President was a distant relative of Princess Diana?

11 Who was the first woman President of Ireland?

12 In which US state did Martin Luther King lead the 1955 bus boycott?

13 Who lost power in Germany in 1998 after 16 years?

14 Who became Secretary General of the UN in 1997?

15 Whom was Bonnie Prince Charlie disguised as when he escaped to France with Flora MacDonald?

16 Who defected to the USSR with Guy Burgess in 1951?

17 Carlos Menem became President of which country in 1989?

18 Who was elected president of France in 2017?

19 What was the alliance between the Germans and the Italians in World War II called?

20 Where in the East End of London did Jack the Ripper operate?

21 As a double agent, Mata Hari was executed by whom?

22 Mrs Meir was the first woman PM in which country?

23 Who was the USA's first Roman Catholic President?

24 Where was Irish prime minister Leo Varadkar's father born?

25 Which Panamanian leader was nicknamed Pineapple Face?

26 Which Pass did Hannibal use to cross the Alps?

27 In 2018, where was a statue of Emmeline Pankhurst unveiled?

28 In which Vietnamese village were 109 civilians massacred by US troops in 1968?

29 Who was the first woman US Secretary of State?

30 In which city was Meghan Markle born?

Answers | Pot Luck 16 *(see Quiz 34)*

1 One square mile. 2 Slaves. 3 Stocks & share prices. 4 Fleet Air Arm. 5 Father of the House. 6 70. 7 Park Lane. 8 Moses. 9 Cunard. 10 Corgi. 11 Kent and Sussex. 12 Red. 13 RAF. 14 Tigris. 15 48. 16 Ageism. 17 Len Goodman. 18 Railway carriage. 19 High blood pressure. 20 Wheel clamp. 21 Vice Squad. 22 Motherwell. 23 The soul. 24 Little Rock. 25 A cough. 26 Westminster Cathedral. 27 Edwin Hubble. 28 Siouxsie and the Banshees. 29 Extinction. 30 Simon Amstell.

1 What is the area of the City of London?
2 What is the last word of Rule Britannia?
3 What does the Footsie show?
4 Which branch of the Royal Navy is concerned with aviation?
5 What name is given to the MP who has served in the House of Commons the longest?
6 A driving licence is issued until the driver reaches what age?
7 In which Lane is London's Dorchester Hotel?
8 In the Old Testament Aaron was the elder brother of which prophet?
9 Which shipping company operated the Queen Mary and the Queen Elizabeth?
10 Which dog's name comes from the Welsh for dwarf dog?
11 In which two English counties are the Cinque Ports?
12 What colour coats do Chelsea Pensioners wear in the summer?
13 Cranwell trains cadets for which of the armed forces?
14 Which river flows through Baghdad?
15 How many kilometres per hour is 30 miles an hour?
16 What is discrimination against the elderly called?
17 Who was the original head judge on "Strictly Come Dancing"?
18 In what type of vehicle was the 1918 World War armistice signed?
19 What is another name for hypertension?
20 What is another name for a Denver boot?
21 Which police department deals with illegal gambling and pornography?
22 James McFadden joined Everton from which club?
23 In religious terms what does absolution purify?
24 What is the capital of the US state of Arkansas?
25 Which condition will an antitussive help alleviate?
26 What is the principal Roman Catholic church in England?
27 Which American astronomer gave his name to the Hubble Space Telescope?
28 Who had hits with "Dear Prudence" and "Hong Kong Garden"?
29 The permanent disappearance of a species is described by which word?
30 Which Simon replaced Mark Lamarr as host of "Never Mind the Buzzcocks"?

Quiz 35 — Sport: Horse Racing

1 Which American was UK champion jockey in 1984, 1985 and 1987?

2 Where is Happy Valley racecourse?

3 Which two races make up the autumn double?

4 How long is the Derby?

5 How many times did Willie Carson win the Derby?

6 Which late Cabinet Minister had been the Glasgow Herald's racing tipster?

7 Desert Orchid raced 70 times, but how many times did he win?

8 Which British racehorse owner sold Vernons Pools in 1988?

9 Who was Champion Jockey a record 26 times between 1925 and 1953?

10 Which Light was a Derby winner for Kieren Fallon?

11 Which Classic was the first to be run on a Sunday in England?

12 In 1995 which horse won the Derby, the King George VI and the Prix de l'Arc de Triomphe?

13 Who founded the online bookmaker bet365?

14 Where is Valentine's Brook?

15 At which racecourse is the Steward's Cup competed for annually?

16 Who was riding Devon Loch when it so nearly won the National?

17 What is Frankie Dettori's real first name?

18 Which Jim was rider for Best Mate's Cheltenham Gold Cup triple triumphs?

19 Which horse won the Cheltenham Gold Cup in 1964, '65 and '66?

20 Who was the UK's first overseas champion jockey after Steve Cauthen?

21 Where is Tattenham Corner?

22 What is the highest jump in the Grand National?

23 Where did Walter Swinburn sustain severe injuries in February 1997?

24 Who won the Grand National in 1993?

25 Which auctioneers were founded in London in 1766 but now have annual sales in Newmarket?

26 Which racecourse is near Bognor Regis?

27 What was unusual about the status of Mr Frisk's winning rider in the 1990 National?

28 How old are horses who run in nursery stakes?

29 In which month is Royal Ascot?

30 What colour was in the name of 2001 Grand National winner Marauder?

Answers | TV: Sitcoms (see Quiz 36)

1 Dermot. 2 Tahani Al-Jamil. 3 Only Fools and Horses. 4 Drop the Dead Donkey.
5 Richard Wilson. 6 Women's pro wrestling. 7 Seinfeld. 8 A wheelchair. 9 Till Death Us Do Part. 10 Fawlty Towers. 11 Porridge. 12 Annie. 13 Cockerel. 14 Thelma.
15 Napoleon. 16 Bubble. 17 After Henry. 18 Are You Being Served?. 19 It was live.
20 As Time Goes By. 21 Barker. 22 Cher. 23 They were witches. 24 Baldrick.
25 Allo Allo. 26 Green. 27 Christopher Biggins. 28 Geraldine Grainger. 29 Bottom.
30 Gordon.

1 What was the name of Harry Enfield's character in "Men Behaving Badly"?

2 What's the name of Jameela Jamil's character in "The Good Place"?

3 What was the most successful sitcom of the 1980s?

4 Which series took place at the Globelink News Office?

5 Which sit com star worked in a hospital laboratory before becoming an actor?

6 What kind of league features in "Glow"?

7 Which US sitcom, which had 180 episodes, finished in May 1998?

8 In "Phoenix Nights" Peter Kay's character used what for mobility?

9 "All in the Family" was a US spin-off from which UK sitcom?

10 Where would you find guests Major Gowen, Miss Tibbs and Miss Gatsby?

11 "Going Straight" was the sequel to what?

12 What was the name of Jim Hacker's wife in "Yes Minister"?

13 In "The Good Life", who or what was Lenin?

14 In "The Likely Lads", whom did Bob marry?

15 In "Dad's Army" what did the air raid warden always call Mainwaring?

16 Who was Edina's PA in "Absolutely Fabulous"?

17 Which series with Prunella Scales as Sarah France had three years on radio before transferring to TV?

18 "Grace and Favour" was a sequel to which sitcom?

19 What was notable about the episode of "Not Going Out" broadcast on 21 December 2018?

20 Which show's theme song begins, "You must remember this..."?

21 Which Ronnie's famous roles have included Arkwright and Fletcher?

22 Which star of "Mermaids" made a guest appearance on "Will & Grace"?

23 What was strange about Samantha Stephens and her mother Endora?

24 Who was Blackadder's servant?

25 Which sitcom was a send-up of "Secret Army"?

26 What was Dorien's surname in "Birds of a Feather"?

27 Who was the effeminate Lukewarm in "Porridge"?

28 What was the Vicar of Dibley's name?

29 In which series did Richie and Eddie first appear?

30 What was Brittas's first name in "The Brittas Empire"?

1 If you nictitate at someone, what do you do?
2 Who offered Demi Moore a million dollars in "Indecent Proposal"?
3 Monument Valley is in which American state?
4 After the age of 70, how frequently must you renew your driving licence?
5 Who is Doria Ragland's famous daughter?
6 On 14 April 1912, what occurred off Newfoundland?
7 Why did Rihanna call her cosmetics line Fenty Beauty?
8 Which instrument was played by David in the Bible?
9 Who is taller, Madonna or Dawn French?
10 Which organisation was founded in 1953 by Reverend Chad Varah?
11 In corned beef what are the corns?
12 Which people used knotted cords called quipu for calculation?
13 Which character was played by Maggie Smith in "Sister Act"?
14 Who wrote the novel "Journey to the Centre of the Earth"?
15 At which school was Thomas Arnold a famous headmaster?
16 Which "Cagney & Lacey" star appeared in the TV thriller "The State Within"?
17 How many squadrons make up a wing in the Royal Air Force?
18 Who followed U Thant as Secretary General of the United Nations?
19 Which high street chain was founded in 1961 by Selim Zilkha?
20 What does the book Glass's Guide contain?
21 Who links "Bob the Builder" and "Line of Duty"?
22 Who directed the epic action movie "Gladiator"?
23 What is an aspen?
24 The Battle of Pinkie of 1547 was fought in which country?
25 What nationality was Amy Johnson?
26 Which animal has the longest pregnancy?
27 Anything above scale 12 on the Beaufort Scale would describe what?
28 Which group were made up of Cass, Michelle, John and Denny?
29 Cars with the international vehicle registration PA come from where?
30 Whom did Shylock want to take his pound of flesh from?

Answers	**Musical Movies** *(see Quiz 38)*

1 Amos Hart. 2 Ursula Andress. 3 Cyd Charisse. 4 Maurice Chevalier. 5 The Philadelphia Story. 6 Martin Scorsese. 7 Keala Settle. 8 Whitney Houston. 9 Richard E. Grant. 10 Master of ceremonies. 11 Antonio Banderas. 12 The Nightmate Before Christmas. 13 Rex Harrison. 14 Beca Mitchell. 15 Marlon Brando. 16 Yul Brynner. 17 Baron Georg Von Trapp. 18 Freddie Eynsford-Hill. 19 Saturday Night Fever. 20 Autry. 21 1950s. 22 Albert Finney. 23 South Pacific. 24 Chim Chim Cheree. 25 Help! 26 Fiddler on the Roof. 27 Jonathan Pryce. 28 Sammy Davis Jr. 29 Cabaret. 30 Monroe.

Quiz 38 | Musical Movies | Answers – page 137

1 Which Chicago character calls himself Mr Cellophane?
2 Which Bond girl starred with Elvis Presley in "Fun in Acapulco"?
3 Who danced with Gene Kelly in the Broadway Ballet section of "Singin' in the Rain"?
4 Who sang "Thank Heaven for Little Girls" in "Gigi"?
5 "High Society" was a musical version of which classic?
6 Which controversial figure directed the musical "New York, New York"?
7 As Lettie Lutz in "The Greatest Showman", who sings "This Is Me"?
8 Who sang most of the soundtrack of "The Bodyguard"?
9 Who had a managerial role in "Spiceworld"?
10 Joel Grey won an Oscar for which role in the 1970s classic "Cabaret"?
11 Who played Che in the film version of "Evita"?
12 Which Tim Burton film featured a hostile takeover of present delivery at Christmas?
13 Who played the Doctor in the musical film version of "Doctor Dolittle"?
14 What is the name of Anna Kendrick's character in "Pitch Perfect"?
15 Which tough guy actor played Sky Masterson in "Guys and Dolls"?
16 Which star of "The King and I" was born in Russia?
17 Whom does Julie Andrews's character marry in "The Sound of Music"?
18 Which character sings "On the Street Where You Live" in "My Fair Lady"?
19 Which 1970s film became a stage musical in London in 1998?
20 Which Gene was the singing cowboy?
21 In which decade does the action of "Grease" take place?
22 Which English actor played the millionaire benefactor in "Annie"?
23 In which musical does Nurse Nellie Forbush appear?
24 Which of the many songs in "Mary Poppins" won the Oscar?
25 What was The Beatles' second film?
26 Which musical is the tale of a Jewish milkman in pre-revolutionary Russia?
27 Who played Eva's husband in "Evita"?
28 Who led "The Rhythm of Life" sequence in Sweet Charity?
29 Which 1970s musical film was set in pre-war Berlin?
30 Which Marilyn sang "Diamonds are a Girl's Best Friend"?

Answers | Pot Luck 17 (see Quiz 37)

1 Wink. 2 Robert Redford. 3 Arizona. 4 Every three years. 5 Meghan Markle. 6 The Titanic sank. 7 It's her surname. 8 Harp. 9 Madonna. 10 Samaritans. 11 Salt. 12 The Incas. 13 Mother Superior. 14 Jules Verne. 15 Rugby School. 16 Sharon Gless. 17 Three. 18 Kurt Waldheim. 19 Mothercare. 20 Vehicle prices. 21 Neil Morrissey. 22 Ridley Scott. 23 A tree. 24 Scotland. 25 British. 26 Elephant. 27 Hurricane. 28 The Mamas and the Papas. 29 Panama. 30 Antonio.

1 What is a pickled gherkin made from?
2 In what year did Terry Jacks score a worldwide hit with "Seasons in the Sun"?
3 What is the name of Britney Spears' second son?
4 Pooh Bah appears in which Gilbert and Sullivan operetta?
5 Which Classic race is run over the longest distance?
6 Who was the brother of Flopsy, Mopsy and Cottontail?
7 What form did the head of the Sphinx take?
8 Which voice in singing is pitched between a tenor and a soprano?
9 Which birds collect in a covey?
10 Which now deposed leader led Iraq into the 1990s Gulf War?
11 Titian is what colour?
12 What part did Madonna play in the film "Shanghai Surprise"?
13 Which actor played the title role in "Quincy"?
14 Which almost eradicated disease was called Phthisis?
15 "The Moonstone" by Wilkie Collins is about a jewel from which country?
16 In which country is Lake Bala the largest natural lake?
17 Who played Sophie Chapman, wife and mother of Mark's child, in "Peep Show"?
18 The US state of Maryland was named after the wife of which King?
19 What type of bars join places of equal atmospheric pressure on a chart?
20 Which tennis star was sued by Judy Nelson for palimony?
21 Who played Mark Antony opposite Liz Taylor in the film "Cleopatra"?
22 What recently discovered element has the symbol Og?
23 Which European city hosted the 2004 summer Olympics?
24 What is the first name of PD James' detective Dalgleish?
25 Which part did Dustin Hoffman play in the film "Hook"?
26 What was the title of the 1994 East 17 Christmas No.1 UK hit?
27 Who was British PM directly before Edward Heath?
28 Which Open win was Nick Faldo's first?
29 What can be solo boxing, a lush mineral or a round timber?
30 Which part did Gene Hackman play in the "Superman" films?

Answers	Living World *(see Quiz 40)*

1 Tidal wave. 2 On the skin. 3 CJD. 4 Worm. 5 Haematology. 6 Hermaphrodite.
7 Falcon. 8 Ear. 9 Marine snail. 10 Knee. 11 Pigeons. 12 Anaemia. 13 Orange.
14 Fungus. 15 Skin. 16 Abdomen. 17 Shoulder blade. 18 Fish. 19 Short-sighted.
20 12. 21 Ivy. 22 Acne. 23 The kiss of life. 24 Tuberculosis. 25 Base of the brain.
26 Achilles tendon. 27 Liver. 28 Green. 29 Kidney. 30 Herring.

Quiz 40 | Living World | Answers – page 139

1 Tsunami is another name for what type of wave?
2 Where would a melanoma appear?
3 Which disease in humans has been linked to the cattle disease BSE?
4 What sort of creature is a fluke?
5 Which branch of medicine is concerned with disorders of the blood?
6 What name is given to an organism which is both male and female?
7 What sort of bird is a merlin?
8 Which part of the body might suffer from labyrinthitis?
9 What sort of creature is an abalone?
10 Where is a bird's patella?
11 Which racing creatures live in lofts?
12 What condition is caused by a shortage of haemoglobin?
13 What colour are the spots on a plaice?
14 What is a puffball?
15 Which part of the body does scabies affect?
16 Which digestive organ lies below the thorax in invertebrates?
17 Where is a human's scapula?
18 What do most sharks live on?
19 If a person has myopia what problem does he or she have?
20 How many pairs of ribs does a human have?
21 One of the UK's few native evergreens, what is the common name of hedera helix?
22 Which skin disorder is caused by inflammation of the sebaceous glands?
23 What is the popular name for mouth-to-mouth resuscitation?
24 A BCG is a vaccination against which disease?
25 Where is the pituitary gland?
26 Which tendon pins the calf muscle to the heel bone?
27 Hepatic refers to which organ of the body?
28 What colour head does a male mallard usually have?
29 The adrenal gland is above which organ?
30 The pilchard is a member of which fish family?

1 Who created sitcoms "Bread" and "Butterflies", and died in 2016?
2 The city of Philadelphia was founded by which religious group?
3 Where would you normally play shovel-board?
4 Which is further north, Blackburn or Blackpool?
5 Which husband of Demi Moore starred in "The Guardian"?
6 Which motor racing team is named after the sacred flower in India?
7 Donald McGill was particularly associated with what seaside art form?
8 Who wrote "Willie Wonka and the Chocolate Factory"?
9 Who narrates "Treasure Island" other than Jim Hawkins?
10 What is the New Zealand National Day called?
11 Paul Merson made his league debut with which club?
12 Which ship sent the first S.O.S.?
13 Which actress penned the autobiography "The Two of Us"?
14 Who wrote "The God Delusion"?
15 Which flower is on the badge of the Boy Scouts?
16 Which former Lebanese hostage wrote a book with Jill Morrell?
17 Maddy Magellan is the partner of which fictional detective?
18 Which Marlon Brando film is based on Conrad's "Heart of Darkness"?
19 In which group of islands is Panay?
20 Which former chimney sweep played Dr Mark Sloan in "Diagnosis: Murder"?
21 The Sierra Nevada mountains are in which American state?
22 Who played Edward in TV's "Edward and Mrs Simpson"?
23 STASHING is an anagram of which famous battle?
24 The TV series "Rebus" was based on the novels of which writer?
25 Whose hits include "Kayleigh" and "Lavender"?
26 Was the Sopwith Camel designed by Sopwith or Camel?
27 Where in the UK is Compton Bay?
28 Who played Dobby in "Peep Show"?
29 Which word links a pastime, a small horse and a small falcon?
30 Which daily food includes the protein casein?

Answers | Pot Luck 20 (see Quiz 42)

1 The surname Smith. 2 William Wordsworth. 3 North. 4 Commonwealth Day.
5 Wessex. 6 Lisbon. 7 Spirit in the Sky. 8 Robert Plant. 9 Freddie Starr. 10 Joseph Lister. 11 Debbie Reynolds. 12 Sweet William. 13 Stoke. 14 Bulgaria. 15 Pickwick Club. 16 Lester Piggott. 17 Stephen Mangan. 18 Windsor. 19 Astronomy.
20 Hercule Poirot. 21 Horses. 22 The Future. 23 Crown Jewels. 24 Study of devil worshippers. 25 A wild pig. 26 A heart attack. 27 Dave Stewart. 28 Canada.
29 Arkansas. 30 Morgan Freeman.

Quiz 42 | Pot Luck 20

Answers – page 141

1 What links the authors of "White Teeth" and "I Capture the Castle"?
2 Dove Cottage was home of which poet?
3 Which Pole was first reached in 1909?
4 Which Day replaced Empire Day in 1958?
5 Alfred the Great ruled which Kingdom?
6 Estoril is a resort north-east of which major city?
7 Which No.1 for Norman Greenbaum was reworked by Gareth Gates?
8 Who was the founder lead singer with Led Zeppelin in 1968?
9 Freddie Powell found fame as which crazy comic?
10 Which British surgeon was a pioneer in improving surgery hygiene?
11 Who was the female lead in "Singing in the Rain"?
12 Which common garden flower has the name Dianthus barbatus?
13 Where were the Spode pottery works established in the 1760s?
14 Cars with the international vehicle registration BG come from where?
15 Which Club included Mr Winkle and Mr Tupman as members?
16 Never Say Die was the first Derby winner for which famous jockey?
17 In 2019, who replaced Frank Skinner as the presenter of "Portrait Artist of the Year"?
18 Which castle is the largest in Britain?
19 Edwin Hubble was concerned with which branch of science?
20 Which part did Albert Finney play in the 1974 film "Murder on the Orient Express"?
21 Sir Alfred Munnings is famous for painting which animals?
22 Comic character Dan Dare was known as the pilot of what?
23 Colonel Thomas Blood tried to steal what in 1671?
24 What is chavezology?
25 What sort of creature was a brawn?
26 If you suffered a myocardial infarction, what would have happened?
27 Who partnered Annie Lennox in the Eurythmics?
28 The Peace River is in which country?
29 In 1957, in which US state were there race riots at Little Rock?
30 Who won a best supporting actor Oscar for a role in "Million Dollar Baby"?

Answers | Pot Luck 19 *(see Quiz 41)*

1 Carla Lane. 2 The Quakers. 3 On a ship's deck. 4 Blackpool. 5 Ashton Kutcher.
6 Lotus. 7 Postcards. 8 Roald Dahl. 9 Dr Livesey. 10 Waitangi Day. 11 Arsenal.
12 Titanic. 13 Sheila Hancock. 14 Richard Dawkins. 15 Fleur-de-lis. 16 John
McCarthy. 17 Jonathan Creek. 18 Apocalypse Now. 19 Philippines. 20 Dick Van
Dyke. 21 California. 22 Edward Fox. 23 Hastings. 24 Ian Rankin. 25 Marillion.
26 Sopwith. 27 Isle of Wight. 28 Isy Suttie. 29 A hobby. 30 Milk.

1 What was the other side of Robson and Jerome's "Up on the Roof"?

2 Which Spice Girl hit came first – "Goodbye" or "Too Much"?

3 Which two singers joined Rod Stewart on the 1994 hit "All for Love"?

4 What night links Whigfield, Alexander O'Neal and Omar?

5 Who featured on East 17's No. 2 "If You Ever" in 1996?

6 Which 1995 hit gave Shaggy his second No.1?

7 Blur were formed in which East Anglian town?

8 What is the title of Amy Winehouse's second album?

9 Which song title links No.1s for Mariah Carey and Nilsson?

10 Which title links the Eurythmics to a 1992 No.1 for Charles and Eddie?

11 Which country did pop/dance act Sash! come from?

12 Which film featured the song that was Whitney Houston's fourth UK No.1?

13 Which dance/rock act was fronted by Keith Flint?

14 What was Simply Red's first UK No.1 in 1995?

15 Who partnered Mariah Carey on "One Sweet Day"?

16 What was "EastEnders'" Michelle Gayle's first hit?

17 What was Curtis Stigers' first UK Top Ten success?

18 Which group held the Christmas single and album top spots in 1996?

19 Which female name was a No. 4 hit for Suggs in 1996?

20 Whose first two UK No.1s were "Flava" and "I Feel You"?

21 What was Jamiroquai's first UK Top Ten hit?

22 Which song title gave The Shamen their only No.1 in 1992?

23 Who was the self-styled "Hardest Working Man in Show Business?"

24 "Better the Devil You Know" was a hit for Sonia and which soap star?

25 What was the first UK No.1 for Celine Dion?

26 What kind of people did R.E.M. take to No. 6 in 1991?

27 What was the one-hit wonder of the Dutch duo Doop?

28 Whose highest chart position was No. 3 in 1991 with "Promise Me"?

29 Which Tony Di Bart No.1 hit from 1994 is the name of a group?

30 Which All Saints No.1 was a cover of a 70s hit for Labelle?

Answers | TV: Soaps (see Quiz 44)

1 Hollyoaks. 2 Davood Ghadami. 3 Alexis Carrington. 4 Family Affairs. 5 Anthony Newley. 6 Matthew Marsden. 7 Beverley Callard. 8 Geoffrey. 9 Home and Away. 10 In a fire. 11 Morgan. 12 South Africa. 13 Billy Hopwood. 14 Emma. 15 Martin. 16 Toyah. 17 Tate. 18 Brookside. 19 Yorkshire TV. 20 Frank Tate. 21 Prince McQueen. 22 Mandy. 23 Trevor Jordache. 24 Bonnie Langford. 25 William Roache's. 26 Lake District. 27 Keith Duffy. 28 Brookside. 29 Bernard Cribbins. 30 Neighbours.

1 Which soap features the unlikely named character Mercedes McQueen?
2 Which actor plays Kush Kazemi in "EastEnders"?
3 What was the name of Joan Collins' character in "Dynasty"?
4 The Hart family appeared in which daily soap?
5 Which ex-husband of Joan Collins appeared on "EastEnders"?
6 Who played mechanic Chris in "Coronation Street" and left to pursue a pop career?
7 Which "Corrie" star produced a fitness video called "Rapid Results"?
8 In "Coronation Street", what is Spider's real name?
9 In which soap were Shane and Angel an item?
10 How did Kathy Glover's husband die in "Emmerdale"?
11 In "Coronation Street" what was Fiona's baby called?
12 Where did Kathy Mitchell go when she left Albert Square?
13 Which badboy Billy was played by David Crellin?
14 Whom did Dannii Minogue play in "Home & Away"?
15 Which Kemp joined Ross Kemp on the "EastEnders" cast?
16 In "Corrie" which of the Battersby girls is Janice's daughter?
17 Which Kim disappeared from "Emmerdale" and was thought to have been murdered?
18 Which soap did "Silent Witness" star Amanda Burton appear in?
19 Which TV company first produced "Emmerdale Farm"?
20 Which role did Norman Bowler play in "Emmerdale"?
21 What is the name of the character played by Malique Thompson-Dwyer in "Hollyoaks"?
22 Which member of Emmerdale's Dingle family went on to present "You've Been Framed"?
23 Who was buried under the patio in "Brookside"?
24 Which former child star and Doctor's assistant joined the cast of "EastEnders" in 2015?
25 Whose son in "Corrie" was once played by his real son Linus?
26 Where did Mavis go when she left The Street?
27 Which one-time boy band member played Ciaran in "Corrie"?
28 "Damon & Debbie" was a short-lived spin-off from which soap?
29 Who links narrating "The Wombles" and playing Wally in a soap?
30 Which soap had a bar called the Waterhole?

1 Alan Shearer's league career finished with a game against which team?
2 Which Kenny Rogers hit starts, "On a bar in Toledo..."
3 In which sport is there a piste other than skiing?
4 Who played Freddie Mercury in the Queen biopic "Bohemian Rhapsody"?
5 Who was appointed Chancellor of the Exchequer by Theresa May in 2016?
6 Which character was played by Dooley Wilson in "Casablanca"?
7 Who wrote the play "Private Lives"?
8 Who invented the bagless vacuum cleaner?
9 Whose hits include "Waterfront" and "Alive and Kicking"?
10 Voords, Krotons and Autons have all appeared on which TV series?
11 Which children's writer's real name was Mrs Heelis?
12 How many seconds are there in three hours?
13 What was the dog called in the Famous Five books?
14 If you were using Dutch or Diaper Bonds what would you be doing?
15 What was Herman's Hermits' only No.1 UK hit?
16 In which country was Salman Rushdie born?
17 What are you doing if you are mendicating?
18 Who wrote the novel "Murder in Mesopotamia" in 1936?
19 Which team from outside Glasgow won the Scottish FA Cup three times from 1982–84?
20 In Monopoly, what is the next property after the Old Kent Road?
21 Whose mountain retreat was at Berchtesgaden?
22 Which programme replaced "Home Truths" on Radio 4?
23 Which was the first British National Park?
24 Fred Perry was world champion in 1929 in which sport?
25 Dendrology is the study of what?
26 The condor belongs to which family of birds?
27 In which country is Arnhem Land?
28 In what year was the final edition of the Yellow Pages published?
29 Which actor was Gandhi in the 1982 film?
30 Who was first to win four World Snooker Championships in a row at the Crucible?

Answers	**Sport: Hot Wheels** *(see Quiz 46)*

1 Tourist Trophy. 2 Malcolm Campbell. 3 Emerson Fittipaldi. 4 Lotus. 5 One.
6 Eddie Merckx. 7 Never. 8 France. 9 McLaren. 10 Peter Sagan. 11 Ayrton Senna.
12 Oulton Park. 13 Stock car racing. 14 Annually. 15 John Surtees. 16 Uncle.
17 Honda. 18 Jack Brabham. 19 London. 20 Iceman. 21 Graham Hill. 22 France.
23 Jackie Stewart. 24 Ferrari. 25 Mini. 26 Chris Boardman. 27 Nigel Mansell.
28 Johnny Herbert. 29 Carl Fogarty. 30 Magny Cours.

1 What does TT stand for in the Isle of Man races?
2 Who first had a record-breaking car and a boat called Bluebird?
3 Who was the youngest F1 world champion before Fernando Alonso?
4 Which team did Jim Clark spend all his racing career with?
5 How many people are in the car in drag racing?
6 Which Belgian cyclist was known as "The Cannibal"?
7 How many times did Stirling Moss win the world championship?
8 In which country was the first organised car race?
9 Who was Lewis Hamilton driving for in 2008 when his won his first world championship?
10 In the 2017 Tour de France Mark Cavendish withdrew after a crash involving whom?
11 Which ex-world champion was killed at the San Marino Grand Prix in 1993?
12 Which motor racing Park is east of Chester?
13 What type of racing is known in the US as Demolition Derbies?
14 How frequently does the Tour de France take place?
15 Who was the first man to be world champion on two and four wheels?
16 What relation was Emerson to Christian Fittipaldi?
17 Which Japanese team won its first F1 Grand Prix in 1967?
18 Who was the first man to win a Grand Prix in a car he designed?
19 Which non-French city was the first to start the Tour de France this century?
20 What is Finnish Formula 1 driver Kimi Raikkonen's nickname?
21 Which Briton was the first world driver's champion to win Le Mans, in 1972?
22 In which country did the first mountain bike world championship take place?
23 Which Briton did Alain Prost overtake for a record number of Grand Prix wins?
24 Which was the first manufacturer to have over 100 Grand Prix wins?
25 Which famous British car won the Monte Carlo Rally in 1967?
26 Who was the first Briton to wear the Tour de France yellow jersey after Tommy Simpson?
27 Who was the first British F1 Champion after James Hunt?
28 Who was the first driver to be sacked by Benetton twice?
29 As of 2018, who has won the most World Superbike Championships?
30 Where is the home of the French Grand Prix?

Answers | **Pot Luck 21** *(see Quiz 45)*

1 Sunderland. 2 Lucille. 3 Fencing. 4 Rami Malek. 5 Philip Hammond. 6 Sam the piano player. 7 Noel Coward. 8 James Dyson. 9 Simple Minds. 10 Dr Who.
11 Beatrix Potter. 12 10,800. 13 Timmy. 14 Bricklaying. 15 I'm into Something Good. 16 India. 17 Begging. 18 Agatha Christie. 19 Aberdeen. 20 Whitechapel.
21 Hitler. 22 Saturday Live. 23 Peak District. 24 Table Tennis. 25 Trees. 26 Vulture.
27 Australia. 28 2019. 29 Ben Kingsley. 30 Ray Reardon.

1 Who wrote "Clothes, Clothes, Clothes. Music, Music, Music. Boys, Boys, Boys?"

2 What constituency did David Cameron represent as an MP?

3 Who produced the Communist Manifesto with Friedrich Engels?

4 What is a firebrat?

5 Where are your fontanelles?

6 Which American protest singer is linked to the "dustbowl ballads"?

7 Who wrote the stories subsequently televised as "Poldark"?

8 In which time device would you find an escapement?

9 The port of Archangel is in which country?

10 The Titanic was launched in which city?

11 Film star Lee Yuen Kam achieved fame as which kung fu expert?

12 Which former tennis player sold Hull City in 1998?

13 Which dirty insects are members of the Diptera family?

14 John Hancock was first to do what at the American Declaration of Independence?

15 In a calendar year what is the third quarter day in England?

16 What is a dirndl?

17 What, in 1902, destroyed the Martinique village of St Pierre?

18 Cork is produced mainly from which species of tree?

19 In which Bond film does the character "Oddjob" appear?

20 What does the word 'Bedouin' mean?

21 Which family made typewriters and invented the breech-loading rifle?

22 Who was the first Roman Emperor?

23 Which word can be a unit of measure, a stick or a fishing implement?

24 Which actor played a black prostitute's minder in the film "Mona Lisa"?

25 Which comedian wrote and performed in "Saxondale"?

26 Who was England's first-choice keeper in the 2002 World Cup?

27 Is St Gabriel the patron saint of messengers, millers or musicians?

28 Which actress played the daughter of Alf Garnett?

29 A love apple is an archaic term for what?

30 Whose hits include "Manchild" and "Buffalo Stance"?

Answers | Movie Superstars *(see Quiz 48)*

1 Clint Eastwood. 2 Australian. 3 Ingrid Bergman. 4 Byron. 5 Sidney Poitier. 6 Fred Astaire. 7 Reynolds. 8 Cleopatra. 9 Saving Mr Banks. 10 Cher. 11 Glenn Close. 12 Dwayne Johnson. 13 Lauren Bacall and Humphrey Bogart. 14 Charlie Chaplin. 15 Dietrich. 16 Clark Gable. 17 Betty Grable. 18 Eight. 19 Cher. 20 Switzerland. 21 Jim Carrey. 22 Cary Grant. 23 George VI. 24 Eddie Murphy. 25 Seven. 26 Robert de Niro. 27 Jane Fonda. 28 Clarice Starling. 29 Robert Redford. 30 Bette Davis.

Quiz 48 | Movie Superstars | Answers – page 147

1 Which actor/director started the trend for spaghetti westerns?
2 What was the nationality of Meryl Streep's character in "A Cry in the Dark"?
3 Who was shunned by Hollywood in the 1940s when she left her husband for Roberto Rossellini?
4 Which poet's name was the middle name of James Dean?
5 Who was Hollywood's first black superstar?
6 Which famous dancer played a straight role in "On the Beach"?
7 Which Burt appeared in "Bean – The Ultimate Disaster Movie"?
8 On the set of which film did the Richard Burton/Elizabeth Taylor affair begin?
9 In what 2013 movie did Tom Hanks play Walt Disney?
10 Who received her first Oscar nomination for "Silkwood"?
11 Whose roles vary from Cruella de Vil on film to Norma Desmond on stage?
12 Whose movies include "Jumanji: Welcome to the Jungle", "Rampage" and "Skyscraper"?
13 Which married superstars starred in "The Big Sleep" in 1946?
14 Which comedian co-founded United Artists in 1919?
15 Dietrich appeared in the German "The Blue Angel"; who appeared in the US version?
16 Which actor's last film was "The Misfits" in 1960?
17 Who was voted No.1 pin-up by US soldiers in WWII?
18 How many parts did Alec Guinness play in "Kind Hearts and Coronets"?
19 Who plays Meryl Streep's mother in "Mamma Mia! Here We Go Again"?
20 In which country did Charlie Chaplin spend the final years of his life?
21 Who was Truman in "The Truman Show"?
22 Which superstar did Tony Curtis parody in "Some Like It Hot"?
23 Which king did Colin Firth play in the 2010 film "The King's Speech"?
24 Who is the physician in the 1990s remake of "Doctor Dolittle"?
25 How many Road films did Crosby, Hope and Lamour make?
26 Who was the psychotic cabbie in Scorsese's "Taxi Driver"?
27 Who announced her retirement when she married Ted Turner in 1991?
28 Who was Jodie Foster's character in "The Silence of the Lambs"?
29 Who directed "The Horse Whisperer"?
30 Who played Margo Channing in "All About Eve"?

Answers | Pot Luck 22 (see Quiz 47)

1 Viv Albertine. 2 Witney. 3 Karl Marx. 4 An insect. 5 Skull. 6 Woody Guthrie.
7 Winston Graham. 8 A clock. 9 Russia. 10 Belfast. 11 Bruce Lee. 12 David Lloyd.
13 Flies. 14 First signatory. 15 Michaelmas Day. 16 A dress. 17 Volcanic eruption.
18 Oak. 19 Goldfinger. 20 Desert-dweller. 21 Remington. 22 Augustus. 23 Rod.
24 Bob Hoskins. 25 Steve Coogan. 26 David Seaman. 27 Messengers. 28 Una Stubbs. 29 Tomato. 30 Neneh Cherry.

1 How many times did Joe Frasier fight Muhammad Ali?
2 What was designed and made in a viable form by Sikorsky in 1941?
3 The TV series "Spooks" is about which organisation?
4 Who had hits with "One Night in Heaven" and "Moving On Up"?
5 Which "dog like" peninsula formed Canada's tenth province in 1949?
6 What was Coco Chanel's Christian name?
7 Quilp appears in a book about what kind of Shop?
8 In which European country are the Pindus Mountains?
9 If a creature is demersal, where does it live?
10 In which county was the first Youth Custody Centre set up in 1908?
11 Espadrilles are a type of what?
12 Who played the part of "Gloria" in "It Ain't Half Hot, Mum"?
13 Michelangelo painted the ceiling of which famous Chapel?
14 In the music world what does MOBO mean?
15 Who was called the "Iron Chancellor"?
16 Where is motor racing's Grand Prix d'Endurance staged?
17 If a creature is succivorous what does it feed on?
18 The source of the Amazon is in which South American country?
19 Al Capone said he was accused of every death except the casualty list of what?
20 If something or someone is gravid what does it mean?
21 Who was the first presenter of the TV series "The Golden Shot"?
22 What was Theresa May's maiden name?
23 What does "chop suey" literally mean?
24 In which city is the University of Surrey?
25 Carisbrooke Castle is on which Isle?
26 In which Disney film is a young lion called Simba?
27 What was the name of Tarzan's monkey friend in the Tarzan stories?
28 Which 2001 film was about real-life events in the Pacific 60 years ago?
29 Which part was played by Herbert Lom in the Pink Panther films?
30 Enigmatology is the study of what?

Answers	On the Map *(see Quiz 50)*

1 Rio de Janeiro. 2 Australia & Tasmania. 3 Cairo. 4 Camp David. 5 Martha's Vineyard. 6 Between East and West Berlin. 7 Florida. 8 Israel & Jordan. 9 Iraq. 10 Nile. 11 Baku. 12 North Sea. 13 Mount Fujiyama. 14 Ecuador. 15 Andes. 16 Death Valley. 17 Berlin. 18 New York. 19 Cape Town. 20 Mediterranean. 21 Mid, South, West. 22 Colorado. 23 Goa. 24 Europe & Asia. 25 Honolulu. 26 Camden. 27 Chile. 28 The Hague. 29 Israel & Syria. 30 Atlantic.

1 Which South American city has a famous Copacabana beach?
2 The Bass Strait divides which two islands?
3 Which Middle East capital is known locally as El Qahira?
4 Where is the official country home of US Presidents?
5 Whose Vineyard is an island off Cape Cod?
6 Where was Checkpoint Charlie?
7 Which US state has a 'pan handle' separating the Atlantic from the Gulf of Mexico?
8 In which two countries is the Dead Sea?
9 The site of ancient Babylon is now in which country?
10 On which river is the Aswan Dam?
11 What is the capital of Azerbaijan?
12 The Fens were formerly a bay of which Sea?
13 What is Japan's highest peak?
14 To which country do the Galapagos Islands belong?
15 Aconcagua is an extinct volcano in which mountain range?
16 Where in California is the lowest point of the western hemisphere?
17 Near which city would you find Müggelsee and Schlachtensee?
18 Ellis Island is in which harbour?
19 Which city is known to Afrikaners as Kaapstad?
20 On which sea is the Gaza Strip?
21 What are the three divisions of Glamorgan?
22 Which river cuts through the Grand Canyon?
23 Where in India are Anjuna beach and Morjim beach?
24 Which continents are separated by the Dardanelles?
25 Which US state capital means "sheltered bay" in Hawaiian?
26 Hampstead is part of which London borough?
27 Which country owns the southernmost part of South America?
28 Where is the seat of the UN International Court of Justice?
29 The Golan Heights are on the border of which two countries?
30 Which is the saltiest of the main oceans?

Answers	Pot Luck 23 *(see Quiz 49)*

1 Three. 2 A Helicopter. 3 MI5. 4 M People. 5 Labrador. 6 Gabrielle. 7 The Old Curiosity Shop. 8 Greece. 9 On the seabed. 10 Kent. 11 Shoes. 12 Melvyn Hayes. 13 Sistine. 14 Music of Black Origin. 15 Bismarck. 16 Le Mans. 17 Sap. 18 Peru. 19 The World War. 20 Pregnant. 21 Jackie Rae. 22 Brasier. 23 Bits and pieces. 24 Guildford. 25 Isle of Wight. 26 The Lion King. 27 Nkima. 28 Pearl Harbor. 29 Commissioner Dreyfus. 30 Puzzles.

Quiz 51 | Pot Luck 24

Answers – page 152

LEVEL 2

1 The song "America" comes from which musical?
2 Which cartoon duo starred in the Oscar-winning film "Quiet Please"?
3 Kate Bush had an album called The Hounds Of ... what?
4 In 1953 who was leader of the British expedition which conquered Everest?
5 Which group had a huge hit with "Millennium"?
6 Who had a UK Top Ten hit with "Can You Feel the Force?"?
7 Which sport was founded in Britain on 28 August 1895?
8 Black Forty Seven in Ireland in the 19th century related to what?
9 What is phonetics the study of?
10 Who was World Heavyweight boxing champion in WWII?
11 Which actor links "Risky Business", "Cocktail" and "Top Gun"?
12 Who was the first president of Zimbabwe?
13 Which element is found in shells, bones and teeth?
14 How old are you if you are a quadragenarian?
15 Which flower is also called the Woodbine?
16 Which item of clothing features on the poster for the movie "The Devil Wears Prada"?
17 A row of windows in the upper wall of a church is known by what name?
18 What is the most times a day of the week can occur in two months?
19 Who was older when he died, Humphrey Bogart or Rock Hudson?
20 Who starred opposite Judy Garland in the film "Easter Parade"?
21 In which sport are there moves called Triffus, Rudolf and Miller?
22 The Horseshoe and American combine to form which famous falls?
23 Which is further west, Bognor or Bournemouth?
24 Who completed ten seasons at Old Trafford in 2006 after playing for Molde?
25 Who has had hits with "Hero" and "Anytime You Need a Friend"?
26 What name is given to a score of 111 in cricket?
27 In Orwell's "1984" what is called Airstrip One?
28 Whose cheap transatlantic air service in 1977 was called "Skytrain"?
29 Who was the third of "Charlie's Angels" with Drew Barrymore and Lucy Liu?
30 In which century was the Battle of Agincourt?

Answers | **Plant World** (see Quiz 52)

1 Barley. 2 Christmas rose. 3 White. 4 Shamrock. 5 Water. 6 Five. 7 Topiary. 8 Monkshood. 9 Yellow. 10 Sweet potato. 11 Bell-shaped. 12 Leaf. 13 Busy Lizzie. 14 Crops and soils. 15 Apple. 16 Strawberry. 17 Deadly nightshade. 18 Paralysis. 19 Female. 20 Tea. 21 Mushroom. 22 Fuchsia. 23 Yellow. 24 South America. 25 Attract pollinators. 26 Herbicide. 27 Red. 28 Flag. 29 Dandelion. 30 Blue.

Quiz 52 | Plant World

Answers – page 151

1 Which cereal can survive in the widest range of climatic conditions?
2 The hellebore is known as what type of rose?
3 What colour are edelweiss flowers?
4 Which plant is St Patrick said to have used to illustrate the Holy Trinity?
5 Succulents live in areas lacking in what?
6 How many points does a sycamore leaf have?
7 What is the ornamental shaping of trees and shrubs called?
8 What is an alternative name for the narcotic and analgesic aconite?
9 What colour are laburnum flowers?
10 What is another name for a yam?
11 What shape are flowers which include the name campanula?
12 What is a frond on a plant?
13 What is the common name of the plant impatiens?
14 Agronomy is the study of what?
15 What is a Sturmer?
16 Which fruit is called "earth berry" in German from where the plant grows?
17 What is another name for belladonna?
18 What is the effect on the nervous system of taking hemlock?
19 Are the male, female or either hop plants used to make beer?
20 What is the most common plant grown in Assam in India?
21 What type of plant is the highly poisonous death cap?
22 Which flowering plant is named after the sixteenth-century German botanist Leonhart Fuchs?
23 The ground powder form turmeric dyes food which colour?
24 The pineapple plant is native to which continent?
25 What is the purpose of a plant's petals?
26 Which type of pesticide is used to kill weeds?
27 What colour are the leaves of a poinsettia?
28 What name is given to the wild yellow iris?
29 Which plant is famous for having a "clock"?
30 What colour are borage flowers?

Answers	**Pot Luck 24** *(see Quiz 51)*

1 West Side Story. 2 Tom and Jerry. 3 Love. 4 John Hunt. 5 Backstreet Boys. 6 The Real Thing. 7 Rugby League. 8 Potato famine. 9 Language sounds. 10 Joe Louis. 11 Tom Cruise. 12 Robert Mugabe. 13 Calcium. 14 40. 15 Honeysuckle. 16 Shoe. 17 Clerestory. 18 Nine. 19 Rock Hudson. 20 Fred Astaire. 21 Trampolining. 22 Niagara Falls. 23 Bournemouth. 24 Ole Gunnar Solskjaer. 25 Mariah Carey. 26 A Nelson. 27 Britain. 28 Freddie Laker. 29 Cameron Diaz. 30 15th.

Quiz 53 Pot Luck 25

Answers – page 154

1 Which former First Lady was nicknamed "The Smiling Mamba"?
2 Who had hits with "Joanna" and "Celebration"?
3 Where would you see a facula?
4 Who played the title character in "The Life and Death of Peter Sellers"?
5 Which country has a unit of currency called the Leone?
6 The seaside town of Westward Ho! is in which county?
7 Oloroso is a type of which drink?
8 What nationality is the singer Sigrid?
9 Which Wonder of the World statue was at Olympia?
10 In which century did William Caxton establish the first English printing press?
11 Cocoa is prepared from the seeds of which tree?
12 Who joined John Torode as a judge on "Celebrity Masterchef"?
13 What is driven by a mahout?
14 What does the cooking expression al dente mean?
15 Which Oliver was Lord Protector of Britain?
16 Which label is distinguished as fashion designed by Armani?
17 Which celeb's childhood nickname was Liver Lips?
18 Who would use a jacquard?
19 In "The Wizard of Oz", which animal was seeking courage?
20 Who captained the US Ryder Cup team in 1997?
21 Who was the Bond girl in "Die Another Day"?
22 Pumpkin pie is the traditional dessert on which special American day?
23 What type of car did Prince Philip flip near Sandringham in January 2018?
24 Who painted "The Starry Night"?
25 Which word can be a swan, a horse, a bread roll and a basket?
26 What was Diana Ross's first solo No.1 in the UK?
27 What are progeny?
28 Who had hits with "I Can't Dance" and "Invisible Touch"?
29 In which part of East London was David Beckham born?
30 If you heard a John Gabel Entertainer, what would be playing?

1 Germany's Red Army Faction was popularly called what after its two founders?
2 The Equal Opportunities Commission was set up to implement which act?
3 Who became US Vice President after Spiro Agnew resigned?
4 Where did the Gang of Four seize power in 1976?
5 Which natural disaster did Guatemala City suffer in 1976?
6 In the Vietnam War who or what was Agent Orange?
7 Who was Nixon's White House Chief of Staff at the height of the Watergate scandal?
8 On which Pennsylvania Island was there a nuclear leak in 1979?
9 In 1978 Mujaheddin resistance began in which country?
10 Who made a precocious speech aged 16 at the 1977 Tory Party conference?
11 Who opened her first Body Shop in 1976?
12 Where was Obote replaced by Amin in 1971?
13 The Pahlavi Dynasty was overthrown by the Islamic revolution in which country?
14 Which Argentine leader died in 1974 and was succeeded by his third wife?
15 Which woman MP did Jack Straw replace as MP for Blackburn?
16 In films, which actor played the comic book character with an S on his chest?
17 Which dictator was deposed in Cambodia in 1979?
18 Which "King" died in 1977 aged 42?
19 What was Harare called until the end of the 1970s?
20 What was inside US incendiary bombs during the Vietnam War?
21 Which title did Quintin Hogg take when made Lord Chancellor in 1970?
22 SALT negotiations took place between which two countries?
23 Which future Labour leader became Trade & Industry Secretary in 1978?
24 Who first charted in the 1970s and had a 2005 No.1 with "Ghetto Gospel"?
25 In which country was a monarchy restored in 1975?
26 The Sandinistas overthrew which government in 1979?
27 Who succeeded Heath as Tory leader?
28 Sapporo was the centre of the 1972 Winter Olympics in which country?
29 Which country did the USSR invade in 1979?
30 In which department was Thatcher a Minister before leading the Party?

Answers	Pot Luck 25 *(see Quiz 53)*

1 Nancy Reagan. 2 Kool & The Gang. 3 The sun (Bright area). 4 Geoffrey Rush.
5 Sierra Leone. 6 Devon. 7 Sherry. 8 Norwegian. 9 Statue of Zeus. 10 15th.
11 Cacao. 12 Gregg Wallace. 13 An elephant. 14 Firm when bitten. 15 Oliver
Cromwell. 16 Emporio Label. 17 Bob Geldof. 18 A weaver. 19 The lion. 20 Tom
Kite. 21 Halle Berry. 22 Thanksgiving Day. 23 Land Rover. 24 Van Gogh. 25 A cob.
26 I'm Still Waiting. 27 Offspring. 28 Genesis. 29 Leytonstone. 30 A juke box.

1 Which actress moved from Madge in "Neighbours" to Millie in "Emmerdale"?
2 Which "Cagney and Lacey" star appeared in the Coen Brothers' 2018 "Ballad of Buster Scruggs"?
3 In 2018, who falsely accused actor Ryan Thomas of punching her on "Celebrity Big Brother"?
4 Superwoman Lynda Carter held which beauty queen title?
5 On which TV show was Jim Davidson "discovered"?
6 In 2018 who took over as the host of "Who Wants to be a Millionaire?"?
7 What is the name of Kath's husband in Australian comedy "Kath & Kim"?
8 In the celeb boxing's "The Fight", Ricky Gervais took on which Grant?
9 The TV profile "Tantrums and Tiaras" was about which pop superstar?
10 Which TV presenter's relationship with Stan Collymore ended violently in Paris during the 1998 World Cup?
11 Which X Factor singer has represented Finland in Eurovision twice?
12 Martin Bashir's 2003 interview led to involvement in a court trial of which celeb?
13 What was Richard Madeley arrested for in 1990?
14 Which TV presenter is joint chief curator at Historic Royal Palaces?
15 In which town was Essex girl Denise Van Outen born?
16 Which "News at Ten" presenter had the first British TV interview with Nelson Mandela after his release?
17 Which game was "Bob's Full House" based on?
18 Which Christmas 2015 series brought together several Dickens characters?
19 Who presented the C5 medical quiz show "Tibs and Fibs"?
20 Who were the first couple to be BBC Sports Personality of the Year?
21 Which cook founded Sainsbury's The Magazine with her husband?
22 In the US Jim Bakker and Jimmy Swaggart are famous for what type of show?
23 Which girl band won the first "Popstars: The Rivals"?
24 Which weather girl went to the same university as Glenys Kinnock?
25 Which character did Ted Danson play in "Cheers"?
26 Which pop group walked out on Clive Anderson on his "All Talk" show?
27 Which comedian's marriage ended after he appeared in "Celebrity Big Brother"?
28 Which talk show hostess appeared in the film "Hairspray" with Divine?
29 Who was the resident snooker player on "Big Break"?
30 Where did Paula Yates conduct her "Big Breakfast" interviews?

Answers	Pot Luck 26 *(see Quiz 56)*

1 Meghan Markle. 2 Domesday Book. 3 A Chorus Line. 4 Republican Party.
5 Stephen Daldry. 6 Games and playing them. 7 Italian. 8 You ain't heard nothing yet.
9 Oil. 10 Galtieri. 11 Balmoral. 12 Mince and slices of quince. 13 Vera Lynn.
14 Yorath. 15 Sid Vicious. 16 Abuja. 17 The Unknown Soldier. 18 Lactic Acid. 19 Kevin Kilbane. 20 Emile Ford. 21 Brandy. 22 David Jason. 23 Russian.
24 Photocopying. 25 The Great Pretender. 26 Delft. 27 A church. 28 Death Penalty.
29 Eddie Shah. 30 Greg Norman.

1 Who was the most Googled person in the UK in both 2017 and 2018?
2 Which famous survey started in 1086?
3 From which musical does the song "One" come?
4 Ronald Reagan was in which political party?
5 Which Stephen directed the movie "Billy Elliot"?
6 Ludology is the study of what?
7 What nationality was Casanova?
8 What was Al Jolson's most famous line?
9 If a substance is oleaginous what does it mainly contain?
10 Which General led the junta in the 1982 seizure of the Falklands?
11 Which famous Castle is on the River Dee?
12 What did the Owl and the Pussycat dine on?
13 Vera Welch sang under what name?
14 What was presenter Gabby Logan's surname before she married?
15 Which outlandish musician's real name was Simon Ritchie?
16 What is the capital of Nigeria?
17 Who is buried at the Arc de Triomphe?
18 During exercise which acid builds up in the muscles?
19 Which Kevin has played for WBA, Sunderland, Everton and Wigan?
20 Which singer had a backing group called the Checkmates?
21 What is added to egg yolks and vanilla to make advocaat?
22 Who played "Blanco" in the TV series "Porridge"?
23 What nationality was Rachmaninov the composer?
24 What is xerography?
25 Which 1956 hit links The Platters with a 1987 Freddie Mercury hit?
26 Which Dutch town is particularly famous for its blue pottery?
27 Where would you find an apse?
28 What was abolished on 18 December 1969 in Britain?
29 Which tycoon started the newspaper called Today?
30 Who was the first golfer to lose play-offs in all four majors?

Answers | TV: TV Times 1 (see Quiz 56)

1 Anne Charleston. 2 Tyne Daly. 3 Roxanne Pallett. 4 Miss America. 5 New Faces.
6 Jeremy Clarkson. 7 Kel. 8 Grant Bovey. 9 Elton John. 10 Ulrika Jonsson.
11 Saara Aalto. 12 Michael Jackson. 13 Shoplifting. 14 Lucy Worsley. 15 Basildon.
16 Trevor McDonald. 17 Bingo. 18 Dickensian. 19 Tony Slattery. 20 Torvill & Dean.
21 Delia Smith. 22 Televangelism. 23 Girls Aloud. 24 Sian Lloyd. 25 Sam Malone.
26 The Bee Gees. 27 Les Dennis. 28 Ricki Lake. 29 John Virgo. 30 On a bed.

1 Who released the album "Auberge"?
2 What was the thirteenth album released by Chicago?
3 Which group's debut album, "Always & Forever", shadowed their name?
4 Whose debut solo album was called "Faith"?
5 Which Queen album shares its name with a newspaper?
6 On the 80s album "Purple Rain" who backed Prince?
7 Which duo released albums called "Introspective" and "Very"?
8 What was George Ezra's 2014 debut album called?
9 What was Radiohead's first album to make No.1 in the British charts?
10 Who guested with Dire Straits on the "Money For Nothing" track?
11 Which phrase with a French flavour was the title of Paul Young's debut album?
12 What was the title of Ike and Tina Turner's only album?
13 Who was the only female solo artist to have a UK Top Ten bestselling album in 2018?
14 A picture of Burt Bacharach appeared on the cover of which bestselling 90s album?
15 Whose debut album was called "Different Class"?
16 "Supposed Former Infatuation Junkie" was whose follow-up to a 30 million-selling album?
17 Which Oasis album came out first – "Be Here Now" or "The Masterplan"?
18 On the Beautiful South's 1996 album what is the "Colour"?
19 Which Olivia Newton-John 1981 album could describe some exercise?
20 Which Bon Jovi album was best kept dry?
21 What was the title of the first album released by The Rolling Stones?
22 What were Madonna's book and 1992 album called?
23 Which musician took Vivaldi's "The Four Seasons" into the charts?
24 Rod Stewart's first album was called after which alley?
25 What animal is on the cover of the Beach Boys' album "Pet Sounds"?
26 Which construction has given its name to a Pink Floyd album?
27 What was the name of Ed Sheeran's third album, released in 2017?
28 Which battle was the title of the first ABBA album?
29 How many Good Reasons had Jason Donovan on his first No.1?
30 Which Annie Lennox album topped the charts in 1993?

1 Who formed the famous dance troupe the Bluebell Girls?
2 Whose CDs include "Seven Year Itch" and "Stickin' to My Guns"?
3 What would you do with a futon?
4 Which play is performed every ten years at Oberammagau?
5 Which wood was mainly used by Thomas Chippendale?
6 In which London area is The Royal Hospital?
7 Where would you be if you were stripping the willow with a dashing white sergeant?
8 Bruce Willis destroyed a plane with his cigarette lighter in which film?
9 What does a blue flag at a beach mean?
10 Which carbohydrate causes jam to gel?
11 If a dog is suffering from "hard pad" what form of disease has it got?
12 What is a hawser?
13 What constituency did Tony Blair represent as an MP?
14 Theophobia is a fear of what?
15 In which French town was Joan of Arc burnt at the stake?
16 What was the name of cowboy Tom Mix's horse ?
17 The quail is the smallest member of which bird species?
18 What is the singular of axes in mathematics?
19 Which actress's real name was Maria Magdalena von Losch?
20 Which port is the most easterly in Britain?
21 What is the common weather in a pluvial region?
22 Which Polynesian word means prohibited or forbidden?
23 What colour is the egg of a kingfisher?
24 The Dodecanese Islands are in which sea?
25 What nationality was Secretary General of the UN Boutros Boutros Ghali?
26 In board games, what colour is the Reverend in Cluedo?
27 Whose hits include "Sunny Afternoon" and "Tired of Waiting for You"?
28 What is on top of the Mona Lisa's left hand?
29 What do Americans call Perspex?
30 Who voices Woody in the "Toy Story" series of animated films?

1 After what sort of activity might you suffer from the bends?

2 What would you buy from Stanley Gibbons?

3 What colour are houses in Monopoly?

4 What shape is a sumo wrestling ring?

5 Which Hindu system of philosophy is used as a means of exercise and meditation in the West?

6 In which game do you score "one for his knob"?

7 The Fastnet race is part of the contest for which Cup?

8 Which game's name comes from a piece of its equipment looking like a bishop's crosier?

9 At which station do you arrive in Paris if you have travelled from the UK by Eurostar?

10 The YOC is the junior branch of which organisation?

11 If you were a collector of Clarice Cliff what would you collect?

12 Alfriston Clergy House was the first what?

13 What is a grand slam in bridge?

14 Camogie is the women's equivalent of which sport?

15 What sort of swimming takes place with musical accompaniment?

16 Which three Quaker families made most of Britain's chocolate?

17 In which country is De Efteling Theme Park?

18 Which sport is played at London's Queen's Club?

19 Which pizza restaurant was the first of a chain founded in London?

20 What sort of club is the Royal and Ancient?

21 Which organisation's anthem is "Jerusalem"?

22 What was the Worldwide Fund for Nature formerly called?

23 Which open-air zoo is near Dunstable in Bedfordshire?

24 Which boy reporter was created by Belgian artist Herge?

25 Where was the first Westfield shopping complex?

26 In athletics, what is attached to a chain and a handle and thrown?

27 Which sport has Greco-Roman and Freestyle, as two distinct styles?

28 The annual Round the Isle race goes round which Isle?

29 La Defence and Les Halles are Christmas markets in which city?

30 Where were Walker's Crisps first made?

Quiz 60 | Pot Luck 28

1 What describes descending a sheer face by sliding down a rope?
2 Donna Reed replaced Barbara Bel Geddes in which TV series?
3 Who won TV's "How Do You Solve a Problem Like Maria?"
4 Which animal is feared by a hippophobe?
5 Whose hits include "Wide Boy" and "Wouldn't It be Good"?
6 The novel "Shirley" was written by which of the Bronte sisters?
7 In which London building does the Lutine Bell hang?
8 Which is further south, Folkestone or Southampton?
9 Which American sportsman was said to be earning more than the US president in 1925?
10 Which famous bear came from Peru?
11 What did the S stand for in Charlie Chaplin's middle name?
12 Zymology is the study of what?
13 What is a passepied?
14 Which species can be Fairy, Black-footed and Crested?
15 Which game uses flattened iron rings thrown at a hob?
16 What was the title of Captain Sensible's No.1 UK hit in 1982?
17 Which mammals will expire when stranded on dry land?
18 In which movie did Ewan McGregor sing Elton John's "Your Song"?
19 What is tansy?
20 Which island is in the Bay of Naples?
21 In which series did Amanda Mealing play Connie Beauchamp?
22 Cyril Mead became known as which comic?
23 Which constituency does Theresa May represent as an MP?
24 In 2018 the first statue of a woman was unveiled in the UK's Parliament Square – whom did it depict?
25 What is a taipan?
26 Is Coventry north or south of Leicester?
27 Which English king was the last to die in battle?
28 Who was older when he died, Peter Sellers or Tony Hancock?
29 What is the smallest administrative unit in the Church of England?
30 In "Pride and Prejudice" whom does Elizabeth Bennet finally marry?

Answers	Leisure (see Quiz 59)

1 Deep sea diving. 2 Stamps. 3 Green. 4 Circular. 5 Yoga. 6 Cribbage. 7 Admiral's Cup. 8 Lacrosse. 9 Gare Du Nord. 10 RSPB. 11 Pottery. 12 National Trust property. 13 13 tricks by one team. 14 Hurling (or hurley). 15 Synchronised swimming. 16 Cadbury, Fry, Rowntree. 17 The Netherlands. 18 Tennis. 19 Pizza Express. 20 Golf Club. 21 Women's Institute. 22 World Wildlife Fund. 23 Whipsnade. 24 Tintin. 25 Sydney, Australia. 26 Hammer. 27 Wrestling. 28 Isle of Wight. 29 Paris. 30 Leicester.

1 Which American was the first to win the Men's Singles Grand Slam?
2 Who in 1979 became the youngest player to complete the double of 1,000 runs and 100 wickets?
3 Which Swede, in 1987, was the first man for 40 years to win a match at Wimbledon without losing a game?
4 Who was the first woman tennis player to win $1 million?
5 Who was the first Briton after 1950 to win the British Open golf three years in succession?
6 Which lady claimed three fastest winning times in the London Marathon?
7 Which woman won 20 Wimbledon titles between 1961 and 1979?
8 Franz Klammer was a record breaker in which sport?
9 Which woman became the youngest Wimbledon semi-finalist for 99 years in 1986?
10 Who broke the world record for an individual innings of 501 in 1994?
11 How many world records did Mark Spitz break when he won his seven gold medals?
12 Who was the first British golfer to win the World Match-Play Championship?
13 Whose 1500m world record did Steve Cram break in 1985?
14 Who was the first British woman swimmer to win a world title?
15 Who was the elder of the motor racing Schumachers – Michael or Ralf?
16 Which Namibian was the first to break the 200m indoors 20-second barrier?
17 Who was the first British winner of the US Masters in 1988?
18 In 1988 who became the first boxer to win world titles at five official weights?
19 What was the first major to be claimed by Tiger Woods?
20 Who was the first Thai snooker player to win a major tournament?
21 In 1972 Mark Spitz broke Olympic records doing which two strokes?
22 October 2018, 1,622 took part and 60 questions were answered – what was it?
23 Who broke Bob Beamon's long jump record set at the 1968 Olympics?
24 Who was the then youngest ever winner of the US Masters in 1980?
25 Who was the first British football player to earn £100 per week?
26 Which US hurdler was undefeated in 122 races?
27 Which British shot putter was world No.1 in 1975?
28 Which Liz won the fastest ever debut marathon when she won in New York in 1991?
29 In 2018, who became the fastest boxer in history to win three titles in three weights?
30 In the modern era, who has won more tennis Grand Slam titles than anyone?

Answers | Pot Luck 29 *(see Quiz 62)*

1 In the blood. 2 Potato. 3 UB40. 4 Tissues of animals and plants. 5 Ant McPartlin. 6 Will Young. 7 2013. 8 Dukes of Bedford. 9 A fruit. 10 Clockwise. 11 Hungary. 12 Pound. 13 Brake horsepower. 14 Darby and Joan. 15 In private. 16 Arnold Schwarzenegger. 17 'Twice-cooked'. 18 Daffodil. 19 A mushroom. 20 Cedric Errol. 21 The Wind in the Willows. 22 Sailing. 23 Bruce Willis. 24 Larch. 25 Free. 26 Blue. 27 Baseball. 28 Poppy. 29 The Moon. 30 A Boom.

1 Where is fibrin found in your body?
2 What is the vegetable common to the Indian dishes of Aloo Gobi and Aloo Palak?
3 Which group had hits including "Homely Girl" and "Kingston Town"?
4 Histology is the study of what?
5 In 2018, which half of a famous duo took time off from his presenting duties after crashing his car?
6 Who first took the much-covered song "Light My Fire" to No.1?
7 In what year did Margaret Thatcher die?
8 Woburn Abbey is the home of which family?
9 What is a durian?
10 Which film starred John Cleese as an under-pressure headmaster?
11 The composer Bela Bartok came from which country?
12 What can be an animal enclosure or a unit of weight?
13 What does the abbreviation BHP stand for?
14 Which poetic names lend themselves to an expression for a devoted, elderly couple?
15 How does a judge hear a case when it is heard In Camera?
16 From 1968 to 1970 which actor was Mr Universe?
17 What does the word 'biscuit' literally mean?
18 The Lent Lily is sometimes used as another name for which flower?
19 What is a Tree Ear?
20 What was Little Lord Fauntleroy's name?
21 Toad of Toad Hall was a dramatised version of which Kenneth Grahame tale?
22 Which sport is Clare Francis famous for?
23 In the film "Look Who's Talking" whose voice was the baby's thoughts?
24 Which tree usually provides the wood for the Highland Games caber?
25 Whose hits include "Wishing Well" and "All Right Now"?
26 What colour is the tongue of a giraffe?
27 Which sport featured in the movie "A League of Their Own"?
28 Californian, Yellow Horned and Opium are all types of which flower?
29 Where is the Sea of Vapours?
30 What is the wading bird the bittern's cry called?

| **Answers** | Record Breakers *(see Quiz 61)* |

1 Donald Budge. 2 Kapil Dev. 3 Stefan Edberg. 4 Chris Evert. 5 Nick Faldo. 6 Paula Radcliffe. 7 Billie Jean King. 8 Skiing. 9 Gabriela Sabatini. 10 Brian Lara. 11 Seven. 12 Ian Woosnam. 13 Steve Ovett's. 14 Karen Pickering. 15 Michael. 16 Frankie Fredericks. 17 Sandy Lyle. 18 Sugar Ray Leonard. 19 US Masters. 20 James Wattana. 21 Freestyle & butterfly. 22 Largest online quiz. 23 Mike Powell. 24 Seve Ballesteros. 25 Johnny Haynes. 26 Ed Moses. 27 Geoff Capes. 28 McColgan. 29 Vasiliy Lomachenko. 30 Roger Federer.

1 Who played Eddie to claim a Best Supporting Actor Oscar in a boxing movie?

2 Which World War II film would have been called Dar el-Beida had it been titled in the local language?

3 Which Michael Cimino film about Vietnam won five Oscars in the 70s?

4 Whom did Daniel Day-Lewis portray in "My Left Foot"?

5 Which veteran won an Oscar in 1981 two years after his daughter?

6 In 2017, which male actor presented the Best Film Oscar to the wrong film?

7 For which film did Tom Hanks win playing a lawyer dying from AIDS?

8 Who overcame deafness to win for "Children of a Lesser God"?

9 Who won the Best Director award for "Titanic"?

10 For which films did Tom Hanks win in successive years?

11 Who won the Best Actor Oscar for "High Noon"?

12 In 2017, which film actually won the Oscar for Best Film?

13 In which decade did Katharine Hepburn win her first Oscar?

14 Who won three Oscars for "Annie Hall"?

15 For which film did Brando win his second Oscar?

16 Who won his first Best Actor Oscar for "Kramer vs. Kramer"?

17 Which singer won an Oscar for "From Here to Eternity"?

18 For which film did Steven Spielberg win his first award?

19 What was unusual about Holly Hunter's performance in "The Piano"?

20 Who won the Best Actress award in both 1997 and 2018?

21 In the year "Gandhi" won almost everything who was Best Actress for "Sophie's Choice"?

22 Who won Oscars for "Dangerous", "Jezebel" and "All About Eve"?

23 Who won as Dan Aykroyd's mother in "Driving Miss Daisy"?

24 How many times between 1990 and 1997 did Best Picture and Best Director Oscars go to the same film?

25 Who played the psychotic nurse in "Misery" and won Best Actress?

26 What did Anthony Hopkins win first, a knighthood or an Oscar?

27 Who won for her role as Blanche in "A Streetcar Named Desire"?

28 Who won Best Director for "The English Patient?"

29 Who won for her first film "Paper Moon"?

30 Which actress was nominated for "The Wings of the Dove"?

---

1 What are Spode, Bow and Chelsea all types of?
2 How old was astronomer Patrick Moore when he died in 2012?
3 Which Italian area produces Chianti?
4 Which scale measures the level of alkalinity and acidity?
5 TV's "Death of a President" was about the fictional assassination of which world leader?
6 Where will you return to if you throw a coin into the Trevi Fountain?
7 What in your body are affected by phlebitis?
8 Who was caretaker manager of Spurs after the departure of Glenn Hoddle in 2003?
9 Whose hits include "Again" and "That's the Way Love Goes"?
10 Which TV character lived on Scatterbrook Farm?
11 Which High Street travel agents devised the holiday package tour?
12 In which UK county was singer George Ezra born?
13 How did Curtis Jackson, born 1976, become known in the music world?
14 What does the Greek odeon mean?
15 If you were using a tambour, what needlecraft would you be doing?
16 On what date did GDPR (data protection legislation) come into force?
17 Which actor co-starred with Juliette Binoche in "Breaking & Entering"?
18 In which century was cockfighting banned?
19 Which supermarket chain paid for the new National Gallery wing opened in 1991?
20 Cars with the international vehicle registration ET come from where?
21 Who started the Habitat chain of shops in 1964?
22 Who is smaller, Janet Street Porter or Naomi Campbell?
23 Edmonton is the capital of which Canadian province?
24 Who played Shirley Valentine in the film?
25 What is the white of an egg called as an alternative to albumen?
26 Which 007 actor was also TV's Remington Steele?
27 The Ashanti tribe live in which African country?
28 Which lady took over as Secretary of State for Education from David Blunkett?
29 What is held annually in London in Ranelagh Gardens?
30 Where was tennis star Monica Seles playing when she was stabbed?

Answers	The Oscars (see Quiz 63)

1 Morgan Freeman. 2 Casablanca. 3 The Deer Hunter. 4 Christy Brown. 5 Henry Fonda. 6 Warren Beatty. 7 Philadelphia. 8 Marlee Matlin. 9 James Cameron.
10 Philadelphia, Forrest Gump. 11 Gary Cooper. 12 Moonlight. 13 1930s.
14 Woody Allen. 15 The Godfather. 16 Dustin Hoffman. 17 Frank Sinatra.
18 Schindler's List. 19 She never spoke. 20 Frances McDormand. 21 Meryl Streep.
22 Bette Davis. 23 Jessica Tandy. 24 Eight (all of them). 25 Kathy Bates. 26 Oscar.
27 Vivien Leigh. 28 Anthony Minghella. 29 Tatum O'Neal. 30 Helena Bonham-Carter.

1 Whose funeral in Milan in 1997 was attended by Elton John and Naomi Campbell?

2 Which Frenchman was the first to launch menswear and ready to wear collections?

3 How was the former Lady Elizabeth Bowes-Lyon better known?

4 What is Donald and Melania Trump's son called?

5 Which oil billionaire founded the world's highest-funded art gallery?

6 Which famous American enrolled her baby daughter at Cheltenham Ladies' College in September 1998?

7 What is the name of Paul McCartney's third wife?

8 Whom did Jerry Hall marry in 2016?

9 Chiang Ching was the third wife of which political leader?

10 Linda Tripp was the confidante of which famous name?

11 Who painted "The Rokeby Venus" in 1647–51?

12 Which Brit began hosting "The Late Late Show" in 2015?

13 The parents of which actress performed as country music duo the Daltons?

14 Who is Dakota Johnson's mother?

15 What did David Frost's and Virginia Wade's father have in common?

16 Whose first names are Anthony Charles Lynton?

17 Which playwright won a BAFTA award for the "Bar Mitzvah Boy"?

18 Which Rolling Stone bought, and died at AA Milne's house?

19 Which director was knighted the year his movie "Matchstick Men" came out?

20 What is Carrie Fisher's actress daughter called?

21 At which sport did Pope John Paul II excel in his youth?

22 Who painted "The Ambassadors" in 1533?

23 American actress Mamie Gummer has a famous mother in the same profession – who is she?

24 Who married millionaire hairdresser Stephen Way in 1998?

25 Who was the wife of Ferdinand Marcos at the time of his death?

26 What relation was Cherie Blair to Pat Phoenix, who played Elsie Tanner in "Coronation Street"?

27 What was the first name of Marks of Marks & Spencer?

28 What links Nataraja in Hinduism and performer Michael Flatley?

29 Who was the first basketball player to declare he was HIV positive?

30 What is the name of David and Victoria Beckham's daughter?

Answers | The Footy *(see Quiz 66)*

1 Gabon. 2 Won gold medal for South Korea in Asian Games. 3 CONCACAF. 4 Thibaut Courtois. 5 Luzhniki Stadium. 6 John Terry. 7 Athletic Bilbao. 8 Steve Finnan. 9 Steve Clarke. 10 Ravanelli, Vialli, Zola and Balotelli. 11 Gordon Strachan (1991). 12 Birds on their crest. 13 Paul Pogba. 14 Roberto Martínez. 15 Fulham. 16 Coventry City. 17 Harry Redknapp. 18 Monaco. 19 Jack Wilshere. 20 Eder. 21 All bitten by Luis Suarez. 22 Copa Libertadores. 23 Celtic. 24 Kolo Toure (Arsenal 03/04, Celtic 16/17). 25 Watford. 26 Kevin Phillips (1999-2000). 27 Blackpool. 28 Griezmann and Lukaku. 29 Salomón Rondón. 30 Bristol City.

1 For which country does Arsenal's Pierre-Emerick Aubameyang play?
2 How did Tottenham's Son Heung-min avoid military service in 2018?
3 Which confederation oversees football in the Caribbean islands?
4 Who was named as the official best goalkeeper of the 2018 World Cup finals?
5 What was the name of the stadium which hosted the 2018 World Cup Final?
6 Who is the only non-Manchester United player to win five or more Premier League title medals?
7 From which club did Manchester City sign Aymeric Laporte in 2018?
8 Which Liverpool full-back was the only player to have been in the Champions League, all four levels of English league football and the Conference?
9 Who replaced Lee Clark as Kilmarnock manager in October 2017?
10 Which four Italians have scored Premier League hat-tricks?
11 Who was the last Scottish player to win the Football Writers Association Footballer of the Year Award?
12 What connects Brighton and Hove Albion, Burnley, Cardiff City, Crystal Palace, Liverpool and Tottenham Hotspur?
13 Griezmann, Lloris, Payet and which other Frenchman were nominated for the 2016 Ballon d'Or?
14 Who was Wigan Athletic's FA Cup-winning manager?
15 Matthew Briggs, youngest player ever in the Premier League, played for who?
16 With which club did striker Callum Wilson begin his professional career?
17 Which Englishman has managed the most Premier League matches?
18 Leicester City manager Claude Puel made 488 senior appearances for who?
19 Which Arsenal midfielder won "Match of the Day" goal of the season in both 2013/14 and 2014/15?
20 Who scored the only goal when Portugal beat France in the Euro 2016 Final?
21 What do Giorgio Chiellini, Otman Bakkal and Branislav Ivanovic have in common?
22 The second leg of which final was played at the Bernabeu Stadium in Dec 2018?
23 Henrik Larsson's last competitive goal at Celtic Park was scored against who?
24 Who played in 'invincible' teams in Scotland and England?
25 With which club did England's Jadon Sanchez begin his career?
26 Who was the last Englishman to win the Golden Boot before Harry Kane?
27 Which club side was Alan Ball playing for during the 1966 World Cup?
28 Harry Kane was top scorer of the World Cup 2018 – who shared second place?
29 Which Premier League striker has scored over 20 goals for Venezuela?
30 Which team has won the most EFL (Checkatrade) trophies?

Quiz 67 | Pot Luck 31

LEVEL 2

1 Nephology is the study of what?
2 What did Robert the Bruce die of?
3 Which constituency did Margaret Thatcher represent as an MP?
4 Dijon is famous for which condiment?
5 Which Robbie Burns hero gave his name to a flat cap?
6 Where is the Bay of Rainbows?
7 A nectarine is a cross between which two fruits?
8 Which top-selling band featured Stuart Cable on drums?
9 What is affected by osteomyelitis?
10 What is Charles II said to have hidden in after the Battle of Worcester?
11 What is the common name for the medication acetylsalicylic acid?
12 How is a Cardinal addressed?
13 When was the wearing of seat belts in the front of a car made compulsory?
14 Thabo Mbeki succeeded which President of South Africa?
15 Which fruit is in creme de cassis?
16 Which beacon was named after a 1930s Minister of Transport?
17 The Painted Desert is in which American state?
18 Who wrote "My Cousin Rachel" and "Frenchman's Creek"?
19 Whose hits include "Moonlighting" and "More Than I Can Say"?
20 Queen Juliana abdicated from which country's throne in 1980?
21 What fraction is a cable of a nautical mile?
22 What is the opposite of hibernation?
23 How many keys does a normal piano have?
24 Who was the most Googled person in Finland in 2016?
25 What is a corn-cockle?
26 What language does the word 'ketchup' derive from?
27 Which part of the body uses forty per cent of the oxygen in blood?
28 Which corpulent TV detective was played by William Conrad?
29 Who was the mother of King Solomon?
30 Who wrote "The Good Companions"?

Answers	Science: Space (see Quiz 68)

1 Arizona. 2 Weightless. 3 Jupiter. 4 Mir. 5 Ultima Thule. 6 Observatory. 7 50s.
8 Four. 9 Helen Sharman. 10 Star sailor. 11 Venus. 12 Comets. 13 European. 14 Far
side of the moon (South Pole-Aitken Basin). 15 Titan. 16 Sea of Tranquillity. 17 Venus.
18 France. 19 Yuri Gagarin. 20 Politics. 21 Cirrus. 22 Tim Peake. 23 Jupiter. 24 Mars.
25 Space station. 26 Space shuttle. 27 Gases. 28 USSR. 29 Orion. 30 Earth.

Quiz 68 | Science: Space

1 In 2004, the Large Binocular Telescope was built on Mt Graham in which US state?
2 Which word describes a body in free fall in space?
3 Which planet has the satellite Europa?
4 Which space station is named after the Russian word for "peace"?
5 In January 2019, Nasa's New Horizons probe sent back pictures of what?
6 What name is given to a site for watching astronomical phenomena?
7 In which decade was Sputnik 1 launched?
8 How many planets in our solar system have rings?
9 Who was Soyuz TM-12's British passenger in 1991?
10 The word astronaut is derived from Greek – what does it mean literally?
11 Uranus and which other planet in our solar system spin clockwise?
12 What is the Oort cloud made out of?
13 Which Space Agency built Ariane?
14 Where did the Chinese land a spacecraft in January 2019?
15 Which rockets shared their name with the giant children of Uranus and Gaia in Greek myth ?
16 Which part of the moon did Armstrong first walk on?
17 Which of our planets is nearest the end of the alphabet?
18 Claudie Andre-Deshays was the first woman in space from which country?
19 Whose spacecraft was Vostok 1?
20 After retiring as an astronaut John Glenn followed a career in what?
21 Which clouds are formed highest above the ground?
22 In 2016, who was the first man to run a marathon in space?
23 What is the largest planet in the solar system?
24 Phobos is a moon of which planet?
25 What was Skylab?
26 Which pioneering spacecraft was first launched in April 1981?
27 What is Jupiter's red spot made from?
28 Which country launched the first space probe in 1959?
29 Which constellation is known as The Hunter?
30 Which is larger, Mars or Earth?

| **Answers** | Pot Luck 31 *(see Quiz 67)* |

1 Clouds. 2 Leprosy. 3 Finchley. 4 Mustard. 5 Tam O'Shanter. 6 On the Moon. 7 Peach & plum. 8 Stereophonics. 9 The bones. 10 An oak tree. 11 Aspirin. 12 Your Eminence. 13 1983. 14 Nelson Mandela. 15 Blackcurrant. 16 Belisha Beacon. 17 Arizona. 18 Daphne du Maurier. 19 Leo Sayer. 20 The Netherlands. 21 1/10th. 22 Aestivation. 23 88. 24 Saara Aalto. 25 A flower. 26 Malay or Chinese. 27 The brain. 28 Cannon. 29 Bathsheba. 30 JB Priestley.

Quiz 69 | Pot Luck 32

1 Which creature do French sports fans traditionally let loose before the start of a big match?
2 Which king unveiled the Victoria memorial?
3 What is made by a testator?
4 Who telephoned Neil Armstrong during his first moon walk?
5 In the 2018 film "Mary Queen of Scots", who played Elizabeth?
6 Which wine-growing region is divided into Baja, Alta and Alavesa?
7 What does fibrin cause to happen to blood?
8 Did Buddy Holly die in 1956, 1959 or 1961?
9 In a retail context, what is a Klippan?
10 Which director appeared in "The Blues Brothers"?
11 In which century was the Taj Mahal constructed?
12 A Bordelaise sauce is flavoured by which vegetable?
13 Ben Nevis is in which mountain range?
14 Where would you probably be looking at a Snellen Chart?
15 In Bingo, what are numbers ending in zero called?
16 What do Sunderland and Benfica football clubs share?
17 Who is the Patron Saint of Venice?
18 What are Mycerinus and Cheprun the second two greatest of?
19 What would you be eating if you ate a Spanish chorizo?
20 Which scientist first discovered the composition of air?
21 Which British actress played Jo Sugden in "Emmerdale" from 2005 to 2008?
22 Which letter and number represent the vitamin riboflavin?
23 Derby, Pelham and Russell have all been what?
24 Who was John the Baptist's father?
25 Alan Stubbs broke his two spells at Everton by playing for which club?
26 Euston became Britain's first railway station to have what in 1848?
27 In 1921 which political party burnt down Dublin's Custom House?
28 Which part of your body is protected by puttees?
29 Which river flows through six different European countries?
30 What is the main ingredient in an Indian raita?

Answers	Performing Arts (see Quiz 70)

1 Glyndebourne. 2 Halle. 3 Voices. 4 Savoy. 5 Opera and ballet. 6 Theatre. 7 Royal Ballet. 8 Piano-style keyboard. 9 Placido Domingo. 10 Four. 11 National. 12 Joey. 13 Triangular. 14 Baritone. 15 Edinburgh. 16 New York. 17 Theatre Royal. 18 Trumpet. 19 George I. 20 Nigel Kennedy. 21 Liverpool Oratorio. 22 Organ. 23 Marcel Marceau. 24 Lin-Manuel Miranda. 25 Mermaid. 26 We never closed. 27 Electric guitars. 28 Tamla Motown. 29 Ayckbourn. 30 Roundhouse.

1 Which opera venue is near Lewes?
2 Sir John Barbirolli was conductor of which orchestra at the time of his death?
3 If a sonata is for instruments what is a cantata written for?
4 Which London theatre was the home of Gilbert & Sullivan operas?
5 Sadler's Wells theatre is famous for which performing arts?
6 Equity in the USA deals only with performers where?
7 Wayne Sleep was principal dancer with which ballet company?
8 What do you press with the right hand on an accordion?
9 Which of the Three Tenors played the title role in the film version of "Otello" in 1986?
10 How many strings are there on a double bass?
11 Richard Eyre replaced Peter Hall as artistic director at which London theatre?
12 What were all Joseph Grimaldi's clowns called?
13 What shape is the sound box on a balalaika?
14 Which male voice is between bass and tenor?
15 Where is an annual Fringe Festival held?
16 In which US city was the Actors Studio founded?
17 What is the official name of London's Drury Lane theatre?
18 Miles Davis is famous for playing which musical instrument?
19 Which king did Handel write The Water Music for?
20 Whose 1986 recording of Vivaldi's "The Four Seasons" sold over a million copies?
21 What was Paul McCartney's first classical oratorio?
22 An anthem is usually accompanied by which musical instrument?
23 Which mime artist created the clown-harlequin Bip?
24 The musical "Hamilton" opened in New York in 2015 – who wrote it?
25 Which theatre near Blackfriars was London's first new theatre in 300 years when opened in 1959?
26 What was the slogan of London's Windmill Theatre?
27 Which musical instruments did Leo Fender create?
28 What was the first black-owned record company in the USA?
29 Who has written more plays, Shakespeare or Ayckbourn?
30 Which Camden theatre re-opened in 2006?

| **Answers** | **Pot Luck 32** *(see Quiz 69)* |

1 Cockerel. 2 George V. 3 A Will. 4 Nixon. 5 Margot Robbie. 6 Rioja. 7 Clot.
8 1959. 9 Sofa, from IKEA. 10 Steven Spielberg. 11 17th. 12 Shallot. 13 The
Grampians. 14 Optician's. 15 Blind. 16 Grounds called The Stadium of Light. 17 St
Mark. 18 The Great Pyramids of Giza. 19 Sausage. 20 Joseph Priestley. 21 Roxanne
Pallett. 22 B2. 23 British Prime Ministers. 24 Zacharias. 25 Sunderland. 26 WH
Smiths. 27 Sinn Fein. 28 Legs. 29 Danube. 30 Yoghurt.

1 Hemel Hempstead and St Albans are in which county?
2 Who would use a quern?
3 Who played the title role in the film "The Wizard of Oz"?
4 Whom did Ricky Gervais play in "Extras"?
5 The Spanish Steps are in which European city?
6 Cars with the international vehicle registration CDN come from where?
7 Which Howard Keel film musical was based on the Roman legend of the rape of the Sabine women?
8 Which Russian-sounding horse won the 2,000 Guineas, St Leger and the Derby in 1970?
9 What kind of a plant is fescue?
10 When Judi Dench was dressed as a lobster for Film Four, how was Ewan McGregor dressed?
11 Which English actor played Lucius Malfoy in six of the eight Harry Potter movies?
12 Musically which note is half the value of a crotchet?
13 "Murder at the..." where was Miss Marple's first appearance?
14 In a retail context, what is a Billy?
15 Which writer Anthony created the county of Barsetshire?
16 What is the largest island in Asia?
17 Which part of an elephant has 40,000 muscles?
18 Who played the lead role in the film "The Prime of Miss Jean Brodie"?
19 Which type of sugar is found in milk?
20 What word can describe a lucky chance and the hook of an anchor?
21 Which female vocalist was known as 'The Force's Sweetheart'?
22 Which novel preceded "Good Wives"?
23 Which pop star married Bianca de Macias in May 1971?
24 Which football team did David Beckham sign for in January 2007?
25 Herod the Great ruled which kingdom?
26 Which Prince's childhood nickname was JAWS?
27 Who succeeded George Carey as Archbishop of Canterbury?
28 Which Blair-ite Alan became Secretary of State for Health?
29 What is the English equivalent of a Scottish Advocate?
30 What shape is a dish called a coquille?

Answers	Country & Western (see Quiz 72)

1 Johnny Cash. 2 D.I.V.O.R.C.E. 3 Pussycat. 4 Shania Twain. 5 Annie's Song.
6 Crazy. 7 1992. 8 Crystal Gayle. 9 Hank Williams. 10 Placido Domingo. 11 Our Song. 12 Kristofferson. 13 LeAnn Rimes. 14 Loretta Lynn. 15 Dolly Parton.
16 Reba McEntire. 17 Yodelling. 18 Chet Atkins. 19 Distant Drums. 20 Glen Campbell. 21 Waylon Jennings. 22 Dollywood. 23 Tammy Wynette. 24 Keith Urban.
25 Justified and Ancient. 26 Willie Nelson. 27 Emmylou Harris. 28 James Taylor.
29 Blue Suede Shoes. 30 Sheena Easton.

Quiz 72 | Country & Western | Answers – page 171

1 Who had a hit in 1972 with "A Thing Called Love"?
2 Which hit in letters followed "Stand by Your Man" for Tammy Wynette?
3 Which group had a No.1 hit in 1976 with "Mississippi"?
4 Which best-selling country and pop star married Mutt Lange?
5 Whose song was a No.1 for John Denver in 1974?
6 Which Patsy Cline hit was covered by Julio Iglesias in 1994?
7 In which year was "Achy Breaky Heart" a hit for Billy Ray Cyrus?
8 Who had a No.11 UK hit with "Talking in Your Sleep" in 1978?
9 Hiram Williams is the real name of which singer?
10 Which opera singer joined John Denver to record "Perhaps Love"?
11 In 2006, Taylor Swift topped the Hot Country Songs chart with which self-penned song?
12 Which Kris wrote "Help Me Make It Through the Night"?
13 Who had a hit in the summer of 1998 with "How Do I"?
14 Who wrote the autobiography "Coal Miner's Daughter"?
15 Who joined Kenny Rogers on the No. 7 hit "Islands in the Stream"?
16 What is Reba McEntire's real name?
17 Which specialist type of singing links Frank Ifield and Slim Whitman?
18 Who duetted with Mark Knopfler on the album "Neck and Neck"?
19 In the No.1, which drums were heard by Jim Reeves?
20 Who sang "All I Have to do Is Dream" with Bobbie Gentry in 1969?
21 Who had a backing band called the Waylors?
22 What is the name of the theme park owned by Dolly Parton?
23 George Jones' 1975 hit "The Battle" told of the split from his wife. Who was she?
24 Which country musician did Nicole Kidman marry in 2006?
25 Which song was a No. 2 UK hit for Tammy Wynette and KLF in 1991?
26 Who wrote the classic song "Crazy"?
27 Who formed the Trio with Dolly Parton and Linda Ronstadt?
28 Taylor Swift was named after which singer-songwriter?
29 Which No. 9 for Elvis was a No.10 for Carl Perkins in 1956?
30 Which "modern girl" joined Kenny Rogers on "We've Got Tonight"?

| **Answers** | Pot Luck 33 *(see Quiz 71)* |

1 Hertfordshire. 2 A miller. 3 Frank Morgan. 4 Andy. 5 Rome. 6 Canada.
7 Seven Brides for Seven Brothers. 8 Nijinsky. 9 Grass. 10 As a tomato. 11 Jason Isaacs. 12 Quaver. 13 Vicarage. 14 Bookcase, from IKEA. 15 Trollope. 16 Borneo. 17 The Trunk. 18 Maggie Smith. 19 Lactose. 20 Fluke. 21 Vera Lynn. 22 Little Women. 23 Mick Jagger. 24 LA Galaxy. 25 Judaea. 26 Prince Edward. 27 Rowan Williams. 28 Alan Milburn. 29 A barrister. 30 Shell-shaped.

1 What was the name of Kate Winslet's character in Titanic?
2 Who was Culture Secretary when the UK won the staging of the 2012 Olympics?
3 Which top-selling band featured Kian Egan on vocals?
4 What is kelp?
5 Who had hits with "Fox on the Run" and "Wig-Wam Bam"?
6 What name is an African lake, a station and a former Queen?
7 What type of vessel was the Torrey Canyon?
8 Which brewing company produces London Pride?
9 What is the more common name for toxaemia?
10 Which members of the big cat family collect in a leap?
11 Who preceded Harold Macmillan as Prime Minister?
12 In the Shakespeare play who killed Macbeth?
13 In which sitcom do Tamsin Greig and Stephen Mangan play Hollywood scriptwriters?
14 Newmarket and Ipswich are both in which county?
15 Reflexology treats your body through what?
16 What can be a short jacket and a dance?
17 What are auctioned at Tattersalls?
18 Who was Phileas Fogg's companion in "Around the World in 80 Days"?
19 Which French-Canadian became Canadian Prime Minister in 1968?
20 Archibald Leach, born in Bristol, became which Hollywood star?
21 In which decade did John Wayne die?
22 What is the capital of Kazakhstan?
23 Which part of your body would interest a rhinologist?
24 In 1926 what was held for the first time at Brooklands?
25 Mesopotamia was the ancient name for which modern-day country?
26 Which female singer made the album "Day without Rain"?
27 Whose report in the 1940s was vital in setting up the welfare state?
28 Which Stevie Wonder No.1 was in the film "The Woman in Red"?
29 What type of animal is a Lippizaner?
30 Which digit is your pollex?

Quiz 74 | Mohamed Salah

Answers – page 173

1 Which Arsenal player is Mo Salah's teammate in the Egypt national side?
2 Against which Premier League team did he score four in March 2018?
3 Who took the Liverpool number 10 shirt to allow him the number 11?
4 What is the name of his daughter – Medina, Malak or Makkah?
5 To which team did Chelsea loan him in 2015?
6 Whom did he beat to win African Player of the Year in both 2017 and 2018?
7 Whose challenge led to his injury in the 2018 Champions League Final?
8 In which year did he play in the Olympic Games?
9 With which Bosnian did he form a strike partnership at Roma?
10 How many million Euros did Liverpool initially pay for him – 35, 42 or 51?
11 In which year did he make his debut for Egypt?
12 Which Chelsea manager bought and sold him?
13 What number shirt does he wear when playing for Egypt?
14 With which team did he win the Super League in 2013?
15 What was his final Premier League goal tally in 2017/18 – 30, 31 or 32?
16 Against which future club did he score in both legs of a Champions League tie in 2013?
17 How old was he when he debuted for El Mokawloon?
18 Which manager bought him for Liverpool?
19 Against which team did he score twice in the 2018 Champions League semi-final?
20 Which former USA manager first picked him for Egypt?
21 How many goals did he score for Chelsea?
22 What part of his body did he injure in the 2018 Champions League Final?
23 How many games did he play in the 2018 World Cup finals?
24 Which award did he win for his 2018 goal against Everton at Anfield?
25 Against which nation did he score his first World Cup finals goal?
26 Which country's leader did he controversially pose with before the 2018 World Cup?
27 What two-word nickname was he given by Liverpool fans?
28 Liverpool fans have based their Salah chant on which 1990 James hit?
29 Whom did he beat to the Golden Boot in the 2017/18 season?
30 How many goals did he score in the 2018 World Cup finals?

Answers | Pot Luck 34 *(see Quiz 73)*

1 Rose. 2 Tessa Jowell. 3 Westlife. 4 Seaweed. 5 Sweet. 6 Victoria. 7 Oil tanker.
8 Fuller's. 9 Blood poisoning. 10 Leopards. 11 Anthony Eden. 12 Macduff.
13 Episodes. 14 Suffolk. 15 Soles of your feet. 16 Bolero. 17 Racehorses.
18 Passepartout. 19 Pierre Trudeau. 20 Cary Grant. 21 1970s. 22 Astana. 23 Nose.
24 British Grand Prix. 25 Iraq. 26 Enya. 27 William Beveridge. 28 I Just Called to Say I Love You. 29 A horse. 30 Thumb.

1 What was the first film in which Clint Eastwood starred as "The man with no name"?
2 Who played the sadistic sheriff in Eastwood's "Unforgiven"?
3 Which actor's films include "Big Jim McLain", "McLintock" and "McQ"?
4 Which star of "Maverick" played Brett Maverick in the TV series?
5 Who wrote the short story which "Brokeback Mountain" is based on?
6 What is the name of the original tale that the "Magificent Seven" is based on?
7 What weather feature was in the title of the song from Butch Cassidy won an Oscar?
8 Who was the star of "Jeremiah Johnson"?
9 Which comedy actor starred in the comedy western "The Paleface"?
10 Who starred with brother Charlie Sheen in "Young Guns"?
11 Which Oscar winner for "Fargo", married director Joel Coen?
12 Who played the woman poker player in "Maverick"?
13 Which actor was "The Bad"?
14 Which "Back to the Future" film returns to the Wild West?
15 In which musical western does the song "Wandrin' Star" appear?
16 Which Hollywood legend was the narrator in "How the West was Won"?
17 Which film was originally called "Per un Pugno di Dollari"?
18 Which country singer was in "True Grit"?
19 How many 'episodes' are there in the anthology movie "The Ballad of Buster Scruggs"?
20 Whom did John Wayne play in "The Alamo"?
21 Clint Eastwood became mayor of which town?
22 Which 1985 film was a revised remake of the classic "Shane"?
23 Where is the village where the action of "The Magnificent Seven" centres?
24 Where was "The Good, the Bad and the Ugly" made?
25 What was the name of Mel Brooks' spoof western?
26 Which English comic appeared in "Desperado"?
27 Which 80s teenage western starred actors known as the Brat Pack?
28 What was Tonto's horse called?
29 Who was Gene Autry's most famous horse?
30 Traditionally, what colour is the western hero's hat?

1 Which Queen wrote the Casket Letters?
2 Yamoussoukro is the capital city of which African country?
3 What can be metric royal, metric demy and metric crown?
4 In which TV series was the character "Boss Hogg"?
5 Who succeeded Charles Clarke as Home Secretary?
6 Which almond cake is traditionally made for Mothering Sunday?
7 Who had hits with "We are Glass" and "Cars"?
8 Ingvar Kamprad founded which retail chain?
9 Which actress had lead roles in the films "Out of Africa" and "Silkwood"?
10 Which two European languages are spoken in Madagascar?
11 Where was actress Saoirse Ronan born?
12 What were the giant insects in the science fiction film "Them"?
13 What lies near Geneva in a tunnel 27km in circumference?
14 During which war does Norman Mailer's "The Naked and the Dead" take place?
15 Aylesbury and Milton Keynes are both in which county?
16 Which film director based "Tea with Mussolini" on his own experiences in 1930s Florence?
17 Which animal was used by Jenner to develop the vaccine against smallpox?
18 What is a davenport?
19 Which singer starred alongside Kyle McLachlan in "Dune"?
20 Who composed the music for "The Good, the Bad and the Ugly"?
21 Who had hits with "Blue Monday" and "World in Motion"?
22 What kind of musical instrument was a kit?
23 In "Peanuts", what is Charlie Brown's little sister called?
24 Which John Carpenter film set in the Antarctic starred Kurt Russell?
25 Name the first yacht to win the America's Cup?
26 Which singing sisters were called Patti, Laverne and Maxine?
27 Who is the Hindu goddess of love and devotion?
28 What name is given to the principal female singer in an opera?
29 The dish Eggs Florentine contains which vegetable?
30 What is Carrie Anne Moss's character's name in the "Matrix" sci-fi thrillers?

| **Answers** | Movies: Westerns *(see Quiz 75)* |

1 A Fistful of Dollars. 2 Gene Hackman. 3 John Wayne. 4 James Garner. 5 Annie Proulx. 6 The Seven Samurai. 7 Raindrops. 8 Robert Redford. 9 Bob Hope. 10 Emilio Estevez. 11 Frances McDormand. 12 Jodie Foster. 13 Lee van Cleef. 14 No. III. 15 Paint Your Wagon. 16 Spencer Tracy. 17 A Fistful of Dollars. 18 Glen Campbell. 19 Six. 20 Davy Crockett. 21 Carmel. 22 Pale Rider. 23 Mexico. 24 Italy. 25 Blazing Saddles. 26 John Cleese. 27 Young Guns. 28 Scout. 29 Champion. 30 White.

1 The Sargasso Sea is part of which ocean?
2 Which US city's name means "The Fields"?
3 How is New York's "Great White Way" also known?
4 Which Canadians speak Inuktitut?
5 Which Cape was originally called the Cape of Storms?
6 In America what type of natural phenomenon is a Chinook?
7 What is the principal island of Japan?
8 Where is the town of Kurri Kurri?
9 The Guangzhou TV & Sightseeing Tower was constructed in which country?
10 By which abbreviation is the mountain Chogori known?
11 What is the only permanent river in the Kalahari Desert?
12 Which ocean's deepest point is the Java Trench?
13 Where would you be if someone put a lei round your neck?
14 Where is the world's longest canal?
15 Afrikaans is the official language of which country in addition to South Africa?
16 In which desert is the Bactrian camel found?
17 What is the name of the index on the New York Stock Exchange?
18 Which group of people have a name meaning "eater of raw meat"?
19 Which is the only Great Lake wholly in the USA?
20 The Kariba Dam is on the border of which two countries?
21 Calypso is the traditional song form of which Caribbean island?
22 Which European language is spoken in Chad?
23 Las Palmas is in which island group?
24 Approximately where was Carthage to be found?
25 Wall Street and Broadway lie on which island?
26 Where is the Magellan Strait?
27 What is the largest island between the North Atlantic and the Arctic?
28 What is Africa's highest volcano?
29 Where is there a Parliament called the Knesset?
30 Which two countries does the Khyber Pass separate?

| **Answers** | Pot Luck 36 *(see Quiz 78)* |

1 A small rock plant. 2 Chrissie Watts. 3 The Old Man of the Sea. 4 Nothing.
5 Jemini. 6 A nap. 7 Harlequins. 8 Baz Luhrmann. 9 Billy Joel. 10 Greenland.
11 Anne Archer. 12 A musical instrument. 13 Antelope. 14 Tom Parker Bowles.
15 Mrs Bridges. 16 Lionel Richie. 17 The Blarney Stone. 18 Richard Chamberlain.
19 Scrumps. 20 George Gershwin. 21 A bird. 22 Crystal Palace. 23 Grange Hill.
24 Derek Wilton. 25 Olive. 26 Hercule Poirot. 27 Jonathan Larson. 28 Violin. 29 A midwife. 30 Morecambe and Wise.

Quiz 78 | Pot Luck 36

Answers – page 177

LEVEL 2

1 What is saxifrage?
2 In "EastEnders" which character killed Dirty Den in February 2006?
3 Who hoisted himself on to Sinbad the Sailor's shoulders?
4 How much are you paid if you hold an honorary post?
5 Which UK act first scored the dreaded "nul points" in the Eurovision Song Contest?
6 What can be a five-card game, a smooth, woolly surface or a sleep?
7 Which club did Will Carling play for?
8 Which Australian movie director links "Romeo and Juliet" and "Strictly Ballroom"?
9 Whose music albums have included "An Innocent Man"?
10 'Englander' is an anagram of which country?
11 Which actress played Michael Douglas's wife in "Fatal Attraction"?
12 What is a melodeon?
13 Which animal family are impala, eland and dik-dik all from?
14 Which famous stepson wrote "The Year of Eating Dangerously"?
15 In TV's "Upstairs Downstairs" what was the name of the cook?
16 Whose hits include "Dancin' on the Ceiling" and "Do It to Me"?
17 Which stone is inscribed "Cormac McCarthy fortis me fieri fecit AD 1446"?
18 Which actor played the leading role in the TV drama "Shogun"?
19 What name is given to withered apples used to make rough cider?
20 Who composed the music for the musical "Lady be Good"?
21 What is a grackle?
22 Which building was erected in 1851 for the Great Exhibition?
23 Which children's TV series has included Tucker Jenkins and Zammo?
24 Which "Corrie" character died with Gilbert and Sullivan playing in his car?
25 Which branch would you hold out to seek peace?
26 Arthur Hastings was the sidekick of which fictional sleuth?
27 Who wrote the musical "Rent"?
28 The leader of an orchestra plays which instrument?
29 What was Mab's job in fairy folklore?
30 Who starred in the film "That Riviera Touch"?

Answers | World Tour *(see Quiz 77)*

1 Atlantic. 2 Las Vegas. 3 Broadway. 4 Inuit (Eskimos). 5 Cape of Good Hope. 6 Wind. 7 Honshu. 8 Australia. 9 China. 10 K2. 11 Okovango. 12 Indian. 13 Hawaii. 14 China. 15 Namibia. 16 Gobi. 17 Dow Jones. 18 Eskimo. 19 Michigan. 20 Zambia and Zimbabwe. 21 Trinidad. 22 French. 23 Canaries. 24 North coast of Africa. 25 Manhattan. 26 Tip of South America. 27 Greenland. 28 Kilimanjaro. 29 Israel. 30 Pakistan & Afghanistan.

Quiz 79 — Past Times: The 80s

Answers – page 180 — LEVEL 2

1 The Hillsborough Agreement was between which two countries?
2 Where was there a major nuclear leak in the USSR in 1986?
3 Who was the last white President of South Africa, elected in 1989?
4 Which former liberal leader was made speaker of the national assembly of Czechoslovakia in 1989?
5 A fatwa calling for the death of which writer was made by Iran in '89?
6 Who succeeded Callaghan as Labour leader?
7 Who became France's first socialist president in 1981?
8 Who was Argentine President during the Falklands Conflict?
9 Which 80s female hit maker is a celebrity gardener this century?
10 Michael Manley became leader of where in 1989?
11 Who owned Rainbow Warrior, sunk by the French in 1985?
12 Vigdis Finnbogadottir became head of state in which country?
13 How many times was Margaret Thatcher elected PM in the 80s?
14 Which film featured "(I've Had) The Time of My Life" in its soundtrack?
15 Who was leader of the GLC from 1981–86?
16 What was the Black day of the week of the 1987 stockmarket crash?
17 Who moved from Transport House to Walworth Road in 1980?
18 In which hotel was the Brighton bomb in 1984?
19 Who became President of Serbia in 1986?
20 Most of which Caribbean island's buildings were destroyed by hurricane Hugo in 1989?
21 Who became Egyptian President after Sadat's assassination?
22 What was the name of the scandal over arms for hostages in which Oliver North was implicated?
23 Which one-time member of Tony Blair's cabinet was leader of Sheffield City Council?
24 Whom did Ronald Reagan defeat to become US President in 1980?
25 Which spin doctor did Neil Kinnock engage to run the 1987 election campaign?
26 In 1989 state schools were allowed to opt out of whose control?
27 Which woman became PM of Pakistan after the death of Zia in a plane crash?
28 Where did the parties of ZANU and ZAPU merge in 1987?
29 In 1986 the pass laws, concerning the carrying of identity documents, were repealed in which country?
30 Which Russian leader introduced the policy of perestroika?

Answers | Pot Luck 37 *(see Quiz 80)*

1 Monkey. 2 Man Utd. 3 James II. 4 Matt LeBlanc. 5 An acre. 6 Dauphin. 7 The Ouse. 8 Sandie Shaw. 9 Clement Attlee. 10 July. 11 Ray Stevens. 12 Ferdinand Marcos. 13 Menin Gate. 14 Peter Sellers. 15 Queen Latifah. 16 Arthritis. 17 A train. 18 Boris Pasternak. 19 The Archers. 20 John Cleese. 21 Kitchen cabinets, from IKEA. 22 Henry VIII. 23 Tommy Steele. 24 Jimmy Young. 25 Supertramp. 26 1979. 27 The Lord is my shepherd. 28 Yaks. 29 A prison camp. 30 Tony Curtis.

Quiz 80 | Pot Luck 37

1 What type of animal is a Sooty Mangabey?
2 Which team lost the first FA Cup Final decided on penalties?
3 Whom did William III defeat in 1690 at the Battle of the Boyne?
4 Which American actor plays a parody of himself in "Episodes"?
5 In Old English which word meant a field?
6 What were the eldest sons of French kings called from the 14th century?
7 Ely stands on which river?
8 Which 60s singer married the designer Jeff Banks?
9 In 1945, who became British Prime Minister?
10 In which month in 2006 was "Top of the Pops" aired for the last time?
11 Who had hits with "The Streak" and "Misty" in the 70s?
12 Who was President of the Philippines from 1965 to 1986?
13 Which Gate is a memorial for British soldiers who fell at Ypres?
14 Who played Fred Kite in the film "I'm Alright, Jack"?
15 In "Bringing Down the House" Steve Martin starred with which rapper?
16 Which complaint was the Jacuzzi originally developed to help?
17 What did Anna Karenina throw herself under in the Tolstoy novel?
18 Who wrote "Dr Zhivago"?
19 In which soap does the Cat & Fiddle rival The Bull?
20 Which comedian was Connie Booth married to?
21 In a retail context, what is Metod?
22 Who preceded Edward VI as Monarch?
23 In the film "The Tommy Steele Story" who played Tommy Steele?
24 Who finished his radio show with "B.F.N. Bye for now"?
25 Who had hits with "The Logical Song" and "Dreamer"?
26 In which year was Lord Mountbatten murdered?
27 What is the start of Psalm 23?
28 Which shaggy horned wild cattle live in the Tibetan mountains?
29 What was a gulag in Russia?
30 In the 1953 film "Houdini" who played the title role?

| **Answers** | **Past Times: The 80s** *(see Quiz 79)* |

1 UK and Eire. 2 Chernobyl. 3 FW de Klerk. 4 Dubcek. 5 Salman Rushdie. 6 Michael Foot. 7 Mitterrand. 8 Galtieri. 9 Kim Wilde. 10 Jamaica. 11 Greenpeace. 12 Iceland. 13 Twice. 14 Dirty Dancing. 15 Ken Livingstone. 16 Monday. 17 The Labour Party. 18 Grand Hotel. 19 Slobodan Milosevic. 20 Montserrat. 21 Mubarak. 22 Irangate. 23 David Blunkett. 24 Jimmy Carter. 25 Peter Mandelson. 26 Local authority. 27 Benazir Bhutto. 28 Zimbabwe. 29 South Africa. 30 Mikhail Gorbachev.

1 In which university city is the Bodleian Library?
2 In which book does Bishop Aringarosa visit Castel Gandolfo?
3 "Uncle Tom's Cabin" was a novel which argued against what?
4 In the US what type of book is Webster famous for?
5 Who is the most famous manservant created by PG Wodehouse?
6 What was Muhammad Ali's autobiography called?
7 Which Dorothy L Sayers' creation was Harriet Vane's husband?
8 Which children's classic was written to encourage adults to be kinder to horses?
9 Which book by ex-intelligence agent Peter Wright, did the British government try to have banned?
10 What was the subject of Benjamin Spock's most famous books?
11 Which soap star wrote "Prime Time"?
12 Which ex-Chancellor of the Exchequer wrote a diet book?
13 Whose first successful novel was "Light a Penny Candle"?
14 What "Are not the Only Fruit" according to Jeanette Winterson?
15 Who wrote the detective novel "Road Rage"?
16 Who wrote "A Walk in the Woods"?
17 "The Murder of Roger Ackroyd" was an early novel by whom?
18 Which is Mario Puzo's most famous novel, first published in 1969?
19 Which Michael Ondaatje book was made into an Oscar-winning film with Ralph Fiennes?
20 Who created George Smiley?
21 Which was the first Thomas Keneally book to win the Booker Prize?
22 Which birth control campaigner wrote the book "Married Love"?
23 What was Frederick Forsyth's follow-up to "The Day of the Jackal"?
24 Which gardening expert wrote "Nobbut a Lad"?
25 "The Woman in White" is the first novel of what type in English?
26 Whose "Not a Penny More, Not a Penny Less" was written to clear bankruptcy debts?
27 In Colin Dexter's books where does Lewis come from?
28 Which Dickens novel is about the French Revolution?
29 What is the second book of the Old Testament?
30 Which Georges wrote over a hundred novels featuring Jules Maigret?

Quiz 82 | Pot Luck 38

LEVEL 2

1 What did MGM stand for?

2 What colour is puce?

3 Which YouTuber was criticized for filming a corpse in Japan's 'suicide forest'?

4 Who was the first presenter of the TV series "Tomorrow's World"?

5 Which cartoon character was the "fastest mouse in Mexico"?

6 Who had 90s No.1 hits with "The Power" and "Rhythm is a Dancer"?

7 Which US state is the second smallest?

8 According to the saying, who rush in where angels fear to tread?

9 What is Blue Vinney?

10 Who wrote "Five Children and It" and "Wet Magic"?

11 Which terrier is the largest of the breed?

12 Who was the head of the German SS?

13 What is studied by a haematologist?

14 Which county is Morganwg Ganol in Welsh?

15 What type of creature is a turnstone?

16 Which country from 1867–1914 had a governor called The Khedive?

17 In the film "The Great Escape" which actor played the Forger?

18 Which Egyptian President was assassinated in 1981?

19 In the TV series "To the Manor Born" what was the name of the butler?

20 In the 2018 film "Mary Queen of Scots", who played Mary?

21 Who had hits with "Kiss from a Rose" and "Crazy"?

22 The town of Newcastle is in which Australian state?

23 What was Marc Bolan's real name?

24 What type of food is a bullace?

25 What is a snake's cast-off skin called?

26 The holiday camp Maplins featured in which TV series?

27 "Did You Hear the Rain" was the October 2013 debut EP of which artist?

28 What is mineral water mixed with quinine called?

29 Jeremy Sandford wrote which 1960s drama about homelessness?

30 What was sought by Jason and the Argonauts?

Answers | Books 2 (see Quiz 81)

1 Oxford. 2 The Da Vinci Code. 3 Slavery. 4 Dictionary. 5 Jeeves. 6 The Greatest.
7 Lord Peter Wimsey. 8 Black Beauty. 9 Spycatcher. 10 Childcare. 11 Joan Collins.
12 Nigel Lawson. 13 Maeve Binchy. 14 Oranges. 15 Ruth Rendell. 16 Bill Bryson.
17 Agatha Christie. 18 The Godfather. 19 The English Patient. 20 John le Carré.
21 Schindler's Ark. 22 Marie Stopes. 23 The Odessa File. 24 Alan Titchmarsh.
25 Detective novel. 26 Jeffrey Archer. 27 Wales. 28 A Tale of Two Cities. 29 Exodus.
30 Simenon.

Quiz 83 | Pop Music: Groups

Answers – page 184

1 What was the name of Georgie Fame's backing group?
2 What nationality were "All That She Wants" group Ace of Base?
3 Whose "Live in Hyde Park" album celebrated the success of the 2004 concerts?
4 What "Sensation" were the Bay City Rollers singing about in 1974?
5 Huey Lewis was vocalist for which group?
6 Which Company band had a hit with "Give Me Just a Little More Time"?
7 What did Go West close in their No. 5 from 1985?
8 What followed in brackets on "I'd Like To Teach the World to Sing"?
9 Who did the Wonder Stuff serve as backing group for?
10 Which heavy band took "When Love and Hate Collide" to No. 2?
11 What was Oasis' first UK Top Ten single?
12 What was The Beach Boys' first UK No.1?
13 Which band made the hit album "Home"?
14 Who is the lead singer of Franz Ferdinand?
15 Ginger, Jack and Eric formed which trio?
16 In which year did Oasis first have a No.1-selling album?
17 Which "Hotel" was visited by the Eagles in 1977?
18 What part of the day took the Stranglers to No. 7 in 1988?
19 In 1982, what was the name of the first UK No.1 by a German group?
20 Which Last Train did KLF catch in their No. 2 UK hit in 1991?
21 Singer/ songwriter David Gates led which group?
22 Who was the brother in the title of a track by Free from 1970?
23 Which girl band had hits with "Manic Monday" and "Walk Like an Egyptian"?
24 Which Irish group had a No. 5 hit with the "Theme from Harry's Game"?
25 What action were M People doing in their No. 2 UK hit from 1993?
26 What relative was "Perfect" according to the hit by the Undertones?
27 Who was the female artist in Vinegar Joe?
28 Which classical crossover/electropop group was formed in Cambridge in 2008?
29 What sort of girl took Jamiroquai to No. 6 in 1996?
30 Where was ZZ Top on the No.10 hit Viva?

Answers	Pot Luck 39 (see Quiz 84)

1 Ray Parker, Jr. 2 Bolton. 3 Twelve. 4 Pigs. 5 Pain. 6 Switzerland. 7 In the morning. 8 The Threepenny Opera. 9 President Marcos. 10 A lie detector. 11 Chicago. 12 D. 13 The Clifton. 14 Krakatoa. 15 A bell. 16 The North Sea. 17 Ant & Dec. 18 Hormones. 19 Deci. 20 16. 21 V & A. 22 Monastery. 23 The bluebell. 24 Newmarket. 25 Martin Luther King. 26 Northern England. 27 San Andreas. 28 Carl Lewis. 29 Spain. 30 Hippocrates.

1 Who was the first Briton to hold a world javelin record?

2 Hidetoshi Nakata of Japan made his Premier League debut with which club?

3 How many players are there in a Canadian football team?

4 Chester Whites, Durocs and Hampshire are all types of what animal?

5 What is killed by an analgesic?

6 The Dufourspitze is the highest mountain where?

7 When do ducks always lay their eggs?

8 In which Bertolt Brecht and Kurt Weill musical play is the song "Mack the Knife"?

9 Who preceded Corazon Aquino as President of the Philippines?

10 Which test would you be taking if you underwent a polygraph test?

11 Which American city's football team is called the Bears?

12 Which vitamin deficiency causes rickets?

13 Which suspension bridge crosses the River Avon?

14 Which volcano erupted in 1883 and lies between Java and Sumatra?

15 What is the vocal tinkling sound made by a deer called?

16 Which sea surrounds Heligoland?

17 Which famous TV duo starred in the sci-fi comedy "Alien Autopsy"?

18 The pituitary gland controls the production of what in the body?

19 Which prefix is a tenth in the metric system?

20 How many pounds does the Olympic hammer weigh?

21 Which museum hosted Kylie: The Exhibition from February to June 2007?

22 What was a Minster originally attached to?

23 What is the popular name for the wood hyacinth?

24 Where is Britain's National Horseracing Museum?

25 Whom did James Earl Ray assassinate?

26 Which area did Rob Brydon and Steve Coogan tour in the first series of "The Trip"?

27 Which fault line is San Francisco on?

28 Who won 100m gold at the 1988 Olympics after Ben Johnson's disqualification?

29 Where was the terrorist group ETA mainly active?

30 Who was called the Father of Medicine?

Answers	Pop Music: Groups *(see Quiz 83)*

1 The Blue Flames. 2 Swedish. 3 Red Hot Chilli Peppers. 4 Summer Love. 5 The News. 6 Chairmen of the Board. 7 Our eyes. 8 In Perfect Harmony. 9 Vic Reeves. 10 Def Leppard. 11 Live Forever. 12 Good Vibrations. 13 Simply Red. 14 Alex Kapranos. 15 Cream. 16 1994. 17 California. 18 All Day and All of the Night. 19 Computer Love/The Model. 20 To Trancentral. 21 Bread. 22 Jake. 23 The Bangles. 24 Clannad. 25 Moving On Up. 26 My Perfect Cousin. 27 Elkie Brooks. 28 Clean Bandit. 29 Cosmic Girl. 30 Las Vegas.

1 Whom did Muhammad Ali beat when he first became world champion?
2 Who was runner up to Jana Novotna in the Wimbledon final in 1998?
3 Who was the first heavyweight boxing champion to retire undefeated?
4 Who was the late Flo Jo's husband?
5 Which husband of Marilyn Monroe was elected to the Baseball Hall of Fame?
6 Whose life was recorded on film in "Raging Bull"?
7 Which British sprinter was 2018 European champion at 100m and 200m?
8 Which snooker champion was unkindly nicknamed Dracula?
9 Who beat Phil Taylor in the 2007 World Professional Darts Championship Final?
10 Whom did Zola Budd trip up at the Los Angeles Olympics in 1984?
11 British-born long jumper Fiona May represents which country in international athletics?
12 Which South African golfer's real first name is Theodore?
13 Which golfer split with his coach and his girlfriend in September '98?
14 Whom did Stephen Hendry replace as world No.1 in the 1989–90 season?
15 Away from cricket, what sort of book did Aussie Matthew Hayden write?
16 Who was appointed USA captain for the 2008 Ryder Cup?
17 Who lost most Ladies Singles finals at Wimbledon in the 80s?
18 Which surname has been shared by three world snooker champions?
19 Peter Nicol won Commonwealth gold for Scotland in which sport?
20 Who successfully defended her heptathlon title at the 1998 Commonwealth Games?
21 Which cricketer with a very English surname was made South Africa captain in 2003?
22 Who is the only 21st century Scottish winner of the BBC Sports Personality of the Year apart from Andy Murray?
23 Which Liverpudlian won the WBC Light Heavyweight Title in 1974?
24 Sharron Davies' one time fiancé Neil Adams was an international in which sport?
25 Who replaced Leon Spinks as Heavyweight Champion in 1987?
26 Who defeated Navratilova in the final at her last Wimbledon?
27 Who captained Europe to Ryder Cup success in 1995?
28 Allison Fisher is a former world champion in which sport?
29 Whom did John McEnroe win five Wimbledon Doubles titles with?
30 Which boxer is nicknamed "The Dark Destroyer"?

1 Which "Game for a Laugh" presenters had the same surname?
2 Who was the subject of "The Naked Civil Servant" with John Hurt?
3 Which sitcom told of Tooting revolutionary Wolfie?
4 Who found fame as "The Saint"?
5 Who played Louie de Palma in "Taxi"?
6 Which spaghetti western star played in "Rawhide" for six years?
7 Who conducted Eric Morecambe playing Grieg's Piano Concerto?
8 Which reporter found fame during her reporting of the Iranian Embassy siege in 1980?
9 In which weekly drama slot was "Cathy Come Home" first shown?
10 Which star of "The Likely Lads" starred in "New Tricks" with Alun Armstrong?
11 Who was the main character on "The Phil Silvers Show"?
12 Who became Mrs Clayton Farlow in "Dallas"?
13 Which series looked back at film clips 25 years old?
14 How were Bruce Wayne and Dick Grayson better known?
15 Which "Carry On" regular was the star of "Bless This House"?
16 Who was "lower class" on "The Frost Report" after John Cleese and Ronnie Barker?
17 Which soap was originally called "The Midland Road"?
18 Which famous singer/actor's daughter shot JR?
19 Which TV veteran narrated "Planet Earth"?
20 What was the surname of Morticia and Gomez?
21 Which area of the country received TV after the area London in 1949?
22 In which sitcom did Richard Beckinsale play Alan Moore?
23 Which series told of the bizarre life of the Clampett family?
24 Polly James and who else were the original Liver Birds?
25 Who played Dr Mark Sloan's son, homicide detective Steve, in "Diagnosis Murder"?
26 What was the BBC's first soap of the 60s?
27 Which actor played the part of Uncle Albert in "Only Fools and Horses"?
28 The controversial "Death of a Princess" caused a rift with which country in 1980?
29 Who had a long-running TV show before starring in "Mary Poppins"?
30 Who is the only "Corrie" star remaining from the original cast?

Answers	**Sport: Who's Who** *(see Quiz 85)*

1 Sonny Liston. 2 Natalie Tauziat. 3 Rocky Marciano. 4 Al Joyner. 5 Joe DiMaggio. 6 Jake La Motta. 7 Dina Asher-Smith. 8 Ray Reardon. 9 Raymond van Barneveld. 10 Mary Decker Slaney. 11 Italy. 12 Ernie Els. 13 Nick Faldo. 14 Steve Davis. 15 Cook book. 16 Paul Azinger. 17 Chris Evert. 18 Davis. 19 Squash. 20 Denise Lewis. 21 Graeme Smith. 22 Chris Hoy. 23 John Conteh. 24 Judo. 25 Mike Tyson. 26 Conchita Martinez. 27 Bernard Gallacher. 28 Snooker. 29 Peter Fleming. 30 Nigel Benn.

1 Who would deliver an edict called a bull?

2 What is a shooting brake?

3 Who does the RNID provide help for?

4 What was the first No.1 single for Stereophonics?

5 Which Danish keeper played for Sunderland and Aston Villa?

6 The Dalai Lama is the spiritual leader of where?

7 In English history what was danegeld?

8 What is the capital of Bavaria?

9 How many days does a decathlon event last?

10 The US Delta Force is based on which British anti-terrorist force?

11 In which country did denim originate?

12 What was the codename for the operation to eject the Iraqis from Kuwait in 1991?

13 Who was the first person to manage and captain a World Cup-winning football side?

14 David was responsible for the adoption of what as a Welsh emblem?

15 What shape is the approved mark of the British Standards Institution?

16 At what occasion do you see a returning officer?

17 Caries is the decay and deterioration of what?

18 Which club's president is the Chief Barker?

19 Where did the UK's first IKEA open?

20 Where in London is the Strangers' Gallery?

21 What is the study of twins called?

22 What sort of institution is UCH?

23 The Battle of Bunker Hill was the first major engagement of what?

24 What name is given to a bump in the road to slow down traffic?

25 What is the profession of an RGN?

26 Whose flag is the red ensign?

27 Which degree of burns is life-threatening?

28 The biography of which late hell-raising actor was called "Behaving Badly"?

29 Which bell is found in the building of Lloyd's of London?

30 What colour is the ceremonial dress of a Yeoman of the Guard?

Answers	Pop: Who's Who? *(see Quiz 91)*

1 Bay City Rollers. 2 Barbra Streisand. 3 Bill Tarmey. 4 Shakin' Stevens 5 Kate Bush. 6 Chris De Burgh. 7 Bruce Springsteen. 8 The Spice Girls. 9 Bono. 10 Richard Clayderman. 11 George Michael. 12 Emerson, Lake & Palmer. 13 Ed Sheeran. 14 Meatloaf. 15 Celine Dion. 16 Michael Caine. 17 Bill Medley. 18 Ken Hutchinson – Hutch. 19 Right Said Fred. 20 David Bowie. 21 Lily the Pink. 22 George Michael. 23 Rod Stewart. 24 Shirley Bassey. 25 Morten. 26 Coco Hernandez. 27 Jarvis Cocker. 28 The Kemp Brothers. 29 Victoria (Posh Spice). 30 Canadian.

Quiz 88 | Freddie Flintoff

Answers – page 191

1 Was Freddie born in 1975, 1977 or 1980?
2 He isn't a Freddie, but what's his real name?
3 How many centuries did he make in the 2005 Ashes series?
4 Freddie first captained England in which country?
5 In 2009, what did he develop after surgery to his knee?
6 At which ground did he make his Test debut?
7 Is his first daughter named Carol, Holly or Ivy?
8 Aged 17 he first appeared for which county?
9 What is Freddie's star sign?
10 In the 2005 Ashes did he score just over 400, 450 or 500 runs?
11 What does he have tattooed on his left shoulder?
12 Against which country did he make his maiden Test century?
13 Although he later came out of retirement, in what year did he first retire from cricket?
14 Freddie's a right-handed batsman, but which is his bowling arm?
15 In 2012, at what sport did he beat American Richard Dawson?
16 His Test debut was against which country?
17 Who was the scheduled series Test skipper when Freddie took over?
18 In the 2014/15 season, which team did he play for in the Australian Big Bash League?
19 He was in which country when his second child was born in 2006?
20 Who shared the ICC joint player of the year award with Freddie in 2005?
21 Who is the other team captain on "A League of Their Own"?
22 What's the name of his Radio 5 podcast?
23 Against which country did he make his one-day England debut?
24 Which famous Lancashire cricketer Neil became Freddie's agent?
25 What did Freddie wear on his face for the official 2005 Ashes celebrations?
26 In March 2006 Freddie became the England player to hit most what in Tests?
27 In 2018 the BBC announced that he would present which flagship show?
28 Against which country did he first have a series batting average of 50 plus?
29 In which London square did the main 2005 Ashes celebrations take place?
30 Which Lancashire skipper Michael watched Freddie break into county cricket?

Answers | Pot Luck 40 (see Quiz 87)

1 The Pope. 2 Estate car. 3 The deaf. 4 Dakota. 5 Thomas Sorensen. 6 Tibet.
7 Tax. 8 Munich. 9 Two. 10 SAS. 11 France (de Nimes). 12 Operation Desert
Storm. 13 Franz Beckenbauer. 14 Leek. 15 Kite-shaped. 16 Election. 17 Teeth or
bone. 18 Variety Club. 19 Warrington. 20 Houses of Parliament. 21 Geminology.
22 Hospital. 23 American Revolution. 24 Sleeping policeman. 25 Nurse.
26 Merchant Navy. 27 Third degree. 28 Richard Harris. 29 Lutine Bell. 30 Red.

Quiz 89 | Pot Luck 41

Answers – page 190

1 Deva was a Roman city now known as what?

2 Spanning 30 years on the charts, how is Tony Fitzgerald better known?

3 What does a kleptomaniac do?

4 What is the popular name for the anaesthetic nitrous oxide?

5 Who was the first woman to be awarded the Order of Merit?

6 The doomed ship Titanic was registered in which English city?

7 In which year did Marc Bolan die?

8 What is made up of the minor arcana and the major arcana?

9 The Romanian dictator Ceausescu was executed on which day in 1989?

10 In "The Life and Death of Peter Sellers", who played his wife Britt Ekland?

11 Dame Eliza Manningham Buller was head of which organisation in 2006?

12 Which Lou was vocalist with the Velvet Underground?

13 Which shipping forecast area is due north of Rockall?

14 Which pier featured in a George Orwell book title?

15 If you are an angler why are you pleased if your monkey starts to climb?

16 In which city was painter LS Lowry born?

17 Where was King Arthur taken after his last battle?

18 Did "Dead Ringers" begin on radio or TV?

19 Which all-male bastion allowed women members for the first time in September 1998?

20 Who made the first televised 147 in snooker, in 1982?

21 Which Prince's childhood nickname was "The Sniggerer"?

22 Who wrote the "Emperor Concerto"?

23 What happened to the Banksy picture "Girl With Balloon" which sold for £1 million at Sotheby's in 2018.

24 How many Inns of Court are there in London?

25 Who is the Hindu goddess of death and destruction?

26 Whose codename was "Pink" before she was surprised on "This is Your Life"?

27 What is a pommel a part of?

28 Cars with the international vehicle registration Z come from where?

29 In which century was the Battle of Naseby?

30 How many pecks are there in a bushel?

Answers	Who was Who? *(see Quiz 90)*

1 James Callaghan. 2 Sgt Pepper's Lonely Hearts Club Band. 3 President Eisenhower. 4 De Gaulle. 5 Nehru. 6 Al Gore. 7 Fuhrer. 8 Alexandra. 9 Andrei Gromyko. 10 Sir Geoffrey Howe. 11 Beeching. 12 Andy Warhol. 13 Baldwin. 14 One day. 15 Shirley Bassey. 16 Sebastian Coe. 17 Nelson Mandela. 18 St Augustine. 19 Gerald Ford. 20 Mussolini. 21 Billy Graham. 22 Edward Heath. 23 Catherine Howard. 24 John Major. 25 George Robertson. 26 Horatia. 27 Ann Widdecombe. 28 Protestant. 29 President Tito. 30 Physics.

1 Who was Chancellor, Foreign Secretary and PM between 1964 and 1979?
2 Artist Peter Blake found fame designing which world-famous Beatles album sleeve?
3 Which American was known as Ike?
4 Which future President organised the Free French Forces in WWII?
5 What was Indira Gandhi's maiden name?
6 Who became US Vice President in 1993?
7 Which title did Hitler take as Nazi leader?
8 Who was the last Tsarina of Russia?
9 Who was Soviet Foreign Minister from 1957 to 1985?
10 Whose resignation on 1 November 1990 began Thatcher's downfall?
11 Whose 1963 Report led to the closure of many railway stations?
12 Who was famous for his pictures of Campbell's Soup cans?
13 Who was British Prime Minister during the abdication crisis?
14 For how long were Hitler and Eva Braun married?
15 Who was the first singer to record two 007 theme tunes?
16 Which athlete became MP for Falmouth and Cambourne in 1992?
17 Which world leader celebrated his 80th birthday in July 1998?
18 Who was the first Archbishop of Canterbury?
19 Which US President publicly pardoned ex-President Nixon?
20 Who had the title Il Duce?
21 Which US evangelist asked his flock to make a "decision for Christ"?
22 In 1990 which ex-PM went to Iraq to try to secure the release of British hostages?
23 Who was the youngest queen of Henry VIII to be beheaded?
24 Which Prime Minister introduced the Citizens' Charter?
25 Who became Defence Secretary in May 1997?
26 What was the name of Horatio Nelson's daughter by Emma Hamilton?
27 Who said her boss Michael Howard had "something of the night about him"?
28 What was the religion of a French Huguenot?
29 Which Communist leader was named Josip Broz at birth?
30 In which category did Einstein win his Nobel prize in 1921?

---

1 The Longmuir brothers were in which 70s teeny bop group?
2 Who partnered Don Johnson on the Goya theme "Till I Loved You"?
3 Which "Coronation Street" star had a hit in 1994 with "Wind Beneath My Wings"?
4 Which UK male vocalist's real name is Michael Barratt?
5 Who duetted with Peter Gabriel on "Don't Give Up"?
6 Christopher John Davidson is the real name of which Irish vocalist?
7 Who had a No.1 on both sides of the Atlantic with "Devils & Dust"?
8 Who launched the British Legion Poppy Appeal with Dame Vera Lynn in 1997?
9 Who featured on the 1986 Clannad hit "In a Lifetime"?
10 Which pianist and instrumentalist's real name is Philippe Pages?
11 Who was the younger of the two Wham! members?
12 Keith, Greg and Carl were the Christian names of which 70s trio?
13 Who was the guest on the first episode of George Ezra's "George Ezra and Friends"?
14 Marvin Lee Aday is better known as which dead ringer vocalist?
15 Who had a No. 5 UK hit with the theme song "Because You Loved Me"?
16 Which actor shares his name with a 1984 hit by Madness?
17 Who sang the theme tune to "Dirty Dancing" with Jennifer Warnes?
18 Which TV detective had a No.1 hit with "Don't Give Up on Us" in 1976?
19 Which group share their name with a Bernard Cribbins 1962 hit?
20 Who joined with Queen in the 1981 No.1 hit "Under Pressure"?
21 Who invented Medicinal Compound according to the 1968 No.1?
22 Which superstar has an autobiography called "Bare"?
23 Which pop legend said, "I really wanted to be a football star"?
24 Who partnered Chris Rea on the 1996 hit "Disco La Passione"?
25 Complete the A-ha trio – Pal, Mags and ....?
26 Which character was played by Irene Cara in "Fame"?
27 Who interrupted Michael Jackson's "Earth Song" at the 1996 Brit Awards?
28 Which brothers were members of Spandau Ballet?
29 Who was the first Spice Girl to get engaged?
30 What nationality is Drake?

Answers Freddie Flintoff *(see Quiz 88)*

1 1977. 2 Andrew. 3 One. 4 India. 5 Deep vein thrombosis. 6 Trent Bridge. 7 Holly. 8 Lancashire. 9 Sagittarius. 10 400 (402). 11 The names of his wife and children. 12 New Zealand. 13 2010. 14 Right. 15 Boxing. 16 South Africa. 17 Michael Vaughan. 18 Brisbane Heat. 19 India. 20 Jacques Kallis. 21 Jamie Redknapp. 22 Flintoff, Savage and Ping Pong Guy. 23 Pakistan. 24 Neil Fairbrother. 25 Dark glasses. 26 Sixes. 27 Top Gear. 28 South Africa. 29 Trafalgar Square. 30 Michael Atherton.

Hard Questions

Ah yes, the hard questions. Cackle fiendishly, and take just a moment to stroke your white, diamond-collared cat before rubbing your hands together gleefully, because these questions are the real McCoy. The posers in this selection will sort the men out from the boys, and no mistake. If you do find any boys in the public bar by the way, be sure to let the landlord know, so he can give them a packet of crisps and a bottle of coke and send them outside. The quizzes in this section will make even the most dedicated trivia hound quake with fear. No one is going to get many of them correct, so if someone turns out an incredible score on these questions, search their coat for a copy of this book.

When you're setting a quiz, use these questions sparingly, like hot chilli powder. Even for teams, they're going to be decidedly tricky. You'll need to allow plenty of time for people to think about each question. What you don't want to do is make an entire night's quizzing out of this section, because you'll only make people feel stupid, and everyone hates a smart aleck who makes them look dumb. A few of these questions, strategically placed, can go a long way.

1 Asuncion is the capital of which country?

2 Which "Pop Idol" star was born Jan 20, 1979, in Berkshire?

3 Who had hits with "Take Your Time" and "Got to Have Your Love"?

4 What is a paravane used for?

5 Dr James Naismith devised which game?

6 In which decade was Jeremy Paxman born?

7 Which worldwide magazine was conceived by DeWitt Wallace?

8 To within two years, when were postcodes introduced to the UK?

9 Waterways Airways operates from which country?

10 Who is the elder – Rowan Atkinson or Clive Anderson?

11 What is prase?

12 Who, in 1890, composed the music for the opera "Ivanhoe"?

13 A poniard is a type of what?

14 Who led the Expedition of the Thousand in 1860?

15 Which 1960s No.1 was written by Madden and Morse in 1903?

16 Which part of the body is affected by thlipsis?

17 Who was found dead in the first episode of "EastEnders"?

18 Which Mel Brooks film was a spoof of Hitchcock movies?

19 Which TV cookery series set out to create a menu for the Queen's 80th birthday?

20 Gabriel Heinze joined Man Utd from which club?

21 Antonio Salazar was dictator for many years in which country?

22 Which US anti-terrorist force is based at Fort Bragg?

23 William Benting was an English pioneer of what?

24 By volume, what makes up about 21% of our atmosphere?

25 Who starred with his wife in the film "Mr and Mrs Bridge"?

26 Whose one and only hit was "I've Never Been to Me" in 1982?

27 Which two political parties aligned to form the Ministry of All-the-Talents in 1806?

28 To which Court are US Ambassadors to Britain officially credited?

29 Which US poet had the middle names Weston Loomir?

30 Which was the first African team to compete in the Cricket World Cup?

Answers | TV Detectives *(see Quiz 2)*

1 Tom Barnaby (Midsomer Murders). 2 Prime Suspect – The Final Act. 3 Liverpool One. 4 Adrian Kershaw. 5 Reginald Hill. 6 Eddie Shoestring. 7 Charlie's Angels. 8 RD Wingfield. 9 CIB. 10 The Remorseful Day. 11 Rupert Davies. 12 Reilly – Ace of Spies. 13 The Rockford Files. 14 Crime Traveller. 15 Denise Welch. 16 Cadfael. 17 Imogen Stubbs. 18 Tom Courtenay. 19 Taggart. 20 Stanton. 21 Van der Valk. 22 Sexton Blake. 23 Gideon's Way. 24 Cordelia Gray. 25 Chief Inspector Haskins. 26 Hercule Poirot. 27 The Body in the Library. 28 Reginald Hill (Dalziel & Pascoe). 29 Henry Crabbe. 30 Simon Templar.

1 Which DCI was first seen in episodes called "The Killings at Badger's Drift" and "Written in Blood"?

2 What was the final drama featuring Det. Supt Jane Tennison called?

3 In which series was Samantha Janus transferred from the Met to Merseyside?

4 Who was Morse's sidekick in "The Wench is Dead"?

5 Which novelist created the characters of Dalziel and Pascoe?

6 Which detective worked for Radio West?

7 Which series centred on Townsend Investigations?

8 Which novelist created Jack Frost?

9 Which acronymic part of the Met did Tony Clark work for in "Between the Lines"?

10 What was the episode called in which Inspector Morse died?

11 Who introduced the very first series of "Detective"?

12 In which series did Inspector Tsientsin appear?

13 Which famous series was introduced with a message on an answering machine?

14 In which series was Slade assisted by Holly?

15 Who played Frances Spender in the Jimmy Nail series?

16 Whose investigations are based in Shrewsbury but often filmed in central Europe?

17 Who played mini-skirted detective Anna Lee?

18 Who played Eric Salter in "Unforgotten" in 2015?

19 Which long running series began with a pilot called "Killer" in 1983?

20 Where did "The Cops" take place?

21 What was the full name of TV's most famous Dutch detective?

22 Who had a Rolls Royce called "The Grey Panther"?

23 Which 60s series had Chief Inspector Keen aiding his Commander?

24 Who is the detective in "An Unsuitable Job for a Woman"?

25 Who was Regan's boss in "The Sweeney"?

26 Which detective lived at Whitehaven Mansions?

27 Which was the first Miss Marple adaptation to star Joan Hickson on TV?

28 Who created the detectives played on TV by actors Clarke and Buchanan?

29 Who had retired from Barstock CID?

30 Claude Eustace Teal was invariably beaten in his dealings with whom?

Answers | Pot Luck 1 *(see Quiz 1)*

1 Paraguay. 2 Will Young. 3 Mantronix. 4 Mine-sweeping. 5 Basketball. 6 1950s. 7 Reader's Digest. 8 1968. 9 New Zealand. 10 Clive Anderson. 11 A type of quartz. 12 Sir Arthur Sullivan. 13 Dagger. 14 Garibaldi. 15 Two Little Boys. 16 The blood vessels. 17 Reg Cox. 18 High Anxiety. 19 Great British Menu. 20 Paris St Germain. 21 Portugal. 22 Delta Force. 23 Slimming diet. 24 Oxygen. 25 Paul Newman. 26 Charlene. 27 Whigs and Tories. 28 St James. 29 Ezra Pound. 30 East Africa (in 1975).

1 Phil Read won several World Championships in which sport?

2 What did an alchemist use an alembic for?

3 What was Eternal's first UK Top Ten hit?

4 In Hindu mythology who was goddess of destruction and death?

5 In which country is the Mackenzie River?

6 Which instrument did Lionel Hampton play?

7 How many Top Five hits did Elvis Presley have in 2005?

8 What was President Carter's wife's first name?

9 Who won the first squash World Open Championship?

10 Where is England's national hockey stadium?

11 Where was the constituency of former Home Secretary Charles Clarke?

12 Who wrote the novel "Rodney Stone"?

13 How many times is Annie mentioned in the lyrics of "Annie's Song"?

14 In Swift's novel what was Gulliver's first name?

15 To which part of the body does the adjective "cutaneous" refer?

16 In which sport were Hildon and Black Bears British Champions?

17 Whose first Top Ten hit was "What a Waste" in 1978?

18 Who was James I of England's father?

19 Which record label did Geri Halliwell sign up with when she left the Spice Girls?

20 What was the old name for stamp collecting?

21 Which "Countdown" regular wrote "The Language Report"?

22 Alfredo di Stefano of Real Madrid fame was born in which country?

23 What is the name of the police officer in "West Side Story"?

24 Which language's name means "one who hopes"?

25 Which public figure resigned over dealings concerning prostitute Monica Coghlan?

26 In the Old Testament which two books are named after women?

27 The Prix Goncourt is awarded for what?

28 Who joined Patrick Macnee on the 1990 No. 5 UK hit "Kinky Boots"?

29 Who or what is a dourousouli?

30 Which team did Nuno Santo manage before joining Wolves?

Answers	Books 1 *(see Quiz 4)*

1 John Cleese. 2 Full Disclosure. 3 Diana Rigg. 4 Martin Amis. 5 Dame Barbara Cartland. 6 Ronnie Spector. 7 Six. 8 Pat Conroy. 9 Clare Francis. 10 Madonna. 11 Isaac Asimov. 12 Darren Gough. 13 Pig. 14 Sussex. 15 Richard Noble. 16 Torvill & Dean. 17 South Africa. 18 Her Majesty's Stationery Office. 19 Stephen Hawking. 20 A Boy from Bolton. 21 Octaves. 22 Noah Webster. 23 Styles. 24 The Rainbow. 25 The Highway Code. 26 Gail Honeyman. 27 Stephen King. 28 Guinness Book of Records. 29 Bridget Jones's. 30 Agatha Christie.

1 Which comedian wrote "Families and How to Survive Them" with psychiatrist Robin Skynner?

2 What was Andrew Neil's autobiography called?

3 Who wrote an anthology of critics' anecdotes called "No Turn Unstoned"?

4 Whose first novel was "The Rachel Papers" in 1974?

5 Which novelist recorded an "Album of Love Songs" in 1978?

6 Which pop celebrity wrote "Be My Baby"?

7 How many Barchester Chronicles are there?

8 Who wrote the novel on which the movie "Prince of Tides" was based?

9 Who went from "Deceit and Betrayal" to "A Dark Devotion"?

10 Whose book "Sex", coincided with a dance album "Erotica"?

11 Which science fiction writer wrote the Foundation Trilogy?

12 Which cricketer wrote "Dazzler on the Dance Floor"?

13 Who or what was PG Wodehouse's Empress of Blandings?

14 The founder of Wisden played for which English county?

15 Whose quest for speed is recorded in his book "Thrust"?

16 Which sports stars' autobiography was called "Facing the Music?"

17 Rider Haggard's colonial service where influenced his books?

18 Who publishes Hansard?

19 Whose 1998 best seller argued that our universe is a part of a super universe?

20 What was boxer Amir Khan's autobiography called?

21 What did Compton Mackenzie refer to each individual volume of his autobiography as?

22 Whose 19th-century dictionary standardised US English?

23 Where was the Mysterious Affair in the first Agatha Christie in Penguin paperback?

24 Which colourful DH Lawrence book was banned because of its sexual content along with "Lady Chatterley" and "Women in Love"?

25 First appearing in 1931, what sold out of its new edition in 3 months in 1996?

26 Who wrote the bestseller "Eleanor Oliphant Is Completely Fine"?

27 The writer of the comic book series "Locke & Key" is the son of which famous author?

28 What is the best-selling copyright book of all time?

29 Whose Diary was written by Helen Fielding?

30 Who wrote romantic novels as Mary Westmacott?

Answers   Pot Luck 2 (see Quiz 3)

1 Motor Cycling. 2 To distil liquids. 3 Stay. 4 Kali. 5 Canada. 6 Vibraphone. 7 17.
8 Rosalyn. 9 Geoff Hunt. 10 Milton Keynes. 11 Norwich South. 12 Sir Arthur Conan
Doyle. 13 Never. 14 Lemuel. 15 Skin. 16 Polo. 17 Ian Dury & The Blockheads.
18 Lord Darnley. 19 Chrysalis. 20 Timbrology. 21 Susie Dent. 22 Argentina. 23
Officer Krupke. 24 Esperanto. 25 Jeffrey Archer. 26 Ruth and Esther. 27 Literature (in
France). 28 Honor Blackman. 29 A monkey. 30 Porto.

Quiz 5 | Pot Luck 3

Answers – page 198

LEVEL 3

1 Who designed the tapestry behind the altar in Coventry Cathedral?
2 An odalisque is a female what?
3 Who founded the record label Maverick Records?
4 Both Clive Woodward and Andy Robinson are linked with which university?
5 Which English poet had the middle name Chawner?
6 The Russian Revolution began in which year?
7 Which notorious serial killer was found hanged in prison in January 2004?
8 Who is the elder – Zoe Ball or Gary Barlow?
9 In the 1980s Greg LeMond became the first American to do what?
10 Whose one and only hit was "Little Things Mean a Lot"?
11 Who created the Statue of Zeus about 430 BC?
12 In which Hertfordshire town was Gareth Southgate born?
13 What was film star Edward G. Robinson's real name?
14 Who was the husband of cellist Jacqueline du Pre?
15 What is the drink kumiss made from?
16 Who came up with "The Book of Heroic Failures"?
17 What was discovered in 1930 by Clyde Tombaugh?
18 In the Bible, who was King David's father?
19 In 1865, where did the Confederates surrender?
20 Wellesley is the family name of which Dukes?
21 What is a dhole?
22 Norman Parkinson made his name in which field of art?
23 How many times did Steve Donoghue win the Derby?
24 Who created the Detective Inspector Anna Travis?
25 Lynn Ripley shone under which name as a pop singer?
26 Which theory was formulated by the German physicist Max Planck?
27 Which poet wrote, "She was a phantom of delight"?
28 Billy Childish and Charles Thompson founded which art movement?
29 The Haber Process manufactures which gas?
30 Who was Banquo's son in Macbeth?

Answers | Albums *(see Quiz 6)*

1 Simon & Garfunkel. 2 If U Can't Dance. 3 Mystery Girl. 4 Vertigo. 5 Innuendo. 6 Alison Moyet (Essex). 7 American Pie. 8 Frank Sinatra. 9 All Things Must Pass. 10 Help! – The Beatles. 11 Sheer Heart Attack. 12 A black dog. 13 Face Value. 14 More Blood, More Tracks. 15 Blue. 16 Mark Coyle. 17 The Police. 18 The Sound of Music. 19 Goodbye Yellow Brick Road. 20 As a soloist, with Style Council and the Jam. 21 Chris De Burgh. 22 Fleetwood Mac. 23 Saturday Night Fever. 24 A postal strike. 25 Postcard. 26 On. 27 WEA. 28 Transformer. 29 Never for Ever. 30 Let England Shake.

197

Quiz 6 | Albums

Answers – page 197

1 Who released the biggest-selling album in Britain in the 70s?
2 What was the final track on "Spice"?
3 Which 1988 album confirmed a comeback by Roy Orbison?
4 Dire Straits first albums came out on which label?
5 Which 6.5-minute hit was the title track of Queen's 7th No.1 album?
6 Who charted with an album named after an English county?
7 Don McLean's "Vincent" came from which album?
8 Which superstar first charted with "Come Fly with Me"?
9 What was George Harrison's first solo album after the Beatles?
10 What was the first album to make its debut into the UK chart at No.1?
11 Which album contains the line, "My kingdom for a horse"?
12 Who is not on the front cover of "Urban Hymns", but features on an inside cover shot?
13 What was Phil Collins' first solo No.1 album?
14 An unreleased version of "Up to Me" featured on which 2018 Bob Dylan official bootleg album?
15 What was the main colour on the cover of Enya's "Shepherd Moons"?
16 Who along with Oasis gets production credits on "Definitely Maybe"?
17 Which group had five consecutive No.1 albums from 1979 to 1986?
18 Which original film soundtrack was on the charts for a staggering 382 weeks?
19 Which album first featured "Candle in the Wind"?
20 Paul Weller has topped the charts in which three guises?
21 Who was the first artist to enter the Swiss album charts at No.1?
22 What was the last Fleetwood Mac album released before the world smash "Rumours"?
23 Which double-album film soundtrack was a 30 million seller in 1978?
24 Why weren't the album charts published in 1971 for eight weeks?
25 What was the name of Mary Hopkin's debut album?
26 Which word appeared in the titles of Will Young's first and third albums?
27 Tubular Bells launched the Virgin label, but which label put out Tubular Bells II?
28 Which album originally featured "Perfect Day"?
29 Which Kate Bush album featured a song about Delius?
30 Which P J Harvey album won her the Mercury Music Prize in 2011?

Answers | Pot Luck 3 *(see Quiz 5)*

1 Graham Sutherland. 2 Slave. 3 Madonna. 4 Loughborough. 5 Rupert Brooke. 6 1917. 7 Dr Harold Shipman. 8 Zoe Ball. 9 Win the Tour de France. 10 Kitty Kallen. 11 Phidias. 12 Watford. 13 Emmanuel Goldenberg. 14 Daniel Barenboim. 15 Milk. 16 Stephen Pile. 17 Pluto. 18 Jesse. 19 Appomattox. 20 Wellington. 21 An Asian wild dog. 22 Photography. 23 Six. 24 Lynda La Plante. 25 Twinkle. 26 Quantum theory. 27 Wordsworth. 28 Stuckism. 29 Ammonia. 30 Fleance.

Quiz 7   Pot Luck 4

1 Who were the first group since The Beatles to have 14 consecutive Top Five singles?
2 What was Golden Earring's first UK Top Ten hit?
3 Started in 1850, what were Children's Temperance Societies called?
4 How long had David Cameron been an MP when he became Tory leader?
5 Gravure is a term connected with which industry?
6 What did Thomas Wheildon make?
7 To the nearest hundred how many islands make up the Maldives?
8 Who was Prime Minister during the General Strike?
9 Once of Newcastle, which country did Hugo Viana play for?
10 Mycology is the study of what?
11 What was the Carla Rosa, existing from 1875 to 1958?
12 Who was the last King of Troy according to legend?
13 What was George Burns' real name?
14 The word Ombudsman comes from which language?
15 Who played the barrel organ in "The Magic Roundabout"?
16 Who wrote the play "The Homecoming"?
17 Who was writer and producer for New Kids on the Block?
18 In which American state were Bonnie and Clyde killed in an ambush?
19 The Statue of Liberty's 100th birthday was celebrated in which year?
20 Which Christmas fruits have the Latin name *vaccinium macrocarpon*?
21 What is studied by a pedologist?
22 Spencer Gore was the first winner of what?
23 George Galvin performed in music-hall under what name?
24 Placido Domingo studied music at which National Conservatory?
25 Who was the last Prime Minister during the reign of Queen Victoria?
26 The star Betelgeuse is in which constellation?
27 Which major pop singer/songwriter was born 13 June 1968, in Manchester?
28 Who was the first woman to be Canadian Prime Minister?
29 What do a tinchel of men do?
30 Which Australian singer often performs in an oversize blonde wig that covers her face?

Answers	**Battle Stations** *(see Quiz 8)*

1 Auchinleck. 2 Panmunjom. 3 Madras. 4 Mohne & Eder. 5 Vidkun Quisling. 6 Right arm. 7 MacArthur. 8 Reims. 9 Richthofen's Flying Circus. 10 Gavrilo Princip. 11 Treaty of Sevres. 12 Switzerland & Luxembourg. 13 Anzio. 14 Second Battle of the Somme. 15 Major Johnny Paul Koroma. 16 29. 17 Contras. 18 Dien Bien Phu. 19 American. 20 Ardennes. 21 Japanese. 22 Tobruk. 23 Near Kiev, Ukraine. 24 Spanish Civil War. 25 Michel Aoun. 26 Boer War. 27 Tutsi v. Hutu. 28 Passchendaele. 29 Von Moltke. 30 Vichy France.

Quiz 8   Battle Stations

Answers – page 199

LEVEL 3

1 Who led the British forces in the First Battle of El Alamein?
2 Where was the peace treaty signed after the Korean War?
3 What was the only place in India attacked by foreign forces in WWI?
4 Which dams were destroyed by bouncing bombs in 1943?
5 Which Norwegian leader aided the 1940 invasion of his country through non-resistance?
6 Which part of his body did Lord Raglan lose at Waterloo?
7 Who was commander of the US forces in the Pacific from March '42?
8 In which city did the German High Command formally surrender to General Eisenhower?
9 What was the German 11th Chasing Squadron known as in WWI?
10 Who assassinated Archduke Franz Ferdinand in 1914 thus precipitating WWI?
11 What was the last of the treaties which ended WWI?
12 Which countries were on either end of the Maginot Line?
13 Which birthplace of Nero was the site of an Allied beachhead invasion in WWII?
14 How is the battle at St Quentin in 1918 also known?
15 Who led the military coup in Sierra Leone's civil war in 1997?
16 How many countries made up the coalition v. Iraq in the Gulf War?
17 In the Nicaraguan Civil War which faction had US support?
18 Where was France's defeat which brought about the division of Vietnam along the 17th parallel?
19 Hitler's plan "Watch on the Rhine" was aimed at which troops?
20 In which area of Belgium/Luxembourg was the Battle of the Bulge?
21 Which navy was defeated at the Battle of Midway Island in 1942?
22 The retreat by the British from which port brought about the replacement of Auchinleck by Montgomery?
23 Where is Babi Yar, where 100,000 people were slaughtered in 1941?
24 In which war did the Battle of Ebro take place?
25 Which General declared a "war of liberation" against Syrian occupation of Lebanon in 1989?
26 Which war was ended with the Peace of Vereeniging?
27 Who were the two opposing factions in the Rwandan Civil War in the mid-1990s?
28 How is the third battle of Ypres in WWI also known?
29 Who was in charge of the German troops in the First Battle of the Marne?
30 What name was given to that part of France not occupied by the Germans until 1942?

Answers | Pot Luck 4 *(see Quiz 7)*

1 Steps. 2 Radar Love. 3 Bands of Hope. 4 Four years. 5 Printing (platemaking).
6 Pottery. 7 1200 (1196). 8 Stanley Baldwin. 9 Portugal. 10 Fungi. 11 An Opera Company. 12 Priam. 13 Nathan Birnbaum. 14 Swedish. 15 Mr Rusty. 16 Harold Pinter. 17 Maurice Starr. 18 Louisiana. 19 1986. 20 Cranberries. 21 Soils. 22 Men's singles, Wimbledon. 23 Dan Leno. 24 Mexico. 25 Marquess of Salisbury. 26 Orion. 27 David Gray. 28 Kim Campbell. 29 Hunt. 30 Sia.

200

1 Which denomination of Ulster banknote featured George Best?
2 What was the middle name of Wallis Simpson, later Duchess of Windsor?
3 Which greedy giant was created by Rabelais?
4 Who is the elder – Tony Blair or Pierce Brosnan?
5 What is sorghum?
6 From what is the writing material true vellum made?
7 What is separated by the oval window and the round window?
8 Whose presidential hopes were ended by model Donna Rice?
9 What fraction of a gold object is a carat as a proportional measure?
10 What is a killick?
11 What is the other job of Conservative MP Sir Paul Beresford?
12 Which team featured in "Footballers' Wives"?
13 What name is given to an animal that may be slaughtered to provide food under Muslim law?
14 In which county did the Tolpuddle Martyrs form a trade union?
15 What is a bowyang ?
16 Which politician said that northerners die of "ignorance and crisps"?
17 In which decade was actress Kristin Scott Thomas born?
18 What is the other job of Conservative MP Sir Paul Beresford?
19 Which country without a D or a Z in its name has the internet code .dz?
20 What relation was Queen Victoria to George IV?
21 Who won the first WBC cruiserweight title in boxing?
22 Why were the Piccard brothers famous in the 1930s?
23 Which Roman god was the god of beginnings and doors?
24 What is gneiss?
25 What was Florence Nightingale the first woman to receive in 1907?
26 What was a "quod" in old slang?
27 Who preceded David II as King of the Scots?
28 How is Julie Anne Smith better known in movies?
29 "The Purple Rose of Cairo" was written and directed by which actor?
30 Which title did Saddam Hussein take first – President or Prime Minister?

Answers	Quiz and Games *(see Quiz 10)*

1 Zoe Tyler. 2 The Moment of Truth. 3 Patrick Kielty. 4 Alan Coren. 5 Kenny Everett. 6 David Sneddon. 7 Child's Play. 8 Vincent Price. 9 Countdown (OED). 10 Ally McCoist. 11 Richard Wilson. 12 Blockbusters. 13 Pat Gibson. 14 Pass the Buck. 15 Max Robertson. 16 John Leslie. 17 Edwina Currie. 18 Newspaper – day of birth. 19 Matthew Kelly. 20 Princess Diana. 21 Blind Date. 22 Max Bygraves. 23 Armand Jammot. 24 Sporting charades. 25 Double Your Money. 26 Paul Daniels. 27 British Museum. 28 Leslie Crowther. 29 The Great Garden Game. 30 Anthea Redfern.

1 Who was the voice coach on "How Do You Solve a Problem Like Maria?"?
2 Which show had a "Dream Directory"?
3 Who joined Anthea Turner on "The National Lottery's Big Ticket"?
4 Who opposed Sandi Toksvig in the 90s "Call My Bluff"?
5 Who was the first male team captain in "That's Showbusiness"?
6 Who was the first winner of "Fame Academy"?
7 In which quiz did Ronnie Corbett replace Michael Aspel as host?
8 Which horror movie actor was on the first "Celebrity Squares"?
9 In which show might Mark Nyman adjudicate?
10 Who was the footballing "A Question of Sport" team captain when Sue Barker took over on a regular basis?
11 Who was the Reverend Green in the second series of "Cluedo"?
12 In which show were you pleased to be on the "Hot Spot"?
13 Which Egghead won "Mastermind", "Brain of Britain" and a million on "Who Wants to Be a Millionaire"?
14 Which weekday elimination quiz was hosted by Fred Dinenage?
15 Who presented the original "Going for a Song"?
16 Which "Blue Peter" presenter took over "Wheel of Fortune"?
17 In "Celebrity Wife Swap" which ex-MP changed places with Mrs John McCririck?
18 What did contestants receive at the end of "Today's the Day"?
19 Who hosted "You Bet" before Darren Day?
20 Who was the subject of an entire show of "100%" in August 1998?
21 Sue Middleton and Alex Tatham famously followed a TV win on which show with marriage?
22 Who presented "Family Fortunes" immediately prior to Les Dennis?
23 Who created Countdown?
24 What happens in the "Sprint Finish" section of "A Question of Sport"?
25 "The Sky's the Limit" was a variation of which show?
26 Whom did Bob Monkhouse replace on "Wipeout"?
27 Which building was central to Tony Robinson's "Codex" challenge?
28 Who first asked contestants to "Come on down"?
29 What was Channel 5's first gardening quiz called?
30 Who was the female half of the first husband-and-wife team to present "The Generation Game"?

Answers | Pot Luck 5 *(see Quiz 9)*

1 £5 2 Warfield. 3 Gargantua. 4 Tony Blair. 5 A cereal crop. 6 Calf skin. 7 Middle ear and inner ear. 8 Gary Hart. 9 1/24th. 10 A small anchor. 11 Saturn. 12 Earls Park. 13 Halal. 14 Dorset. 15 String tied to the knee to hitch trousers up. 16 Edwina Currie. 17 1960s. 18 Dentist. 19 Algeria. 20 Niece. 21 Marvin Camel. 22 Balloonists. 23 Janus. 24 A type of rock. 25 The Order of Merit. 26 A prison. 27 Robert the Bruce. 28 Julianne Moore. 29 Woody Allen. 30 President (1979).

1 Who led the British force in 1898 at Omdurman?

2 What was Adam Ant's first UK Top Ten hit?

3 How many cubic centimetres in a cubic metre?

4 Jeet D. Patel is a world champion of which fusion sport?

5 Which real island, famed in fiction, is some 25 miles south of Elba?

6 Who would use a fyke?

7 Who was the first Irish cyclist to win the Tour de France?

8 What first did Bernard Harris achieve when he did his space walk?

9 Who or what is Katherine Gorge?

10 Which two countries are separated by the Kattegat?

11 In which decade did Picasso die?

12 Houses in Sherwood Crescent were destroyed in which disaster?

13 Which classic film was billed as "The Eighth Wonder of the World"?

14 Which Royal House ruled from 1461 to 1485 in England?

15 What is a gribble?

16 How many books are there in the New Testament?

17 How many FA Cup Finals did Roy Keane play in?

18 Which city is the capital of Tibet?

19 "In No Way to Treat a Lady" what did the killer leave on the brow?

20 What is bohea?

21 The Greek goddess Nyx was the personification of what?

22 Ion Iliescu has twice been President of which country?

23 What form did the Yahoos have in Gulliver's Travels ?

24 "I Didn't Get Where I am Today" was which comedy writer's autobiography?

25 In which country is the national drink called pisco?

26 Whose one and only hit was "First Time" in 1988?

27 Which place is in Berkshire in England and Pennsylvania in America?

28 Unlucky for some, what was Westlife's 13th No.1 single?

29 When George Bush Snr was elected president who was his Democrat opponent?

30 Which rock star has children called Rufus Tiger and Tiger Lily?

Answers   Around the UK (see Quiz 12)

1 Ipswich. 2 Heriot-Watt. 3 Cowdray Park. 4 The Pit. 5 Orkney. 6 Holy Loch. 7 Hampstead. 8 Finisterre. 9 Buckinghamshire. 10 Suffolk. 11 Three. 12 Antonine Wall. 13 Middlesex Street. 14 Northamptonshire. 15 Mount Pleasant. 16 Man of Kent. 17 Durham. 18 The Boston Stump. 19 PM Earl of Liverpool. 20 Carlton House Terrace. 21 Trowbridge. 22 Westminster Abbey. 23 Mansion House. 24 The Burrell Collection. 25 Blenheim Palace. 26 Bush House. 27 Preston. 28 Banqueting House. 29 Shetlands. 30 Hereford and Worcester.

1 The Euroroute E24 is from Birmingham to which county town?
2 Which Scottish university was named after a jeweller and an inventor?
3 Which polo ground is in the park of a burnt-down former country house?
4 What is the smallest theatre at the Barbican in London called?
5 Where is Grimsetter Airport?
6 Which inlet of the Clyde was used as a US submarine base from the early 60s?
7 In which part of London is Kenwood?
8 Which shipping area is due north of Trafalgar?
9 In which county was the Open University founded?
10 John Peel lived in which county for the latter part of his life?
11 How many national parks does the Pennine Way pass through?
12 Which wall runs from the river Forth in the east to the Clyde in the west?
13 What is the real name of "Petticoat Lane"?
14 Which county is due north of Buckinghamshire?
15 Where is the Post Office's main sorting office?
16 What name is given to someone born east of the Medway?
17 Which county is due south of Tyne and Wear?
18 Which colloquial name of the main church in Boston serves as a landmark for ships?
19 Who or what was London's Liverpool Street station named after?
20 Where is the official London residence of the Foreign Secretary?
21 What is the administration centre of Wiltshire?
22 How is London's Collegiate Church of St Peter better known?
23 Which House has an Egyptian Hall for banqueting?
24 Which important collection was given to the city of Glasgow in 1944?
25 Which World Heritage Site was built for the Duke of Marlborough?
26 Which house is headquarters and home to the BBC World Service?
27 Where would you find Ove Arup's brutalist bus station?
28 Which famous House is the only surviving part of Whitehall Palace?
29 Where is Scatsa Airport?
30 Which county is due south of Shropshire?

Answers	**Pot Luck 6** *(see Quiz 11)*

1 Lord Kitchener. 2 Dog Eat Dog. 3 One million. 4 Chess boxing. 5 Monte Cristo.
6 A fisherman. 7 Stephen Roche. 8 First black man to walk in space. 9 National Park in Australia. 10 Denmark and Sweden. 11 1970s. 12 Jumbo jet crash, Lockerbie. 13 King Kong. 14 York. 15 A crustacean. 16 27. 17 Seven. 18 Lhasa. 19 A lipstick kiss. 20 Tea. 21 Night. 22 Romania. 23 Human. 24 David Nobbs. 25 Peru. 26 Robin Beck. 27 Reading. 28 You Raise Me Up. 29 Michael Dukakis. 30 Roger Taylor.

1 Where on your body is your philtrum?

2 In which decade was Delia Smith born?

3 Inigo Jones was famous in which profession?

4 Who discovered carbon dioxide in 1754 and called it "fixed air"?

5 Who was the first musician to be made a life peer?

6 In which sport did Ariya Jutanugarn top the rankings in January 2019?

7 Who defeated Sweden's forces at Poltava in 1709?

8 What was the last film directed by Alfred Hitchcock?

9 Which country known by two words since 1970 was long ago known as Serendip?

10 Where is the Louis Armstrong Stadium?

11 Who wrote Gary Barlow's second solo No.1?

12 In "Brideshead Revisited" which actor played the father of Jeremy Irons?

13 What was John Lennon's middle name?

14 Mikel Arteta joined Everton from which club?

15 Whose only UK Top Ten hit from 1971 was called "Rose Garden"?

16 What is the more common name for the flower called the Kingcup?

17 What odds is a horse if it is "Burlington Bertie" in rhyming slang?

18 Who wrote "Tropic of Cancer" and "Tropic of Capricorn"?

19 Which ballet dancer died on the same day as Dizzy Gillespie?

20 What was Chris Rea's first UK Top Ten hit?

21 Amboyna is a richly coloured type of what?

22 What was Sir John Gielgud's first name?

23 Which poet wrote, "I have measured out my life with coffee spoons"?

24 What was Timothy Dalton's last film as James Bond?

25 Plasma in blood consists of platelets and red and white what?

26 Who was the drummer in the group Police?

27 Who invented the Polaroid camera in 1947?

28 "Barefoot in the Park" was written by which US playwright?

29 What is opposed by the John Birch Society in the USA?

30 Which famous inventor had the middle name Alva?

Answers | Books 2 *(see Quiz 14)*

1 Clive James. 2 Melvyn Bragg. 3 Charlie Parker. 4 Bob Dylan. 5 Blue. 6 Mae West. 7 The Rainmaker. 8 Britain. 9 French Revolution (Tale of Two Cities). 10 Margaret Mitchell. 11 Disraeli. 12 Without Remorse. 13 Michael Ondaatje. 14 Dr No. 15 Curtain. 16 Children's Hospital. 17 The Wonky Donkey. 18 Women in Love. 19 Sapiens. 20 Ken Follett. 21 Ruth Rendell as Barbara Vine. 22 Raymond Chandler. 23 Oliver Twist. 24 William Blatty. 25 Ellery Queen. 26 Jehovah's Witnesses. 27 Conan Doyle. 28 Jeffrey Archer. 29 Jilly Cooper. 30 Quintin Jardine.

1 Which TV presenter published his "Unreliable Memoirs" in 1980?

2 Whose novel "A Time to Dance" was adapted into a controversial TV drama?

3 In "From One Charlie to Another", whom did Charlie Watts write about?

4 Which singer wrote the book "Tarantula"?

5 What was the colour of the first Penguin paperback?

6 Which blonde wrote "The Constant Sinner"?

7 Which John Grisham book set a record initial print run of 2.8 million?

8 To be considered for the Booker Prize a book has to be published where first?

9 What according to Dickens was "the best of times, the worst of times"?

10 Whose only novel won the Pullitzer Prize in 1937?

11 Which PM wrote "Sybil"?

12 For which novel did Tom Clancy receive an advance of $14 million?

13 Which joint 1992 Booker Prize winner had his book made into an Oscar-winning film?

14 Which Ian Fleming novel has the shortest title?

15 What was Hercule Poirot's last case called?

16 What did JM Barrie give the royalties from Peter Pan to?

17 A viral video of a 'Scottish Granny' reading which book to her grandchild made it a 2018 bestseller?

18 What was the sequel to DH Lawrence's "The Rainbow"?

19 "Homo Deus" was a sequel to which bestseller?

20 Whose early thrillers include "The Eye of the Needle"?

21 Who wrote "The House of Stairs" under a pseudonym?

22 Which detective novelist wrote the screenplay for "Strangers on a Train"?

23 What was Charles Dickens' second novel, after "Pickwick Papers"?

24 Who wrote "The Exorcist" which was made into a successful film?

25 How are Patrick Dannay and Manfred B. Lee better known?

26 Who produced "The Truth That Leads to Eternal Life"?

27 Who wrote the historical romance "Micah Clarke"?

28 Which novelist once owned a Rolls registration number ANY 1?

29 Whose early novels were "Bella", "Harriet" and "Prudence"?

30 Bob Skinner is the creation of which crime/thriller writer?

Answers | Pot Luck 7 (see Quiz 13)

1 Groove between nose and lip. 2 1940s. 3 Architecture. 4 Joseph Black. 5 Benjamin Britten. 6 Golf (women's). 7 Russia. 8 Family Plot. 9 Sri Lanka. 10 Flushing Meadow, New York. 11 Madonna. 12 John Gielgud. 13 Winston. 14 Real Sociedad. 15 Lynn Anderson. 16 Marsh Marigold. 17 100-30. 18 Henry Miller. 19 Rudolf Nureyev. 20 The Road to Hell (Part 2). 21 Wood. 22 Arthur. 23 TS Eliot. 24 Licence to Kill. 25 Corpuscles. 26 Stewart Copeland. 27 Edwin Land. 28 Neil Simon. 29 Communism. 30 Thomas Edison.

1 Cetewayo, Dingaan and Chaka have all led which people?

2 Whose one and only hit was "Move Closer" in 1985?

3 Which painting attributed to Leonardo da Vinci became the most expensive ever in 2017?

4 Which Suffolk town was the first in Britain to have a woman mayor?

5 Who played Yvonne Hartman, head of the Torchwood Institute in "Doctor Who"?

6 What is the correct name for chickenpox?

7 Which top-selling band featured Richard Jones on bass?

8 Who is the elder – Phil Collins or Robbie Coltrane?

9 In the 80s which building did Prince Charles compare to a "nuclear power station"?

10 Which US actor's autobiography was titled "Never Have Your Dog Stuffed"?

11 The brown pigment bistre is prepared from what?

12 Maureen Connolly was the first female to perform what?

13 Which two "Corrie" actresses were awarded the MBE in millennium year?

14 In which FIFA World Cup were red and yellow cards first used?

15 What did Jack Ketch do for a living?

16 Van Gogh's "Sunflowers" used to hang in the bedroom of which other famous artist?

17 In mythology, whom did Leander swim the Hellespont nightly to see?

18 What would you do with a filibeg?

19 Bert Hardy was a staff photojournalist for which periodical?

20 Madonna's first British TV appearance was on which show?

21 Who was George Clooney's co-star in the movie "Out of Sight"?

22 Which battle was the decisive one in the English Civil War?

23 To ten years, when was the National Rifle Association of Great Britain formed?

24 In which country are the Sutherland Falls?

25 What is an alpaca?

26 In which metropolitan borough was MP Jo Cox assassinated in 2016?

27 What was American comedian Jack Benny's signature tune?

28 Who had UK Top Ten hits in the 90s with "Don't Worry" and "G.L.A.D."?

29 Who wrote "The Handmaid's Tale"?

30 What did businessman Peter de Savray buy for £6.7 million in 1987?

Answers Musical Greats *(see Quiz 16)*

1 Without You. 2 The Miracles. 3 12 years. 4 Georgia. 5 Mary's Boy Child. 6 The Doors. 7 In the Summertime. 8 Christie Brinkley. 9 Can't Help Falling in Love. 10 Mistletoe and Wine. 11 Tears. 12 What a Wonderful World. 13 She Loves You. 14 Jimmy Young. 15 Bright Eyes. 16 Far Corporation. 17 Rodgers and Hammerstein. 18 Sun. 19 Gary Busey. 20 Otis Redding. 21 Morning Has Broken. 22 Release Me. 23 Roy Orbison. 24 24 weeks. 25 I'm Into Something Good. 26 Imagine. 27 Green. 28 Waterloo by ABBA. 29 Cook without an "e". 30 I Wanna Hold Your Hand.

1 Which Pete Ham and Tom Evans song has been at No.1 with two different artists?

2 The Isley Brothers and which other Motown act recorded "Grapevine" before Marvin Gaye?

3 To the nearest year, how long was there between Sinatra's first and second UK No.1s?

4 Where is the singer's home in the lyrics of "On the Dock of the Bay"?

5 What was the first song to be Christmas No.1 in two different versions?

6 Which group wrote the song that was Will Young's second No.1?

7 Which 1970 seven-week No.1 was best selling UK single of the year?

8 Whom did Billy Joel dedicate his 1983 version of "Uptown Girl" to?

9 What was Elvis Presley's closing number in his Las Vegas stage act?

10 What was Cliff Richard's first self-produced No.1?

11 What was the chief of the Diddymen's only UK No.1?

12 Which standard has the line, "I see friends shaking hands saying how do you do"?

13 Which Beatles hit stayed in the UK Top 50 for 33 weeks in 1963?

14 Who had the first UK No.1 with "Unchained Melody"?

15 Which film theme was the biggest-selling single of 1979?

16 Who took Led Zeppelin's "Stairway To Heaven" into the singles charts before Rolf Harris?

17 Who wrote "You'll Never Walk Alone"?

18 Which heavenly body is mentioned in the title of the song that gave George Michael his 4th solo and Elton John his 3rd No.1?

19 Who played Buddy Holly in the 1978 movie "The Buddy Holly Story"?

20 Who wrote Aretha Franklin's first UK hit "Respect"?

21 What was Yusuf Islam's, once known as Cat Stevens, last Top Ten hit before "Father and Son"?

22 Which 1967 No.1 recorded the longest-ever stay in the UK Top 50?

23 Which 1960s star, who died in 1988, charted with "Love Songs" album in 2001?

24 How many weeks in total did Whitney Houston top the US and UK charts with "I Will Always Love You"?

25 Which hit was the first No.1 for writers Gerry Goffin and Carole King?

26 Which song includes the line, "nothing to kill or die for"?

27 What was the colour mentioned in the title of Tom Jones' final No.1 in the 1960s?

28 What is the biggest international hit from Eurovision Song Contest?

29 What was Sam Cooke's real name?

30 What was the Beatles' first No.1 in America?

Answers	Pot Luck 8 *(see Quiz 15)*

1 The Zulus. 2 Phyllis Nelson. 3 Salvator Mundi. 4 Aldeburgh. 5 Tracy-Ann Oberman. 6 Varicella. 7 Stereophonics. 8 Robbie Coltrane. 9 National Theatre. 10 Alan Alda (of M*A*S*H fame). 11 Soot. 12 The tennis Grand Slam. 13 Betty Driver and Elizabeth Dawn. 14 1970. 15 A hangman. 16 Paul Gauguin. 17 Hero. 18 Wear it. 19 Picture Post. 20 The Tube. 21 Jennifer Lopez. 22 Battle of Naseby. 23 1860. 24 New Zealand. 25 A hoofed mammal. 26 Kirklees. 27 Love in Bloom. 28 Kim Appleby. 29 Margaret Atwood. 30 Land's End.

1 Which christian name derives from the Germanic for "strong ruler"?
2 Between 1963 and 2006, how many Bond films featured the Aston Martin DB5?
3 The novel "Robinson Crusoe" was based on whose experiences?
4 What important post did Millard Fillmore hold?
5 Which magazine serialised "The Adventures of Sherlock Holmes" in the 1890s?
6 Which group features Peter Salisbury on drums and Simon Jones on bass?
7 Where were the first Winter Olympics held in 1924?
8 Who preceded John Bruton as Prime Minister of Ireland?
9 What can be a type of musket or a type of rhomboid?
10 Which frontman of rock band Soundgarden committed suicide in 2017?
11 Which long-running radio quiz show was hosted by Wilfred Pickles?
12 In which John Braine book is Joe Lampton the central character ?
13 What does a manometer measure the pressure of?
14 What was R.E.M.'s first UK Top Ten hit?
15 Otto Lilienthal was associated with what form of transport?
16 In furniture, what can be bracket, bun and stile on a chest?
17 What amalgamated in 1918 with the Royal Naval Air Service to form the RAF?
18 What did the M stand for in EM Forster's middle name?
19 Where is the poet Wordsworth buried?
20 What is your columella?
21 In "Big Brother 3" who made a memorable escape by climbing over a roof?
22 Who was the first UK golfer to win the World Match-Play Championship?
23 In folktales a silkie was half man and half what?
24 Who was Prince Philip's father?
25 Jose Barroso took over as Prime Minister of which European country in 2002?
26 Who composed "Clair de Lune"?
27 Players of which club died in a plane crash en route to the 2016 Copa Sudamericana final?
28 Who was Transport Secretary at the time of the King's Cross tube fire disaster?
29 Whose only UK Top Ten hit was "Pick Up the Pieces" in 1975?
30 Black Friars are members of the religious order established by whom?

Answers | Football *(see Quiz 18)*

1 Wilf McGuinness. 2 First woman ref of men's football. 3 Italy (1990). 4 Man City.
5 Richard Branson. 6 Javi Gracia. 7 Everton. 8 Wigan Athletic. 9 67 games. 10
Morocco. 11 Torino. 12 Brazil. 13 Peter Schmeichel. 14 Thomas Ravelli. 15 Diego
Maradona. 16 Bari. 17 Chesterfield. 18 Bulgaria. 19 Inter Milan. 20 Gillespie Road.
21 Arnold Muhren. 22 West Brom. 23 Spurs v. Wolves. 24 Ajax. 25 90. 26 Matěj
Vydra. 27 Boston, USA. 28 Santos. 29 Ugo Ehiogu. 30 Rangers and Hearts.

1 Who preceded Frank O'Farrell as Man Utd manager?
2 How did Joan Bazely make history in 1976?
3 Who were the opponents in Peter Shilton's last game for England?
4 Which Premier League side lost nine of its last ten games in 2006 but stayed up?
5 Who offered the England and Scotland squads a week on his Caribbean island if they won the World Cup in 1998?
6 Which Premier League manager was in charge of Rubin Kazan in 2016/17?
7 Which club's motto is "Nil Satis Nisi Optimum"?
8 John Benson, Bruce Rioch and Steve Bruce have all managed which club?
9 To three, for how many games was Sven-Goran Eriksson in charge of England?
10 Ray Wilkins was sent off while playing for England against which country?
11 Who did Denis Law play for immediately before Man Utd?
12 Who was the only side to beat England over 90 minutes when Venables was manager?
13 Who appeared in a TV ad for bacon before the 1998 World Cup?
14 Who is Sweden's most capped player of all time?
15 Who led Naples to their first ever Italian championship?
16 Which of the Italian sides David Platt played for had the shortest name?
17 Bolton's Kevin Davies has played over 100 games for three clubs – which was first?
18 Who was fourth in the 1994 World Cup?
19 Roy Hodgson joined Blackburn Rovers from which club?
20 What was Arsenal tube station called before it was called Arsenal?
21 Who was the first Dutchman to play in an FA Cup Final?
22 Whom were Man Utd playing when George Best made his debut?
23 Which sides competed in the first all-British UEFA Cup Final?
24 Who were the first winners of the Inter Toto Cup?
25 How many times did Bobby Moore captain England in 108 internationals?
26 Who was the leading goalscorer in the Championship in 2017/18?
27 Where did Paul Ince captain England for the first time?
28 Which club side were the first to win the South American Cup?
29 Which defender scored his only England goal in Sven-Goran Eriksson's first game?
30 Which two Scottish sides did Antti Niemi play for prior to moving to England?

1 Which singer's 2018 autobiography was titled "Brutally Honest"?
2 Which creature is represented in the year the Chinese call hou?
3 A fear of cats is known as what?
4 Which country ruled Greece until 1830?
5 Who wrote the line: "The female of the species is more deadly than the male"?
6 How many species of ostrich are there?
7 Dakar is the capital of which country?
8 Which theme gave Clannad their first UK Top Ten hit?
9 Who is the elder – John Prescott or Trevor McDonald?
10 The spice allspice is made from which part of a plant?
11 Which "E" number is used to represent Tartrazine in products?
12 What is the main language of Andorra?
13 Which elderly couple were immortalised in a poem by Henry Woodfall?
14 Where on Dartmoor is Dartmoor prison?
15 Which jazz festival is held annually in Rhode Island?
16 What does the Latin ab initio mean?
17 Which Prime Minister was offered a dukedom when he retired in 1955?
18 The constellation Aquila has which name in English?
19 In which country is the city of Baku?
20 What does the musical term "con fuoco" mean?
21 Which bird appears with two heads on the Albanian flag?
22 Which letter in Braille comprises a single raised dot?
23 Which Noel Edmonds show featured the ill-fated Whirly Wheeler?
24 Subtitled "The Time-Torn Man", Claire Tomalin's book was about which writer?
25 What are separated by the Cook Straits?
26 In which year did the UK become a member of the UN?
27 Which country has the internet code .pi?
28 Which country's team dominated World Fly Fishing at the start of this century?
29 Prime Minister Wilfried Martens was leader of which country?
30 How would the letter E be formed in Morse Code?

1 In whose home is "The Green Green Grass" set?

2 "Thirtysomething" was set in which US state?

3 Who did "Casualty's" George play in "May to December"?

4 What were Private Godfrey's sisters called in "Dad's Army"?

5 Which bookie did Vince Pinner work for?

6 Who had a wife, daughter and mother-in-law who were witches?

7 In which real-life town was "Jam and Jerusalem" filmed?

8 Who sang the theme music for "You Rang M'Lord" with Bob Monkhouse?

9 What was Richard's mother called in "To the Manor Born"?

10 What was Super Hans going to open in Macedonia at the end of "Peep Show"?

11 In which series did George, Kramer and Elaine appear?

12 Which TV husband and wife lived in Lanford Illinois?

13 Who was the first manager of the Bayview Retirement Home?

14 Who in his later years had a black home help called Winston?

15 What was the US series on which "The Upper Hand" was based?

16 Which property was left to Jim Davidson in "Up the Elephant and Round the Castle"?

17 In which hospital did Sheila Sabatini work?

18 Which sitcom was first called "You'll Never Get Rich" in the US?

19 What was Reg Varney's character called in "On the Buses"?

20 What was Thelma's surname before she married Likely Lad Bob?

21 Elaine Nardo was the only female cabbie in which company?

22 What job did Michael Douglas do when he guested on "Will and Grace"?

23 What were Harold Steptoe's middle names?

24 Which character in "Soap" was later given his own series?

25 Who wrote the original series of "Shine on Harvey Moon"?

26 Which sit com star played Vera Hopkins in "Coronation Street"?

27 Who was the mayor of Royston Vasey in the 2017 anniversary episodes?

28 Who was the barman of the Nag's Head as frequented by the Trotters?

29 Who created the theme music for "One Foot in the Grave"?

30 Which show centred round the 1-2-1 Club?

---

1 Who crossed Niagara Falls in 1859 on a tightrope?
2 What did the Romans call the Isle of Wight?
3 Who is the voice of a 1951 Hudson Hornet in the Pixar movie "Cars"?
4 What are gar, wrasse, alewife and blenny?
5 What was Jim Reeves' first UK Top Ten hit?
6 Who is the actress daughter of actress Phillida Law?
7 Who composed the music for "Jaws" and "Star Wars"?
8 What was the capital of the ancient empire of Assyria?
9 On what date in 1986 did Prince Andrew marry Fergie?
10 Which part did Prunella Scales play in "A Question of Attribution"?
11 Which David was FA executive director during the Faria Alam affair?
12 Which presenter of "That's Life" was famous for his odd odes?
13 What is a futtock?
14 Which film star married Robyn Smith in 1980?
15 Which alloy contains 2% antimony, 8% copper and 90% tin?
16 Liane Carroll is famous for which type of music?
17 Jörg Meuthen is the leader of which German far-right party?
18 Which son of Henry VII married Catherine of Aragon in 1501?
19 In what year did Classic FM begin?
20 What are Lambda, Omicron and Tau all found in?
21 Charing, as in Charing Cross, comes from an Old English word meaning what?
22 What can be a trump at cards or a type of sandpiper?
23 The major town of Herat is in which war-torn country?
24 Where is English actor David Garrick buried?
25 Which Argentinian has twice been the joint leading scorer in Serie A this century?
26 Walter Gropius was famous in what field?
27 In 2015 who became the first and only woman to be awarded the Royal Gold Medal by RIBA?
28 Famed as Alfie Moon, what part did this actor play in "Grease" in the West End?
29 Which celebrated novelist lived at Greenaway house?
30 Who directed the film "You Can't Take It with You"?

Answers	**Animal World** *(see Quiz 22)*

1 Vampire bat. 2 Blue whale. 3 One. 4 Capybara. 5 Algae which grow on it. 6 Mount Everest pika. 7 Exmoor ponies. 8 Bat. 9 Intestine. 10 Behind its eyes. 11 Bootlace worm. 12 On its skin. 13 Canine teeth. 14 Anywhere above ground. 15 Balaenoptera musculus. 16 Flemish horse. 17 Yellow. 18 Europe (bison). 19 Madagascar. 20 Maine coon. 21 Poisonous frog. 22 Couple of hours. 23 Collagen. 24 Tarsiers. 25 Herd reindeer. 26 Argentina. 27 Lemur. 28 Asian elephant. 29 Forehead horn. 30 Warm-blooded.

1 What is the only mammal to live as a parasite?
2 How is a Sibbald's rorqual also known?
3 For how many hours in a period of 24 does a giraffe sleep?
4 What is the world's largest rodent?
5 What gives the sloth its greenish appearance?
6 Which mammal lives at the highest altitude?
7 Which animals are famously sold at Bampton Fair?
8 The mammal which can live at the greatest depth is a species of what?
9 From which part of a sperm whale is ambergris obtained?
10 Where does a cane toad squirt poison from?
11 What is the longest type of worm?
12 Where would you find a shark's denticles?
13 What does the male mouse deer have that no other deer has?
14 Where does a browser find food?
15 What is the Latin name for the Blue Whale?
16 A Clydesdale was originally a cross between a Scottish draught horse and a what?
17 What colour is a mandrill's beard?
18 The wisent is native to where?
19 Lemurs are only found in their natural habitat where?
20 What is the oldest indigenous breed of cat in the US?
21 What is a koikoi?
22 What is the average life expectancy of the mayfly?
23 Which protein is cartilage made up of?
24 The term monkey refers to all primates except apes, humans and what?
25 Why were Samoyeds originally bred?
26 Falabellas are native to where?
27 What is another name for the aye-aye?
28 Which animal has the longest tail?
29 What name is given to the smaller of a rhino's horns?
30 What does it mean if an animal is homoiothermic?

1 Which English football club were the first to clock up 105 points in a season?

2 What was the trade of John Galliano's dad?

3 In the Beckett play which characters were Waiting for Godot?

4 Which disease is diagnosed by the Wasserman Test?

5 The King of Alba ruled in which country?

6 In which decade was Sting born?

7 Whose one and only hit was "No Charge" in 1976?

8 What does a petrologist study?

9 Which African country lies between the sea and Zimbabwe?

10 What are Temple-Tuttle and Kohoutek both types of?

11 In which London hall was England's first official showjumping event held in 1869?

12 Rod Stewart donated the royalties from which single to the Dunblane fund?

13 The ship Petit Pierre was the first to be driven by what in 1902?

14 Which island is in the middle of Niagara Falls?

15 Who was the first "Blue Peter" presenter to be sacked?

16 For what did John Singer Sargent achieve fame?

17 In which country is the majority of the Yucatan Peninsula?

18 The statue of Albert opposite the Albert Hall is made from what?

19 In "Corrie" who was Leanne Battersby's first mother-in-law?

20 Why was the Roman consul Incitatus unusual?

21 Who composed "God Bless America"?

22 Violinist Arthur Grumiaux came from which country?

23 When can a woman suffer puerperal fever?

24 What was Jack Rosenthal's autobiography called?

25 "The Dambusters" film was based on which book?

26 Who is the elder – Michael Crawford or Eric Clapton?

27 Which of Jesus' disciples were sons of Zebedee?

28 In a 2001 census what was Canada's population to the nearest million?

29 Who plays at the Stade Ernest-Wallon (formerly Stade des Sept Deniers)?

30 Rozonda Thomas was part of which top-selling girl group?

Answers	60s Films (see Quiz 24)

1 Doctor Dolittle. 2 Bryan Forbes. 3 New York & Paris. 4 John Ford. 5 Kenneth Williams. 6 David Bailey. 7 He has no dialogue. 8 When Dinosaurs Ruled the Earth. 9 Gillian Lynne. 10 George Segal. 11 Peter Cushing. 12 Brief Encounter. 13 Claudia Cardinale. 14 Joseph Mankiewicz. 15 Jimmy Bryant. 16 Maurice Jarre. 17 A Walk with Love and Death. 18 Stoke Poges. 19 Guess Who's Coming to Dinner. 20 Jess Conrad. 21 Gregory Peck. 22 Tom Courtenay. 23 Tom Jones. 24 Lee Marvin. 25 Big Sam. 26 Who's Afraid of Virginia Woolf?. 27 Ratso Rizzo. 28 Corin. 29 Rod Steiger. 30 Katharine Hepburn.

Quiz 24 | 60s Films

1 In which 60s film did Richard Attenborough sing?
2 Who became head of production at EMI in 1969?
3 Between which two cities is "The Great Race" set?
4 Who directed the Civil War sequences of "How the West was Won"?
5 Who was Camembert in "Carry On – Don't Lose Your Head"?
6 Who inspired the David Hemmings role in Antonioni's "Blow Up"?
7 What is unusual about Christopher Lee's terrifying role in "Dracula –
  Prince of Darkness"?
8 What was the sequel to "A Million Years BC"?
9 Who devised the dance routines in "Half a Sixpence"?
10 Who is the only American in "King Rat"?
11 Who was the Doctor in the big screen "Doctor Who and the Daleks"?
12 Which film classic inspired Billy Wilder to make "The Apartment"?
13 Who played Princess Dala in "The Pink Panther"?
14 Who took over directing "Cleopatra" mid way through production?
15 Who was the singing voice of Tony in "West Side Story"?
16 Who wrote the music for "Lawrence of Arabia"?
17 In which film of her father's did Anjelica Huston make her screen debut?
18 Which golf course featured in "Goldfinger"?
19 What was Tracy and Hepburn's final movie together?
20 Which pop star starred in "Rag Doll" in 1960?
21 Which '62 Best Actor studied medicine at the University of California?
22 Who was Oscar-nominated for Pasha in "Doctor Zhivago"?
23 Which 60s Oscar winner was narrated by Michael MacLiammoir?
24 Who killed Ronald Reagan in his last film "The Killers"?
25 Whom did John Wayne play in "North to Alaska"?
26 For which film did Elizabeth Taylor win her second Oscar?
27 For which role was Dustin Hoffman nominated in 1969?
28 Which of the Redgrave clan appeared in "A Man for All Seasons"?
29 Who played opposite then wife Claire Bloom in "The Illustrated Man"?
30 Who was the older winner of the shared Best Actress Oscar in 1968?

Quiz 25 | Pot Luck 13 | Answers – page 218

1 A zinfandel is used for making what?

2 What separates Alaska from the other 48 US states?

3 How many times is "Um" sung in the chorus of 60s hit "Um Um Um Um Um Um"?

4 What is the capital of the US state of New Jersey?

5 On which island which is also a country is Adam's Peak?

6 In which year did London Underground's Bakerloo Line open?

7 Who won Best Actor Oscar for his part in the musical film "Amadeus"?

8 If you have comedos, what are you suffering from?

9 What is the third largest city in Britain?

10 What was Susie Cooper famous for?

11 What is Warwickshire's county motif?

12 Which former PM became President of the Czech Republic in 2003?

13 What kind of weapon was an arbalest?

14 Which Austrian physicist gave his name to perceived frequency variations under certain conditions?

15 Imran Khan played cricket for which two English counties?

16 What is the meaning of the legal expression "caveat emptor"?

17 Which optical aid was invented by Benjamin Franklin?

18 What was the Bay City Rollers' first UK Top Ten hit?

19 Where are the ethmoid, vomer and zygomatic bones in your body?

20 Who was Severus Snape when Robbie Coltrane was Rubeus Hagrid?

21 The capital of Japan is an anagram of which former capital?

22 Who rode both Toulon and Moonax to St Leger triumphs?

23 Who wrote "All Quiet on the Western Front"?

24 Where did John McGregor found the first Canoe Club in 1866?

25 Benny of ABBA has a cameo in "Mamma Mia! Here We Go Again" – as what?

26 Michael Jackson, Billie and Alicia Keyes have had different singles with which same title?

27 Which European country lost the battle of Ulm in 1805?

28 On TV, who was the victim in the first series of "The Murder Game"?

29 Which country has Guyana to the east and Colombia to the west?

30 How did Emiliano Zapata, the Mexican revolutionary, die in 1919?

Answers	**Kings & Queens** (see Quiz 26)

1 17 Bruton St, London. 2 King George V and Queen Mary. 3 Edward VII. 4 Adelaide.
5 George I. 6 Hit with a cricket ball. 7 George V. 8 Henry II's wife Eleanor of
Aquitaine. 9 Edward I (19). 10 It was his second. 11 The Pope. 12 Dunfermline.
13 Square, she was so obese. 14 Richard II. 15 River Soar. 16 Tax collectors. 17
Charles II. 18 St Stephen's Abbey Caen. 19 Henry I. 20 Edward VIII. 21 George I. 22
William IV. 23 Edward VII. 24 Christian IX of Denmark. 25 William II. 26 Four. 27
Norfolk. 28 Two. 29 Jane Seymour & Catherine Parr. 30 Gloucester Cathedral.

1 At which address was Elizabeth II born?
2 Who were the parents of the subject of "The Lost Prince" by Stephen Poliakoff?
3 Who was the only British monarch from the House of Wettin?
4 Who was William IV's queen?
5 Which monarch's mother was Sophia of Bohemia?
6 How did George II's eldest son die?
7 Who was the first British monarch to make a Christmas Day broadcast?
8 Which English king's wife was a former wife of Louis VII of France?
9 Which British monarch produced the most legitimate children?
10 What was notable about Henry VI's coronation in 1470?
11 Who made Henry VIII Fidei Defensor?
12 Where was Charles I born?
13 What shape was Queen Anne's coffin and why?
14 Which English king is reputed to have invented the handkerchief?
15 Where were Richard III's bones thrown when his grave was desecrated?
16 Why was Henry VIII's execution of Richard Empson and Edmund Dudley a popular move?
17 Who was threatened by the Rye House Plot?
18 Where is William the Conqueror buried?
19 Which king founded the first English zoo?
20 Who was the penultimate Emperor of India?
21 The Duchess of Kendal was mistress of which king?
22 Who was the first monarch born in Buckingham Palace?
23 Who was the first Emperor of India?
24 Who was Edward VII's father-in-law?
25 Which English king was killed by Walter Tyrel?
26 How many English kings reigned in the first half of the twentieth century?
27 In which county did George V die?
28 How many shirts did Charles I wear for his execution?
29 Who were Henry VIII's two oldest wives?
30 Where was Henry III crowned?

| **Answers** | **Pot Luck 13** *(see Quiz 25)* |

1 Wine. 2 British Columbia. 3 24. 4 Trenton. 5 Sri Lanka. 6 1906. 7 F. Murray Abraham. 8 Blackheads. 9 Glasgow. 10 Ceramic design. 11 A standing bear next to a ragged staff. 12 Vaclav Klaus. 13 A giant crossbow. 14 Christian Doppler. 15 Worcestershire and Sussex. 16 Let the buyer beware. 17 Bifocal lenses. 18 Keep On Dancing. 19 Skull. 20 Alan Rickman. 21 Kyoto. 22 Pat Eddery. 23 Erich Remarque. 24 Richmond, Surrey. 25 Pianist in a restaurant. 26 Girlfriend. 27 Austria. 28 Catherine Prior. 29 Venezuela. 30 Assassinated.

Quiz 27 | Pot Luck 14

Answers – page 220

LEVEL 3

1 Who directed the 1930s film "Mr Deeds Goes to Town"?
2 Who was the first Spaniard to win the French Open in tennis this century?
3 Shogi is a Japanese form of which game?
4 "Same Trailer Different Park" was the debut album for which country singer?
5 Which bird would you find in a squab pie?
6 Who played the lead character in the film "The Loneliness of the Long Distance Runner"?
7 Whose fourth volume of memoirs was called "North Face of Soho"?
8 Which football club's crest consists of two sets of stripes, a cross and a ball?
9 Which famous actor played Philo Beddoe in two films?
10 Whom did Australia beat when they first won cricket's World Cup?
11 What is the legendary ship The Flying Dutchman doomed to do?
12 Which queen of England had most fingers?
13 Who wrote the novel "Fair Stood the Wind for France"?
14 Who is the elder – Joan Collins or Michael Caine?
15 Whose one and only hit was "Eye Level" in 1973?
16 To three years, when did the M1 motorway open?
17 What was found in 1939 at Sutton Hoo, in Suffolk?
18 What is of interest to a thanatologist?
19 Where would you find calderas?
20 Who wrote the novel "The Lost World"?
21 If something is napiform which vegetable shape is it?
22 What part of the body is studied by a myologist?
23 Which song features the words, "Here am I floating round my tin can"?
24 What was the Triangular Trade mainly concerned with?
25 What, in America, is a cayuse?
26 How many strokes underwater may a competitive breast-stroke swimmer make at the start and turn?
27 The town of Carrara in Italy is famous for what?
28 Who wrote humour books naming Mussolini and Hitler in the titles?
29 Which gallery won the Art Fund Museum of the Year prize in 2018?
30 The Battle of Antietam was in which war?

Answers | **Classic No.1s** (see Quiz 28)

1 Wet Wet Wet. 2 Unchained. 3 My Sweet Lord. 4 Wooden Heart. 5 Maggie May. 6 Frankie Laine. 7 Gary Jules (Mad World). 8 Ticket to Ride. 9 Peter Cetera. 10 Herbert Kretzmer. 11 Girls' School. 12 Elton John. 13 The Fly (U2). 14 The Fleet's In. 15 Hole in the Head. 16 I Know Him So Well. 17 Whatever Will be Will be. 18 Mandy 19 Hello Goodbye. 20 Careless Whisper. 21 Bridge Over Troubled Water. 22 Who's Sorry Now? 23 Three Times a Lady. 24 John Travolta. 25 Hung Up. 26 Claudette. 27 Craig David. 28 Stranger on the Shore (Acker Bilk). 29 Bohemian Rhapsody. 30 Living Doll.

219

Quiz 28 | Classic No.1s

Answers – page 219

LEVEL 3

1 Who were the first Scottish group to have three No.1s?
2 Which 1955 American movie had "Unchained Melody" as theme tune?
3 Which No.1 was the first solo single by George Harrison?
4 Which Elvis hit made him the first artist with three consecutive British No.1s?
5 Which Rod Stewart hit was originally the B-side of "Reason to Believe"?
6 Who was on top of the charts the week Everest was first climbed?
7 Who featured on the first No.1 for Michael Andrews?
8 What was the first No.1 from the Beatles' second film "Help!"?
9 Who wrote Chicago's No.1 classic "If You Leave Me Now"?
10 Which lyricist of Aznavour's "She" was a writer on "Les Mis"?
11 What was on the other side of the double A No.1 "Mull of Kintyre"?
12 Who co-wrote a No.1 duet song under the pseudonym Ann Orson?
13 What finally knocked "(Everything I Do) I Do It for You" off the No.1 spot?
14 Which film did Frank Ifield's "I Remember You" originally come from?
15 What was the third UK No.1 single for the Sugababes?
16 What became the all-time best-UK selling single by a female duo?
17 Which Doris Day Oscar-winning song was from "The Man Who Knew Too Much" in 1956?
18 What was the first Westlife No.1 single with a one-word title?
19 Which No.1 hit by the Beatles equalled 7 weeks at the top with "From Me to You"?
20 What is the only George Michael song for which Andrew Ridgeley takes equal writing credit?
21 Which album title track gave Simon and Garfunkel their biggest hit?
22 Which 1920s standard gave Concetta Franconero a 6-week No.1 hit?
23 Which Commodores classic became Motown's best UK seller?
24 Who is the male half of the duo that have spent most weeks at No.1?
25 Which single marked Madonna's 20-year span of having UK No.1s?
26 Apart from "Cathy's Clown", which other No.1 for the Everly Brothers had a girl's name in the title?
27 In 2000, who became the youngest male to write and perform a UK No.1 single?
28 Which single was the first by a UK performer to top the US charts in the 1960s?
29 Which 1975 megahit remained at No.1 for 9 weeks?
30 Which No.1 hit was Cliff Richard's first million-seller?

| **Answers** | Pot Luck 14 *(see Quiz 27)* |

1 Frank Capra. 2 Juan Carlos Ferrero. 3 Chess. 4 Kacey Musgraves. 5 Pigeon. 6 Tom Courtenay. 7 Clive James. 8 Barcelona. 9 Clint Eastwood. 10 England. 11 Sail for ever. 12 Anne Boleyn (11). 13 HE Bates. 14 Michael Caine (by 2 months). 15 Simon Park Orchestra. 16 1959. 17 A Saxon ship. 18 Death. 19 Volcanoes (they are craters). 20 Sir Arthur Conan Doyle. 21 Turnip. 22 Muscles. 23 Space Oddity. 24 Slaves. 25 A horse. 26 One. 27 White marble. 28 Spike Milligan. 29 Tate St Ives. 30 American Civil War.

220

1 What is Kyzyl Kum in Russia?
2 Neville Cardus was associated with which sport?
3 Who played Paul Henreid's wife in the film "Casablanca"?
4 Which "Simpsons" catchphrase was first to make the on-line version of Oxford English Dictionary?
5 Where did the Dryad nymphs live in Greek mythology?
6 What sort of creature is a killdeer?
7 What type of music is Ira D. Sankey particularly noted for composing?
8 How old was Louis Braille when he invented his reading system for the blind?
9 Which actor starred in the silent films "Robin Hood", "The Three Musketeers" and "The Black Pirate"?
10 What was Five Star's first UK Top Ten hit?
11 Ficus Elastica is the Latin name for which plant?
12 In which sport is there a bonspiel?
13 Arch, loop and whorl are all parts of what?
14 What is pishogue a form of?
15 Permission was given to whom in 1988 to rebuild London's Globe Theatre?
16 Which country has the internet code .at?
17 A fylfot is better known as a what?
18 Alton Byrd was famous in which sport?
19 Who played the magical Supergran in the 1985 TV series?
20 Which 1990s Oscar Best Film did Colin Firth appear in as well as "Shakespeare in Love"?
21 Which actor was "The Virginian" on TV?
22 Which band's albums include "Load" and "Reload"?
23 Richard Meade won Olympic gold in which sport?
24 What is the main difference between squash and rackets?
25 In which year was the CBI set up?
26 Whose first Top Ten hit was "House of Love"?
27 In what unusual type of location was the late, great Jack Lemmon born?
28 In which country did the UK first score a Eurovision Song Contest no points?
29 Who would use a trochee?
30 Who wrote the play called "A Taste of Honey"?

Answers | **London Buildings** *(see Quiz 30)*

1 Elizabeth Tower. 2 Joanna Lumley. 3 The Cheesegrater. 4 The V&A. 5 The Goodies. 6 USA. 7 61 metres. 8 Erno Goldfinger. 9 London Eye. 10 Sir John Soane. 11 52 metres. 12 Chamberlin, Powell and Bon. 13 1951. 14 George Gilbert Scott. 15 72. 16 Southwark Cathedral. 17 Foster and Partners. 18 Gothic revival. 19 30 St Mary Axe. 20 Pink Floyd – Animals. 21 English Baroque. 22 191 metres. 23 Horace Walpole. 24 Alexandra Palace. 25 Zaha Hadid. 26 St Paul's Cathedral. 27 William Morris. 28 Liberty department store. 29 Largest Hindu temple outside India. 30 Norman Foster.

1 What is the official name of the famous tower known as Big Ben?
2 The garden bridge over the Thames was whose original idea?
3 What is 122 Leadenhall Street, London, more commonly known as?
4 Who salvaged part of East London's Robin Hood Gardens council estate?
5 A giant kitten crushed St Paul's Cathedral in which comedy series?
6 Which country opened a new embassy in London's Nine Elms in January 2018?
7 How far is the Monument from where the Great Fire of London started?
8 Which architect made his home in Willow Road?
9 Marks Barfield Architects designed which London structure?
10 Who was the architect of the Dulwich Picture Gallery?
11 How tall is Nelson's Column?
12 Which architecture firm designed the Barbican?
13 In what year did the Royal Festival Hall open?
14 Who designed the Midland Grand Hotel at St Pancras Station?
15 How many habitable floors has the Shard?
16 What stands at the site of the oldest crossing point of the Thames?
17 Who designed City Hall, HQ of the Greater London Authority?
18 What style of architecture was Augustus Pugin known for?
19 What is the address of the Gherkin?
20 A pig floats over Battersea Power Station – name the band and album.
21 Nicholas Hawksmoor was a leading proponent of which architectural style?
22 In total, how many metres high is the BT Tower?
23 Who built and lived at Strawberry Hill House?
24 The first public TV transmissions were made in 1936 – from where?
25 Who designed the London Aquatics Centre, used for the 2012 London Olympics?
26 In 2011 an anti-capitalist Occupy London camp was established where?
27 Who lived at the Red House in Bexleyheath?
28 HMS Impregnable and HMS Hindustan timbers were used in what?
29 Why did the Shri Swaminarayan Temple in Neasden enter the 2000 Guinness Book of Records?
30 Which architect roofed over the British Museum's Great Court?

Answers	Pot Luck 15 *(see Quiz 29)*

1 A desert. 2 Cricket. 3 Ingrid Bergman. 4 D'oh. 5 In trees. 6 A bird (type of plover). 7 Hymns. 8 15. 9 Douglas Fairbanks. 10 System Addict. 11 Rubber plant. 12 Curling. 13 Fingerprints. 14 Sorcery. 15 Sam Wanamaker. 16 Austria. 17 Swastika. 18 Basketball. 19 Gudrun Ure. 20 The English Patient. 21 James Drury. 22 Metallica. 23 3 Day Eventing. 24 Squash uses a softer ball. 25 1965. 26 East 17. 27 In a lift. 28 Latvia. 29 A poet. 30 Shelagh Delaney.

1 With which police identification system is Francis Galton associated?

2 Which trees mainly produced the fossilised resin which becomes amber?

3 Sissoko, Ameobi and Krul played together for which Premier League team?

4 If a ship is careened, what has happened to it?

5 What did Henry Segrave break at Daytona in 1927 and 1929?

6 What is the nickname of Callum Highway in "EastEnders"?

7 Which event is the first in a Decathlon?

8 Which US President died on the same day as Aldous Huxley?

9 When is Haley's Comet predicted to make its next visit in Earth's vicinity?

10 Who wrote the "Gormenghast Trilogy"?

11 In which county is Chequers?

12 The King of which country was the "Prisoner of Zenda"?

13 Who was the first jockey to record three consecutive Derby wins?

14 What relation to King Arthur was Mordred?

15 Who designed the first lightning conductor?

16 Iraq's prime minister Nuri al-Maliki is a member of which party?

17 What is matzo?

18 Which actor played Captain Bligh, Quasimodo and Henry VIII in films?

19 Which Archbishop of Canterbury was burnt at the stake in 1556?

20 What is the capital of the US state of North Dakota?

21 In London's Hampstead, what is also known as the Lawn Road Flats?

22 Who played King Arthur in "First Knight"?

23 Whose one and only hit was "Michelle" in 1966?

24 What can be grapnel, sheet and bower?

25 A trudgen is used in which sport?

26 Which river was first explored by Mungo Park, a Scottish surgeon?

27 To five years, when were Nobel Prizes first awarded?

28 In the poem "Beowulf", what kills Beowulf?

29 What would you do with a gigot?

30 The sitcom in which Warren Mitchell made his name took its title from which book?

Answers	**Periodic Table** *(see Quiz 32)*

1 Dmitri Mendeleev. 2 Hydrogen. 3 1869. 4 Primo Levi. 5 Left. 6 Periods. 7 Thorium. 8 Ammonia. 9 Groups. 10 Charcoal. 11 Retinol (vitamin A). 12 The first 98. 13 Atomic number. 14 Hydrogen. 15 Oganesson (118). 16 Ascorbic acid (vitamin C) 17 Ytterby. 18 As. 19 Hydrogen. 20 Colour. 21 Noble gases. 22 Tennessine. 23 1890s. 24 Rubidium. 25 N and O. 26 Gallium. 27 Goblin. 28 Chloroform. 29 Neon. 30 H_2SO_4.

Quiz 32 | Periodic Table

Answers – page 223

1 Which Russian chemist published the first recognisable periodic table?
2 What is the lightest element?
3 In what year was the first recognisable periodic table published?
4 Who wrote the 1975 short story collection "The Periodic Table"?
5 Are metals generally on the left or the right of the periodic table?
6 What are the rows of the periodic table called?
7 Which element is named after the Norse god of thunder?
8 NH_3 is the chemical formula for what?
9 What are the columns of the periodic table called?
10 The name carbon comes from the Latin word for what?
11 $C_{20}H_{30}O$ is the chemical formula for what?
12 How many elements occur naturally?
13 What indicates the number of protons in an element's nucleus?
14 The name of which element comes from the Greek for 'water-forming'?
15 Which element has the highest atomic number and atomic mass?
16 $C_6H_8O_6$ is the chemical formula for what?
17 Which Swedish village has four elements named after it?
18 What is the chemical symbol for arsenic?
19 What is the most abundant chemical in the universe?
20 Chromium gets its name from the Greek word for what?
21 What are odourless, colourless and have very low chemical reactivity?
22 As of 2018, what is the most recently discovered element?
23 In which decade did the Curies report their discovery of radium?
24 The name of which element means 'deepest red' in Latin?
25 What are the chemical symbols of the two most common gases in the air?
26 Which element's name comes from the Latin name for France?
27 The name cobalt comes from the German word for what?
28 $CHCl_3$ is the chemical formula for what?
29 The Greek word for new gave which element its name?
30 What is the chemical formula for sulphuric acid?

Answers | **Pot Luck 16** *(see Quiz 31)*

1 Fingerprints. 2 Coniferous trees. 3 Newcastle United. 4 Turned on one side for cleaning. 5 Land Speed record. 6 Halfway. 7 100 metres. 8 JF Kennedy. 9 2061. 10 Mervyn Peake. 11 Buckinghamshire. 12 Ruritania. 13 Steve Donoghue. 14 Nephew. 15 Benjamin Franklin. 16 Dawa party. 17 Unleavened bread. 18 Charles Laughton. 19 Thomas Cranmer. 20 Bismarck. 21 The Isokon. 22 Sean Connery. 23 Overlanders. 24 Anchors. 25 Swimming. 26 River Niger. 27 1901. 28 A dragon. 29 Eat it. 30 The Book of Common Prayer.

Quiz 33 Pot Luck 17

Answers – page 226

LEVEL 3

1 What was discovered by Garcia Lopez de Cardenas in 1540?
2 Whose first Top Ten hit was titled "September"?
3 In the Seven Years War who were Britain's two allies?
4 On which label did Gorillaz first have a No.1 album?
5 Who was the first player to score 100 points in a NBA basketball game?
6 Rose Louise Hovick achieved fame under what name?
7 Who is the father of Marsha Hunt's daughter Karis?
8 What is the final line in the film "Gone with the Wind"?
9 Which newspaper was featured in the TV series "Hot Metal"?
10 The gemstone ruby is associated with which month?
11 What is the name of Phil and Jill Archer's farm?
12 What is the most populous state and largest economy that is not a member of the UN?
13 Which comic actor's father was the deputy speaker of the Irish Parliament?
14 Where on your body are the Mounts of the Sun, Mercury and Venus?
15 Which fungal disease has the name Ceratostomella Ulmi?
16 Who created the cartoon character Colonel Blimp?
17 Where is the village of Skara Brae?
18 Who won the 1989 Best Actor Oscar for the film "My Left Foot"?
19 Who is the elder – Ian Botham or Jim Davidson?
20 Which actor played the title role in the TV series "Dear John"?
21 Whose theme was a No. 4 UK hit in 1959 for Elmer Bernstein?
22 If you are an encratic person, what do you possess?
23 Who said, "There never was a good war, nor a bad peace"?
24 David Beckham made his league debut on loan at which club?
25 Who wrote "The White Company"?
26 Which general was the youngest in the American Civil War?
27 Who was top scorer for Man Utd in 1997–98 and Man City in 2005–06?
28 With which profession is the organisation RIBA associated?
29 Who founded the record label Respond?
30 Who in 1632 painted "The Anatomy Lesson of Dr Tulip"?

Answers	Pot Luck 18 *(see Quiz 34)*

1 Major Hugh Lindsay. 2 Colin Powell. 3 336. 4 Sir Ranulph Fiennes. 5 Flags. 6 Sir Francis Walsingham. 7 Mountaineering. 8 Philosopher's Stone. 9 Paraguay. 10 Abraham Darby. 11 Denise La Salle. 12 Daniel Day-Lewis. 13 Juventus. 14 Cockerel. 15 Sumatra. 16 Thin. 17 China. 18 Edinson Cavani. 19 Julia Somerville. 20 Peacock. 21 Sphalerite. 22 Chess. 23 A stream. 24 President Truman. 25 Helston, Cornwall. 26 Ocean depths. 27 Sri Lanka. 28 Raw Meat. 29 Dieting. 30 How am I Supposed to Live without You.

325

Quiz 34 | Pot Luck 18

1 Who died in the avalanche in Klosters in 1988 involving Prince Charles' party?

2 Who was chairman of the Joint Chiefs of Staff during the Gulf War?

3 How many hours are there in a fortnight?

4 Which modern-day explorer has Twisleton-Wykeham as part of his name?

5 Vexillology is the study of what?

6 Who was Elizabeth I's State Secretary from 1573 to 1590?

7 Edward Whymper is associated with which leisure activity?

8 What did alchemists call the imaginary object that would turn base metals to gold?

9 Nicanor Duarte Frutos became President of which South American country?

10 Who designed and built the world's first iron bridge?

11 Who took her "Toot Toot" into the pop charts in the 80s?

12 Who is the elder – Sean Bean or Daniel Day-Lewis?

13 What was Michel Platini's club when he was three times European Footballer of the Year?

14 On the Chinese calendar, what is the only bird?

15 Where are the Padang Highlands?

16 What are you if you are described as being an ectomorph?

17 Where did Indian ink originally come from?

18 Who was the Ligue 1 top goalscorer in 2016-17 and 2017-18?

19 Who was the first female to present the main news on BBC and ITV?

20 What bird was the symbol of Persia's monarchy from 1739 to 1979?

21 What is the metal zinc extracted from?

22 Which game uses the expression "J'adoube"?

23 In London what was the Tyburn?

24 Who attempted the programme of social reform called Fair Deal?

25 Where in England might you do a Furry Dance?

26 What are measured in hadal, abyssal and bathyl zones?

27 Which country has the internet code .lk?

28 The word Eskimo means the eaters of what?

29 If you were banting, what would you be doing?

30 What was the Michael Bolton's first UK Top Ten hit?

Answers | Pot Luck 17 (see Quiz 33)

1 The Grand Canyon. 2 Earth, Wind & Fire. 3 Hanover and Prussia. 4 Parlophone.
5 Wilt Chamberlain. 6 Gypsy Rose Lee. 7 Mick Jagger. 8 Tomorrow is another day. 9 Daily Crucible. 10 July. 11 Brookfield. 12 Taiwan. 13 Ardal O'Hanlon. 14 Your hand. 15 David Low. 16 Dutch elm disease. 17 The Orkneys. 18 Daniel Day-Lewis. 19 Jim Davidson. 20 Ralph Bates. 21 Staccato's Theme. 22 Self-control. 23 Benjamin Franklin. 24 Preston. 25 Sir Arthur Conan Doyle. 26 George A. Custer. 27 Andy Cole. 28 Architects. 29 Paul Weller. 30 Rembrandt.

Quiz 35   JK Rowling

Answers – page 228

1 In which year was JK Rowling born?
2 In which year was the first Harry Potter book published?
3 At which University did she study?
4 Although she wanted to study English what did she study?
5 Who became her literary agent?
6 Which publisher and which division of it published her first book?
7 Both of JK's parents came from which city?
8 Who worked on the Latin translation of "Philosopher's Stone"?
9 What was the name of JK's first daughter?
10 Whom is "Chamber of Secrets" dedicated to?
11 The second, third and fourth Harry Potter books were published in which month?
12 Where did her parents meet?
13 All titles begin "Harry Potter and the" what other word is in titles two to five?
14 JK worked for a while in London for which worldwide organisation?
15 Who is the resident ghost of Ravenclaw House?
16 Who first directed a Harry Potter movie – Chris Columbus or Mike Newell?
17 Which Scottish city did JK Rowling move to when teaching English?
18 Which national wizarding newspaper did JK create in her books?
19 Which word was changed to Sorceror in the title of a US edition?
20 Which novel starts with Harry going to the Quidditch World Cup?
21 What is JK's word for a wizard that can talk to snakes?
22 Under what pseudonym did she write the "Cormoran Strike" series?
23 Which Hogwarts House did JK say she would like to have been in the most?
24 What was the title of her 2016 e-book guide to Hogwarts and its secrets?
25 Harry Potter is in which year at Hogwarts for "The Half-Blood Prince"?
26 What were the names of Harry's parents?
27 Which secondary school did JK Rowling attend?
28 What is the name of the red ball used for scoring in quidditch?
29 On the cover of "Order of the Phoenix" does the bird look to its left or right?
30 Which character is the only one that depicts someone JK Rowling knew?

Answers   Pot Luck 19 *(see Quiz 36)*

1 Chord. 2 Can The Can. 3 Lexington. 4 John Schlesinger. 5 Edward I. 6 John Major. 7 The central nervous system. 8 Mary Arden. 9 Ainsley Harriott. 10 Kurt Hahn. 11 Blue IKEA bag. 12 73. 13 Eat it. 14 Seaweed. 15 In the veins of Greek gods. 16 Kalin Twins. 17 Boils. 18 Palk Straits. 19 Harold Wilson. 20 Harry Secombe. 21 Lord Tweedsmuir. 22 Nigeria. 23 Rosinante. 24 Prokofiev. 25 Under the Eye of the Clock. 26 Nutria fur. 27 Bill Bryson. 28 Churchill. 29 Medvedev. 30 Tim Roth.

1 What is a line joining any two points on a curve called in geometry?
2 What was Suzi Quatro's first UK Top Ten hit?
3 Which battle is remembered in the USA in April on Patriots' Day?
4 Who directed the films "Marathon Man" and "Billy Liar"?
5 Who was the eldest son of Henry III?
6 Who preceded Douglas Hurd as Foreign Secretary?
7 Which part of the body is affected by chorea?
8 Who was William Shakespeare's mother?
9 Which celeb chef spent nine years as head chef at the Long Room at Lord's?
10 Who founded the Outward Bound Trust?
11 In a retail context, what is Frakta?
12 How old was Klaus Barbie when he was sentenced to life for wartime atrocities?
13 What would you do with a kaki?
14 What are Purple Laver and Devil's Apron types of?
15 Where would ichor supposedly have flowed?
16 Which singing twins were Hal and Herbert?
17 In the Bible, what did Job suffer with?
18 Which straits separate India from Sri Lanka?
19 Who referred to international financiers as "gnomes of Zurich"?
20 Who was the second oldest Goon?
21 What was author John Buchan's real title?
22 Which country do the Hausa people live in?
23 What was the name of Don Quixote's horse?
24 Who wrote the opera "The Love for Three Oranges"?
25 Christopher Nolan was a Whitbread Book of the Year winner with what?
26 Which fur comes from the coypu?
27 Who wrote the travelogue: "I come from Des Moines. Somebody had to"?
28 Who became Minister of Defence when Churchill became PM in 1940?
29 Which name is shared by a senior Russian politician and an ATP tennis player?
30 In Tarantino's directorial debut, Harvey Keitel was White – who was Orange?

Answers	JK Rowling (see Quiz 35)

1 1965. 2 1987. 3 Exeter. 4 French. 5 Christopher Little. 6 Bloomsbury Children's Books. 7 London. 8 Peter Needham. 9 Jessica. 10 Sean Harris. 11 July. 12 On a train (from King's Cross). 13 Of. 14 Amnesty International. 15 The Grey Lady. 16 Chris Columbus. 17 Edinburgh. 18 The Daily Prophet. 19 Philospher. 20 Goblet of Fire. 21 Parselmouth. 22 Robert Galbraith. 23 Gryffindor. 24 Hogwarts: An Incomplete and Unreliable Guide. 25 Year Six. 26 James & Lily. 27 Wydean. 28 Quaffle. 29 Left. 30 Gilderoy Lockhart.

1 What is hanepoot?
2 Who or what was Buck's Fizz named after?
3 Which snack's name comes from the Turkish for rotating?
4 Where is the yeastless beer faro made?
5 Where was Anton Mosimann's first position as chef in the UK?
6 Kummel is a Russian liqueur extracted from what?
7 The macadamia is native to where?
8 What is the main ingredient of a brandade?
9 Who opened the Miller Howe restaurant in 1971?
10 In his diary what did Pepys call "jucalette"?
11 Where in a dish would you put gremolata?
12 Which country has a wine-growing area called O'Higgins?
13 Which term indicates the amount of wine by which a container falls short of being full?
14 Who is credited with creating camembert cheese in about 1790?
15 What is the base of a florentine biscuit made from?
16 Where did malmsey wine originate?
17 Balti is the Indian word for what?
18 Which abbreviation indicates wine between the qualities of vin de pays and appellation contrôlée?
19 What are the ingredients of a Mr Callaghan?
20 What is cocose?
21 What is Deliciously Ella's real name?
22 In Swiss cooking what is a leckerli?
23 What is added to an omelette to make an omelette Argenteuil?
24 Which herbs are put in a béarnaise sauce?
25 Which fruit is used to make slivovitz?
26 Foie gras is the liver of which creatures?
27 In ceviche raw fish is marinated in what?
28 What is a mesclun?
29 A brochette is another name for what?
30 In Mexican cookery what is a quesadilla?

1 What was Sting's debut movie?
2 What was Justin Henry's surname in a 70s Oscar winner?
3 In which film does railwayman Cleavon Little become sheriff?
4 "That's Entertainment" was a compilation of clips from which studio?
5 Who played Siegfried to Simon Ward's James in "All Creatures Great and Small"?
6 Which music plays in the background in "10"?
7 What was Alan Parker's first feature film?
8 Who starred in and produced "The China Syndrome"?
9 What was Tom Selleck's first film, in 1970?
10 Who played Winston's father in "Young Winston"?
11 Whose was the disembodied voice narrating Agatha Christie's "And Then There were None"?
12 Who wrote the music for "Shaft"?
13 Who was the landlord of "10 Rillington Place"?
14 Who sang the title song in "The Aristocats"?
15 For the trailer of which Hitchcock film was the director seen floating in the Thames?
16 Stacy Keach starred in "Fat City" after who turned it down?
17 Who directed "Death Wish"?
18 Who was the first director to cast Goldie Hawn in a non-comedy film?
19 Whom did Jane Fonda play in "Julia"?
20 Why did Peter Finch not collect his Oscar for "Network"?
21 Whose music did Malcolm McDowell like in "A Clockwork Orange"?
22 Who was the only female Oscar winner for "One Flew Over the Cuckoo's Nest"?
23 Who played the editor of the Washington Post in "All the President's Men"?
24 Which club features in "Cabaret"?
25 Who played the brother in "The Railway Children"?
26 Who was Maid Marian opposite Sean Connery in "Robin and Marian"?
27 What was the first film in which Julie Christie and Warren Beatty starred together?
28 What was Peter Ustinov's first film as Hercule Poirot?
29 What was the sequel to "Love Story"?
30 Which film of a Frederick Forsyth novel starred Jon Voight?

Answers | **Food & Drink** *(see Quiz 37)*

1 Type of grape. 2 Buck's Club in London. 3 Doner kebab. 4 Belgium. 5 The Dorchester. 6 Caraway seeds. 7 Australia. 8 Salt cod. 9 John Tovey. 10 Chocolate. 11 Top (garnish). 12 Chile. 13 Ullage. 14 Madame Harel, a French farmer's wife. 15 Chocolate. 16 Greece. 17 Bucket. 18 VDQS. 19 Cinzano, apricot brandy & angostura bitters. 20 Butter made from coconut. 21 Ella Mills. 22 Biscuit. 23 Asparagus. 24 Tarragon, chervil. 25 Plums. 26 Geese or ducks. 27 Lime juice. 28 Mixed green salad. 29 Kebab. 30 Filled tortilla or pancake.

Quiz 39 Pot Luck 20

Answers – page 232

1 What is eaten by a pantophagist?
2 Who were the Fuggers?
3 What do isohyet lines indicate on a map?
4 What are the dark, lowland plains on the moon known as?
5 Where, in 1855, is ice hockey thought to have originated?
6 What was the only UK Top Ten hit for the group Black Sabbath?
7 In which country was musician Leopold Stokowski born?
8 Saddam's death sentence in Nov. 2006 related to a massacre in which town?
9 What was the name of Fingal's dog in Gaelic legend?
10 The Schich Test can be used to test for which disease?
11 In the Oliver Stone film "Natural Born Killers", who played Mickey?
12 What do you do with a maduro?
13 How many albums had Eva Cassidy made before the top-selling "Songbird"?
14 Which novel starts "The past is a foreign country: they do things differently there"?
15 Which TV celeb advertised pizza with Caprice?
16 What is the main colour on the cover of the album "Spice"?
17 In which decade was Betty Boothroyd born?
18 Coptic Christians are found in Egypt and which one other country?
19 Which 1996 tennis tournament saw the debut of a fluorescent ball?
20 What was Errol Flynn's last film in 1959?
21 In which decade was playwright Sir Alan Ayckbourn born?
22 Which son of English parents was the voice of the Scottish ogre in "Shrek"?
23 Which part did Brian Wilde play in the TV series "Porridge"?
24 Which phobia describes a fear of marriage?
25 What was Bjork's first UK Top Ten hit from 1995?
26 Which female media personality has been President of the Ramblers Association?
27 What was a carrack?
28 What term describes using a gentler expression to soften a hard one?
29 Who is the elder – Lynsey de Paul or Noel Edmonds?
30 Which club did Gianluigi Buffon join in 2018?

Answers | TV Gold (see Quiz 40)

1 1969. 2 Sally James. 3 A poppy field. 4 Pauline Collins. 5 Dusty Springfield. 6 Stars and Garters. 7 Anne Aston. 8 Mrs Edna Hall. 9 Eamonn Andrews. 10 Cabbage. 11 Kate, Avril & Victoria. 12 Sherman. 13 Dawn. 14 Harry Worth. 15 Sheila Hancock. 16 Len Fairclough's son in Corrie. 17 Donatello. 18 Bernard Hill. 19 Robert Robinson. 20 Barbara Windsor. 21 Ronnie Corbett. 22 Dorothy McNab. 23 Steptoe & Son. 24 Noah Beery Jr. 25 Keith Partridge. 26 Mollie Sugden. 27 Wilbur Post. 28 Obadiah Slope. 29 Hughes. 30 Maxwell Klinger.

Quiz 40 TV Gold

1 In what year was the first "Monty Python" show broadcast?
2 Who was the female presenter of "Tiswas"?
3 What was the final view at the end of "Blackadder Goes Forth"?
4 Which future Oscar nominee played Samantha Briggs in "Dr Who"?
5 Who was the only female on the first "Top of the Pops"?
6 In which TV pub did Vince Hill find fame?
7 On "The Golden Shot" who famously always got her sums wrong?
8 Who was the housekeeper in "All Creatures Great and Small"?
9 Who was the first presenter of "World of Sport" on ITV?
10 What was the booby prize on "Crackerjack"?
11 Who were the trio in "Take Three Girls"?
12 In "Fawlty Towers", what was Polly's surname?
13 Who originally shared a flat with Sandra in "The Liver Birds"?
14 Which comedian starred as himself in the northern town of Woodbridge?
15 Who played the shop treasurer in "The Rag Trade"?
16 The lead singer of Herman's Hermits played whose son on TV?
17 Who was the first Teenage Mutant Hero Turtle alphabetically?
18 Who played Yosser in "Boys from the Blackstuff"?
19 Who was doing the asking in "Ask the Family"?
20 Who frequently appeared as Nymphia in "Up Pompeii"?
21 Who starred as Charley Farley, partner of Piggy Malone?
22 Who was the author played by Elaine Stritch in "Two's Company"?
23 Which sitcom began with a one-off play called "The Offer"?
24 Who played Jim Rockford's father, Rocky, in "The Rockford Files"?
25 As which character did David Cassidy shoot to fame in the 70s?
26 In "My Wife Next Door" which sitcom doyenne played George's mother?
27 Who was the only person the horse Mr Ed would talk to?
28 Which character shot Alan Rickman to fame in "The Barchester Chronicles"?
29 In "Fawlty Towers", what was Terry's surname?
30 Which corporal in "M*A*S*H" took to wearing women's clothes in order to be discharged?

Quiz 41 | Pot Luck 21

Answers – page 234

LEVEL 3

1 Which Yorkshire gallery won the Art Fund Museum of the Year prize in 2017?
2 In which year did Channel 4 start to broadcast?
3 What was the Scavenger's Daughter used for in the 16th century?
4 What can be sornick, nainsook and samite?
5 Who wrote "Life Before Man" and "The Edible Woman"?
6 Which country launched a strike against Russia's fleet in 1904 at Port Arthur?
7 What is the collective name for a group of rhinoceroses?
8 Who created the character Doctor Finlay?
9 Which British-born Hollywood star has children called Rafferty, Iris and Rudy?
10 "The Flame Trees of Thika" was set in which country?
11 What was Boney M's first UK Top Ten hit from 1976?
12 What was the Derby Scheme of 1915?
13 Who wrote "A Farewell to Arms"?
14 Who is the elder – Dawn French or Jennifer Saunders?
15 What name was given to George Stephenson's first locomotive?
16 At which ceremony are coins of the realm tested?
17 Who was Britain's first Minister for the Arts in 1967?
18 Which northern city was given the Latin name Pons Aelius?
19 In "The Politician's Wife" who played the adulterer opposite Juliet Stevenson?
20 When was Exchange & Mart first published?
21 Whom did Buddha marry before searching for enlightenment?
22 Alphabetically what is the last of the Chinese Zodiac signs?
23 Did Geoff Hurst's World Cup final shirt fetch around £50,000, £92,000 or £130,000 at auction?
24 What was the profession of the pneumatic tyre patentee John Dunlop?
25 What, on 3 December 1923, gave its first broadcast?
26 Whose final movie as Q was in "The World is not Enough"?
27 Which Lord headed the investigating committee into "sleaze" in public life in 1995?
28 Who said, "Don't point that beard at me: it might go off"?
29 Who has a cousin called Scampi?
30 What ceased to be legal at midnight, December 31, 1960?

Answers | Girl Power *(see Quiz 42)*

1 Every Night. 2 Gwen Stefani. 3 Girl Power. 4 Mel and Kim Appleby. 5 1970. 6 You Don't Know. 7 Briana Corrigan. 8 Freda Payne's Band of Gold. 9 Michael Jackson. 10 Sandie Shaw. 11 Louise. 12 Lola Lovell. 13 Eithne Ni Bhraonain. 14 Siobhan Fahey. 15 Into the Groove. 16 Alison Moyet. 17 1957. 18 The Bangles. 19 Don't be a Stranger. 20 Jacqui Abbott. 21 Hunchback of Notre Dame. 22 Mica Paris. 23 Jump to the Beat. 24 Cissy Houston. 25 Kim Wilde. 26 Steps. 27 Desire. 28 Kim Gordon. 29 Sugababes. 30 Mariah Carey.

Quiz 42 | Girl Power

Answers – page 233

1 What are Celine Dion's first two words on "My Heart Will Go On"?
2 Which artist became the first to achieve one million paid downloads in the US?
3 What did Geri write by her signature on the cover notes of "Spice"?
4 Which sisters gave Stock/Aitken/Waterman their first No.1 hit?
5 In which year was Diana Ross's first UK solo Top Ten hit?
6 Which hit made Helen Shapiro the youngest British artist to reach No.1?
7 Who sang female vocals on the Beautiful South's first No.1?
8 Belinda Carlisle and Bonnie Tyler both covered which 1970 No.1?
9 Who partnered Janet Jackson on her UK No. 3 hit "Scream"?
10 Who was the first British female soloist to have three chart No.1 hits?
11 Whose first UK Top Ten hit as a solo artist was "Light of My Life"?
12 Which character was played by Kylie Minogue in "The Delinquents"?
13 What is Enya's full name?
14 Which Bananarama star went on to join Shakespear's Sister?
15 What was Madonna's first UK No.1?
16 Whose first UK Top Ten hit was "Love Resurrection"?
17 When did Shirley Bassey first reach the UK Top Ten?
18 Formed in 1981, girl band The Colours charted under which name?
19 What was Dina Carroll's first solo Top Ten hit?
20 Which former Beautiful South singer reunited with Paul Heaton in 2013?
21 Which film featured the Eternal hit "Someday" in 1996?
22 Whose first UK Top Ten hit was "My One Temptation"?
23 Which UK No. 3 for Stacy Lattisaw was a No. 8 for Dannii Minogue?
24 Which lady recorded the original "Midnight Train To Georgia"?
25 Which lady was "Rockin' Around the Christmas Tree" in 1987?
26 Lisa Scott-Lee and Faye Tozer were members of which top-selling pop quintet?
27 What was Geri Halliwell's first single with a one-word title?
28 Who wrote the 2015 memoir "Girl in a Band"?
29 In which girl group did Heidi Range replace Siobhan Donaghy?
30 Who was the first solo female to enter the UK charts at No.1?

| **Answers** | **Pot Luck 21** *(see Quiz 41)* |

1 Hepworth Wakefield. 2 1982. 3 A torture device. 4 Fabrics. 5 Margaret Atwood. 6 Japan. 7 A crash. 8 AJ Cronin. 9 Jude Law. 10 Kenya. 11 Daddy Cool. 12 Conscription. 13 Ernest Hemingway. 14 Dawn French. 15 Blucher. 16 Trial of the Pyx. 17 Jennie Lee. 18 Newcastle-upon-Tyne. 19 Trevor Eve. 20 1868. 21 Princess Yashara. 22 Tiger. 23 £92,000. 24 Veterinary Surgeon. 25 Big Ben. 26 Desmond Llewelyn. 27 Lord Nolan. 28 Groucho Marx. 29 Sooty. 30 The farthing.

1 How did Marie Curie's husband Pierre die?
2 Which group of people were once known as Millennial Dawnists?
3 In which decade was musician Mark Knopfler born?
4 What are you like if you are described as being saurian?
5 Who was the father of Enoch in the Bible?
6 Who created the character Tristram Shandy?
7 By which name is Denis Charles Pratt better known?
8 In which country is there a political party called Likud?
9 What was Tammy Wynette's real first name?
10 Which part did Carl Weathers play in the Rocky movies?
11 Where is a howdah normally found?
12 Which Spaniard painted the picture "The Rokeby Venus"?
13 Which River mouth was discovered by Amerigo Vespucci in 1499?
14 In "Corrie", what was the late Mike Baldwin's middle name?
15 What did PT Barnum allegedly say is born every minute?
16 Richard Kuhn, Jutus Liebig and Harold Urey were famous in which scientific field?
17 Who was the first undisputed heavyweight world champion boxer to be European?
18 As of 2018, what is the tallest unfinished building in the world?
19 Which Diane featured in the original cult movie "The Wicker Man"?
20 Horace Saussure made the first ascent of where in 1787?
21 Which title is traditionally given to the second son of the monarch?
22 What sort of food is Dunlop?
23 What is a cow's first milk after calving called?
24 Which country celebrates the National holiday, the "Day of the Dead"?
25 Who wrote "A Handful of Dust"?
26 What's Geri Halliwell's middle name?
27 The train the Cornish Riviera ran from where to where?
28 In the Second World War what did the Germans send out in "wolf packs"?
29 What was Bow Wow Wow's first UK Top Ten hit?
30 Who wrote the poems "Maud" and "Locksley Hall"?

Answers	**Sport Moments** *(see Quiz 44)*

1 Corbiere. 2 Beethoven. 3 Paul Scholes (in 2005). 4 Carlos Bacca. 5 Ohio State University. 6 The Ryder Cup. 7 Iffley Road. 8 200,000. 9 Said Aouita. 10 Lotus. 11 Chris Brasher (pacemaker for Bannister). 12 Esha Ness. 13 18-17. 14 Adrian Moorhouse. 15 Andrew Holmes. 16 Steve Cram. 17 First woman to take part in the boat race. 18 Mill Reef (1971). 19 Seven. 20 7hr 54 mins. 21 Mike "Fluff" Cowan. 22 Nine. 23 Alan Shearer. 24 Hickstead. 25 Betty Stove. 26 700. 27 800m, 1000m, 1500m. 28 25,095-1. 29 Noureddine Morceli. 30 Trevor Berbick.

Quiz 44 | Sport Moments

Answers – page 235

LEVEL 3

1 Which Grand National winner was the first to be trained by a woman?
2 David Broome was the first British showjumping champion on which horse?
3 Who had his spot kick saved in the first FA Cup Final decided on penalties?
4 Which Colombian's penalty did Jordan Pickford save in the 2018 World Cup shoot-out?
5 Jesse Owens was part of which university team when he set his three world records?
6 What competition did 'Moliwood' help win in 2018?
7 In which road in Oxford did Roger Bannister run his four-minute mile?
8 How many people witnessed Brazil's defeat by Uruguay in the 1950 World Cup Final?
9 Who was the first athlete to break 13 minutes for the 5000m?
10 Who made Chris Boardman's winning bicycle in Barcelona?
11 Which famous pacemaker founded the London Marathon?
12 Which Grand National horse was the first to cross the line the year the race was abandoned?
13 By what score did Steve Davis lose the World Professional Championship Final in 1985?
14 Who was the first man to break one minute for 100m breaststroke in a 25m pool?
15 With whom did Steve Redgrave take the second of his four Olympic golds?
16 Which British man ran the fastest mile in the 1980s?
17 Why did Susan Brown make history in 1981?
18 Which was the last horse before Lammtarra in 1995 to win the classic triple?
19 How many times did Nadia Comaneci score a perfect 10 at Montreal in 1976?
20 To the nearest 10 minutes, how long did it take Brian Lara to score his record 501 against Durham in 1994?
21 Who caddied for Tiger Woods on his first US Masters victory?
22 How many races out of the 16 did Nigel Mansell win to become World Champion?
23 Who was the first player since WWII to score more than 30 goals in three consecutive seasons?
24 Where was Harvey Smith when he made his infamous V sign?
25 Whom did Virginia Wade beat to win her Wimbledon Singles title?
26 How many League games had Stanley Matthews played before his final match aged 50?
27 Seb Coe simultaneously held three world records, at which distances?
28 To the nearest 100 what were the odds against Frankie Dettori's seven Ascot wins?
29 Who broke the 1500, 3000 and 5000m records in 1994?
30 Whom did Mike Tyson beat to become the youngest WBC champion?

Answers | Pot Luck 22 *(see Quiz 43)*

1 In a road accident. 2 Jehovah's Witnesses. 3 1940s. 4 A Lizard. 5 Cain. 6 Laurence Sterne. 7 Quentin Crisp. 8 Israel. 9 Virginia. 10 Apollo Creed. 11 Seat placed on the back of an elephant. 12 Velasquez. 13 Amazon. 14 Vernon. 15 A sucker. 16 Chemistry. 17 Max Schmeling (German). 18 Ryugyong Hotel, North Korea. 19 Diane Cilento. 20 Mont Blanc. 21 Duke of York. 22 Cheese. 23 Beestings. 24 Mexico. 25 Evelyn Waugh. 26 Estelle. 27 London to Penzance. 28 U-boats. 29 Go Wild in the Country. 30 Tennyson.

1 How many chapters are in the book of Genesis in the Bible?
2 The Salk vaccine was developed against which disease?
3 What is a Venus's Looking Glass?
4 What is the maiden name of White House press secretary Sarah Sanders?
5 What were constructed in the Highlands by General Wade in 1724?
6 What was the name of the John Gielgud character in the film "Arthur"?
7 What is a dossal?
8 At which club did Nigel Worthington replace Bryan Hamilton?
9 What was Meg Ryan filming as her marriage to Dennis Quaid hit the rocks?
10 Who is the elder – Chris Evans or Paul Gascoigne?
11 In the film "Isadora" who played the role of Isadora Duncan?
12 What is a barrico?
13 How many American colleges and universities are in the Ivy League?
14 Who played the lead role in the film "Take Me High"?
15 Cicadas are types of what?
16 Who are in charge in a theocracy?
17 How many lines has a clerihew?
18 What was Patty Sheehan the first woman to do in the same year?
19 "Breathe Again" was the first UK Top Ten hit for which female vocalist?
20 Who had been Britain's youngest cabinet member before William Hague?
21 Frederick is born on which date in "The Pirates Of Penzance"?
22 Who was Archbishop of Canterbury from 1974 to 1980?
23 Who left F1 team Sauber to drive for Ferrari in 2019?
24 What was the name of the first baby born to contestants who met on "Big Brother"?
25 Which unit of measurement is equal to 3.2616 light years?
26 Which Man Utd manager appeared in a film called "Cup Fever"?
27 What was sendal?
28 What is a firearm called if it has a calibre over 20mm?
29 Which British liner was the first to be sunk by a U-boat on the first day of the Second World War?
30 In which decade was actor David Jason born?

Answers	20th Century *(see Quiz 46)*

1 Manchu or Qing ("Ching"). 2 Ekofisk. 3 Mario Frick of Liechtenstein. 4 Seychelles.
5 Arts & Science. 6 Konrad Adenauer. 7 Jeffrey Archer. 8 Liberals and SDP. 9 Arafat, Rabin, and Peres. 10 Warner Brothers. 11 Committee to Re-Elect the President. 12 Pope John Paul II. 13 British Empire Exhibition 1924. 14 Rievaulx. 15 Winter of discontent. 16 Vote to women over 21. 17 Rafsanjani. 18 Samora Machel. 19 Methodism. 20 Irangate. 21 Japan. 22 Nicholas Ridley. 23 Radio Keith Orpheum. 24 Bugs Moran. 25 Onions. 26 25. 27 Romania. 28 Jacques Delors. 29 Apartheid. 30 Falange.

1 What was the last ruling dynasty of China?
2 Which oil field blow-out caused an 8.2 million gallon spill in April 1977?
3 Who became Europe's youngest head of state at 28 in 1993?
4 Where was Archbishop Makarios exiled by the British in the mid-50s?
5 Which Deputy Ministerial post did Winnie Mandela hold in Nelson Mandela's first government?
6 Which German Chancellor achieved post-war reconciliation with France in the 50s and early 60s?
7 Who became the youngest ever member of the GLC in 1969?
8 Which political parties linked in the UK in the 80s to form the Alliance?
9 Which Middle East leaders were awarded the Nobel Peace Prize in 1994?
10 Which film studio released the first talking film?
11 In the Watergate scandal, who or what was CREEP?
12 Who was the third-longest-serving Pope in history?
13 Wembley Stadium was completed for which event?
14 Harold Wilson became Baron of where on his elevation to the peerage?
15 Which quotation from "Richard III" was used to describe the end of 1978 and beginning of 1979?
16 What was nicknamed 'The Flapper Vote' in 1928?
17 Who succeeded the Ayatollah Khomeini as political leader of Iran?
18 Who was the first president of an independent Mozambique?
19 J. Arthur Rank entered films in the 30s to promote which cause?
20 In 1987, what did the Tower Commission investigate in the US?
21 Where was the Recruit Scandal of 1988?
22 Which minister in Thatcher's government shared his name with Henry VIII's chaplain?
23 What did the initials of film company RKO stand for?
24 Whose gang did Al Capone's men massacre on Valentine's Day 1929?
25 A shortage of which commodity was a major issue in the 1998 Indian election?
26 At what number Cromwell Street did Rose and Fred West live?
27 King Michael abdicated which throne in 1947?
28 Whom did Jacques Santer replace as President of the European Commission?
29 The 1964 Rivonia Trial involved those opposed to what?
30 What was the name of Franco's fascist party in Spain?

Answers | **Pot Luck 23** *(see Quiz 45)*

1 50. 2 Polio. 3 A plant. 4 Huckabee. 5 Roads. 6 Hobson – the butler/valet. 7 An ornamental hanging in a church. 8 Norwich. 9 Proof of Life. 10 Chris Evans. 11 Vanessa Redgrave. 12 A small barrel. 13 Eight. 14 Cliff Richard. 15 Insects. 16 Priests. 17 Four. 18 Win golf's British and US Opens. 19 Toni Braxton. 20 Harold Wilson. 21 29 February. 22 Donald Coggan. 23 Charles Leclerc. 24 Pierce. 25 Parsec. 26 Sir Matt Busby. 27 A silken fabric. 28 Artillery. 29 Athenia. 30 1940s.

1 What is the name of the fitness instructor in "Balamory"?

2 In which city in 1882 were the Phoenix Park murders?

3 What is Roxburghe a style of?

4 Which world leader married Graca Machel in 1998?

5 Which writer died in Zurich after an operation for an ulcer in 1941?

6 Which city's underground has more stations than any other?

7 Which weaving invention was invented by John Kay?

8 Who was first to take "Everything I Own" to No.1 ?

9 What is hydroponics?

10 The Rye House Plot of 1683 was aiming to assassinate which king?

11 What is a quirt?

12 Who wrote "A Connecticut Yankee in King Arthur's Court"?

13 The Christian name Kenneth derives from the Gaelic for what?

14 Which Soviet dictator died on the same day as composer Prokofiev?

15 What is the unit of currency in The People's Republic of Congo?

16 Which MP controversially blocked parliamentary bills concerning upskirting and FGM?

17 Which animals can suffer the disease strangles?

18 Janet Leigh's car was registered in which American state in "Psycho"?

19 In which decade was Gloria Hunniford born?

20 What were discovered by David Livingstone in 1855?

21 What is a strobilus another name for?

22 The name Commandos comes from an Afrikaans word for what?

23 Where did Nick Faldo win his first British Open?

24 Which European king died in 1993?

25 Which Biblical woman is the Jewish festival Purim a celebration to?

26 In which month is Prince Harry's birthday?

27 In America what is 2 February called?

28 What was Boyz II Men's first UK Top Ten hit?

29 In 2017 who gave birth to a daughter named Alexis Olympia Ohanian Jr.?

30 Grilse, Alevins and Kelts are all forms of what?

Answers	**Hobbies 1** *(see Quiz 48)*

1 Thailand. 2 River Cafe. 3 The Manager. 4 Bridge. 5 Abraham Saperstein. 6 144.
7 Armani. 8 Art Nouveau. 9 23m or 75 feet. 10 20 minutes. 11 Silk screen printing.
12 Monoboarding. 13 Son et lumière. 14 Macramé. 15 Uruguay. 16 7 & 11. 17
Raymond Blanc. 18 Swimming. 19 28. 20 Bowling green. 21 Cricket. 22 Angling.
23 Dragons. 24 Super Smash Bros. 25 Small cart in harness racing. 26 Potholing. 27
Basketball. 28 Arms and hands. 29 Taekwondo. 30 Kneeling.

Quiz 48 | Hobbies 1

Answers – page 239

LEVEL 3

1 Phi Phi Island is a popular holiday destination in which country?
2 Which eating house did Ruthie Rogers found?
3 Which football board game was launched by Terry Venables?
4 For what game is the Camrose Trophy awarded?
5 Who founded the Harlem Globetrotters?
6 How many tiles are there in a game of mah-jong?
7 Who designs clothes for younger people under the Emporio label?
8 What type of art was known as Jugenstil in Germany?
9 How long is the rope in water skiing?
10 In the early days of cinema how long would a "two reeler" last?
11 Serigraphy is also known as what?
12 What name is given to the style of skiing on a single broad ski?
13 Which type of outdoor spectacular was created by Paul Houdin and first shown at the Chateau de Chambord in 1952?
14 Which craft takes its name from the Arabic for "striped cloth"?
15 Where did canasta originate?
16 What are the two winning numbers made with two dice in craps?
17 Who opened Les Quat' Saisons in 1977?
18 If you follow FINA rules which sport do you practise?
19 How many dominoes are there in a double six set?
20 Southampton boast of having the first sports area of what type in the country?
21 Which sport would interest you if you followed the work of the ACS?
22 Ellem in Scotland is the oldest club of what type?
23 In the role-playing game known as D&D, what does the second D stand for?
24 Which video game series features 'fighters' from "Pokémon", "Super Mario", "Donkey Kong" and other games?
25 If you spent your leisure time in a sulky where would you be?
26 If you were spelunking in the US what would you be doing?
27 In 1976 the NBA and the ABA merged in which sport?
28 In sepek takrow you can hit the ball with any part of the body except which?
29 General Choi Hong Hi is responsible for the development of which martial art?
30 What position does the canoeist adopt in Canadian canoeing?

Answers	Pot Luck 24 *(see Quiz 47)*

1 Josie Jump. 2 Dublin. 3 Bookbinding. 4 Nelson Mandela. 5 James Joyce. 6 New York. 7 The flying shuttle. 8 Ken Boothe. 9 Cultivation of plants without soil. 10 Charles II. 11 A whip. 12 Mark Twain. 13 Handsome. 14 Stalin. 15 The Zaire. 16 Christopher Chope. 17 Horses. 18 Arizona. 19 1940s. 20 The Victoria Falls. 21 A pine cone. 22 Troops. 23 Muirfield. 24 King Baudouin (Belgium). 25 Esther. 26 September. 27 Groundhog Day. 28 End of the Road. 29 Serena Williams. 30 Salmon.

1 In whose stately home was the Tarzan film "Greystoke" filmed?
2 What was Sharon Stone's first film, in 1980?
3 "Uncle Buck" was the debut of which movie star?
4 May Day was the Bond girl in which film?
5 What was the occupation of Madame Sousatzka in the Shirley Maclaine film?
6 Who had a lead role in the movie version of "Rising Damp" who wasn't in the TV sitcom?
7 Whom did Alan Rickman play in "Die Hard"?
8 Who are the two letter writers in "84 Charing Cross Road"?
9 Which son of a pop star appears as Jackson's friend in "Moonwalker"?
10 In which film did Jack Nicholson say the catchphrase "Here's Johnny"?
11 Who played Mrs La Motta in "Raging Bull"?
12 Which film all but bankrupted United Artists in 1980?
13 Which ailing actor's voice was dubbed by Rich Little in "Curse of the Pink Panther"?
14 Who played Meryl Streep's eccentric friend in "Plenty"?
15 Who won an Oscar for his first major role in 1982?
16 Who was Glenn Close's character in "Dangerous Liaisons"?
17 Which film included the song "It Might be You"?
18 Who was the only Cambodian Oscar winner of the 80s?
19 Who was the only winner of an Oscar and a BAFTA for "Platoon"?
20 Who was nominated as Best Supporting Actress for "The Color Purple"?
21 In the film "A Royal Love Story", who played Princess Diana?
22 "The Color of Money" re-created the character from which film?
23 Which father and son appeared in "Wall Street"?
24 Which role did Kevin Kline play in "A Fish Called Wanda"?
25 Which presidential candidate's cousin won an Oscar for "Moonstruck"?
26 Apart from Music and Visual Effects, which other Oscar did "E.T." win?
27 Who directed "Psycho III"?
28 Whose music features on the soundtrack of "When Harry Met Sally"?
29 Whose novel was Warren Beatty's "Reds" based on?
30 Who was the aerobics instructor in "Perfect"?

Answers | Pot Luck 25 (see Quiz 50)

1 Spooner. 2 United We Stand. 3 Warwickshire. 4 Sweden. 5 1950s. 6 The Rose Theatre. 7 Norman Wisdom. 8 Mike Atherton. 9 Henry Fonda. 10 Five. 11 John Cleese. 12 Insecticide. 13 Dali. 14 Bedtime Story. 15 St Aubrun. 16 Two-Faced Woman. 17 Water skiing. 18 Mass of gases. 19 New York. 20 A surveyor. 21 95 goals. 22 Sweden. 23 Living in America. 24 Joanna Lumley. 25 Accented (Forzato). 26 Lima. 27 1972. 28 Glasgow. 29 A card game. 30 An imp.

Quiz 50 | Pot Luck 25

Answers – page 241 LEVEL 3

1 In "Family Guy", the Griffin family live on which street?
2 What was Brotherhood of Man's first UK Top Ten hit?
3 In which county did the battle of Edgehill take place?
4 Which country does chart-topping Eric Prydz come from?
5 In which decade was TV presenter Eamonn Holmes born?
6 Which theatre foundations were discovered in London in 1988?
7 Who was lead in the films "Man of the Moment" and "The Square Peg"?
8 Who became England cricket captain to replace Graham Gooch?
9 Which actor won Best Actor Oscar for "On Golden Pond" aged 76?
10 How many countries surround Botswana?
11 Barbara Trentham was the second wife of which English comic?
12 What is Bordeaux Mixture a blend of?
13 Which Spanish artist painted "The Persistence of Memory"?
14 Which film was remade as "Dirty Rotten Scoundrels"?
15 What is the middle name of knighted cricketer Garry Sobers?
16 What was Greta Garbo's last film?
17 The WWSU is the governing body of which sport?
18 What mass is measured in Criths?
19 In which city is the Verrazano Narrows Bridge?
20 Which profession did George Washington start out in?
21 To five, how many Premier League goals did Ruud van Nistelrooy score for Manchester United?
22 Which country celebrates the crayfish with a party in August?
23 What was the title of the only UK Top Ten hit for James Brown?
24 Who is the elder – Joanna Lumley or Maureen Lipman?
25 What does the abbreviation 'fz' mean in music?
26 Spaniard Francisco Pizarro founded which city?
27 When was the magazine Cosmopolitan first published?
28 Which city was the first to erect a monument to Lord Nelson in Britain?
29 What was Angel Beast an old type of?
30 What is the county emblem of Lincolnshire?

| Answers | 80s Films (see Quiz 49) |

1 Duke of Roxburghe's. 2 Stardust Memories. 3 Macaulay Culkin. 4 A View to a Kill. 5 Piano teacher. 6 Denholm Elliott. 7 Hans Gruber. 8 Helene Hanff & Frank Doel. 9 Sean Lennon. 10 The Shining. 11 Cathy Moriarty. 12 Heaven's Gate. 13 David Niven. 14 Tracey Ullman. 15 Ben Kingsley. 16 Marquise de Merteuil. 17 Tootsie. 18 Haing S. Ngor. 19 Oliver Stone. 20 Oprah Winfrey. 21 Catherine Oxenberg. 22 The Hustler. 23 Martin & Charlie Sheen. 24 Otto. 25 Olympia Dukakis. 26 Sound. 27 Anthony Perkins. 28 Harry Connick Jr. 29 John Reed's. 30 Jamie Lee Curtis.

1 A branch of which Paris arts centre opened in Metz in 2010?
2 Tarom Airlines are based in which country?
3 What is the capital of Georgia?
4 Which capital is further north – Budapest or Vienna?
5 Which Gulf is to the west of Estonia and Latvia?
6 Where is the news agency Centre d'Information Presse based?
7 In which country is Kranebitten International airport?
8 What is the chief port of Slovenia?
9 The Pelagian islands belong to which European country?
10 Bornholm is an island in which Sea?
11 Hoge Veluwe National Park is in which country?
12 Which European country has the internet code .ee?
13 St Petersburg is at the head of which gulf?
14 What is the largest island in Europe?
15 Which two Italian volcanoes erupted in 1994?
16 What is the world's highest dam?
17 Which country is called Suomen Tasavalta in its own language?
18 Which capital is further north – Berlin or London?
19 Aero Lloyd Airlines are based in which country?
20 Which European country has the highest life expectancy for men and women?
21 What is the highest waterfall in Europe?
22 Brest is a major town in which country other than France?
23 In which town did an earthquake claim nine lives in 1997?
24 In which country is the city of Bochum?
25 To which country do the islands of Stromboli and Vulcano belong?
26 What is the prominent religion of Lithuania?
27 Which is the northernmost and second largest of the Ionian islands?
28 What are Andorra's two main industries?
29 In which country is Sondica International airport?
30 Hardangervidda National Park is in which country?

Answers | Pot Luck 26 *(see Quiz 52)*

1 A type of theatre. 2 Tom Dixon. 3 A sword. 4 Carl Davis. 5 John Huffham. 6 San Francisco 49ers. 7 Edinburgh. 8 Duffel in Belgium. 9 Charles Lindbergh. 10 Glastonbury. 11 My Kind Of Town. 12 A straw hat. 13 Omicron. 14 Gulf of Taranto. 15 Alexander the Great. 16 Kipps. 17 1843. 18 1500 metres. 19 Richey Edwards. 20 Vision of Love. 21 Barber. 22 Bert Oldfield (Australia). 23 Kenwood House. 24 Pentecost Island. 25 Phileas Taylor. 26 1993. 27 Kitty Kallen. 28 James I. 29 Surface tension. 30 Ukraine.

Quiz 52 — Pot Luck 26

Answers – page 243

LEVEL 3

1 What is No in Japan?
2 In 2018, IKEA announced it was developing urban farming products with which British designer?
3 What is a tulwar?
4 Who, with Paul McCartney, composed the "Liverpool Oratorio"?
5 What were Charles Dickens' two middle names?
6 Which team was the first to top the 50 points mark in a Super Bowl final?
7 In which city is Fettes College?
8 Where was the cloth used to make duffel coats first made?
9 On May 21, 1927, who landed at Le Bourget airport?
10 Where did Joseph of Arimathea's staff take root and bud, in legend?
11 Which song did Frank Sinatra feature in the film "Robin and the Seven Hoods"?
12 What is a skimmer to an American?
13 What name is given to the Greek letter that is the equivalent of letter O?
14 Which gulf is between the heel and sole of Italy?
15 Which famous leader brought an end to the Pharaohs in Egypt?
16 Which HG Wells novel is the musical "Half a Sixpence" based on?
17 To ten years, when was the magazine The Economist founded?
18 What is the final event in a decathlon?
19 Which of the Manic Street Preachers was officially declared dead in 2002?
20 What was Mariah Carey's first UK Top Ten hit?
21 In "Peanuts", what was the profession of Charlie Brown's father?
22 Who was the first wicketkeeper to claim 50 stumping victims in Tests?
23 Which elegant white villa dating from the eighteenth century is situated on Hampstead Heath?
24 On which island is bungee jumping said to have originated?
25 What were the Christian names of the showman Barnum?
26 To three years, in which year did Audrey Hepburn die?
27 Whose one and only hit was "Little Things Mean a Lot" in 1954?
28 Which monarch introduced the sedan chair into England?
29 What physical property lets a needle float on water?
30 Which country has the internet code .ua?

Answers	**Euro Tour** *(see Quiz 51)*

1 Pompidou. 2 Romania. 3 Tbilisi. 4 Vienna. 5 Gulf of Riga. 6 Brussels. 7 Austria. 8 Koper. 9 Italy. 10 Baltic. 11 Netherlands. 12 Estonia. 13 Gulf of Finland. 14 Great Britain. 15 Mount Etna and Stromboli. 16 Grande Dizence in Switzerland. 17 Finland. 18 London. 19 Germany. 20 Liechtenstein. 21 Ormeli in Norway. 22 Belarus. 23 Assisi in Central Italy. 24 Germany. 25 Italy. 26 Roman Catholic. 27 Corfu. 28 Tourism and tobacco. 29 Spain. 30 Norway.

1 What was the first UK No.1 in which the title posed a question?
2 Which traditional song provided instrumental and vocal versions that charted for 94 weeks?
3 What was Roy Orbison's final chart topper from 1964?
4 Which "Women" was the longest ever at No.1 for the Rolling Stones?
5 Graham Gouldman and Eric Stewart wrote which 1975 classic No.1?
6 Which 1950s vocalist began singing with the Tony Pastor band?
7 What are the first three words of "San Francisco (Be Sure To Wear Flowers In Your Hair)"?
8 How were the birds singing in the original title of the No.1 "Why Do Fools Fall in Love"?
9 Which 1986 No.1 was a cover of a 1970 No.1?
10 Which artist took over the title of the youngest No.1 hitmaker in 1972?
11 What is Ray Charles' only UK No.1?
12 Which Canadian was next to No.1 after Paul Anka?
13 Which hit gave producer Norrie Paramour his 27th and final No.1?
14 Emile Ford shared his first week at No.1 with which artist?
15 Which Chuck Berry hit was No.1 at the same time in the UK and US?
16 Steve Miller's "The Joker" hit No.1 in 1990 but when was it recorded?
17 Which hit gave The Searchers their second No.1?
18 Who had a No.1 with the original version of "Young Love"?
19 Who wrote and produced Nancy Sinatra's "These Boots are Made for Walking"?
20 Which John Leyton hit was covered in 1985 by Bronski Beat and Marc Almond?
21 Whose only UK hit was "Here Comes Summer"?
22 Who wrote "See My Baby Jive"?
23 What film theme gave Danny Williams his only No.1 in 1961?
24 What was the first instrumental No.1 after the Shadows' "Foot Tapper"?
25 What was the Kinks' third and final No.1 hit in the summer of 1966?
26 What was the only Cliff Richard & the Shadows No.1 double-A-side?
27 Which 1968 No.1 was revived in the film "Good Morning Vietnam"?
28 What was Wonderful in the Shadows hit which stayed longest at No.1?
29 Which act was the first beginning with a letter Z to have a No.1 single?
30 What was Cilla Black's only US Top 40 hit?

Answers | Pot Luck 27 *(see Quiz 54)*

1 Turkish. 2 Francis Drake's. 3 Adnan Syed. 4 Montague Rhodes. 5 Ballard Berkeley.
6 1950s. 7 Sankey and Moody's. 8 An oak tree. 9 Chelsea F.C. 10 Richard Burton
and John Speke. 11 Zsa Zsa Gabor. 12 Darkness. 13 Sousaphone. 14 Black. 15
Pennsylvania. 16 Gertrude Ederle. 17 Luanda. 18 Harry Horse. 19 A metallic
element. 20 Los Angeles Angels. 21 Duke of Wellington. 22 Rome. 23 Australian. 24
A poem. 25 Finland. 26 Belgium. 27 Next to You. 28 Could It Be Forever/Cherish.
29 Hungary. 30 Marlon Brando.

Quiz 54 | Pot Luck 27

Answers – page 245

LEVEL 3

1 Which language do the words kiosk, tulip and caviar come from?
2 Whose Drum can be seen at Buckland Abbey in Devon?
3 Which convicted prisoner was the subject of the first season of the podcast "Serial"?
4 What do the initials stand for in the name of ghost story writer MR James?
5 Which actor played Major Gowen in "Fawlty Towers"?
6 In which decade was Loyd Grossman born?
7 Whose hymn book was first published in 1873?
8 A durmast is a variety of what?
9 Whose only UK Top Ten Hit was "Blue is the Colour" from 1972?
10 Which Europeans discovered Lake Tanganyika in 1858?
11 Who said, "I never hated a man enough to give him his diamonds back"?
12 Achulophobia is the fear of what?
13 Which brass instrument is wrapped around the player's body?
14 What colour appears with white and green on the Afghanistan flag?
15 In which US state was there a nuclear accident at Three Mile Island in 1979?
16 Who was the first woman to swim the English Channel in 1926?
17 What is the capital of Angola?
18 Under what pseudonym did Richard Horne write "The Last Polar Bears" and other children's books?
19 What is indium?
20 For which baseball team does Mike Trout play?
21 Who lived at No.1, London?
22 Where are the Aventine, Viminal and Quirinal Hills?
23 What nationality was Sir Robert Helpmann?
24 What is a clerihew?
25 In which country can you visit Espoo and Vantaa?
26 In which European country is the province of Brabant?
27 What was the title of Gloria Hunniford's book about her late daughter Caron Keating?
28 What was David Cassidy's first UK Top Ten hit?
29 Where did Kun's Red Terror exist in 1919?
30 Which actor was first to sign a $1 million deal for a single picture?

Answers	Oldies & Goldies (see Quiz 53)

1 (How Much is) That Doggie in the Window? 2 Amazing Grace. 3 Oh Pretty Woman.
4 Honky Tonk. 5 I'm not in Love. 6 Rosemary Clooney. 7 If you're going. 8 So Gay.
9 Spirit in the Sky. 10 Little Jimmy Osmond. 11 I Can't Stop Loving You. 12 Terry
Jacks. 13 Lily the Pink. 14 Adam Faith. 15 My Ding-a-Ling. 16 1973. 17 Needles
and Pins. 18 Tab Hunter. 19 Lee Hazlewood. 20 Johnny Remember Me. 21 Jerry
Keller. 22 Roy Wood. 23 Moon River. 24 The Good, the Bad and the Ugly. 25 Sunny
Afternoon. 26 The Next Time/Bachelor Boy. 27 What a Wonderful World. 28 Land. 29
Zager & Evans. 30 You're My World.

1 What was different about the diving pool in Rio 2016?
2 At which sport did future tennis star Jaroslav Drobny win a medal in 1948?
3 Who won the men's cycling road race in London 2012?
4 Where were the Winter Olympics held in 1928 and 1948?
5 On which apparatus did Nadia Comaneci score perfect tens in 1976?
6 Who was the first man to win Olympic gold at 200m and 400m?
7 In which event did Carl Lewis win his ninth and final gold medal?
8 Who won the first of four discus golds in Melbourne in 1956?
9 How many silver medals did skier Raisa Smetanina win with her four golds and one bronze?
10 How many gold medals did Mark Spitz win in his first Olympics?
11 Which amazing treble did Emil Zatopek achieve at the 1952 Games?
12 After which event did Bert le Clos famously celebrate his son's gold medal in London 2012?
13 On which lake did Steve Redgrave win his record-breaking fourth gold medal?
14 Who was the only British woman sprinter to compete in all Olympics between 1984 and 1996?
15 Under what name did Mrs Erik de Bruin win gold at Atlanta?
16 What was the name of the Olympic mascot in Atlanta?
17 Where did Linford Christie run his first Olympic race?
18 Who was the oldest Olympic 100m champion when he won in 1980?
19 In 2016, which Olympian wasn't robbed at gunpoint in Rio after all?
20 Which is the only Olympic yachting event for three-person crews?
21 Which Canadian sprinter won silver in the 200 metres and bronze in the 100 metres in Rio 2016?
22 Who won Britain's first tennis medal since 1924 in Atlanta?
23 Who replaced her partner Michael Hutchinson before winning gold in 1984?
24 Other than 400m hurdles for which event did Sally Gunnell win a medal in Barcelona?
25 In which year did women first compete in the Olympics?
26 Why were equestrian events held in Sweden in 1956 when the Games were held in Australia?
27 Who was Britain's only female medallist at the Atlanta games?
28 Where did Daley Thompson compete in his first Olympics?
29 Which son of a former Millwall goalie won gold in the USA in 1980?
30 What was the first Asian country to have staged the Winter Olympics?

| **Answers** | Pot Luck 56 *(see Quiz 28)* |

1 Simon Fuller. 2 A shark. 3 Artie Shaw. 4 Bellini. 5 Bowls. 6 Exile. 7 Sheila. 8 Cyan, magenta. 9 Bulimia. 10 Nora Ephron. 11 Special Brew. 12 A viewing turret. 13 March. 14 Australia. 15 Donald Dewar. 16 Leeds. 17 The Floaters. 18 David Ben-Gurion. 19 Central Park. 20 1986. 21 A top hat. 22 John Flamsteed. 23 Humphrey Bogart. 24 Franck Ribery. 25 David. 26 Gymnastics. 27 1937. 28 America. 29 Adelaide. 30 Whistle.

Quiz 56 | Pot Luck 28

Answers – page 247

1 Whom did the Spice Girls sack as their manager in early 1998?
2 What is a porbeagle?
3 Which bandleader married both Ava Gardner and Lana Turner?
4 What was the family name of artists Jacopo and his sons Gentile and Giovanni?
5 Scottish solicitor William Mitchell drew up the rules for which sport?
6 Which group had a 70s hit with "Kiss You All Over"?
7 What is the first name of John Peel's widow?
8 What two colours go with black and yellow in printing's four-colour process?
9 What did Diana Princess of Wales describe as "a shameful friend"?
10 Who won an Oscar for her first screenplay "Silkwood"?
11 What was Bad Manners' first UK Top Ten hit?
12 What is a belvedere?
13 In which month is the feast day of St Cuthbert?
14 In which country are the mountains called the Stirling Range?
15 Which late politician was the first leader of the Scottish Parliament?
16 Which football club has been managed by both Jimmy Armfield and Brian Clough?
17 Whose one and only hit was "Float On" in 1977?
18 Who was the first Prime Minister of Israel?
19 Where is New York's Metropolitan Museum of Art?
20 In what year did the London Stock Exchange go computerised?
21 What is a gibus?
22 Who was the first man to hold the post of Astronomer Royal?
23 Who numbered Helen Menken and Mary Philips among his wives?
24 Between 2010 and 2018, who was the only European Player of the Year who didn't play for a Spanish club?
25 Which Michelangelo statue is in Florence?
26 Vera Caslavska was Olympic and World Champion in which sport?
27 In which year was Wimbledon first televised?
28 Where was the first woman MP to enter the Commons born?
29 Who ceased to be queen when Victoria became queen?
30 What do you do if you siffle?

Answers | Olympics *(see Quiz 55)*

1 The water was green. 2 Ice hockey. 3 Alexander Vinokourov. 4 St Moritz. 5 Bars and beam. 6 Michael Johnson. 7 Long jump. 8 Al Oerter. 9 Five. 10 Two. 11 Retained 10,000m and won 5000m and marathon. 12 200m butterfly. 13 Lake Lanier. 14 Simone Jacobs. 15 Michelle Smith. 16 Izzy. 17 Seoul. 18 Allan Wells. 19 Ryan Lochte. 20 Soling. 21 Andre De Grasse. 22 Tim Henman & Chris Broad. 23 Jayne Torvill. 24 4 x 400m relay. 25 1900. 26 Quarantine laws. 27 Denise Lewis. 28 Montreal. 29 Robin Cousins. 30 Japan.

1 What is the range of numbers on a roulette wheel?
2 Where would you watch FC Jazz and what would they be doing?
3 FIDE is the governing body of which game?
4 Which furniture-making wood can be Cuban, Honduras and San Domingan?
5 In athletics how much does a hammer weigh?
6 Where is the Guggenheim Museum in Europe?
7 In abseiling what are karabiners?
8 Who first appeared in a strip cartoon "in the Land of the Soviets"?
9 Which UK tourist attraction is on the site of an 8th-century fortress?
10 Where in Normandy would you visit Monet's garden?
11 If you collected Bizarre pottery whose work would you have?
12 Paintball is a simulation of what?
13 How many zones does an archery target have?
14 In which London street was the first artificial ice rink opened?
15 In shinty what is the curved stick called?
16 Which radio star appeared in films such as "The Wrong Box"?
17 In which sport does a match last for a certain number of heads?
18 Whose art collection sold for a record $832 million in 2018?
19 Which activity has two main types, tomiki and uyeshiba?
20 How many more people are there in an outer handball team than there are in an indoor one?
21 John Tomlinson is credited with starting which hobby?
22 Which form of flying was perfected by Francis Rogallo in the 1970s?
23 In which mountains is the Brockenbahn steam railway?
24 Which restaurateur owned Daphne's and founded The Collection?
25 In cyclocross what do you do with your bike when you're not riding it?
26 Where is the Liseberg theme park?
27 Who opened the Braeval restaurant in Scotland in 1986?
28 In which activity do you "dive for the horizon"?
29 Wing Chun is a popular form of which art?
30 In which Botanic Gardens was the tulip first introduced in 1594?

| **Answers** | Pot Luck 29 *(see Quiz 58)* |

1 Paul McCartney. 2 Sweden. 3 Heights. 4 Ivory Coast. 5 Should I Stay or Should I Go. 6 Red. 7 Spider. 8 Johnny Depp. 9 Connecticut. 10 1960s. 11 None. 12 Sarah. 13 Rachmaninov. 14 7th. 15 1770. 16 My Lord. 17 Thailand. 18 Tom Kerridge. 19 Buffalo Stance. 20 William. 21 Bulgaria. 22 210mm x 297mm. 23 Sweden. 24 Hyde. 25 Thomas Gainsborough. 26 Sydney. 27 Renée Zellweger. 28 Sandra Howard (wife of Michael). 29 William IV. 30 Manama.

Quiz 58 | Pot Luck 29

LEVEL 3

1 Bernard Webb was a pseudonym used by which famous song writer?
2 In which country is the royal family the House of Bernadotte?
3 Acrophobia is the fear of what?
4 In which country is the city of Abidjan?
5 What was the only No.1 UK hit for the Clash?
6 What colour is the circle on the Bangladesh flag?
7 A Brazilian Huntsman is a type of what?
8 Who played director Ed Wood in the 1994 film biography?
9 A Nutmegger is an inhabitant of which American state?
10 In which decade did South Africa resign from the Commonwealth?
11 How many locks are there on the Suez Canal?
12 What is Mrs Gordon Brown's first name?
13 Who composed Rhapsody on a Theme of Paganini for Piano?
14 What was the number of the British Armoured Division nicknamed the "Desert Rats"?
15 In which year did James Cook land at Botany Bay, Australia?
16 What is the correct form of address to begin a letter to a Baron?
17 In which country is the town of Nakhon?
18 Whose Michelin-starred gastropub is called the Hand and Flowers?
19 What was Neneh Cherry's first UK Top Ten hit?
20 What was the Christian name of aeroplane manufacturer Mr Boeing?
21 In which European country are the provinces of Sofiya and Burgas?
22 What size is A4 paper in millimetres?
23 Australia hosted the 1956 Olympics but equestrian events were held in which other country?
24 Murderer Dr Harold Shipman worked in which Greater Manchester district?
25 Which artist painted "The Watering Place" in 1777?
26 INXS singer Michael Hutchence was born in and died in which city?
27 Who played Russell Crowe's wife in "Cinderella Man"?
28 Whose first novel was called "Glass Houses"?
29 Clarence House was built for which monarch when he was still Duke of Clarence?
30 What is the capital of Bahrain?

Answers | Hobbies 2 *(see Quiz 57)*

1 0 to 36. 2 Finland, playing football. 3 Chess. 4 Mahogany. 5 16lb. 6 Bilbao. 7 Steel links. 8 Tintin. 9 Alton Towers. 10 Giverny. 11 Clarice Cliff. 12 Military combat. 13 10. 14 Baker Street. 15 Caman. 16 Tony Hancock. 17 Curling. 18 Peggy and David Rockefeller. 19 Aikido. 20 Four (11 and 7 respectively). 21 Stamp collecting. 22 Hang gliding. 23 Harz Mountains (Germany). 24 Mogens Tholstrup. 25 Carry it. 26 Gothenburg, Sweden. 27 Nick Nairn. 28 Bungee jumping. 29 Kung fu. 30 Leiden.

1 Who played Mike Channel in "KYTV"?
2 Who is the smallest Teletubby?
3 Who found fame as Egg in "This Life"?
4 "Prove It!" was a CITV series about what?
5 Who is the largest Teletubby?
6 Where did the first outside broadcast on "Grandstand" come from?
7 Who is Postman Pat's wife?
8 In which docu soap did Emma Boundy find fame?
9 Which "Casualty" character played a midwife in "Spice World"?
10 Which two words has Nicole uttered to advertise Renault?
11 Who played Inspector Crome in the BBC's 2018 adaptation of "The ABC Murders"?
12 Which TV presenter made the cake when Jemima Goldsmith married Imran Khan?
13 What was Michael Barrymore's talent-spotting TV show called?
14 Which late actress won a BAFTA for "A Cream Cracker Under the Settee"?
15 What was the name of the David Furnish-directed documentary about Elton John?
16 Who played the Englishwoman in "Parnell and the Englishwoman"?
17 In which series did Lynda La Plante introduce Dolly Rawlings?
18 Who was the first woman presenter of "Grandstand"?
19 Who replaced Richard Baker as the presenter of the Proms?
20 What role did Dominic West play in the 2019 BBC adaptation of "Les Misérables"?
21 How is TV playwright Romana Barrack better known?
22 In which show was Harry S Truman the sheriff?
23 In which town would you read "The Daily Slate"?
24 The music from "Raging Bull" was used to advertise which lager?
25 Where is Chris Evans' home town?
26 Who had a pet octopus called Aristotle?
27 Who played the title role in Alan Bleasdale's "The Monocled Mutineer"?
28 Anthea Turner was replaced at GMTV by whom?
29 Where did the Munsters live?
30 On a Friday, on children's TV who were Jenny & Willy?

Answers | Pot Luck 30 (see Quiz 60)

1 Switzerland. 2 Ambrose Burnside. 3 Sierra Leone. 4 Switzerland. 5 River Cafe. 6 Portuguese. 7 Extinguished by a cloudburst. 8 Connecticut. 9 Thomas Gainsborough. 10 1843. 11 Send in the Clowns. 12 Cheimaphobia. 13 Dorset (figure carved in chalk hillside). 14 Gambia. 15 Clothes were removed before bathing. 16 Claudius. 17 LAR. 18 Seeds. 19 Royal Horse Guards, Whitehall. 20 Derbyshire. 21 Easy. 22 Witness. 23 Paris. 24 Trans-uranic elements. 25 Green and Red. 26 Janet Guthrie. 27 Caveat emptor. 28 1971. 29 Mali. 30 Rice Krispies.

Quiz 60 | Pot Luck 30

1 Players of which country made two-handed eagle gestures in the 2018 World Cup finals?
2 After which American General were sideburns named?
3 Freetown is the capital of which country?
4 Villinger and Couchepin have been Presidents of which country this century?
5 Which eating house was founded by Ruth Rogers?
6 What is the main language of Angola?
7 What happened to the Olympic flame during the 1976 games?
8 Hartford is the capital of which American State?
9 Which 18th-century artist painted "Peasant Girl Gathering Sticks"?
10 To five years, when was the News of the World founded?
11 What, other than "Amazing Grace", was a Top Ten hit for Judy Collins?
12 A fear of the cold is known as what?
13 In which county is the Rude Man of Cerne?
14 Which country has the dalasi as its currency?
15 What was done in an apodyterium?
16 Emperor Nero was the adopted son of which other emperor?
17 What is the international car index mark for a car from Libya?
18 The spice annatto is made from which part of a plant?
19 Other than Buckingham Palace, which venue sees the daily Changing of the Guard?
20 Which English county does actor Robert Lindsay come from?
21 What was the Commodores' first UK Top Ten hit?
22 In which movie did Harrison Ford play the character John Book?
23 Painter Georges Seurat was born, died and worked in which city?
24 What name is given to elements with atomic numbers 93 to 112?
25 What two colours appear with yellow on the Cameroon flag?
26 Who was the first woman to qualify for the Indy 500 motor race?
27 Which Latin phrase means, "Let the buyer beware"?
28 In which year did women gain the vote in Switzerland?
29 In which country is the city of Bamako?
30 As a child Jonathan Ross appeared in an ad for which food product?

Quiz 61 90s Films

Answers – page 254

LEVEL 3

1 Which Barry Levinson film was used to satirise the US presidency during the Lewinsky crisis?
2 Who is the subject of "Love is the Devil"?
3 Which tough guy directed "Christmas in Connecticut"?
4 Who died during the filming of "Dark Blood" in 1993?
5 Which war is depicted in "Land and Freedom"?
6 Who was Lyon Gaultier in "AWOL"?
7 In which film did Tom Hanks make his directorial debut?
8 Which film's initial title was "$3,000"?
9 Who or what is Andre in the film of the same name?
10 Who was Leonardo DiCaprio's mother in "This Boy's Life"?
11 Who is Leslie Nielsen in the "Naked Gun" films?
12 What is Jim Carrey's job before he finds the mask in the hit movie?
13 Who was Tinkerbell when Spielberg met JM Barrie?
14 Who was the butler in "Princess Caraboo"?
15 What was director Tony Richardson's final film?
16 Which US presidents does Gump meet in "Forrest Gump"?
17 Who was the voice of Mufasa in "The Lion King"?
18 Muriel is a fan of which band in "Muriel's Wedding"?
19 Whom did Woody Allen cast as his ex-wife in "Deconstructing Harry"?
20 What was Hugh Grant's first Hollywood movie?
21 Who was Oscar-winning best screenwriter for "Sense and Sensibility"?
22 Who was John Goodman's mother-in-law in "The Flintstones"?
23 What is Macaulay Culkin's full name in the "Home Alone" movies?
24 Who designed The Riddler's costume in "Batman Forever"?
25 Who directed "White Men Can't Jump"?
26 In which film did Kate Winslet have her first nude scene?
27 Who played rat catcher Caesar in "Mousehunt"?
28 Who was the author in "The Muppet Christmas Carol"?
29 Which film was Gary Oldman's directorial debut?
30 In which comic did Sylvester Stallone's '95 futuristic police character appear?

| **Answers** | **Living World** *(see Quiz 62)* |

1 Whippoorwill. 2 Isabelle Diniore. 3 Sleeping sickness. 4 Internal. 5 Keratin. 6 Single set of chromosomes. 7 Kola nuts. 8 Human's forearm. 9 Red blood cell. 10 Beachflea. 11 Bird droppings. 12 South America & Antarctica. 13 Weil's disease. 14 Seaweed. 15 Head. 16 Ruppell's vulture. 17 Excretory organs. 18 Not hooded. 19 Cerebellum. 20 Penguin. 21 Salamander. 22 Male malle fowl. 23 Goliath. 24 Wishbone. 25 Alcoholism. 26 Butterfly. 27 Cuba. 28 Kiwi. 29 Harvest mite (which bites). 30 Ten.

1 What is another name for the North American nightjar?

2 Who was the first woman to have a partial face transplant?

3 How is the disease trypanosomiasis also known?

4 What is meant by a haemorrhage which is "occult"?

5 Which protein is present in a hair?

6 What does it mean if a cell is haploid?

7 In addition to tea and coffee where is caffeine found?

8 Where is the flexor carpi radialis?

9 What is an erythrocyte?

10 How is the sand hopper also known?

11 Guano is used as fertiliser but what is it made from?

12 Cranes are found on all continents except which two?

13 What is an alternative name for leptospirosis?

14 Carragheen is a type of what?

15 Where is a caterpillar's spinneret?

16 Which bird flies highest?

17 What is an insect's Malpighian tubes?

18 How does a mamba differ from a cobra?

19 Which part of the brain controls muscular movements, balance and co-ordination?

20 Which bird can swim as fast as a seal?

21 An urodele is another name for which reptile?

22 Which bird builds the largest nest?

23 The world's largest spider is named after which Biblical character?

24 What is a bird's furcula?

25 Disulfiram is used in the treatment of what?

26 What is a hairstreak?

27 On which island would you find the bee hummingbird?

28 Which bird produces the largest egg in relation to its body size?

29 Why should you avoid a chigger?

30 How many hearts does an earthworm have?

Answers	90s Films *(see Quiz 61)*

1 Wag the Dog. 2 Francis Bacon. 3 Arnold Schwarzenegger. 4 River Phoenix. 5 Spanish Civil War. 6 Jean-Claude Van Damme. 7 That Thing You Do!. 8 Pretty Woman. 9 Seal. 10 Ellen Barkin. 11 Frank Drebin. 12 Banker. 13 Julia Roberts. 14 Kevin Kline. 15 Blue Sky. 16 Kennedy & Nixon. 17 James Earl Jones. 18 ABBA. 19 Kirstie Alley. 20 Nine Months. 21 Emma Thompson. 22 Elizabeth Taylor. 23 Kevin McCallister. 24 Jim Carrey , who played The Riddler. 25 Ron Shelton. 26 Jude. 27 Christopher Walken. 28 Gonzo. 29 Nil by Mouth. 30 2000 AD.

1 Who was the first person to receive a heart transplant?

2 In which European country are the counties of Viborg and Aarhus?

3 Who composed the music for the ballet "The Wooden Prince"?

4 Who played the lead role in the film "Two a Penny"?

5 As PM Tony Blair first lost a Commons vote on which high-profile subject?

6 Who was Vice President when Ronald Reagan was President?

7 Which animal head represents the Hindu god Ganesa?

8 Keying in the word DAMSON which row of letters is used the most?

9 In which country is the city of Adana?

10 Which type of fish gives its name to a particular patterning of the sky?

11 In which year did Roy Plomley last present "Desert Island Discs"?

12 The first men's hockey club in England was founded in which London suburb?

13 Who were the movie stars when Ralph Fiennes voiced Victor Quartermaine?

14 Who was chip shop owner Harry Ramsden's famous nephew?

15 What was Randy Crawford's first UK Top Ten hit?

16 Which Oscar and BAFTA nominee was a one-time face of Yardley cosmetics?

17 How many seconds are there in half a day?

18 What was the nationality of the astronomer Nicolaus Copernicus?

19 Geri Halliwell became a UN ambassador specialising in what?

20 Who wrote the novels "London Fields" and "Time's Arrow"?

21 How is the letter S formed in Morse Code?

22 Bjorn of ABBA has a cameo in "Mamma Mia! Here We Go Again" as what?

23 Which public figure was shot dead by John Bellingham?

24 Which country won the Copa América for the first time in their history in 2015?

25 Changed in 1868, what was the former name of Tokyo?

26 What do you suffer from if you have acromegaly?

27 The yacht Black Magic won the America's Cup for which country?

28 A Hoosier is an inhabitant in which American state?

29 Who had hits with "Stool Pigeon" and "I'm a Wonderful Thing, Baby"?

30 Haphephobia is the fear of what?

Answers	Rockers *(see Quiz 64)*

1 Sweetie Pie. 2 Dennis Quaid. 3 Pilot in the crash that killed Holly. 4 Colette. 5 Athens, Georgia. 6 Black Rebel Motorcycle Club. 7 Paul Anka. 8 Jailhouse Rock. 9 AC/DC. 10 Decca. 11 The Post Office. 12 Cum On Feel the Noize. 13 An arm (in a car crash). 14 Kurt Cobain's body. 15 Little Richard. 16 Iggy Pop. 17 Sun Studio, Memphis. 18 July. 19 St Martin's School of Art. 20 Christmas Alphabet. 21 Guildford. 22 Alan Lancaster. 23 Rollin' Stones. 24 What'd I Say. 25 Norman Petty. 26 The Pixies. 27 Status Quo. 28 John Bonham. 29 Malcolm McLaren. 30 Blackboard Jungle.

Quiz 64 | Rockers

Answers – page 255

LEVEL 3

1 What was Eddie Cochran's next UK single after "Three Steps to Heaven"?
2 Who played Jerry Lee Lewis in the 1989 biopic of his life?
3 How does Roger Peterson figure in rock history?
4 What was Billy Fury's first UK Top Ten hit from 1960?
5 In which city were R.E.M. formed?
6 What is the full name of the band BRMC?
7 Who wrote the Holly classic "It Doesn't Matter Anymore"?
8 Which Elvis No.1 is the only one written solely by Leiber and Stoller?
9 Which hard-rock band did the Scottish Young brothers form in Australia?
10 "Rock Around the Clock" came out on which label?
11 Whom did Keith Richards work for before coming a full-time Stone?
12 Which Slade hit was No.1 when US soldiers left Vietnam in 1973?
13 What did Rick Allen of Def Leppard lose in 1984?
14 What did an electrician fitting a burglar alarm find in Seattle in 1984?
15 Who first charted with "Rip It Up"?
16 James Jewel Osterberg took the stage under which name?
17 At which studio did the "Million Dollar Quartet" get together in the 50s?
18 In which month did Jim Morrison die in 1971?
19 Where in London was the Sex Pistols' first concert?
20 Which Dickie Valentine hit replaced "Rock Around the Clock" at No.1?
21 Which place used to form part of The Stranglers name?
22 Who was Francis Rossi's school mate and long-time bass player in Status Quo?
23 How were the Rolling Stones billed for their first live concert?
24 Which Jerry Lee Lewis hit is the only version of the Ray Charles classic to reach the British charts?
25 Who ran the Clovis, New Mexico studio where Buddy Holly recorded?
26 Which group did Black Francis get back together in 2018?
27 Who recorded the album "Ma Kelly's Greasy Spoon"?
28 Which Led Zeppelin drummer died in 1980?
29 Who ran the Chelsea clothes shop called Let It Rock?
30 Which 1955 Glenn Ford movie featured "Rock Around the Clock"?

Answers | **Pot Luck 31** *(see Quiz 63)*

1 Louis Washkansky. 2 Denmark. 3 Bela Bartok. 4 Cliff Richard. 5 Terrorism. 6 George Bush. 7 Elephant. 8 Second or middle row. 9 Turkey. 10 Mackerel. 11 1985. 12 Blackheath. 13 Wallace & Gromit. 14 Harry Corbett (Sooty). 15 One Day I'll Fly Away. 16 Helena Bonham Carter. 17 43,200. 18 Polish. 19 Sexual health in the Third World. 20 Martin Amis. 21 Dot, dot, dot. 22 University professor. 23 Spencer Perceval (British PM). 24 Chile. 25 Edo. 26 Excessive growth. 27 New Zealand. 28 Indiana. 29 Kid Creole and the Coconuts. 30 Touch.

1 Which former cricketer was appointed chancellor of Bradford University in 2018?

2 In the 1980s, who wrote the short-story collection "A Twist in the Tale"?

3 What is the Parliament of Sark called?

4 What colour appears with white and red on the Faroe Islands flag?

5 In 1995 Hugh Grant got into trouble for performing a lewd act with whom?

6 What is the capital of Belize?

7 The North American Nebula is a region in which constellation?

8 What was The Damned's one and only UK Top Ten hit?

9 Which Inspector did Johnny Depp play in the movie "From Hell"?

10 What is a golomyanka?

11 Who was unbeaten as England rugby union captain in 2018?

12 Bombay, Chartreux and Japanese bobtail are all types of what?

13 Which war is Stephen Crane's novel "The Red Badge of Courage" set in?

14 In which country is the city of Alma-Ata?

15 The writer Thomas Keneally comes from which country?

16 In which decade was actor Colin Firth born?

17 Prithwi Narayan Shah was the first King of which kingdom?

18 Where were William Hague, Jesse Owens and Pele brought together?

19 Homichlophobia is the fear of what?

20 What are Vera Small and Irene Spencer known as?

21 Who or what was a piggin?

22 In which year was the Women's International Bowling Board formed?

23 Which media presenter left his wife Carol McGiffin in 1993?

24 Which ex-Monkee was in a band called Shoe Suede Blues?

25 Among which hills does Chequers lie?

26 Who composed the opera "Noye's Fludde"?

27 The band Coldplay formed while attending which educational establishment?

28 Under which name did Leslie Charles sail to pop success?

29 Which city has the oldest stock exchange in the USA?

30 What does the musical term "giocoso" mean?

Answers | Pot Luck 33 *(see Quiz 66)*

1 Francis Ford Coppola. 2 Earl of Liverpool. 3 The Valley of the Queens. 4 Alexander. 5 John Constable. 6 New Orleans. 7 Fruits. 8 1969. 9 The Ivy League (US colleges). 10 RC. 11 Doctor. 12 The Breeders. 13 String. 14 Walter F. Mondale. 15 Sir William Walton. 16 Lord Lovat (1747). 17 1970s. 18 Hamburger SV. 19 The Hob. 20 Titanic. 21 The Milan – San Remo (Primavera). 22 The Times. 23 Solomon Islands. 24 Gordonstoun. 25 A black star. 26 Four. 27 Milk and Alcohol. 28 Buenos Aires. 29 Gordon setter. 30 Madagascar.

1 Who directed the 1992 film "Bram Stoker's Dracula"?
2 Robert Banks Jenkinson was British PM under which title?
3 Which cemetery is to the south of the Valley of the Kings?
4 What is Nick Faldo's middle name?
5 Which artist painted "The White Horse" in 1819?
6 The Lake Pontchartrain Causeway links Mandeville, Louisiana with where?
7 The spice coriander is made from which part of a plant?
8 When was The Sun newspaper founded?
9 Brown, Cornell and Dartmouth are all members of what?
10 What is the international car index mark for a car from Taiwan?
11 Neil Diamond started to train – but didn't qualify – as what?
12 Which band featured Kim and Kelley Deal?
13 What type of musical instrument is the Japanese koto?
14 Who was Vice President when Jimmy Carter was President of USA?
15 Which British composer died on the island of Ischia in 1983?
16 Who was the last person to be executed by beheading in the UK?
17 In which decade did Agatha Christie die?
18 Son Heung-min played for Bayer Leverkusen and which other German team?
19 In quoits, what name is given to the target at which the rings are thrown?
20 What was the first movie to make $1,000 million at the box office?
21 In cycling what is the first major classic of the season?
22 Which newspaper in the UK was the first to publish a daily weather chart?
23 In which island group is Guadalcanal?
24 Prince Charles, Prince Edward and Prince Philip were all head boys at which school?
25 What appears in the centre of the national flag of Ghana?
26 How many symphonies did Brahms compose?
27 What was the title of Dr Feelgood's only Top Ten hit?
28 Which South American city has a name meaning "fair winds"?
29 Alexander Gordon 1743–1827 gave his name to what?
30 In which country is the city of Antananarivo?

1 Where is Baltasound Airport?
2 What was Blue's first single not to make the Top Ten?
3 Grand Duke, Stanley and Lombard are all varieties of which fruit?
4 In which country is the city of Cali?
5 Comedian Greg Davies was in a long-term relationship with which MP?
6 Who was the actress mother of actor Daniel Day-Lewis?
7 What is the correct form of address to begin a letter to a Lady Lord Mayor?
8 What was Frank Sinatra's first UK No.1?
9 Demophobia is the fear of what?
10 Which creature is represented in the year the Chinese call gou?
11 What is the most southerly London borough?
12 Anne Bonney and Mary Read famously carried out which trade?
13 Who composed the opera "Death In Venice"?
14 What have you had if you've just had a dog's nose?
15 During which decade did the Orient Express first run?
16 The Court of Arches is the chief court of whom?
17 Which country has the austral as a unit of currency?
18 Which island is the largest of the Dodecanese group?
19 Emanuel Lasker was undisputed world champion for over 26 years at what?
20 Which former Premier League star became manager of Nice in 2018?
21 Whose one and only UK Top Ten hit was "Kung Fu Fighting"?
22 What are the initials IPA an abbreviation of, as well as being an ale?
23 How many league goals did Jimmy Floyd Hasselbaink score for Chelsea?
24 The landau carriage takes its name from a town in which country?
25 Who wrote the novel "A Time to Dance"?
26 Talia Shire is the sister of which film director?
27 What have you got with a plateful of Pisum satvium?
28 Which country left the Commonwealth in 1949?
29 Who directed the movie "Men in Black"?
30 Which two colours appear on the national flag of Honduras?

Answers	Children's Literature *(see Quiz 68)*

1 Clive King. 2 Alex Rider. 3 John Green. 4 The Wolves of Willoughby Chase. 5 JD Salinger. 6 Norton Juster. 7 Skulduggery Pleasant. 8 Forks. 9 Robert C. O'Brien. 10 Catching Fire. 11 Tove Jansson. 12 Paul Zindel. 13 The Goblet of Fire. 14 Madeleine L'Engle. 15 Coram Boy. 16 The Mortal Instruments. 17 Patrick Ness. 18 The Hate U Give. 19 Charlie. 20 Newt Scamander. 21 Diary of a Wimpy Kid. 22 Charlie Higson. 23 Watership Down. 24 Iorek Byrnison. 25 Sally Gardner. 26 How I Live Now. 27 Noughts and Crosses. 28 La Belle Sauvage. 29 Boneland. 30 Babe.

1 Who wrote "Stig of the Dump?"
2 Who is the hero of Anthony Horowitz's spy novels?
3 Whose debut novel was "Looking for Alaska"?
4 Cousins Bonnie and Sylvia Green first appear in which novel?
5 Who was the author of "The Catcher in the Rye"?
6 "The Phantom Tollbooth" was written by whom?
7 Who is Valkyrie Cain's co-star in Derek Landy's comedy-fantasy books?
8 What was Stephenie Meyer's "Twilight" originally called?
9 Who wrote "Mrs Frisby and the Rats of NIMH"?
10 What is the second novel in the "Hunger Games" series called?
11 Who created Snufkin, Sniff and the Snork Maiden?
12 Who wrote "The Pigman"?
13 What is the fourth Harry Potter book called?
14 Who wrote "A Wrinkle in Time"?
15 Jamila Gavin won the Whitbread children's book prize in 2000 with what?
16 Clary Fray and Jace Wayland appear in which Cassandra Clare series?
17 Who wrote the "Chaos Walking" series?
18 Starr Carter is the protagonist in Angie Thomas' debut – what is it called?
19 Who is the wallflower in Stephen Chbosky's "The Perks of Being a Wallflower"?
20 What is the name of Eddie Redmayne's "Fantastic Beasts" character?
21 What was Greg Heffley's diary published as?
22 Who was the author of the "Enemy" series?
23 Where did Hazel and Fiver move to?
24 The armoured bear in Philip Pullman's "His Dark Materials" is called what?
25 Who was the author of "Maggot Moon"?
26 What was Meg Rosoff's first novel called?
27 Sephy and Callum feature in which Malorie Blackman novel?
28 What is the first book in Philip Pullman's "Book of Dust" trilogy?
29 "The Weirdstone of Brisingamen", "The Moon of Gomrath" and, eventually, what?
30 What was the film adaptation of Dick King-Smith's "The Sheep-Pig" called?

---

1 Which country has the forint as its unit of currency?
2 A fear of dreams is known as what?
3 What was Stephen "Tin Tin" Duffy's only Top Ten hit?
4 How long is the Suez Canal?
5 In the military, what is an AFV?
6 Which UK No.1 was written by Red Dwarf creators Robert Grant and Doug Naylor?
7 Which letter is two dots in Morse Code?
8 In which decade was Rory Bremner born?
9 Mbabane is the capital of which country?
10 What popular pub name comes from the title held by soldier John Manners?
11 What colour are the stars on the national flag of the Republic of Iraq?
12 What does the Latin deo volente mean?
13 At the departure of Arsène Wenger who was the Premier League's longest-serving manager?
14 Raleigh is the capital of which US state?
15 What size is B4 paper in millimetres?
16 Who stood against Jeremy Corbyn in the 2016 Labour leadership election?
17 In which of his many movies did Anthony Hopkins play Dr Frederick Treves?
18 What is the administrative centre for the Welsh county of Powys?
19 Stotinki can be spent in which country?
20 Where in Westminster Abbey was the Stone of Scone?
21 What is the international car index mark for a car from Chile?
22 To five years when was the magazine Country Life founded?
23 Which late singer was the lead guitarist with the Grateful Dead?
24 In which country is the city of Dalian?
25 Who was the Roman God of death?
26 Whose top hat sold for £22,000 at Sotheby's in 1988?
27 The spice fenugreek is made from which part of a plant?
28 What was Dollar's first UK Top Ten hit in 1979?
29 In the film "Ace Ventura: Pet Detective" Ace is hired to find what?
30 Who was known as "Joltin Joe" and "the Yankee Clipper"?

Answers	**World Tour** *(see Quiz 70)*

1 Boliviano. 2 Hudson & East. 3 Beslan. 4 Brazil. 5 Bandar Seri Begawan. 6 Angola. 7 Macao. 8 Uruguay. 9 Khartoum. 10 Dzongkha. 11 Australia. 12 Brazil. 13 Algeria and Mauritania. 14 Namib desert. 15 Bogota. 16 Pennsylvania Station. 17 New Providence Island. 18 Wyoming. 19 Mount McKinley. 20 Eilat. 21 Edwin Lutyens. 22 Niger. 23 Nigeria. 24 Kilauea. 25 Indonesia. 26 Bujumbura. 27 Bloemfontein. 28 Maine. 29 Honduras. 30 Java.

1 What is the currency of Bolivia?
2 Between which two rivers does Manhattan lie?
3 Where in Russia was a school besieged by extremists in September 2004?
4 In which country is the city of Curitiba?
5 What is the capital of Brunei?
6 In which country is the deep-water port of Lobito?
7 The islands of Taipa and Coloane are part of which possession?
8 Pluna Airlines are based in which country?
9 Which capital is further north – Khartoum or Addis Ababa?
10 What is the official language of Bhutan?
11 In which country is Kakadu National Park?
12 Which country is due north of Uruguay?
13 Which two countries border Morocco?
14 Which desert lies between the Kalahari and the Atlantic Ocean?
15 Where is the news agency Colprensa based?
16 What is Madison Square Garden situated over?
17 On which island is Nassau, the capital of the Bahamas?
18 In which US state was the first National Park?
19 How is Denali in Alaska also known?
20 The Negev desert tapers to which port?
21 Who designed New Delhi?
22 What is the third longest river in Africa?
23 Which country has the largest oil resources in Africa?
24 Which volcano erupted on Hawaii's Big Island in May 2018?
25 In which country is the city of Medan?
26 What is the capital of Burundi?
27 What is South Africa's judicial capital?
28 What is the most north-eastern US state?
29 SAHSA Airlines are based in which country?
30 Which island is situated between Sumatra and Bali?

Answers | Pot Luck 35 *(see Quiz 69)*

1 Hungary. 2 Oneirophobia. 3 Kiss Me. 4 100 miles (161 km). 5 Armoured Fighting Vehicle. 6 The Chicken Song. 7 I. 8 1960s. 9 Swaziland. 10 Marquis of Granby. 11 Green. 12 God willing. 13 Eddie Howe. 14 North Carolina. 15 250mm x 353mm. 16 Owen Smith. 17 The Elephant Man. 18 Llandrindod Wells. 19 Bulgaria. 20 Under the Coronation Chair. 21 RCH. 22 1897. 23 Jerry Garcia. 24 China. 25 Orcus. 26 Winston Churchill's. 27 Seeds. 28 Love's Gotta Hold on Me. 29 A dolphin. 30 Joe DiMaggio.

1 Both Emma Bunton's dad and Robert Redford's dad worked as what?
2 London's Royal College of Music is in which regal-sounding road?
3 Which actress starred in "Thelma and Louise" and "Lorenzo's Oil"?
4 In which European country are the regions of Kitaa and Tunu?
5 By what name do we know Calvin Cordozar Broadus Jr.?
6 What name is given to the Greek letter that is the equivalent of letter M?
7 Sophie Okonedo was Oscar-nominated for which film based on real life?
8 Who joined the European Union in 1995 with Finland and Sweden?
9 Which sea would you cross if you sailed from Corfu to Cephalonia?
10 Who has been married to Catherine Deneuve, Marie Helvin and Catherine Dyer?
11 What expenses claim made Tory MP Peter Viggers feel "ashamed and humiliated"?
12 What was Celine Dion's first solo UK Top Ten hit?
13 Which US state is called the Bullion State?
14 What name did former Mayfair hairdresser Nigel Davies adopt in the 1960s ?
15 What colours appear with black and red on the Jordanian flag?
16 In which year did Dennis the Menace first appear in the Beano?
17 Which British army officer invented shells containing bullets to inflict more casualties?
18 Who was the longest-serving British PM?
19 What was Donovan's autobiography called?
20 What is the capital of Djibouti?
21 Which English seaside resort is associated with Count Dracula?
22 What was Donny Osmond's last UK No.1?
23 Who wrote "Chicken Soup with Barley"?
24 Doraphobia is the fear of what?
25 What was the pirate Blackbeard's real name?
26 What is the name Blimp derived from in the character Colonel Blimp?
27 Which fund pays the Queen's private expenses as sovereign?
28 Martin Short played Franck Eggelhoffer in a 1990s remake of which movie?
29 Where was Captain James Cook killed in 1779?
30 Who composed the opera "Billy Budd"?

Answers | Plant World *(see Quiz 72)*

1 Ginkgo. 2 Oxalic. 3 Callus. 4 Cherokee leader. 5 It dissolves blood corpuscles. 6 Italy. 7 Rockies. 8 North & South Carolina. 9 Blue. 10 Ferns & mosses. 11 Pacific coast of North America. 12 Stalk. 13 African violet. 14 From insects. 15 It loses its green colour. 16 Matchbox bean. 17 Rose of Jericho. 18 Sloes. 19 Cactus. 20 Poppy. 21 General Sherman. 22 Lettuce. 23 On dung. 24 Sierra Nevada. 25 Belladonna. 26 Stalk. 27 By the sea. 28 Silver Fir. 29 Praslin & Curiense. 30 Giant waterlily.

Quiz 72 | Plant World

Answers – page 263

LEVEL 3

1 How is the maidenhair tree also known?
2 Which acid makes rhubarb leaves poisonous?
3 What is a tissue which forms on a damaged plant surface called?
4 The Sequoia takes its name from what?
5 What makes the death cap mushroom so toxic?
6 Which European country produces more than half of Europe's rice?
7 Where would you find the home of the bristlecone pine?
8 The Venus flytrap is found naturally in which US states?
9 A meadow clary has flowers of what colour?
10 What sort of plants are cryptogams?
11 The world's tallest tree is native only to where?
12 If a leaf is sessile what is missing?
13 What is another name for the Saintpaulia?
14 How does a bladderwort receive its nourishment?
15 If a plant suffers from chlorosis what happens to it?
16 How is the entada known in Australia?
17 What is the only plant which can change its shape?
18 What is the fruit of the blackthorn bush?
19 What type of plant is a saguaro?
20 To which family does the greater celandine belong?
21 The largest known giant redwood is named after whom?
22 How is the plant lactuca sativa better known?
23 If something is coprophilous where does it grow?
24 The tree sometimes known as Wellingtonia is native to which mountains?
25 Atropine is derived from which plant?
26 Which part of the flax plant is used to make linen?
27 If a plant is halophytic where does it grow?
28 Which tree is the tallest native to Europe?
29 On which two islands would you find the sea coconut?
30 Which plant has the largest leaves?

| **Answers** | Pot Luck 36 *(see Quiz 71)* |

1 Milkmen. 2 Prince Consort Road. 3 Susan Sarandon. 4 Greenland. 5 Snoop Dogg. 6 Mu. 7 Hotel Rwanda. 8 Austria. 9 Ionian. 10 David Bailey. 11 Duck house. 12 The Power of Love. 13 Missouri. 14 Justin de Villeneuve. 15 White and green. 16 1951. 17 Shrapnel (Sir Henry). 18 Earl of Liverpool. 19 The Hurdy Gurdy Man. 20 Djibouti. 21 Whitby. 22 Young Love. 23 Arnold Wesker. 24 Fur. 25 Edward Teach. 26 The word for an airship in WWI. 27 Privy Purse. 28 Father of the Bride. 29 Hawaii. 30 Benjamin Britten.

1 A sentence containing all the alphabet's letters is known as a what?
2 What is the international car index mark for a car from Singapore?
3 Who is the elder – Terry Wogan or Bill Wyman?
4 Which two clubs had Ole Gunnar Solskjaer managed before Manchester United?
5 In which decade did Fiji leave the Commonwealth?
6 Who wrote the novel "The Pathfinder"?
7 Columbus is the capital of which US state?
8 Who directed the 1991 film "The Silence of the Lambs"?
9 What was Duran Duran's first UK Top Ten hit?
10 Which post was held by William Gilbert at the courts of Elizabeth I and James I?
11 Which poet was awarded an Order of Merit in 1953, three years before his death?
12 A 25-foot high statue of which celebrity appeared next to London's Tower Bridge in June 2018?
13 Which river was explored by Scotsman Mungo Park?
14 Bill Robertie became the first person to win which World Championship twice?
15 Mogadishu is the capital of which country?
16 Where did the married Princess Elizabeth live before she came to the throne?
17 In music what does the expression "pesante" mean?
18 Who was the Greek goddess of victory?
19 On the first of which month is Canada Day celebrated?
20 What is the title of the head of the College of Arms?
21 In which movie did Hitchcock first appear in one of his cameo roles?
22 Which TV character drove a yellow car called Bessie?
23 In which country is the city of Douala?
24 Whose only UK Top Ten hit was "Jeans On"?
25 For which film did Geena Davis first win an Oscar?
26 In 1860 Willie Park became the first winner of which sporting trophy?
27 Which TV series was set in Atlantic City in the Prohibition era and starred Steve Buscemi?
28 What colour separates the black, red and green bands on the Kenyan flag?
29 What part of your body is initialised as the ANS?
30 Which artist painted "Dancer at the Bar" around 1900?

Answers	**Music Superstars** (see Quiz 74)

1 Tina Turner. 2 Carole King. 3 Neil Diamond. 4 Girls! Girls! Girls! 5 Sorry Seems to be the Hardest Word. 6 When I Need You. 7 1960s. 8 Bohemian Rhapsody. 9 Bob Dylan. 10 Eleven. 11 Kate Bush. 12 Dancing Queen. 13 Turandot. 14 Barry, Robin & Maurice Gibb. 15 Let's Dance. 16 Jean Terrell. 17 Mark McGrath. 18 Madonna. 19 Epic. 20 1962. 21 Gladys Knight. 22 Roxy Music. 23 Rod Stewart. 24 Thunderclap Newman. 25 Celine Dion and Peabo Bryson. 26 Love Me for a Reason. 27 Zubin Mehta. 28 Hot Chocolate. 29 Blinded by the Light. 30 Rock On.

1 Which veteran singer's first No.1 album was "Foreign Affair"?
2 Who became the first female recipient of the Library of Congress Gershwin Prize for Popular Song in 2013?
3 Who wrote "I'm a Believer" for The Monkees?
4 From which film was Elvis Presley's 2005 hit "Return to Sender"?
5 What was Elton John's first solo hit on his own Rocket label?
6 Which Leo Sayer hit gave the Chrysalis label their first No.1?
7 In which decade did Barbra Streisand first make the UK charts?
8 Which hit was the first to be No.1 over two separate Christmases?
9 Which singer/songwriter penned the lines, "The carpet, too, is moving under you"?
10 How many consecutive UK No.1 hits did the Beatles have?
11 Who duetted with Peter Gabriel on "Games without Frontiers"?
12 What was ABBA's only No.1 in the USA?
13 Which opera does Pavarotti's anthem "Nessun Dorma" come from?
14 Which of the Gibb brothers wrote their first UK No.1 "Massachusetts"?
15 Which David Bowie hit was his fourth UK and second US No.1 in 1983?
16 Who replaced Diana Ross when she left The Supremes?
17 Who was the first person to duet on a single with Shania Twain?
18 Stephen Bray and Patrick Leonard have both co-written No.1s with which singer?
19 Michael Jackson's "Thriller" and "Bad" came out on which label?
20 When did Tony Bennett first record "I Left My Heart in San Francisco"?
21 Who sang the national anthem at Super Bowl LIII (2019).
22 A John Lennon song gave which group their only UK No.1?
23 Which singing superstar once had a trial for Brentford FC?
24 Pete Townshend's first No.1 as a producer was for which group?
25 Who sang the theme song to the film "Beauty and the Beast"?
26 What was the final No.1 by any of the Osmond family?
27 Who conducted the Three Tenors for their Italia 90 concert?
28 Who is the only group to appear in the charts in every year of the 1970s?
29 Which Springsteen song was a hit for Manfred Mann's Earth Band?
30 Which David Essex hit was the soundtrack for "That'll be the Day"?

Quiz 75 | Pot Luck 38

Answers – page 268

1 Which US state is called the Gopher State?
2 From which musical is the song "June is Bustin' Out All Over"?
3 In which decade was Frankie Dettori born?
4 The French physician Laennec invented which medical aid?
5 Nelophobia is the fear of what?
6 Who wrote the novel "Death In The Afternoon"?
7 In which country is the city of Fortaleza?
8 In what year did the UK's first IKEA open?
9 Which tree appears on the Lebanese flag?
10 What's the English name of the constellation Dorado?
11 Whose only UK Top Ten hit was "The Final Countdown"?
12 Who is the most photographed person to attend Riddlesdown High school, Croydon?
13 In which country are the regions of Liguria and Calabria?
14 Which studio produced the series of "Scream" slasher horror movies?
15 The majority of tourists to the USA are from which country?
16 Who composed the opera "The Golden Cockerel"?
17 Who was the youngest performer last century to win an Oscar open to adults?
18 Which country has the ngultrum as a unit of currency?
19 Who is the elder – Ruby Wax or Victoria Wood?
20 How old was James Herriot when he began writing books?
21 Which King of Spain was known as Charles the Mad?
22 Who joined the European Union in the same year as Portugal?
23 What is the Swedish plattar?
24 Which media celeb founded a magazine called "Passing Wind"?
25 Who had flaming locks of auburn hair with ivory skin and eyes of emerald green?
26 What was Earth, Wind and Fire's first UK Top Ten hit?
27 The wall, bar and frog are all part of a horse's what?
28 What is the capital of the Dominican Republic?
29 What is Julie Andrews' full real name?
30 In which decade was the first Archery World Championship?

Answers	Tennis (see Quiz 76)

1 Borotra, Brugnon, Cochet & Lacoste. 2 Vijay Amritraj. 3 Martina Navratilova. 4 Arthur Ashe. 5 Gabriela Sabatini. 6 Pete Sampras. 7 French Open. 8 Margaret Smith. 9 Plus an Olympic gold medal. 10 Karen Hantze. 11 1968. 12 Michael Stich. 13 Richard Krajicek. 14 Andy Roddick. 15 Bethanie Mattek-Sands. 16 Nick Kyrgios. 17 The Queen. 18 Men's doubles. 19 French. 20 Australia. 21 Michael Stich. 22 Lindsay Davenport. 23 Kevin Curren. 24 Tony Pickard. 25 Stefan Edberg. 26 Tim Gullikson. 27 Roger Taylor. 28 Kosice, Slovakia. 29 Pat Cash. 30 Sukova.

1 Who were tennis's "Four Musketeers"?

2 Which tennis player appeared in "Octopussy"?

3 Who had the car number plate X CZECH?

4 Who won the first US Men's Open?

5 Who, in 1986, became the youngest woman semi-finalist at Wimbledon for 99 years?

6 Who won the inaugural Grand Slam Cup in Munich in 1990?

7 What was Monica Seles's first Grand Slam title?

8 Who was the first Australian woman to win the Wimbledon Singles?

9 How does a Golden Grand Slam differ from a Grand Slam?

10 With whom did Billie Jean Moffitt win her first Wimbledon Doubles title?

11 What year was the world's first Open tournament?

12 Who was the first German to win the Wimbledon Men's Singles after reunification?

13 At Wimbledon who won an unseeded men's final in the 90s?

14 Whom did Roger Federer beat to win his third US Open?

15 Which US player did Jamie Murray partner to win the US Open Mixed Doubles in 2018?

16 Who won the boys' singles at the Australian Open and Wimbledon in 2013?

17 Who gave Virginia Wade her trophy when she won Wimbledon?

18 Which new competition was included in the Wimbledon championships in 1884 along with the Women's Singles?

19 Which Grand Slam title has Boris Becker never won?

20 Where did Caroline Wozniacki win her maiden Grand Slam title in 2018?

21 In 1992 John McEnroe won the Wimbledon Doubles title with whom?

22 Who replaced Martina Hingis as World No.1 in October 1998?

23 Whom did Boris Becker beat to become Wimbledon's youngest Men's Singles winner?

24 Whom did Greg Rusedski sack as his coach during Wimbledon 1998?

25 Who won his first Open title in 1985 two years after winning the Junior Grand Slam?

26 Which mentor of Pete Sampras died in May 1996?

27 Who was the last British man before Tim Henman to reach a Wimbledon quarter-final?

28 Where was Martina Hingis born?

29 In 2013 who became the first player to win junior, tour and legends titles at Wimbledon?

30 Which Helena won two titles in one day at Wimbledon 1996?

Answers | Pot Luck 38 *(see Quiz 75)*

1 Minnesota. 2 Carousel. 3 1970s. 4 Stethoscope. 5 Glass. 6 Ernest Hemingway.
7 Brazil. 8 1987. 9 Cedar tree. 10 Swordfish. 11 Europe. 12 Kate Moss. 13 Italy.
14 Dimension Films. 15 Canada. 16 Rimsky-Korsakov. 17 Tatum O'Neal. 18 Bhutan.
19 Ruby Wax. 20 50 years old. 21 Charles II. 22 Spain. 23 Pancake. 24 Ian Hislop.
25 Jolene. 26 September. 27 Hoof. 28 Santo Domingo. 29 Julia Elizabeth Wells. 30 1930s.

1 What was the christian name of chocolate founder Mr Cadbury?
2 In which country is the city of Gwangju?
3 Bill Perks the son of a bricklayer became known as who?
4 What does the Latin mea culpa mean?
5 Which creature is represented in the year the Chinese call "long"?
6 Which country has the rufiyaa as a unit of currency?
7 2000 saw the first "X-Men" film – which decade saw the comic characters first appear?
8 What was Enrique Iglesias's first US No.1 single?
9 What was Foreigner's first UK Top Ten hit in 1981?
10 Who is the elder – Bob Geldof or Nigel Kennedy?
11 Which Hitchock film title ties in with his father's field of work?
12 In 2018 who became the first Brighton and Hove Albion player for over a century to win a full England cap?
13 Whose nickname was "Stormin' Norman"?
14 Who directed the 1987 film "Good Morning Vietnam"?
15 Columbia is the capital of which US state?
16 What is a honey locust?
17 Born Marie Grosholtz, under what name is this French lady remembered?
18 What could be signed by Hardy Bros of Ainwick or Charles Forlan?
19 Which saints share their names with three of the five inhabited Scilly Isles?
20 Maputo is the capital of which country?
21 What does the medical term D & C stand for?
22 Who played Marsellus Wallace in "Pulp Fiction"?
23 Which artist painted "Toledo Landscape" around 1610?
24 How is the letter O formed in Morse Code?
25 How many square chains make one hectare in surveying?
26 In which county was Sir Humphry Davy, inventor of the miner's safety lamp, born?
27 What did Terry Wogan study at Belvedere College, Dublin?
28 Who was the Greek god of vegetation and rebirth?
29 Which seasonal rose is from the genus Helleborus?
30 What is the international car index mark for a car from Lebanon?

1 How old was David Cameron when he was elected Tory leader?
2 Who was Sue Lawley's final guest on "Desert Island Discs"?
3 Which celeb chef appeared in "Adrian Mole: The Cappuccino Years" and "Footballers' Wives"?
4 Who is known to his family as "Yog"?
5 Who became Mrs Taylor Hackford in 1997?
6 Who changed his name from Jim Moir so it didn't clash with the BBC's Head of Light Entertainment?
7 Why was Cliff Richard banned from entering Singapore in 1972?
8 How is the former Miss Katharine Worsley better known?
9 In whose family home did Charles and Diana spend the first night of their honeymoon?
10 Who was Margaret Thatcher's press secretary when she resigned?
11 Which "Baywatch" star's autobiography was called "Making Waves"?
12 Who founded the Chelsea Design Company in 1976?
13 Which Leeds-born chef won three Michelin stars by his early thirties?
14 Who opened the punk boutique Seditionaries in the 70s with Vivienne Westwood?
15 Which famous name is the mother of Blue Ivy?
16 Who was André Previn's fifth wife?
17 Who was Mohammed Al Fayed's first wife and Dodi Al Fayed's mother?
18 Who is London's largest landowner?
19 Who is the son of former rugby league international Danny Wilson?
20 Who was raised by his grandmother Olga Winogradsky?
21 Which former editor is Lady Lucinda Lambton's third husband?
22 Who are the parents of George, Harry, Tobias and Angus?
23 Who has "100% Blades" tattooed on his left arm?
24 William Hague's father's business produced what?
25 In 1998 Stella McCartney designed for which fashion house?
26 What relation is Natasha Richardson to Jemma Redgrave?
27 After whom or what did Lady Helen Taylor (née Windsor) name her first son?
28 Which Hamlet ran off with his mother Gertrude in 1995?
29 Which singer and songwriter was born Peter Gene Hernandez?
30 Who succeeded John Galliano at Givenchy in 1996?

Answers | Pot Luck 39 *(see Quiz 77)*

1 John. 2 South Korea. 3 Bill Wyman (Rolling Stones). 4 Through my fault. 5 Dragon. 6 Maldives. 7 1960s. 8 Bailamos. 9 Waiting for a Girl Like You. 10 Bob Geldof. 11 The Birds (Dad a poultry trader). 12 Lewis Dunk. 13 US General Norman Schwarzkopf. 14 Barry Levinson. 15 South Carolina. 16 A tree. 17 Madame Tussaud. 18 Fishing reel. 19 Agnes, Mary & Martin. 20 Mozambique. 21 Dilation and Curettage. 22 Ving Rhames. 23 El Greco. 24 Dash, dash, dash. 25 Ten. 26 Cornwall. 27 Philosophy. 28 Adonis. 29 Christmas Rose. 30 RL.

1 Which occupation was shared by the fathers of Roger Moore and Burt Reynolds?
2 What are the two colours of the national flag of Pakistan?
3 Who was the elder – Liam Gallagher or Ryan Giggs?
4 What was Gerald Ford's middle name?
5 What was the profession of escapologist Harry Houdini's father?
6 Over 700 people died in Greece in July 1987 due to what?
7 Who composed the opera "The Rape of Lucretia"?
8 Ian Thorpe announced his retirement from swimming at what age?
9 Which gallery is located at Bankside, London SE1 9TG?
10 Which friend and rapper does Drake have a picture of tattooed on his left arm?
11 Which prince was born in the year Ted Hughes became Poet Laureate?
12 If a wine is said to be flabby what does it lack?
13 What is the capital of Greenland?
14 In music, what does the expression "strepitoso" mean?
15 For a role in which film did Vanessa Redgrave shave her head?
16 Which country has the lev as a unit of currency?
17 For what offence did Sophia Loren spend 17 days in prison in 1982?
18 In which decade was Richard Branson born?
19 In which European country are the regions of Beja and Guarda?
20 Which playwright was born in Whiston on Merseyside in 1947?
21 Which American state is called the Hawkeye State?
22 Which vitamin is also known as biotin?
23 Which singer played a bouncer in "Wayne's World"?
24 What is the name of Bob Mortimer and Andy Dawson's surreal sporting podcast?
25 Who played Ron Jenkins in "Coronation Street"?
26 "Lost Souls" was the first chart album for which act?
27 Which hit got to No. 2 simultaneously in November 1995 with two separate groups?
28 On TV, James Bolam's Arthur and Michael French's Tom came from which town?
29 Who in Gilbert and Sullivan is "a dealer in magic and spells"?
30 Alphabetically, what is the first English parliamentary constituency?

Answers | Screen Greats *(see Quiz 80)*

1 None. 2 Betty Grable. 3 Peter Lorre. 4 Goldfinger. 5 Errol Flynn. 6 20th Century-Fox. 7 Charles Bronson. 8 Tony Curtis. 9 Barbara Stanwyck's. 10 Bela Lugosi. 11 Gene Kelly. 12 Audrey Hepburn. 13 Marlon Brando. 14 Ingrid Bergman. 15 Rita Hayworth. 16 Rebecca. 17 Sophia Loren. 18 One Night in the Tropics. 19 Dustin Hoffman. 20 George C. Scott. 21 Julie Andrews. 22 Lola-Lola. 23 His wife Carole Lombard. 24 Ginger Rogers. 25 Charlotte Brontë. 26 Twenty. 27 Anchors Aweigh. 28 The Big Broadcast. 29 The Barkleys of Broadway. 30 Making a Living.

Quiz 80 Screen Greats

1 What is the total number of Oscars won by Errol Flynn, Peter Cushing and Richard Burton?

2 Who once had her name changed to Frances Dean by Goldwyn?

3 Who is mentioned by name in Al Stewart's song "The Year of the Cat"?

4 Which Bond film did Sean Connery make prior to Hitchcock's "Marnie"?

5 Eric Porter played Soames on TV but who played Soames in "That Forsyte Woman"?

6 Which was the first US studio Richard Burton worked for?

7 Who was known in Italy as "Il Brutto"?

8 Who changed Bernie for Tony in his first film "Criss Cross"?

9 Bette Midler recreated whose 1930s role in "Stella"?

10 Which screen great did Martin Landau play in "Ed Wood"?

11 Who was lent to Columbia by MGM for "Cover Girl"?

12 Sean Ferrer was the son of which Hollywood Oscar winner?

13 Whose first Oscar was for playing Terry Malloy in a 1950s classic?

14 Who was the mother of actress Isabella Rossellini?

15 Whose pin-up was pinned to the atomic bomb dropped on Bikini?

16 What was Hitchcock's first Hollywood film?

17 Who was the first performer to win an Oscar for a performance entirely in a foreign language?

18 What was Abbott and Costello's first feature film?

19 Who played Sean Connery's son in "Family Business"?

20 Who was the first actor ever to refuse an Oscar?

21 Who was the first British-born British actress of British parents to win an Oscar?

22 What was the name of Marlene Dietrich in "The Blue Angel"?

23 Whose death in 1942 spurred Clark Gable to join the US Air Corps?

24 Whose first film was "Campus Sweethearts" with Rudy Vallee?

25 Which author did Olivia de Havilland play in "Devotion"?

26 How old was Debbie Reynolds when she made "Singin' in the Rain"?

27 What was the first film which teamed Gene Kelly with Frank Sinatra?

28 In which film did Bob Hope find his theme tune?

29 In which 1949 film were Rogers and Astaire reunited after a ten-year break?

30 In which film did Chaplin make his screen debut, in 1914?

Answers | Pot Luck 40 (see Quiz 79)

1 Police officers. 2 White and green. 3 Liam Gallagher. 4 Rudolph. 5 A Rabbi. 6 Heatwave. 7 Benjamin Britten. 8 24. 9 Tate Modern. 10 Lil Wayne. 11 Prince Harry. 12 Acidity. 13 Godthab. 14 Noisy, boisterous. 15 Playing for Time. 16 Bulgaria. 17 Tax evasion. 18 1950s. 19 Portugal. 20 Willy Russell. 21 Iowa. 22 B6. 23 Meat Loaf. 24 Athletico Mince. 25 Ben Kingsley. 26 Doves. 27 Wonderwall. 28 Ormston (Born & Bred). 29 John Wellington Wells (The Sorcerer). 30 Aldershot.

1 Who was the first post-war German Chancellor to have been brought up in the former DDR?

2 The Isle of Man belonged to which two countries before it came under UK administration in 1765?

3 What name meaning "achievement of universal peace" is given to the reign of Emperor Akihito?

4 How did the former Princess Alix of Hesse meet her death?

5 Who did not seek re-election as Austrian President in 1991 after revelations about his activities in WWII?

6 Who was the first President of Israel?

7 How many days after Waterloo did Napoleon resign?

8 Which governor of Sumatra was responsible for the founding of Singapore?

9 What did the Rarotonga Treaty secure in 1987?

10 What does Rasputin mean, as a name given to Grigory Efimovich?

11 Where were all but six French kings crowned?

12 Which country had a secret police force called the securitate which was replaced in 1990?

13 Which President Roosevelt was Republican?

14 What name was given to the incorporation of Austria into the Third Reich?

15 What did Haile Selassie's title Ras Tafari mean?

16 Who was Nazi minister of eastern occupied territories from 1941–44?

17 Who was secretary of state to Kennedy and Johnson?

18 Which French Prime Minister asked Anthony Eden to have the Queen as head of state?

19 In which country was the Rosetta Stone found in in 1799?

20 What name was given to the socialist movement which carried out the Nicaraguan Revolution?

21 Which Conference drew up the United Nations Charter?

22 How many German Popes were there before Benedict XVI?

23 In which year did Baroness Elliott become the first woman to address the House of Lords?

24 Who succeeded Ian Smith as Prime Minister of Rhodesia which then became known as Zimbabwe?

25 Where was the first Marxist state in Africa created?

26 Where was the Maoist guerrilla group Sendero Luminoso active in the 1980s?

27 Who became New Zealand PM in December 1997?

28 Who was joint secretary general of the ANC with Mandela in 1964?

29 Who were the first three states to break away from Yugoslavia in 1991?

30 Where did the Hundred Flowers Movement encourage government criticism in the 50s?

Answers | Pot Luck 41 *(see Quiz 82)*

1 Flight of the Conchords. 2 Brighton & Hove Albion. 3 South Dakota. 4 Joan Crawford. 5 Edward Heath. 6 Boa snakes. 7 Rosemary Conley. 8 Anita Lonsbrough. 9 She fell down a flight of stairs. 10 Ouranophobia. 11 Ben E. King. 12 MC. 13 Henri Matisse. 14 Ronnie Barker. 15 Myalgic Encephalitis. 16 Eltham. 17 Steven Spielberg. 18 Mali. 19 Hugh Grant. 20 Catherine Zeta Jones. 21 Delia Smith. 22 Universal Credit.. 23 Mauritania. 24 Samuel. 25 Balamory. 26 Lewis Carroll. 27 Taiwan. 28 American. 29 Winifred Holtby. 30 2,197.

Quiz 82 | Pot Luck 41

1 Together Bret McKenzie and Jemaine Clement are whom?
2 Which football team does Des Lynam support?
3 Pierre is the capital of which American State?
4 Which actress was also known as Lucille Le Sueur?
5 Which ex-PM died on 17 July 2005?
6 Which reptiles come from the family Boidae?
7 Who produced a fitness video called "Ultimate Fat Burner"?
8 Who was the first female winner of the BBC Sports Personality of the Year?
9 How did fashion empress Laura Ashley die?
10 A fear of heaven is known as what?
11 Which singer's real name is Benjamin Earl Nelson?
12 What is the international car index mark for a car from Monaco?
13 Which artist painted "La Desserte" in 1908?
14 Who presented David Jason with his BAFTA Fellowship?
15 What is the full name for the medical condition known as ME?
16 Where in the UK did Bob Hope have a theatre named after him?
17 Who directed the 1992 film "Hook"?
18 Bamako is the capital of which country?
19 Who links the movies "Extreme Measures" and "The Remains of the Day"?
20 Who duetted with David Essex on "True Love Ways" in 1994?
21 Whose first book was "How to Cheat at Cooking"?
22 On which reform was Theresa May's government first defeated in October 2017?
23 Which country has the ouguiya as a unit of currency?
24 What was the christian name of shipowner Cunard?
25 In which town would you find Edie McCredie the minibus driver?
26 Which children's author appeared on the cover of "Sgt Pepper"?
27 In which country is the city of Kaohsiung?
28 What is the nationality of writer and chef Ken Hom?
29 "Testament of Friendship" is about Vera Brittain's friendship with which author?
30 What is 13 cubed?

| **Answers** | **World History** *(see Quiz 81)* |

1 Angela Merkel. 2 Norway & Scotland. 3 Heisei. 4 Shot with her husband Tsar Nicholas II. 5 Kurt Waldheim. 6 Chaim Weizmann. 7 Four. 8 Thomas Stanford Raffles. 9 Nuclear-free South Pacific. 10 Dissolute. 11 Reims. 12 Romania. 13 Theodore. 14 Anschluss. 15 Lion of Judah. 16 Alfred Rosenberg. 17 Dean Rusk. 18 Guy Mollet. 19 Egypt. 20 Sandanista. 21 San Francisco. 22 Seven. 23 1958. 24 Bishop Abel Muzorewa. 25 Mozambique. 26 Peru. 27 Jenny Shipley. 28 Walter Sisulu. 29 Slovenia, Macedonia & Croatia. 30 China.

Quiz 83 | Who's Who? | Answers – page 276 | LEVEL 3

1 Who starred with Steve Coogan on "The Dead Good Show"?
2 Who was the real-life husband of the first girl in the famous Nescafe commercials?
3 How was comedy writer Gerald Wiley better known?
4 Who found fame with Emma Thompson playing Danny McGlone?
5 Who starred in and produced a mini-series called "Sins"?
6 Who was a regular in "Crown Court" as barrister Jeremy Parsons QC?
7 Who hosts TV talk show "The Last Leg"?
8 What was presenter Matthew Wright's job before moving to TV in 2000?
9 Whose first pop TV series was called "The Power Station"?
10 Which Moll Flanders lost husband Ralph to Francesca Annis?
11 Who was the first male presenter of "Live & Kicking"?
12 Who directed and produced the documentary "They Shall Not Grow Old"?
13 Who came to fame as "Q" of "The Little Ladies"?
14 Who was Cherie Lunghi's character in "The Manageress"?
15 Who played Fletch's son Raymond in "Going Straight"?
16 Which Andy was the 32nd presenter of "Blue Peter"?
17 Who was Eurus?
18 Who was the first female presenter of "Top Gear"?
19 Who wrote the "Magic Roundabout" scripts when they were first broadcast in the UK?
20 Which actresses created "The House of Elliott"?
21 Who appeared in "Dixon of Dock Green" aged ten and found fame as Mrs Theodopolopoudos?
22 Who was Eric Monkman's rival and friend?
23 Which "EastEnders" star used to be better known by his catchphrase "Terr-i-fic"?
24 Who played Marjory in "The Outside Dog" in the "Talking Heads" series?
25 Who won "New Faces" and went on to present it?
26 Who is the real-life mum of Grace and Henry Durham?
27 Still popular, who broke into TV with the 1986 series "Pet Watch"?
28 Who adapted his novel of the same name into "Men Behaving Badly"?
29 Who played the seventh Doctor Who?
30 Who was the only female presenter at the Live Aid concert?

Answers | Pot Luck 84 (see Quiz 42)

1 Betty Joan Perske. 2 Margaret Thatcher. 3 Tennyson. 4 Jeweller. 5 Good Evening Britain. 6 Scilly Isles. 7 RM. 8 Iran. 9 Oops Up Side Your Head. 10 Conakry. 11 Karpov. 12 Oriental rug. 13 Liberator. 14 Bolivia & Peru v. Chile. 15 Little Sioux River. 16 Children. 17 Conservatives. 18 Michael Ramsey. 19 Brighton. 20 Jane Seymour. 21 Trans-Canada Highway. 22 Kris Kristofferson & Rita Coolidge. 23 Complete works of Shakespeare. 24 Maine. 25 Phil Collins. 26 Myanmar. 27 Sir Edward Heath. 28 Gannex. 29 Romania. 30 It was gatecrashed by his children.

275

1 What is Lauren Bacall's full real name?
2 About whom did Cliff Richard say, "She really is a woman just like my Mum"?
3 Who wrote the poem "The Idylls of the King"?
4 What was the profession of fizzy drinks maker Jacob Schweppes?
5 On which one-off special show did Danny Dyer deliver a sweary rant about Brexit?
6 Saint Mary's airport serves which Isles?
7 What is the international car index mark for a car from Madagascar?
8 Which country did Hollywood director Barbet Schroeder come from?
9 What was the Gap Band's first UK Top Ten hit?
10 What is the capital of Guinea?
11 Whom did Kasparov beat to become world chess champion in 1985?
12 What is a kelim?
13 What was the by-name for the B24 bomber?
14 Which countries fought the Pacific War in the 19th century?
15 On which river does the US city of Cherokee lie?
16 What or who does UNICEF benefit?
17 Which political party did Mrs Pankhurst join in 1925?
18 Who was the first Archbishop of Canterbury to meet a Pope since the 16th century?
19 The first Body Shop opened in which town?
20 Who was Elizabeth I's first stepmother?
21 What runs for 4,860 miles from St John's to Victoria?
22 Which husband-and-wife team had a hit with "A Song I'd Like to Sing"?
23 What was the first text to be 'bowdlerised' by Thomas Bowdler?
24 Which American state is called the Pine Tree State?
25 Who is taller – Mick Jagger or Phil Collins?
26 Which country has the kyat as a unit of currency?
27 Who according to Denis Healey, "represented the sensible wing of the Tory party"?
28 What make of raincoat did Harold Wilson popularise?
29 In which European country are the counties of Arad, Arges and Cluj?
30 What made Professor Robert Kelly's 2017 news interview a classic?

Answers | Who's Who *(see Quiz 83)*

1 Caroline Aherne. 2 Trevor Eve. 3 Ronnie Barker. 4 Robbie Coltrane. 5 Joan Collins. 6 Richard Wilson. 7 Adam Hills. 8 TV editor of The Sun. 9 Chris Evans. 10 Alex Kingston. 11 Andi Peters. 12 Peter Jackson. 13 Rula Lenska. 14 Gabriella Benson. 15 Nicholas Lyndhurst. 16 Akinwolere. 17 Sherlock Holmes's long-lost sister. 18 Angela Rippon. 19 Eric Thompson. 20 Jean Marsh & Eileen Atkins. 21 Pauline Quirke. 22 Bobby Seagull. 23 Mike Reid. 24 Julie Walters. 25 Marti Caine. 26 Victoria Wood. 27 Dale Winton. 28 Simon Nye. 29 Sylvester McCoy. 30 Janice Long.

1 What was Bob Geldof's TV production company called?
2 When were downloads added to physical sales in the UK singles chart?
3 Who led the protest about Murdoch's buying of ITV shares in Nov. 2006?
4 What was the first INR radio station?
5 Kelly's Directories catalogue what?
6 Which female Russian journalist was murdered in a high-profile case in 2006?
7 What was the first magazine in the UK in 1691?
8 In which magazine did the Addams Family first appear?
9 Which American syndicated a newspaper column called "My Day"?
10 Who founded the Daily Mail?
11 Where is the newspaper ABC from?
12 Which two UK national newspapers were founded in 1990?
13 Apart from the Tribune, which other US newspaper has Chicago in its name?
14 Which press agency has the abbreviation IRNA?
15 Which newspaper proprietor was born Jan Ludvik Hoch?
16 In 1989 Richard Murdoch bought a 50% stake in which Hungarian tabloid?
17 Which Sunday Times editor made headline news himself regarding details of his affair with Pamella Bordes?
18 Loyd Grossman was restaurant critic of which magazine in the 1980s?
19 Who took over The Observer in 1981?
20 Apart from the Guardian, which other newspaper did James Naughtie work for before joining the BBC?
21 What type of correspondent for the BBC was Michael Cole before he went to work for Mohammed Al Fayed?
22 Who was chairman of Saatchi & Saatchi when they took over the Tory Party account?
23 Which agency did the Saatchi brothers found in 1995?
24 Which famous columnist is married to Lady Camilla Harris?
25 Whose affair with David Mellor brought media man Max Clifford into the public gaze?
26 Which media man's sons all have the middle name Paradine?
27 Which track became the first to achieve one million paid downloads in the US?
28 Which co-founder of TV-am was married to a future Leader of the House of Lords?
29 What was Ted Turner's family business before he turned to TV?
30 Which media magnate has owned AC Milan and been his country's PM?

Answers | Pot Luck 43 *(see Quiz 86)*

1 Blue and white. 2 Maldives. 3 20th. 4 BDS. 5 Rob Reiner. 6 Talking Pictures. 7 Paradise. 8 Paramount Studios. 9 Angola. 10 Mona Lisa. 11 Rwanda. 12 Mongolia. 13 Eliza Rose. 14 Prince Edward Island. 15 Jacopo Robusti. 16 Dunfermline Athletic. 17 Arabian Sea. 18 Sierra Leone & Liberia. 19 Iris. 20 British United Provident Association. 21 House painting. 22 David Thewlis. 23 Texas. 24 Securities and Investments Board. 25 Reptiles. 26 Sea. 27 Games without Frontiers. 28 Yeah!. 29 John Osborne. 30 Spanish.

1 What two colours appear on the flag of San Marino?

2 Male is the capital of which country?

3 In which century was Dame Barbara Cartland born?

4 What is the international car index mark for a car from Barbados?

5 Who directed the 1992 film "A Few Good Men"?

6 Which channel launched in 2015 is dedicated to showing vintage British films?

7 Which Persian word means "pleasure garden"?

8 Which film production company began as the Famous Players Film Company?

9 In which country is the port of Lubango?

10 Which painting did Arthur Scargill choose as his luxury on "Desert Island Discs"?

11 Paul Kagame became President of which country plagued by internal fighting?

12 Which country has the tugrik as a unit of currency?

13 What was the name of TV historian Lucy Worsley's debut novel?

14 In which Canadian province is the novel "Anne of Green Gables" set?

15 What was painter Tintoretto's real name?

16 Which 1968 Scottish Cup winners did not make another final until 2004?

17 Which sea, after the Coral Sea, is the largest in area in the world?

18 From which countries do the Mende people originate?

19 Who was the Greek goddess of the rainbow?

20 What does BUPA stand for?

21 What trade did playwright Brendan Behan learn on leaving school?

22 Who played Paul Verlaine in the film "Total Eclipse" to Leonardo DiCaprio's Rimbaud?

23 What is the only US state to have been an independent republic?

24 In monetary and banking terms, what do the initials SIB stand for?

25 The Gladys Porter Zoo in Texas is noted for its collection of what?

26 Thalassophobia is a fear of what?

27 What was Peter Gabriel's first UK Top Ten hit?

28 What was Usher's first single to top both the UK and US charts?

29 Who wrote the screenplay for the 1963 film "Tom Jones"?

30 What is the main language of the Dominican Republic?

Answers	The Media *(see Quiz 85)*

1 Planet 24. 2 April 2005. 3 Richard Branson. 4 Classic FM. 5 Towns and cities. 6 Anna Politkovskaya. 7 Compleat Library. 8 New Yorker. 9 Eleanor Roosevelt. 10 Lord Northcliffe. 11 Madrid. 12 The Independent on Sunday & The European. 13 Chicago Sun-Times. 14 Islamic Republic News Agency. 15 Robert Maxwell. 16 Reform. 17 Andrew Neil. 18 Harpers and Queen. 19 Tiny Rowland. 20 The Scotsman. 21 Royal. 22 Tim Bell. 23 M & C Saatchi. 24 Nigel Dempster. 25 Antonia de Sancha. 26 David Frost. 27 Hollaback Girl. 28 Peter Jay. 29 Advertising. 30 Silvio Berlusconi.

Quiz 87 Whose Music?

LEVEL 3

1 Who was knocked off No.1 position by "Wannabe"?
2 Whose record has the longest playing time of any to make No.1?
3 Howie Dorough was in which best-selling boy band?
4 Whose one-hit wonder replaced "Honky Tonk Women" at No.1 in US and Britain?
5 Which singer left school in 1961 to appear in the film "It's Trad, Dad"?
6 Which No.1 singer was born Arnold George Dorsey in Madras?
7 Which top musician produced Shakin' Stevens' "Merry Christmas Everyone"?
8 Who sang lead vocal on the chart topper "Babe"?
9 In whose song did an old man sing "The Rare Old Mountain Dew"?
10 Who has recorded singles with Paul McCartney, Julio Iglesias and Diana Ross?
11 Who was the first drummer with The Stone Roses?
12 Joyce Vincent and Thelma Hopkins were the girls in which 1970s group?
13 Who joined Wendy Richard in the No.1 from 1962 "Come Outside"?
14 Craig David's "Woman Trouble" featured Robbie Craig and who else?
15 Which chart topper started life at Leigh, Lancashire as Clive Powell?
16 Who set up the DEP record label?
17 Which 60s artist was the first British-born artist with three No.1 hits?
18 To two years, when did Tony Christie's "Amarillo" first hit the charts?
19 Who wrote "Chain Reaction" for Diana Ross?
20 Who joined the Beatles on their first hit to enter the charts at No.1?
21 Who recorded the 1993 No.1 written and produced by Shaw and Rogers?
22 Which actor was talking to the trees on the B side of "Wand'rin' Star"?
23 Who was No.1 in the UK and US singles and album charts at the same time in 1971?
24 How many versions of "Spirit in the Sky" had made No.1 before Gareth Gates' did?
25 Which Creation Records boss signed Oasis?
26 Which duo made up the Righteous Brothers?
27 Who joined Calvin Harris for "One Kiss" in 2017?
28 Whose death moved Don McLean to write "American Pie"?
29 The Beatles apart, who first took a Lennon & McCartney song to No.1, with the Dakotas?
30 In the 1950s who was the first instrumentalist to achieve two No.1s?

Answers Pot Luck 44 (see Quiz 88)

1 Liberia. 2 Arnold Wesker. 3 Man City. 4 Five. 5 A blue moon eclipse. 6 John Malkovich. 7 God. 8 Alaska. 9 John Donne. 10 Dreams. 11 Physics. 12 Spain. 13 An antelope. 14 Colombia. 15 1900. 16 The Red House Mystery. 17 Five. 18 Drowning. 19 Romania. 20 Charles Buchinski. 21 MA. 22 San Quentin prison. 23 Rho. 24 Veterans Day. 25 Great Ultimate Boxing. 26 British Open 2006. 27 Mozambique. 28 Brian Johnston. 29 Michael Tippett. 30 People Just Do Nothing.

1 Which country has the ports of Buchanan and Grenville?
2 Who wrote "Chips with Everything"?
3 Who were the first English team outside London to claim the European Cup Winners' Cup?
4 In Scrabble what would the word DOG score without any bonus points?
5 What kind of eclipse took place at the end of January 2018 for the first time since 1983?
6 Who played Poirot in the BBC's 2018 adaptation of "The ABC Murders"?
7 Theophobia is the fear of what?
8 Which American state is called the Last Frontier?
9 "For whom the bell tolls" is a quote from whom?
10 What was Gabrielle's first UK Top Ten hit?
11 What did Olivia Newton-John's grandfather win a Nobel Prize for in 1954?
12 In which European country are the regions of Vigo and Murcia?
13 What type of animal is a kudu?
14 Peter Crouch made his England debut against which country?
15 In which year did Michelin produce the first of its Red Guides?
16 Which detective novel did AA Milne write in 1922?
17 How many stripes are there on the Thai flag?
18 What was the first Backstreet Boys' hit with a one-word title?
19 In which country is the town of Constanta?
20 What was Charles Bronson's full real name?
21 What is the international car index mark for a car from Morocco?
22 Where had Jim Rockford been in the years preceding "The Rockford Files"?
23 What name is given to the Greek letter that is the equivalent of letter R?
24 What is Remembrance Sunday called in the US?
25 What does "tai chi chuan" mean in Chinese?
26 What was the first Major won by Tiger Woods after his father's death?
27 In which country is the city of Maputo?
28 Which cricket commentator was awarded the Military Cross in WWII for his "cheerfulness under fire"?
29 Who wrote the opera "The Knot Garden"?
30 Kurupt FM was the focus of which mockumentary series?

Answers | Whose Music? *(see Quiz 87)*

1 Gary Barlow. 2 Meat Loaf. 3 Backstreet Boys. 4 Zager and Evans – In the Year 2525. 5 Helen Shapiro. 6 Engelbert Humperdinck. 7 Dave Edmunds. 8 Mark Owen. 9 The Pogues. 10 Stevie Wonder. 11 Alan "Remi" Wren. 12 Dawn. 13 Mike Sarne. 14 Artful Dodger. 15 Georgie Fame. 16 UB40. 17 Frank Ifield. 18 1971. 19 The Gibb Brothers. 20 Billy Preston on Get Back. 21 Mr Blobby. 22 Clint Eastwood. 23 Rod Stewart. 24 Two versions. 25 Alan McGhee. 26 Bill Medley and Bobby Hatfield. 27 Dua Lipa. 28 Buddy Holly. 29 Billy J. Kramer. 30 Eddie Calvert.

1 Who beat Jahangir Khan's five-year unbeaten record in 1986?
2 Who had the car number plate 1 CUE?
3 How was Walker Smith better known?
4 Who captained the England netball team in the January 2019 Quad Series of test matches?
5 Whom did Andy Robinson name as his first captain when appointed head coach?
6 What was the nickname of baseball player Ty Cobb?
7 Which woman was undefeated over 400m between 1977 and 1981?
8 Which horse did Willie Shoemaker ride in his last race?
9 Who was the only person to beat Sugar Ray Leonard in a professional fight?
10 Which athlete was nicknamed "The Flying Finn"?
11 Who beat Babe Ruth's long-standing record of 714 home runs in 1974?
12 Who was the first jockey to saddle more than 8,000 winners?
13 Who was the first skier to overtake Pirmin Zurbriggen's four overall world championship titles?
14 Which American football player was nicknamed "Sweetness"?
15 Who in 1985 was the first man for 30 years to hold the 1500m and 5000m world records at the same time?
16 Whose triple jump world record did Jonathan Edwards break?
17 Who was the first South African to win the Benson & Hedges Masters snooker title?
18 Where did Nelson Piquet win his first Grand Prix?
19 Who won Olympic gold in the table tennis men's singles in Rio 2016?
20 Who won the Moto Cross des Nations for the first time in 1975?
21 Who was dubbed the Louisville Lip?
22 Whose record of 24 Grand Prix wins was broken by Jim Clark?
23 Who was the first non-European to win the Tour de France?
24 Who won the 1988 Jesse Owens Award as the year's most outstanding athlete?
25 Which Northern Irishman was Superbike World Champion in 2015, 2016, 2017 and 2018?
26 In January 2019, who lost her landmark employment case against British Cycling and UK Sport?
27 Which French cyclist's nickname means "The Badger"?
28 Gene Tunney was only beaten once, by whom?
29 Who was the first Australian to win the Women's World Open Snooker Championship?
30 Who was the first racing driver to win 500 points in Formula 1?

Answers	**Gareth Southgate's England** *(see Quiz 93)*

1 Tom Heaton. 2 47. 3. Trent Alexander-Arnold. 4 Malta. 5 Wayne Rooney. 6 Bottom. 7 Daniel Sturridge. 8 Rijeka. 9 Raheem Sterling. 10 Five. 11 Dele Alli. 12 Jesse Lingard. 13 57. 14 Theo Walcott. 15 Southgate London Underground Station. 16 Belgium. 17 Harry Kane. 18 Kyle Walker. 19 Inflatable Unicorns. 20 Panama. 21 Head of People and Team Development. 22 Ruben Loftus-Cheek. 23 Slovenia. 24 St Petersburg. 25 Five. 26 Adnan Januzaj. 27 At corners. 28 Kieran Trippier. 29 2-1 defeat to Spain. 30 Bear Grylls.

Quiz 90 | Pot Luck 45

Answers – page 285

1 What's the most number of raised dots in a single letter of Braille?
2 Which 'E' number is used to represent riboflavin in products?
3 Who was actress Jane Seymour's first father-in-law?
4 In which country is the city of Maracaibo?
5 In which decade was Mohammed Al Fayed born?
6 Who, on the cover of "Sgt Pepper", was known by his three names?
7 What is Sven-Goran Eriksson's star sign?
8 What was David Gray's next Top Ten single hit after "Babylon"?
9 Which two colours form the background for the Vatican City flag?
10 What is the capital of the American state of Wisconsin?
11 Who was Henry IV's father?
12 In Bangladesh what is kabaddi?
13 Which actress links "Goldeneye" and "X-Men"?
14 Which Spice Girl once appeared as an extra in "Emmerdale"?
15 What's the English name of the constellation Pictor?
16 Who directed the 2017 coming-of-age film comedy "Lady Bird"?
17 Which country has the dirham as a unit of currency?
18 What is the main food of baby whales?
19 What is the international car index mark for a car from Tanzania?
20 In which US state is a university endowed by Cornelius Vanderbilt?
21 Which comedian played Tollmaster in "Doctor Who" in 1987?
22 What is the main language of Ethiopia?
23 Who played the black film detective Shaft?
24 Which Nobel Prize was won in 1975 by Andrei Sakharov?
25 Who had a No.1 UK hit with "Seven Tears" in 1982?
26 Lauren Laverne presents which late night Radio 4 spin-off programme?
27 Who wrote the "Leatherstocking Tales"?
28 Tegucigalpa is the capital of which country?
29 What was the Christian name of frozen food man Mr Birdseye?
30 Who directed the 1991 film "JFK"?

Answers | Whose Sport? *(see Quiz 89)*

1 Ross Norman. 2 Jimmy White. 3 Sugar Ray Robinson. 4 Ama Agbeze. 5 Jonny Wilkinson. 6 The Georgia Peach. 7 Marita Koch. 8 Patchy Groundfog. 9 Roberto Duran. 10 Paavo Johannes Nurmi. 11 Hank Aaron. 12 Willie Shoemaker. 13 Marc Girardelli. 14 Walter Paynton. 15 Said Aouita. 16 Willie Banks. 17 Perrie Mans. 18 Long Beach USA. 19 Ma Long (China). 20 Czechoslovakia. 21 Muhammad Ali. 22 Juan Manuel Fangio. 23 Greg LeMond. 24 Florence Griffith-Joyner. 25 Jonathan Rea. 26 Jess Varnish. 27 Bernard Hinault. 28 Harry Greb. 29 Lesley McIlraith. 30 Alain Prost.

1 What is chiefly grown in Alabama's Canebrake country?
2 The Julian and Dinaric Alps extend into which two countries?
3 The Amur river forms much of the boundary between which two countries?
4 What is the Maori name for New Zealand?
5 Which two main metals are found in the Atacama Desert in Chile?
6 What is the currency of Malaysia?
7 Which country has the highest density of sheep in the world?
8 Which African country takes its name from the Shona for "House of Stone"?
9 Which volcanic peak is west of Cook inlet in Alaska?
10 San Miguel is the main island of which group?
11 What is the capital of the Lazio region of Italy?
12 What is the former name of the capital of Dominica?
13 Which Brazilian state is the centre of Amazonian tin and gold mining?
14 Aqaba is which country's only port?
15 On which island of the Philippines is Manila?
16 What is the world's flattest continent?
17 Which former fort in New York State is the home of the US Military Academy?
18 Which US state capital lies on the river Jordan?
19 In which country is Africa's lowest point?
20 What is the largest primeval forest left in Europe?
21 The Red Sea is the submerged section of which valley?
22 Regina in Saskatchewan was originally called what?
23 How many countries do the Andes pass through?
24 In which country do the Makua live?
25 What is the highest peak of the Apennines?
26 Which city south-east of St Malo was the old capital of Brittany?
27 Which Alps lie north-east of the Sea of Showers?
28 Robben Island is a prison in which bay?
29 What is Malawi's largest city?
30 Which South American port's name means River of January?

Answers	Pot Luck 46 *(see Quiz 92)*

1 Maltesers. 2 Wood not metal resonators. 3 Indonesia. 4 Tippett. 5 Dick Tracy.
6 Amy Grant. 7 Tea. 8 Geoffrey Boycott. 9 St. Raymond Nonnatus. 10 Henry. 11 Crimean. 12 Doris Kappelhoff. 13 Kansas. 14 Z. 15 Jawaharlal (Pandit) Nehru. 16 Man City. 17 Sousaphone. 18 Journalism, literature & music. 19 Turkey. 20 Ghosts. 21 Czech Republic. 22 Light My Fire. 23 Max. 24 Ice cream. 25 Muscat. 26 The Phantom. 27 Sian Williams. 28 Puppetry. 29 Kidney. 30 William I.

1 Which chocolate brand's TV ad campaign used diverse women with disabilities?

2 How does a marimba differ from a xylophone?

3 In which country is the city of Surabaya?

4 Who composed the opera "The Ice Break"?

5 Which comic strip character was played by Warren Beatty?

6 Whose first UK Top Ten hit was "Baby Baby"?

7 What would you drink from a cha-no-yu?

8 Who said they'd hang their MBE round their cat's neck when they got back home after the 2006/07 Ashes whitewash?

9 To which order do the nuns of "Call the Midwife" belong?

10 What did the last emperor of China Hsuan Tung ask to be called after he was deposed?

11 In which war was the Battle of Inkerman?

12 What is Doris Day's full real name?

13 Which American state is called the Sunflower State?

14 Which letter is two dashes and two dots in Morse Code?

15 Who preceded Lal Shastri as Prime Minister of India?

16 Which club moved from M14 7WN to M11 3FF?

17 According to the Bonzo Dog Doo-Dah Band's "The Intro and the Outro" what is Princess Anne playing?

18 The Pulitzer Prize is awarded in which three categories?

19 In which European country is the region of Anatolia?

20 Phasmophobia is the fear of what?

21 Which country has the koruna as a unit of currency?

22 Which song links UB40 and Will Young?

23 Who is the male hero of the children's book "Where the Wild Things are"?

24 What is cassata a type of?

25 What is the capital of Oman?

26 In the first "Pink Panther" film what was the professional jewel thief called?

27 Which BBC Breakfast host became a Channel 5 news anchor?

28 In Japan what type of entertainment is bunraku?

29 Pyelitis affects which organ of the body?

30 Which king of England was crowned on Christmas Day?

| **Answers** | **Exploration** *(see Quiz 91)* |

1 Cotton. 2 Albania & Yugoslavia. 3 China & Russia. 4 Aotearoa. 5 Silver & copper. 6 Ringgit. 7 Wales. 8 Zimbabwe. 9 Mount Redoubt. 10 Azores. 11 Rome. 12 Charlotte Town. 13 Rondonia. 14 Jordan. 15 Luzon. 16 Australia. 17 West Point. 18 Salt Lake City. 19 Djibouti. 20 Hainburg in Austria. 21 Great Rift Valley. 22 Pile of Bones. 23 Seven. 24 Mozambique. 25 Gran Sasso d'Italia. 26 Rennes. 27 Lunar Alps. 28 Table Bay. 29 Blantyre. 30 Rio de Janeiro.

1 Who was England's standby keeper for the 2018 World Cup?
2 How old was Southgate when he was named England manager?
3 Who was the only uncapped player in his 2018 World Cup Squad?
4 Who was England's first opposition under Southgate?
5 Who captained England in Southgate's first match?
6 Where did his Under-21 England team finish in their group in the 2015 European Championships?
7 Who scored England's first goal under Southgate?
8 Where did England play Croatia behind closed doors in 2018?
9 Who scored twice in England's UEFA Nations League win over Spain in Seville?
10 After how many minutes did Kieran Trippier score against Croatia in the World Cup semi-final?
11 Dele Alli, Michael Keane, Jack Cork – who didn't make their England debut under Southgate?
12 Which player did substitute Wayne Rooney replace in England's 2018 friendly against USA?
13 Who was not selected again for England after his 47th appearance against Spain in November 2017?
14 How many England caps did Southgate win?
15 What building temporarily changed its name to honour England's campaign in the 2018 World Cup finals?
16 Who defeated England in the third place play-offs in Russia?
17 Whose late goal against Croatia sent England into the finals of the UEFA Nations League?
18 Who gave away England's penalty against Tunisia in their first 2018 World Cup match?
19 On what did England's players race in the swimming pool during the 2018 World Cup finals?
20 Which country scored their first ever World Cup goal against England in 2018?
21 What role does psychologist Pippa Grange have at the FA?
22 Who replaced Dele Alli after 80mins of England's first World Cup finals match?
23 An injury-time victory over which team in November 2017 saw England qualify for the World Cup finals?
24 England's base in Russia was just outside which city?
25 How many Tottenham Hotspur players were in his 2018 World Cup squad?
26 Who scored for Belgium against England in the group stage of the 2018 World Cup?
27 When did England deploy the 'Love Train' during the World Cup finals?
28 Who took England's penultimate penalty in the shoot-out against Colombia in 2018?
29 What was the result of England's first game after the 2018 World Cup finals?
30 With whom did Southgate go on a TV 'survival' mission in December 2018?

Answers Pot Luck 45 *(see Quiz 90)*

1 Five. 2 E101. 3 Richard Attenborough. 4 Venezuela. 5 1920s. 6 George Bernard Shaw. 7 Aquarius. 8 The One I Love. 9 White & yellow. 10 Madison. 11 John of Gaunt. 12 Team sport (like tag). 13 Famke Janssen. 14 Mel B. 15 Easel. 16 Greta Gerwig. 17 United Arab Emirates. 18 Milk. 19 EAT. 20 Tennessee. 21 Ken Dodd. 22 Amharic. 23 Richard Roundtree. 24 Peace. 25 Goombay Dance Band. 26 Late Night Woman's Hour. 27 James Fenimore Cooper. 28 Honduras. 29 Clarence. 30 Oliver Stone.

How to Set Up Your Own
Pub Quiz

It isn't easy, get that right from the start. This isn't going to be easy. Think instead of words like "difficult", "taxing", "infuriating", consider yourself with damp palms and a dry throat and then, when you have concentrated on that, put it out of your mind and think of the recognition you will receive down the local, imagine all the regulars lifting you high upon their shoulders dancing and weaving their way around the pub. It won't help but it's good to dream every once in a while.

What you will need:

- A good selection of Biros (never be tempted to give your own pen up, not even to family members)
- A copy of *The Pot Luck Pub Quiz Book*
- A set of answer sheets
- A good speaking voice and possibly a microphone and an amp
- A pub
- At least one pint inside you
- At least one more on your table
- A table

What to do:

Choose your local to start with; there is no need to get halfway through your first quiz and decide you weren't cut out for all this and then find yourself in the roughest pub in Christendom 30 miles and a long run from home.

Chat it through with the landlord and agree on whether you will be charging or not; if you don't then there is little chance of a prize for the winners other than a free pint each and this is obviously at the landlord's discretion – if you pack his pub to bursting then five free pints won't worry him, but if it's only you and a couple of others then he may be less than unwilling, as publicans tend to be.

If you decide on an entry payment keep it reasonable; you don't want to take the fun out of the quiz; some people will be well aware that they have very little hope of winning and will be reluctant to celebrate the fact by mortgaging their house.

Once location and prize are all sorted then advertising the event is paramount. Get people's attention, sell, sell, sell or, alternatively, stick up a gaudy-looking poster on the door of the bogs. Be sure to specify all the details, time, prize and so on – remember you are selling to people whose tiny attention span is being whittled down to nothing by alcohol.

After this it is time for the big night. If you are holding the event in the "snug" which seats ten or so you can rely on your voice, if not you should get hold of a good microphone and an amplifier so that you can boom out your questions and enunciate the length and breadth of the pub (once again, clear this with the landlord and don't let liquid anywhere near the electrical equipment). Make sure to practise, and get comfortable with the sound of your own voice and relax as much as possible, try not to rely on alcohol too much or "round one" will be followed by "rown' too" which will eventually give way to "runfree". Relax your voice so that you can handle any queries from the teams, and any venomous abuse from the "lively" bar area.

When you enter the pub make sure you take everything listed above. Also, make sure you have a set of tie-break questions and that you instruct everybody who is taking part as to the rules – and be firm. It will only upset people if you start handing out impromptu solutions, and let's face it the wisdom of Solomon is not needed when you are talking pub quiz rules; "no cheating" is a perfectly healthy stance to start with. Keep people happy by double-checking your questions and answers; the last thing you need is a mix-up on the prize-winning question.

Finally, keep the teams to a maximum of five members, hand out your answer papers and pens and, when everybody is good and settled, start the quiz. It might not be easy and it might not propel you to international stardom or pay for a life of luxury but you will enjoy yourself. No, really.